T0323978

Emerging Technologies, Novel Crimes, and Security

This book provides a holistic overview of the complexities of modern technological advances and their implications for crime and security. It examines the societal dilemmas that accompany these technologies, their strategic impact on geopolitics, governments, business, and civil society.

The increasingly interconnected world gives rise to novel crimes and creates a new, complex set of threats. Understanding this landscape is essential to strategizing for the prevention, protection, mitigation, and risk assessment of technology-related crime.

Practical and approachable, this book builds knowledge and awareness of the impact of emerging technologies on crime and security among professionals, students, academicians, researchers, and policymakers.

Hedi Nasheri is a Professor of Cybercriminology and Global Security at Kent State University and a Visiting Professor of Technology Crimes in the Faculty of Law at the University of Turku in Finland. Her academic and practical experiences have focused for a number of years on cybercrime, global security, and intellectual property crimes. She has collaborated with members of the Intellectual Property Section of the Department of Justice and the Federal Bureau of Investigation on a number of domestic and international educational and research projects related to cybercrimes and intellectual property.

More recently, Professor Nasheri served as a Visiting Scholar at the Max Planck Institute for Innovation and Competition in Germany and as a Senior Fellow in the Policy Division of the Business Executives for National Security (BENS) in Washington DC. She has held a number of Visiting Scholar appointments at New York University School of Law, Columbia University, Case Western Reserve University School of Law, and the University of London's Institute of Advanced Legal Studies.

"Hedi Nasheri's latest book challenges interdisciplinary scholars to understand and respond to the legal, social, and policy issues created by emerging technologies in the globalized, digital age. This comprehensive volume also seeks to encourage industry and governments to predict and address potential harms that emerging devices possess and to be aware of the unintended, counterproductive consequences of innovation. Essential reading for all."

Professor Russell G Smith, *College of Business Government and Law, Flinders University, Australia*

"Professor Nasheri has performed an important service with this readable and thoughtful account of changing technologies, the threats they pose, and the appropriateness of enforcement responses to them."

Michael Levi, *PhD, DSc (Econ.), FaCSS, FLSW, Professor of Criminology, Cardiff University*

"*Emerging Technologies, Novel Crimes, and Security: The Good, the Bad, and the Ugly* is a must-read for anyone seeking to understand the critical role of emerging technologies in shaping our collective security and society. Professor Nasheri addresses big questions from novel crimes, to benefits and risks of emerging tools, and policy considerations. The book fills the knowledge gap describing the general landscape of latest technologies and challenges associated with them."

Prof. Dr. Jelle Janssens, *Associate Professor of Criminology and Vice-Head of the Department of Criminology, Criminal Law and Social Law, Ghent University*

Emerging Technologies, Novel Crimes, and Security

The Good, the Bad, and the Ugly

Hedi Nasheri

Routledge
Taylor & Francis Group

NEW YORK AND LONDON

Designed cover image: Alamy

First published 2025
by Routledge
605 Third Avenue, New York, NY 10158

and by Routledge
4 Park Square, Milton Park, Abingdon, Oxon, OX14 4RN

Routledge is an imprint of the Taylor & Francis Group, an informa business

© 2025 Hedi Nasheri

ISBN: 9781032436579 (hbk)
ISBN: 9781032432984 (pbk)
ISBN: 9781003368304 (ebk)

DOI: 10.4324/9781003368304

Typeset in Sabon
by Newgen Publishing UK

Dedicated to all my students

Contents

Acknowledgments

I am indebted to many colleagues and friends for their mentorship and inspiration throughout the years and in particular to those who provided encouragement during the writing of this book.

I want to extend my gratitude to the late Professor James B. Jacobs, Chief Justice Warren E. Burger Professor of Constitutional Law and the Courts and Director, Center for Research in Crime and Justice at New York University School of Law, who played a significant role in my academic career, with offering wisdom, support, and guidance. I am also much obliged to the late Professor Alan Lizotte, Distinguished Professor at the School of Criminal Justice, University at Albany, who was a great mentor and always there to offer counsel.

I am grateful to Professor David Farrington, Professor of Psychological Criminology at the Institute of Criminology, Cambridge University, who throughout the years offered scholarly insight and encouragement for my academic pursuits.

I want to thank Professor Peter Grabosky, School of Regulation and Global Governance, at the Australian National University, Canberra, and Professor Russell G Smith, at Flinders University, South Australia and the Deputy Director of Research at the Australian Institute of Criminology, who I have learned a lot from on cybercrime and for their continued collaboration over the years.

I am grateful to Professor Steven Belenko at Temple University's Department of Criminal Justice for his mentorship from the outset of my academic career to the present time. We collaborated over the years on significant projects at the Center on Addiction and Substance Abuse at Columbia University as well as the Treatment Research Institute at the University of Pennsylvania.

I am thankful to Professor Wim Hardyns at the Institute for International Research on Criminal Policy, Department of Criminology, Criminal Law and Social Law at the University of Ghent and Dr Noël J. Klima at IDC,

Crime, Criminology & Criminal Policy Institute at the University of Ghent for their transatlantic criminological collaborations, and who teamed up with me on a number of cyber-related projects.

I want to express my gratitude to General Norton A. Schwartz, Chief of Staff of the United States (US) Air Force, who was the general in charge of leadership at BENS in Washington, during my residency as a visiting scholar. It was a real privilege and a learning experience to have the opportunity to work at BENS under General Schwartz's leadership.

I am thankful to Professor Josef Drexl, the Director of the Max Planck Institute for Innovation and Competition and Intellectual Property. Most of my writing for this book took place at Max Planck during my visiting scholar appointment in Germany.

I am grateful to my bright and hardworking student mentees at Kent State University who assisted me with different tasks during the writing of this book.

Preface

My interest in crime and technology began more than 20 years ago. I was asked to develop a graduate course on technological crimes during a visiting professorship at the University of Turku in Finland. The course development tied directly to my primary research on the social, economic, and security impact of information theft, in particular, the theft of proprietary information, that is, trade secrets. I had already been working for a number of years on cybercrime and security before these topics became more prevalent in discussions among academicians and governmental bodies. Soon after, my research was funded by the US Department of Justice which led to an appointment as a research scholar at the University of London's Institute of Advanced Legal Studies, giving me an opportunity to study this topic from a comparative perspective in two common law systems. Subsequently, my work on the topic resulted in a series of lectures globally.

Fast forward to more recent times, my focus logically extended to emerging technologies, like artificial intelligence (AI) and their impact on crime in cyberspace. I began working on AI in 2016, while serving as a fellow in the Policy Division of BENS in Washington. The purpose of my work at BENS was to translate my research into actionable policy focusing on state-sponsored espionage activities and their national security implications for the US.

The decision to write this book stemmed from an invitation by the Australian Government's Institute of Criminology in 2017, where I first presented my research that was very much in its infancy stages. I envisioned that AI would play a critical role in driving changes in society, transforming warfare, the way commerce would be conducted, and how the threat landscape would change. The changes that rapidly unfolded included the automation of social-engineering attacks, vulnerability discovery, influence campaigns, terrorist repurposing of commercial AI systems, increased cyberattacks, and manipulation of information, adding another layer of complexities on top the preexisting risks and challenges.

Innovation is playing a critical role in today's world order, affecting global economies, militaries, and societies. The cumulative effect of these technologies is powerful; it was clear to me even back then, that AI was a going to be a strategic technology and would become a new focus of international competition for economic superiority and geopolitical positioning.

My policy work in Washington provided me with an opportunity to meet with national security professionals from across government agencies. I met with a wide range of individuals, organizations, and trade associations, some of which included United Nations (UN) agencies, representatives of financial institutions, cybersecurity professionals, advocacy groups, international law enforcement agencies, government officials and policymakers, discussing the use and implications of emerging technologies in different sectors, including the criminal justice system. My outreach was focused on the state of emerging technologies, how they were being used, for what purpose, and what risks they posed. The testimonials from discussions, forums, and conferences, nationally and internationally, provided me with a synthesis of practitioner knowledge related to issues of equity, privacy, fairness, accountability, and governance. The testimonials illustrated that leaders often struggled to balance innovation with risk management, like how to safeguard sensitive data from threat actors.

I had already completed my research of open-source and publicly available materials that offered valuable insight into the understanding of the entirety of the cyber ecosystem. This process synthesized social science and practitioner knowledge as a starting point to fill the knowledge gaps. Building a higher level of awareness on this topic for all stakeholders is essential and the approach must be multidisciplinary. There is a lack of knowledge about what these technologies are, their implications, capabilities, limitations, promises, and the role that they play in decision-making processes. The new emerging technologies have brought antidemocratic forces with them, and we need to think about how government, industry, and civil society can work together to ensure that these technologies are safe for adoption and use.

One of the main objectives of this book is to serve as a road map for future research. The book raises important questions at the core of these technologies, like what does it mean to be human and to have the freedom to choose? Our present approach to life and its meaning is changing quickly and therefore, it is important to start discussing these changes as soon as possible.

We are at a critical juncture and need to develop strong pragmatic policies on technologies like AI; this is a period where practical ideas and common sense are desperately needed in order to be able to solve the twenty-first century security problems. The potential of AI is vast and transformative, it is critical to approach its adoption with a strategic mindset. For the most part, people think that they need technical skills to be able to understand this topic, however, it is not actually technical skills that they need, it is logic, reasoning, and understanding of cause and effect.

With more geopolitical tensions on the horizon, governments need to engage in international conversations and global cooperation on the trustworthiness of these technologies. Regulatory cooperation between advanced economies should take place to align standards in order to advance an international vision that can be translated into policies and law. An alignment across sectoral and national lines is needed in order to be able to navigate the geopolitical and technological challenges. The book's goal is to promote a better understanding for policymakers, scholars, journalists, and the public on how deployment and adoption of these technologies influence the threats, vulnerabilities, and criminal activities, and what factors will accelerate or mitigate risks in the cyber ecosystem.

Introduction

The Technological Revolution in Action

The Purpose and the Audience

This book aims to provide a conceptual overview of the scope and importance of the topic of emerging technologies, novel crimes, and the risks and threats associated with these technologies. The book tackles key intellectual, ethical, cultural, and policy questions. Overall, it weaves together the critical policy questions in the context of the current shifting megatrends and global crises. It provides a summary of the good, the bad, and the ugly nature of these technologies. It examines the societal dilemmas that accompany these technologies, and their strategic impact on geopolitics, governments, business, and civil society. The forthcoming chapters discuss the future uncertainties and how governments and law enforcement bodies have to cope with these complexities and the disruptions that are unfolding.

The pace of change is accelerating, and challenges and opportunities have never been more interconnected. Global access to emerging technologies, such as robotics, AI, machine learning (ML), the fifth generation of mobile communications (5G), and quantum computing are evolving rapidly, amplifying the best and worst of human behavior. There is a need to better understand how emerging technologies are shaping crime, impacting governments, and drastically reshaping national and global security.

Prevention, protection, and mitigation of threats in a digital world require a comprehension of the significance of connectivity and its risks. Understanding the cyberthreat landscape and the regulatory framework is important for assessing the ultimate impact of emerging technologies. This book further explores the collision of technological competition and the development of new forms of cybercrime.

New technologies bring new questions. This book focuses on the big-picture questions that policymakers have to grapple with in addressing the risks and threats posed by emerging technologies. In order to provide an awareness of how emerging technologies are giving rise to novel crimes,

DOI: 10.4324/9781003368304-1

the book aims to illustrate the broader societal impact of these technologies. Decision-makers, law enforcement professionals, legislative bodies, researchers, and policymakers have to process tough questions and must be able to make sense of the fast-changing environment. The book strives to outline a wide range of why and what questions, namely, how do emerging technologies fit into the big societal picture? How are they connected to future topics? How will the law enforcement community cope with emerging crimes? How does the adoption of these technologies impact crime in a digital world? How are emerging technologies used by criminals, nation-states, and terrorist organizations? Will data be weaponized? Will there be a poor outcome for humanity?

Everyone Needs to Learn About Emerging Technologies

Generally, most people shy away from subjects like technology and cyberspace, because they believe that they require a highly technical background and skills to be able to understand them. As previously mentioned, it is important to recognize that emerging technologies, cybercrime, and cybersecurity are no longer solely an engineering discipline. Building an understanding of emerging technologies requires background knowledge from a wide range of disciplines; therefore, a holistic approach is required in order to gain the necessary knowledge. Cybersecurity and cybercrime are inherently multidisciplinary subjects, as they entail technical and mathematical as well as social, behavioral, and forensic insight.

Effective prevention, protection, mitigation, and risk assessment of technological crimes will require an awareness of a wide range of disciplines. The challenges facing the world are more complex and cannot be solved from a narrow perspective. Emerging technologies such as AI, quantum computing, and the Internet of Things (IoT) cannot be centered on one group but will need to appeal to a much wider audience and be accessible to everyone.

A Multidisciplinary Approach

The expansion of emerging technologies such as AI into many aspects of public life requires a perspective beyond a technical approach to one that encompasses the social factors in which these technologies operate. Awareness of technical and non-technical capabilities of emerging technologies can provide a better understanding of the implications for societies. Anything short of a holistic approach will lack the fundamental ingredient for establishing a trustworthy framework for their development, deployment, and usage. Awareness of and education and workforce training on emerging technologies should be a priority for all governments[1] taking into consideration the broader issues like the future coming of quantum computing, space technology, and the development of sector-specific regulations for these technologies.

It is imperative to develop a multidisciplinary approach to the understanding of emerging technologies and their relation to novel crimes. This book aims to inform the reader on global technology trends, while considering other disciplinary perspectives. It is intended to provide an awareness of how these evolving technologies—such as drones, robots, AI, 5G, and autonomous weapons—create new risks and threats.

Benefits of This Approach

Analyzing issues from a multidisciplinary perspective can lead to a better understanding of this complicated topic. Computer scientists and the technical community of researchers must integrate humanities and social sciences into their analysis in order to provide a holistic picture of emerging technologies. Therefore, the issues highlighted in this book will draw from other disciplines, such as philosophy, economics, information technology, criminology, political science, and sociology, weaving together the critical trends in order to provide a more comprehensive understanding of this technological revolution.

The potential threats that governments, law enforcement agencies, and the global community are facing in the current digital environment cannot solely be explained from a technical perspective. There is no crystal ball for predicting the future; nevertheless, there is a need for preparedness for what is unfolding. Building awareness is essential to stopping the massive growth of bad actors utilizing emerging tools for malicious purposes.

Technology is Unstoppable

People are more connected than ever, and as a result of this connectivity are more vulnerable and less secure than ever before. The world is getting more complex. Technological advances have drastically changed the nature of daily lives and people's interactions. Logically, this technological acceleration has prompted an open information society, facilitating communications among people, industries, and nations everywhere.

People must constantly adapt and keep up with their technological tools. For instance, each time one gets comfortable with the network operation at the workplace, changes like new software or updates mandate that they adapt and learn new skills in order to function. Whether it is a new email system, application, or a new tool like a tablet or a handheld device, people are continuously in the process of updating the technological devices they depend on to communicate and conduct their daily lives.

Regardless of the risks and challenges that emerging technologies pose, they will continue to emerge despite people's personal preferences and opinions. The way people live now has been shaped by technological innovations. Emerging technologies have the potential to shatter existing limits in medicine, knowledge, memory, and cognition, transforming the quality of life for people globally, but there are no guarantees that these technologies will deliver on their promise. Balancing the possibilities of technological innovations with cascading security threats, namely privacy, mass surveillance, and novel crimes, will define the future.

Geopolitics

Geopolitics now plays a key role in the digital infrastructure as nations race to dominate the development and deployment of emerging technologies. Household names such as Open AI, Facebook, Meta, Google, X (formerly known as Twitter), TikTok, Amazon, and Zoom exemplify the nexus of politics, culture, cybercrime, and conflict felt by individuals, organizations, governments, and societies.

The Race

The race for dominance in the marketplace is shaping societies and creating an uncertain future in which criminals and hostile states may be the winners. The best way to confront risks and challenges is to raise awareness, which can lead to effective policies and regulations for prevention, risk assessment, and preparedness.

Why Should We Care?

Technological developments are giving rise to new risks and threats, adding to the preexisting layers of security challenges. Emerging threats are often derived from the application of new technologies in novel ways, which result in new or unanticipated risks. Emerging crimes are becoming more sophisticated and creating additional levels of complexity and challenges for nations and law enforcement bodies. Traditional crimes are taking on different forms, and law enforcement agencies must be prepared to confront these novel crimes. Adequate training and understanding of the impact of AI and robotics for fighting emerging crimes is critical.

Science Fiction and Reality

Humanity has always been fascinated by science fiction and predictions about the future. Science fiction has been characterized by some as the glue that binds the distant future and the real world that people live in. Human interest in the future has always been an important topic of conversation as it relates to the relationship between technology and society. Societies shape technologies that are developed and used and, in turn, these technologies shape societies. Oftentimes, thinking of science fiction, the first thing that comes to mind may be the blockbuster movies produced in Hollywood in which concepts are exaggerated for dramatic impact.

We Are Living in a Science Fiction World

The line between science fiction and the real world has become blurred, and the two concepts are increasingly intertwined through the development, deployment, and sales of technological tools and products that are pushed onto markets and consumers through advertisements. A digital world is being created on top of the real physical world, which seems irregular and at odds with public sentiment. Emerging technologies such as AI are shaped by a small group of individuals and companies, not by the scientists and engineers that are designing and building them, or by the governments that ultimately have to mitigate risks and harm to protect their citizens. AI is changing the world, but improving and integrating the technology into the physical world is raising more difficult and complex questions than first envisioned, and no chatbot has the magic answers.

Humanity and Technology

Emerging technologies have modified how people socialize, shop, interact with one another, and conduct business. The internet has made vast amounts of information instantly available, and smartphones have put it at people's fingertips everywhere.[2] Human interaction with the physical world is now being altered by the IoT. For instance, drone delivery is no longer a fantasy; it is already taking place in certain cities and is becoming mainstream. Biotechnologies, synthetic biology, and genetic engineering are no longer the work of science fiction; they enable critical advancements in areas like drug development, agricultural enhancement, and novel research. The rewards, however, are not without risks.

The emerging digital tools provide opportunities and risks and have the potential to shatter existing limits in knowledge, memory, and human lifespan. Balancing the possibilities of emerging technologies with concerns about security, privacy, transparency, accountability, and ethics is not a simple task that can be accomplished by one nation.

Figure 0.1 Female Robot

The Internet Was Meant to Make the World a Smaller Place

The internet is a double-edged sword, a source for tremendous good and dreadful evil. As seen over recent decades, advances in technology have facilitated easy access to information and also made the theft of proprietary information much easier. As a mechanism to improve business performance and for efficiency, businesses everywhere engaged in comprehensive automation of their operations to maximize their profitability. A wide range of automation from secretarial and clerical tasks such as contact logs, telephone operations, calendar updates, bookkeeping, accounting, and other financial-related tasks, to name a few, took place in all business settings. Automation of business operations occurred in many industries like manufacturing, trade, mining, utilities, construction, travel, banking and finance, automotive technology, software, biotechnology, pharmaceuticals, and healthcare. An important part of the automation process is that most data, whether design, research and development, formulas, business processes, customer lists, or product information, were computerized from hard copy to digital data files stored on systems networks and via cloud computing. Businesses turned to technological solutions for their data retrieval and storage purposes. Retrieving information no longer required sifting through boxes of documents. At the same time, government agencies followed the same automation model businesses adopted in the private sector.

These technological advances created new opportunities for those who target proprietary information. For example, historically, to steal proprietary information one would need to have physical access to the documents and physically remove boxes of documents, and would probably need a truck to move the boxes to a different location. Now all one needs is a thumb drive if the theft is being carried out by someone who has internal access and if by an outside person or group, all that is required is a computer.[3]

The development of the internet gave rise to today's cybercrime, security threats, and vulnerabilities.[4] Institutions, people, and businesses are vulnerable to internet-based attacks precisely because they increasingly rely on digital infrastructure. Additionally, a growing quantity and quality of data about persons and organizations are stored online and transmitted online, providing attack opportunities.

AI, robotics, 5G, and quantum computing all hold promising possibilities; however, those involved in the development and deployment of these technologies must carefully consider the threats and risks that these systems pose.

How Did We Get Here?

The technological innovations, automation, and impact of globalization on the business sector worldwide have created a platform of interdependence through connectivity of global social networks. The nature of entrepreneurship has changed forever and adapted to a new set of rules in a borderless cyberspace of commerce. At the same time as businesses across the world are making the necessary adjustments to operate in global markets, criminal enterprises are making the same adjustments in order to conduct their operations globally.[5]

Technology has not only increased the importance of technological crimes, but at the same time has created an enabling environment for criminal groups and organizations. Mobility is not an issue for criminals, since they only need to have access to technology. Physical contact is not necessary, and profits are extremely high. Elements of low risk and high profits are the motivating factors for transnational organized criminal groups and terrorist organizations.[6]

Risks in a Digital World

Cybercrime and security challenges are global in nature. With networked services, attacks are rarely confined to a single jurisdiction. Understanding how cybersecurity breaches occur, the nature and the extent of the threats, and the increasingly sophisticated attack methods are the basis for mitigation, prevention, and preparedness. For example, data storage has shifted to the cloud, increasing its availability and usefulness; but also increasing its exposure to vulnerabilities and breaches. Digital systems are complex because of their large and distributed nature. With many subsystems and interconnections, there is a mix of human, legal, regulatory, and technological components involved. The scale and interactions of these systems makes it difficult to predict their risks and outcomes.

Layers of Complexity

Globalization has provided tremendous opportunities for both commerce and criminals. Criminal groups increasingly take advantage of globalization and emerging technologies to engage in sophisticated and expansive criminal activities. One can sit in a kitchen in St. Petersburg, Russia, and steal from a bank in New York; that is how easy it is. Products can be manufactured in one country, assembled in another, transported through a third one, and eventually sold in a fourth country. As an example, with a lack of borders in cyberspace, international intellectual property theft and violations by transnational criminal groups, terrorist organizations, and hostile states present not only great economic loss but threaten a nations' national security and pose a risk to global markets. Technological advances, including AI, biotechnology, and IoT, provide new opportunities for criminals to conduct high-profile attacks by developing new attack methods and collaborating with other criminal networks across borders.[7]

Overseas networks of cybercriminals have hacked into the computer networks of businesses, stealing their valuable intellectual property in order to produce cheap competitor or counterfeit products. Large-scale criminal enterprises are openly engaged in the online sale of massive amounts of stolen software and counterfeit goods. Some of the overseas criminal networks that engage in intellectual property theft are linked to terrorist organizations. Investigators tracking international criminal groups regularly work with their international counterparts and other law enforcement agencies to build a single case. The laws and practical circumstances in each country are different and result in investigatory and evidentiary challenges to actions like being able to interview witnesses or locate suspects.

In today's digital world, adversaries have the potential to make attacks harder to detect, prosecute, and prevent. Challenges related to public safety; maintaining border security; protecting the critical infrastructure; preventing cyberattacks; protecting against foreign and domestic terrorism; preventing chemical, biological, radiological, and nuclear threats (CBRN); protecting against foreign misinformation and disinformation; preventing manipulation of markets; and preventing economic espionage represent a sample of today's security threats.[8]

The Greater the Opportunity, the Greater the Risks

AI chatbots and related tools, like Open AI's ChatGPT or Google's Gemini, have been hailed as powerful productivity enhancements; nonetheless, these tools also can augment hackers' abilities to carry out cyberattacks and more credible social-engineering scams. A recent report released by the US Department of the Treasury[9] highlights the risks associated with AI, such as data poisoning, data leakage, and data integrity attacks, all of which target the sensitive information used to train AI models. By compromising the foundational information within source data, attackers can permanently alter a large-language model's output, leading to an AI system producing biased, unethical, or false answers in response to a given prompt. The report identifies industries that are at risk like financial services, education, housing, law, healthcare, and transportation, which are prone to suffer from the misuse of a given AI technology. While foundational training data are a prime target for hackers, all data handled throughout an AI system's development and production cycle demand protocols that would protect them from cybercriminal access. For instance, cybercriminals that deploy hacking techniques driven by tools like generative AI chatbots are likely to have a leg up against financial institutions.

Preparedness

People and institutions have been left unprepared on many fronts due to the rapid growth and distribution of emerging technologies like AI. These technological advances have dramatically increased vulnerabilities of the interconnected complex systems and the multidimensional interdependence of these systems.

Rapid technological and social changes have the potential to broadly improve quality of life while at the same time providing new avenues of risk and exposure. The changing dynamics of emerging technologies and cybersecurity require an understanding of how societal, economic, commercial, and cultural factors impact security as a whole. It is imperative to have an adequate understanding and knowledge in order to develop effective policies and solutions to tackle the risks and threats that are unfolding.

Strategic Foresight

If nations are unable to resolve the security threats and risks that they are currently confronting from emerging crimes, they most likely will not be able resolve tomorrow's threats, as risks posed by AI, quantum computing, IoTs, and other emerging technologies are still unknown. Addressing the implications of accelerated digital transformation and making sense of these complex technologies cannot be ignored. The corporations responsible for making and distributing emerging products and tools are not advocating for any regulations; in fact, they largely view enactment of any legislation or regulation as a barrier to innovation.

Predictive tools such as those using AI are already globally in use by law enforcement agencies. AI and robotics are complex and highly interconnected. It is conceivable that law enforcement agencies globally may become dependent on these technologies without adequately understanding their implications and shortcomings.

An important question to consider is whether the extensive network of surveillance and predictive devices used by law enforcement agencies around the world will serve as a test case for issues related to privacy, accountability, trustworthiness, and ethics. Achieving the delicate balance between privacy and security is not an easy task to accomplish for any liberal society with democratic principles, and it cannot simply be ignored either.

Building awareness and knowledge about the risks and benefits of emerging technologies is a necessity. Knowledge and awareness of economic, social, and cultural aspects and consequences of these technologies will serve as the foundation for crafting effective policies and regulations governing them. The primary objective of this book is to raise awareness of this timely subject, as these technologies will deeply impact the future of crime and criminal activity in the digital world.

Notes

1 Department of Defense. (2020, September). *2020 Department of defense artificial intelligence education strategy.*
2 Nasheri, H. (2023, May). *State-sponsored economic espionage in cyberspace: Risks and preparedness, in cybercrime in the pandemic digital age and beyond* (Chang, L. Y-C., Sarre, R., & Smith, R. G., Eds.). Springer International Publishing.

3 Nasheri, H. (2005). *Economic espionage and industrial spying.* Cambridge University Press.
4 For more background on this topic, see Grabosky, P. (2007). *Electronic crime.* Pearson Prentice Hall. Wall, D. S. (2007). *Cybercrime: The transformation of crime in the information age* (1st ed.). Cambridge: Polity. Grabosky, P., Smith, R. G., & Urbas, G. (2004). *Cyber criminals on trial.* Cambridge University.
5 Nasheri, H. (2018). The impact of intellectual property theft on national and global security. In Reichel, P., & Randa, R. (eds.) *Transnational crime and global security* (Vol. 1). Praeger.
6 Nasheri, H. (2005). *Economic espionage and industrial spying.* Cambridge University Press.
7 Nasheri, H. (2012). *New developments in intelligence and espionage.* World Politics Review.
8 U.S. Department of Homeland Security. (2023, September 14). *Homeland threat assessment 2024.* www.dhs.gov/sites/default/files/2023-09/23_0913_ia_23-333-ia_u_homeland-threat-assessment-2024_508C_V6_13Sep23.pdf
9 U.S. Department of the Treasury. (2024, March). *Managing artificial intelligence-specific cybersecurity risks in the financial services sector.* https://home.treasury.gov/system/files/136/Managing-Artificial-Intelligence-Specific-Cybersecurity-Risks-In-The-Financial-Services-Sector.pdf

1 What Do Emerging Technologies Mean and Why Do They Matter?

Emerging technologies are those technologies that use algorithmic or ML technology and are different in that respect from previous technologies. Technologies such as AI, biotechnology, and quantum technology, as well as new weapons' technologies such as hypersonic weapons and directed energy weapons, continue to mature and hold significant implications for societies.[1]

The development and deployment of these technologies has been much faster than the law enforcement capabilities. The public's knowledge and understanding of what these technologies are and how they are used is very limited. People are facing AI agents like ChatGPT and are worried about their potential negative impact on society according to the Pentagon's AI chief.[2]

As the technological transformation is unfolding, the world order and democracies are being tested by geopolitical conflicts and global power struggles.[3] Seemingly endless threats like cyberspace security, the Covid-19 economic impact, the surge of far-right nationalist and extremist groups across the West, global warming, food and water security are all serious crises that are coinciding with one another.[4] Currently, the development and deployment of emerging technologies can best be characterized as the "Wild Wild West," as the commercial sector is eager to get these technological tools into the market. Public awareness and legislative initiatives have not been able to keep up with the pace of development and deployment of these technologies. At the same time, the internet has enhanced and augmented the daily lives of people around the world despite the fact that it has given rise to new emerging crimes.[5]

The Good and the Bad

Emerging technologies combined with AI, like robotics, have led to positive advances in various fields, like medicine, transportation, telecommunications, housing, and scientific research and discoveries.[6]

DOI: 10.4324/9781003368304-2

These technologies, such as, robotics, AI, machine learning (ML), quantum computing, drones, 3D, biotech, nanotechnology, 5G, 6G, supercomputers, automation, biotechnology, and the IoT, are transforming the current world into a digital world.[7] The Fourth Industrial Revolution refers to an era of connectivity, advanced analytics, automation, and advanced manufacturing technology, resulting in a narrowing of the gap between the digital, physical, and biological worlds.[8]

Despite the profound opportunities, the proliferation of technologies like AI is not without risks. While the advances have provided great benefits to society in general, they are often abused, or exploited for criminal intent. For example, generative AI is not just teaching the bad cyber actors new attack methods, it is also making it easier for anyone to become a bad actor. Technology is now a key component of most, if not all, criminal activities. Technology is enabling crime to be delivered at scale in an almost industrial fashion. The range and variety of technological advances that can be exploited by criminals is extensive. Criminals are particularly flexible in adapting to technological changes in society. There is a significant demand for these technologies, as they are versatile and powerful due to their capabilities to transform entire industries and fields of science, and that is why criminals, governments, and corporations all want to acquire these technologies. Emerging technologies all rely on their digital nature, which makes them easily accessible, and regulating them is a challenging task.[9]

In the meantime, emerging technologies continue to invade the natural world. 3D-printed food systems are being explored by scientists, and some businesses are in the process of figuring out what astronauts would eat on deep-space missions. 3D visualization highlights, for example, the potential damage from a hurricane; it helps coastal communities to understand better the flooding patterns that may occur. This technology creates an increased community awareness around potential hurricanes and flooding. At the same time, if these technologies are not used properly or governed, they can pose an existential threat to civilization and humanity in its current form.[10] Machines with superhuman intelligence, built by humans, but not fully understood, could endanger humanity.[11] Geoffrey Hinton, a well-known figure in the field of AI, left his position at Google, voicing concerns about the risks associated with AI, including AI chatbots' potential to surpass human intelligence.[12] Technological singularity,[13] the idea that AI could surpass human intelligence and bring about irreversible changes, is also worrying to many global technologists, including those at Open AI, Google, and DeepMind who emphasize the urgent need for a global priority on AI risk mitigation.[14] According to a survey conducted in 2023 in the US, most Americans hold the belief that AI poses a danger to humanity.[15]

Although there is an enormous and growing number of policy initiatives to keep the potential harms in check, as of the writing of this book, there are no international regulations or legislation in place to protect against its misuse. Some have pointed out that the inventors of these technologies have been naïve about the technology that they champion and its consequences.[16] At the present time, all business, government, and law enforcement agencies are at liberty to commission these tools as they deem appropriate for use. The manner in which these technologies are adopted will have tremendous ramifications for national security and economic well-being.[17] For the most part, people may not realize that they are surrounded in their daily lives by these emerging technologies, regardless of their personal views, preferences, or feelings.

New Tools

As previously described, technological innovations hold many positive prospects for businesses and people alike; however, they also create brand new opportunities for criminals who want to capitalize on these developments.[18] Today's connectivity, for all its advantages, brings an increased risk of theft, fraud, and abuse. As more people become reliant on modern technologies, more will become vulnerable to cyberattacks, security breaches, spear phishing, and social media fraud, and these examples do not even cover the wide spectrum of attack possibilities.

Government agencies and industries have been using a wide range of emerging technologies to support their work for decades. Online databases, satellites, video conferencing, and automated plate recognition are some examples of these technological tools that were considered new at one point, but are now common.

The Pandemic

With the inevitable impact of the Covid-19 pandemic, contactless biometrics' technology was used for applications like border control, law enforcement surveillance, healthcare, and biotechnology. For example, facial recognition biometric systems were adopted in some countries to detect individuals that were not abiding by mask-wearing rules that were implemented and mandated during the pandemic period.[19]

Traffic

The latest tools, such as electronic toll collection, drone traffic management, and blind-spot detection, have all resulted in a heightened expectation of achieving efficiency for traffic and transportation networks. The growing adoption of telecommunications' technology and evolution of IT systems are expected to result in less traffic congestion and air pollution.[20]

Cars

Most people consider their cars as a private space. A recent report by the *Mozilla Foundation* reveals that cars have the power to monitor, listen, and gather data about the drivers' actions and location; furthermore, these data can be shared and sold to various entities, including law enforcement agencies.[21] Cars with automated systems are considered to be a rolling platform for software-controlled features and functions.[22] These features and functions can frequently be updated automatically over the air. In the future, cars may be equipped with detection technology systems that will detect the driver's alcohol level.[23] Cars that can chat with drivers or that come with swappable body types have been among the transportation innovations featured in recent years at trade shows.

Smart Cities

The concept of smart cities, known as arcologies, with all the essential components incorporated, was introduced in 1969 by Paolo Soleri, and the notion was also used in science fiction movies.[24] Smart cities became apparent in the 1990s and were broadly referred to as an urban premise that used information and communications technology to increase operational efficiency. Smart cities have been gaining increased traction in recent years, with several nations engaging in initiatives for building them. Intelligent transportation systems are one of the integral functional components of smart cities.[25] As mentioned earlier, part of smart cities' infrastructure, like traffic surveillance cameras, parking guidance systems, weather forecasting information, and satellite communications systems, are built in for functional purposes.[26]

Risks

It is beyond dispute that the integration of AI and digital systems introduces new attack opportunities and vulnerabilities; therefore, their susceptibility to cyberattacks poses a major security concern. Safeguarding the digital networks of smart cities is important.[27] The US has teamed up with partner nations to release *Smart City Cyber Guidelines*. With respect to security risks, breaking into a smart home and hijacking a smart assistant through exposed audio devices is a very likely scenario. An additional security issue concerns the smart assistant being in control of the entire home automation system. An attack can target the AI assistant by either exploiting its presence in the household or abusing its development model prior to being used in a home setting. For instance, if a speaker is connected to the internet, it is vulnerable and can be exploited.

Criminals have also been using automation for their scamming operations, as they realize that automating all operations is a more effective and efficient way of doing business. A security reality is that attacks themselves are becoming increasingly automated.[28]

Automated Decision-Making

New technologies are being used by a wide range of services to make important societal decisions in fields like healthcare, policing, banking, education, housing, and employment. The Federal Trade Commission (FTC) in the US is concerned about the deceptive design elements in AI and companies that are steering people to utilize generative AI for their decision-making processes.[29] People should have the right to know if they are interacting with a machine or a real person.

Machines are making decisions using algorithms based on past data. The nature of AI decision-making increases the possibility of unintentional bias, discrimination, unexpected outcomes, and intentional misdirection.[30] The use of automated decisions in the context of the criminal justice system includes surveillance and algorithm systems like risk assessments, predictive policing, automated license plate readers, real-time facial recognition systems (especially those used in public places like airports, or during a protest), social media monitoring, and ankle-worn monitoring devices.[31]

Automated systems are now widely used to make determinations in employment decisions and credit ratings and are shaping the public's experiences from courtrooms to online classrooms. For instance, an applicant might not know whether a person rejected their résumé or a hiring algorithm moved their résumé to the bottom of the consideration list. A defendant in the courtroom might not be aware if an actual judge is denying their bail, or if the denial decision originated from an automated system labeling them as high risk. People are often denied the necessary information that they need in order to assess the impact of automated systems on their lives.[32]

In the law enforcement context, these technologies have the potential to help solve crimes and identify unknown suspects; nonetheless, they also have the potential to make errors, resulting in misidentification, arrest, and prosecution of innocent people.[33] AI's involvement in human decision-making processes will continue to raise ethical concerns.

Cloud

Cloud computing services have been growing exponentially in recent years. Cloud platforms provide on-demand access to large-scale and big data computing much faster than in the past.[34] They can support important new modalities of data, such as streaming real-time data and therefore, enabling advanced analytics.[35] They are capable of providing large data storage capabilities and backup functions that can be accessed remotely from anywhere. Using cloud resources is much faster than buying, installing, and operating a data storage facility on a premises. Of course, this convenience is not risk-free, since cloud computing systems are internet-based and are therefore susceptible to unauthorized access and security breaches.[36]

Internet of Things (IoT)

The Internet of Things (IoT) is the networking capability that allows information to be sent to and received from devices like kitchen appliances or garage door openers. The benefit stems from the shift to a more digital and connected world, but nonetheless, these connections create new avenues for security breaches like espionage and sabotage operations. As mentioned earlier, the increase in connectivity via the internet has resulted in an unprecedented number of devices and sensors.[37] All internet-enabled devices are vulnerable to malicious actors. IoT devices may not have the same level of security that a computer does and therefore, are susceptible to unauthorized access. IoT devices cause systemic risks, because each device provides an opportunity for a malicious actor to access other connected systems. For example, hackers can use unsecured IoT devices to access home-based routers; therefore, allowing the hacker access to everything else that operates on home networks.[38]

Automated Vehicles (AVs)

Automated vehicles (AVs) have the potential to boost the auto economy, reduce traffic, improve road safety, energy consumption, and pollution.[39] AVs rely on sensors and software that allow for an enhanced view of the environment like lighting and weather conditions. The economic benefit and societal benefits of AVs can be substantial, including increased economic productivity and efficiency, reduced commuting time, and overall energy efficiency.[40] Other potential benefits include improved safety and reduction in roadway fatalities; access and mobility; lower energy usage; and improved supply chain management. In the near future, AVs and driverless taxis (robotaxis)[41] will be more widespread, despite the fact that companies are hesitant to roll out their products due to a lack of confidence in safety and that existing infrastructures are not suited for AVs. The current public sentiment reflects that AVs, pedestrians, and traditional vehicles cannot all mix on the roadways.[42]

Risks

The US government until recently had chosen a more passive approach of "wait and see," in the hope of letting the market develop and thrive before introducing legislation.[43] The computer systems involved in the operation and communications of AVs make the vehicle a potential target for bad actors. The AVs' computer systems have to be designed with adequate cybersecurity measures and must be able to combat criminal exploitation. For example, software vulnerabilities and other risks can cause an accident. AI systems behaving in unintended ways can result in accidents, like a self-driving car failing to understand its environment or distinguishing between an object and a person. As AVs' technologies are designed and deployed, concerns regarding data security and privacy will emerge.[44]

Recently, the US Department of Commerce launched an inquiry into the risks associated with importing AVs from foreign adversaries. In the future, connected vehicles will be able to communicate with smart cities to optimize traffic management and with other connected vehicles to enhance road safety.[45] Nonetheless, this means that connected vehicles represent a vulnerable endpoint that can create attack opportunities. Hackers can target the vehicle's control systems causing serious safety issues. Connected cars collect large amounts of sensitive data on their drivers and passengers and regularly use their cameras and sensors to record detailed information on infrastructure. These vehicles are essentially giant sensors capturing data from everywhere they travel, including military bases and government facilities. With vehicles increasingly becoming data collection points, there is a legitimate concern that sensitive personal information can be transmitted to servers in other jurisdictions, prompting national security red flags.[46]

Robots

A robot is defined by the Department of Defense as a powered machine capable of executing a set of actions by direct human control, computer control, or a combination of both. At a minimum it is comprised of a platform, software, and a power source.[47] Robotics' advances combined with AI and ML, are creating autonomous machines that can perform far more complex tasks. Traditional industrial robots and AI-powered task automation robots are spreading rapidly as companies look for ways to replace and augment an aging workforce. Most industries have established first,

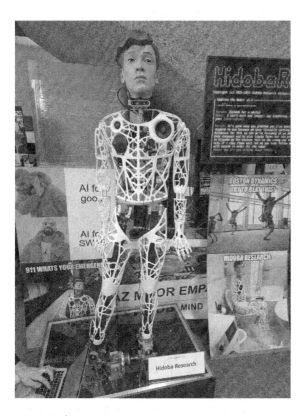

Figure 1.1 Robot

second, and third generations of robots in the workforce.[48] Creativity in the field of robotics continues to flourish as software becomes cheaper and more advances are made in the field. Humanitarian, recreational, military, and commercial applications of robots are taking place globally.

Different Applications

Advances in AI and robotics have generated interest in household robots for domestic chores. Special-purpose robots like vacuum cleaners or kitchen robots target specific tasks, but achieving general purpose home robots is still in the developmental phase.[49] Robots struggle with delicate, irregular shapes and lack humanlike control and feedback. While robots have improved in picking and placing objects, mastering diverse kitchen tools remains a challenge. Long-term labor shortages have pushed companies increasingly in the direction of adopting robotics' automation. More recently, the retail and e-commerce sectors have notably shifted toward automation in response to labor challenges and consumer demand.[50] Lately, a robot that stocks drinks was introduced in Japanese convenience stores to enhance the efficiency of restocking beverages. These types of robots are designed to collaborate with humans, assisting with routine responsibilities.[51] Recently, an AI-powered legal assistant "robot lawyer" offered guidance to a defendant in a US court. This experiment highlights the potential of AI in the justice system.[52] Some pharmacies have created "micro-fulfillment centers" with robots filling prescriptions.[53]

Advanced humanoid robots are being developed for different purposes. Recently, a robot that reads human emotions and serves as a companion for individuals with autism or Alzheimer's disease was developed for the purpose of aiding in therapeutic treatment for mental illness and conducting diagnoses of learning disabilities.[54] Another example of a humanoid robot that can assist with repetitive tasks is a robot that has been developed by Tesla, which combines AI and autopilot technologies for navigating labor-related work.[55] Humanoid robots are now assisting humans in warehouses, handling heavy objects.[56]

The delivery market is another field of growth for robot utilization. A company recently partnered with 7–11 gas station convenience stores to deliver its product to select locations in the US. Age-restricted items such as alcohol and other drugs can be delivered by these robots. One of the issues that needs to be worked out is how autonomous robots will be regulated. With regard to delivery of alcohol and other drugs, biometric analysis can be used to match the face and identity of the individual who is receiving the delivery.[57] In the UK, grocery bots have been used to deliver groceries. The bots have cameras and an alarm system in case of interference, and can cross the street without getting hit.[58] A number of tech firms have developed robots that can cook and plate up large quantities of food. The robot can do everything from turning the oven or stove on or off, to chopping vegetables and whisking eggs.[59] Robots have also been used for taking food orders in restaurants and delivering them to customers while being remotely monitored by an operator.[60] Chatbots are also assisting employees at drive-through fast food giants. They operate through drive-through speakers, and relay order details on a screen for customers to review.[61]

Criminal Justice

In light of the recent accelerated distribution and production of robots, they are now making their way into the criminal justice system.[62] There is a growing interest among law enforcement and counterterrorism agencies globally in exploring robotic technology for their investigative

Figure 1.2 Robot

and operational processes. For example, robots are used for bomb disposal and reconnaissance in dangerous situations. A robot dog was used
by the New York Police Department (NYPD) for patrolling public housing
neighborhoods.[63] The use of the robot dog by the NYPD caused outrage
when it was used to help detain a man who had been holding a woman
and her baby hostage at gunpoint.[64] The use of the robotic dog raised serious concerns about privacy rights.[65] Eventually, the robot dog had to be
returned in light of the controversy.[66]

Military and Defense

While robots are used in many applications, as one might imagine, there is
a significant demand for their use in the military and for defense purposes,
particularly as they can operate in extreme environments. Swarm robotics,
which consists of the coordination of multiple robots as a system, has
applications in defense and security scenarios, including surveillance and
battlefield operations. Swarms of autonomous robots can be deployed

for coordinated missions, target tracking, or perimeter defense.[67] Human moderators will enter a command and the drones will respond through their sensors in order to take the best course of action. The moderator will have a virtual reality headset, used to instruct the drone to cover surveilling areas.[68] The purpose of the drone swarms is to collect information and complete tasks with more efficiency. A command is sent to the drones and collectively they must all work together to reach and complete challenges.[69]

Risks

There are cross-cutting issues stemming from the intersection of cybersecurity and increasingly autonomous cyber-physical systems. The dissemination of robots to a large number of human-occupied spaces makes them potentially vulnerable to remote manipulation for physical harm. For example, a service robot can be compromised, by being hacked from far away to carry out an attack indoors. With regard to cyber-physical systems, the IoT is often heralded as a source of greater efficiency and convenience, but it is also important to recognize that it is highly insecure and represents an additional attack point, as mentioned earlier.

Autonomous security robots are used for suspicious activity and patrol intersections in parts of the world. These security robots have patrolled stores and parking lots. For instance, a company that uses autonomous robots for patrolling, boasts IP address tracking technology that can ping and track Wi-Fi-enabled cellphones, while most wireless access points are also capable of doing the same. This illustrates the risks associated with autonomous robots for surveillance purposes.[70]

There is some evidence suggesting that people are unduly trusting of autonomous mobile robots. This trust can potentially create additional sources of vulnerabilities as more robots are deployed.[71] The consequences of these cyber vulnerabilities are particularly acute for autonomous systems that conduct high-risk activities such as self-driving cars or autonomous weapons.[72]

Drones

Drones have advanced in the last decade from relatively unstable and hard-to-fly drones to ones that can stabilize themselves automatically. Like other emerging technologies, drones bring great promise, including the ability to deliver medicines and supplies to remote locations. More recently drones have been used in Ukraine to search for mines.[73] Drones are being used increasingly these days by the police to observe an area safely, particularly to get the aerial view of an area when protests are taking place. Advances in drone technology have enabled remotely piloted aircraft devices to carry larger payloads, fly faster and longer distances, and operate at lower costs. The Transportation Security Administration (TSA) has a drone security program for security assessments at airports and other locations, primarily focusing on evaluating location security.[74]

Several technology companies are attempting to demonstrate that drones can be a part of the solution for securing ocean safety for supply cargo vessels. Long-range unmanned helicopter systems that specialize in satellite-based monitoring and surveillance can in the near future monitor the seas and look out for pirates.[75] Electric jet skis that can be converted into autonomous drones for military use are being explored by the military, and are also being considered for search and rescue missions.[76] Self-docking boats and flying taxis powered by AI have been on display at trade shows.

Risks

Advances in drone technology have also aided criminal activity; essentially any crime can exploit a low-profile mechanism of transporting or delivering illicit goods. The availability of drones has provided a number of opportunities for criminals and other malicious actors. For example, criminals have deployed drone pirates to home porches to steal packages left by delivery services. The trafficking and distribution of drugs or other contraband are some other obvious examples of criminals employing drone technology.[77]

Drones capable of carrying heavier loads provide the opportunity for drug traffickers to avoid checks at border crossings, ports, and airports. A camera-equipped drone would allow the operator to be able to aim at specific targets within a certain proximity. These targets can include nuclear power plants, fuel storage facilities, chemical production and storage plants, and shipments of highly toxic industrial chemicals.[78] A recent US intelligence report from 2021 detailed a drone used in an attack on an electrical grid substation. The drone was a consumer-level drone, modified with a large supply of copper wire. If it had come into contact with the high-voltage equipment in the substation, it would have resulted in equipment failures and fires.[79]

Commercial systems can be used in harmful and unintended ways, such as using drones or AVs to deliver explosives and cause crashes. For instance, suspected cartel members in Mexico have used drones to drop explosives on police forces.[80] Drones have been used for surveillance and have already been used with firearms, including automatic weapons and explosives.

3D Printing

3D printing, also called additive manufacturing, is used to build physical objects from scratch in shapes and to standards that would be impossible to build with existing traditional methods. The major component is a digital build file that contains a 3D blueprint of the object to be built. Raw materials are needed to build the object. More advanced 3D printing machines can print in metal, ceramics, and even biological tissue. Researchers have already used 3D printing to print individual body parts. It is possible now to 3D-print drones, handguns, and microreactors that can synthesize chemicals.[81] A 100-foot tall rocket with entirely 3D-printed parts of an innovative copper alloy was launched by the National Aeronautics and Space Administration (NASA) in 2023, underscoring the utilization of alloys in future space missions.[82] 3D printing is also being used in the US to tackle the problem of homelessness and to construct homes quickly for homeless individuals.[83]

3D printing was explored in the 2016 opening sequence of a television series called *Westworld*, which offered a glimpse of the possible future of additive manufacturing 3D printing. One might argue that this fictional technology is similar to what many envision the IoT will be presenting in the real world. The "eye in the sky" capabilities shown in *Westworld* would be welcomed and desired by governments for combating crime and terrorism. Shows like *Westworld* not only make good entertainment, but can also be inspirational to the next generation of engineers, scientists, and technicians. As scientists and engineers are turning today's science fiction into tomorrow's engineering fact, they need to contemplate the implications of what they are building.[84] An important question that comes to mind is what would stop us from eventually putting all these parts together to create a complete life, human or animal?

Risks

3D technology has already demonstrated its potential for criminal abuse. For example, 3D printer digital files to print a gun can be downloaded or searched on the dark web before any authority would be able to close a website that hosts a digital file. Almost any object can be printed with these materials. Europol notes the synergies between firearms' trade and cybercrime in production, sale, and possession. The advancing technology of 3D printing poses a significant future threat, like 3D weapons being used in mass-casualty attacks as well as 3D-printed drones in the wrong hands. Handguns and magazines have already been printed,[85] and larger objects have been printed with larger printers. Such technology has already been used by ATM skimmers to produce skimming devices and equipment (such as ATM panels). It is easy for criminals to acquire this technology. They can make any custom components using a 3D printer for any illicit purposes.[86]

Data

Data transform into information, and information transforms into knowledge.[87] Data fuel the development of AI. AI requires vast and diverse amounts of data, whether derived from an authoritative source or generated from people's daily digital footprint that they leave behind. The creation of data and information will not slow down any time soon in our society.[88]

Today's digital economy is fueled by data, and data are considered as one of the most valuable resources in today's economy. Any action taken in the digital economy, whether it be buying food, selling a service, or accessing a piece of information, requires the creation and transfer of data and lots of it.[89] Data are a crucial component for the operation of many emerging tools. Without data, none of this would be possible.

The commercial sector uses an enormous amount of data for their automated systems. The information technology evolution and advances in emerging tools has made it possible to collect and analyze large data sets. Data have transformed the global landscape in both saving and threatening life. Emerging technologies such as 5G, sensor technology, cloud-based storage, connected AVs, and many other activities have dramatically increased the volume and types of public and private data produced around the globe.[90]

The decisions about which data to use for AI models are often made based on what data are available, rather than what data might be suitable. Even if datasets are reflective of the real world, they may still exhibit entrenched historical and societal biases. AI image generators often overlook gender and cultural biases in their art creation using ML algorithms.[91] AI and ML are both sensitive to the type of data that they are trained on, so bad data could produce poorly performing AI.[92] For example, AI can behave in antisocial ways because their training data were full of antisocial behavior.[93] Data can be easily shared, copied, and repurposed freely across the globe. If an incomplete, biased dataset is used to build an AI tool, it could lead to unforeseen consequences.

AI is used to automate tasks in surveillance; for example, analyzing mass-collected data, or creating targeted propaganda and deception, like manipulating videos, can threaten invasion of privacy and social manipulation. Novel attacks in the future can take advantage of an improved capacity to analyze human behaviors, moods, and beliefs on the basis of available data. These concerns are significant and undermine democratic principles.

Data Infrastructure

Data infrastructure includes both traditionally structured data collection systems, like government-run health information systems; as well as more nascent approaches to data collection. Metadata, for example, generated through the use of digital tools, or private-sector data collected through consumer activities like internet searches or online purchases, can power AI models. Especially in the context of privately held data resources, data infrastructure must carefully balance individual protections, such as privacy, and provide mechanisms for redress. Examples of automated systems with a potential privacy impact include smart home systems and associated data, systems that use or collect health-related data, ad-targeting systems, and systems that perform big data analytics in order to build profiles or infer personal information about individuals; and any system that has the meaningful potential to lead to algorithmic discrimination.[94] Another example is the popular voice assistant Alexa, sold by Amazon, that retained sensitive data. The Alexa recordings were not deleted for an extended period of time. Additionally, Amazon Ring doorbell cameras were providing employees with unrestricted access to customer data.[95] Law makers voiced privacy concerns with Amazon when the company was sharing its Ring doorbell camera footage with law enforcement agencies without user consent.[96]

Data analysis software and tools are being used to create insights and guide decision-making. The analysis is used to primarily predict future

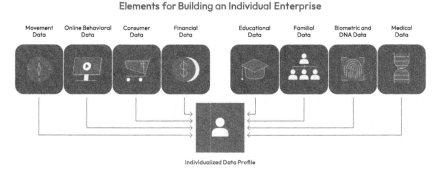

Elements for Building an Individual Enterprise

| Movement Data | Online Behavioral Data | Consumer Data | Financial Data | Educational Data | Familial Data | Biometric and DNA Data | Medical Data |

Individualized Data Profile

Figure 1.3 Elements for Building an Individualized Data Profile

Source: Special Competitive Studies Project. (2022, September). Mid-decade challenges to national competitiveness. www.scsp.ai/2022/09/special-competitive-studies-project-releases-first-report-sept-12-2022/

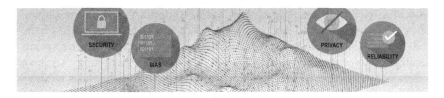

Figure 1.4 Data Used for AI Model Development

Source: United States Government Accountability Office. (2021, June). *Artificial intelligence: An accountability framework for federal agencies and other entities* (GAO-21-519SP). www.gao.gov/assets/gao-21-519sp.pdf

risks based on past data. There needs to be trust in the integrity of the data and the security of the data that are being used to train ML systems. High-stake safety decisions must be based on quality data.[97]

Data Flow

Despite cross-border data flow, there are few globally agreed rules governing data collection, storage, processing, and transfer. Instead, global data flow through an increasingly complicated and conflicting framework. The European Union has a digital ecosystem shaped by heavy regulation, in contrast to US, which does not have any comprehensive federal digital privacy legislation.[98] In 2019, the European Union Agency for Fundamental Rights released a report titled: *Data Quality and Artificial Intelligence – Mitigating Bias and Error to Protect Fundamental Rights.* The report emphasizes the need for high-quality data and algorithms in ML systems and AI. The report draws attention to the requirement for data transparency, data that are used in training the AI systems. It also explains how AI systems use data and provides examples of how biases could be introduced and how low-quality data might affect accuracy and outcomes. A list of criteria for assessing data quality in the report includes completeness, accuracy, consistency, timeliness, duplication, validity, availability, and whether the data are fit for the purpose that they are used for.[99]

Risks

Companies use commercial surveillance technology that tracks individuals across various devices and the internet, creating risks of data breaches, data misuse, manipulation, and discrimination.[100] The increase in sensors has contributed to massive data collection on private citizens.

Individuals leave a digital footprint on the internet through their everyday searches, reading, streaming shows, online shopping, and dating habits. These data are collected and harvested. Depending on the nature of the collected data and whose data are collected, the collection process can facilitate microtargeting particular individuals. Microtargeting can have a devastating security impact for key personnel in government or military positions.[101] Adversaries can also acquire personal identifiable information on particular officials that can contribute to espionage activities.

Lack of Awareness

Individuals' awareness and familiarity with emerging tools is an important security factor. Oftentimes, people are purchasing and using tools without completely understanding their consequences. For example, they are unaware that each time they access their device, their personal data are collected. Generally, people are unaware that their data are being harvested by a third party, and that their data will be sold to commercial data brokers.[102] Subsequently, the harvested data will be used for training AI models. Data brokers frequently collect consumer data from numerous sources without the consumer's consent or knowledge.[103] Data brokers also sell consumer's data to law enforcement and government agencies.[104]

Lack of Explanation

Automated systems usually rely on data from other systems, including historical data, allowing irrelevant information from past decisions to infect decision-making in unrelated situations. For example, some systems awarding benefits changed their criteria invisibly, and individuals were denied benefits due to data entry errors and other system flaws. These flaws were only revealed when an explanation of the system was demanded and produced. The lack of explanation made it harder for the errors to be corrected in a timely manner.[105]

Artificial Intelligence (AI)

Artificial intelligence (AI) refers to automated, machine-based technologies with at least some capacity for self-governance that can, for a given set of human-defined objectives, make predictions, recommendations, or decisions influencing real or virtual environments.[106] This includes the ability of machines to perform tasks that normally require human intelligence, like, recognizing patterns, learning from expertise, drawing conclusions, making predictions, or taking action (whether digitally or as the smart software behind autonomous systems).[107]

What Is AI?

AI refers to the ability of machines to perform tasks that normally require human intelligence, for example, recognizing patterns, learning from experience, drawing conclusions, making predictions, or taking actions.[108] Almost all academic literature on AI acknowledges that no commonly accepted definition of AI exists, in part because of diverse approaches to research in this field.[109] For the purposes of this book, the following definition established by the National Institute of Standards and Technology (NIST)[110] will be used:

> An AI system is an engineered or machine-based system that can, for a given set of objectives, generate outputs such as predictions, recommendations, or decisions influencing real or virtual environments. AI systems are designed to operate with varying levels of autonomy.[111]

Why Is AI Used?

AI has a number of unique characteristics. It has the potential to be integrated across a variety of applications, improving the so-called IoT in which devices are networked together to optimize their performance. Many AI applications are dual-use, meaning they have both military and civil applications. For instance, image recognition algorithms can be trained to recognize cats in YouTube videos as well as terrorist activity. AI can be integrated into a product that may not be immediately recognizable.[112]

Systems That Think Like Humans	Systems That Think Rationally
"The Automation of activities that we associate with human thinking, activities such as decision making, problem solving, and learning." —Bellman, 1978	"The study of computations that make possible to perceive, reason, and act." —Winston, 1992
Systems That Act Like Humans	Systems That Act Rationally
"The art of creating machines that perform functions that require intelligence when performed by people." —Kurzweil, 1990	"The branch of computer science that is concerned with the automation of intelligent behavior". —Luger and Stubblefield, 1993

Figure 1.5 Historical AI Definitions

Source: Congressional Research Service. (2020, November 10). *Artificial intelligence and national security* (CRS Report No. R45178). https://crsreports.congress.gov/product/pdf/R/R45178/10

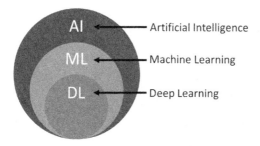

Figure 1.6 AI Capabilities

Source: Science Council of the National Oceanic and Atmospheric Administration. (2020). *NOAA Artificial Intelligence Strategy: Analytics for next-generation earth science.* https://sci encecouncil.noaa.gov/wp-content/uploads/2023/04/2020-AI-Strategy.pdf

AI has already become mainstream and is shaping the existing world. This trend will grow. AI is reshaping society and opening up new opportunities and will have a profound impact on all aspects of everyday life. AI is no longer limited to science fiction and is no longer newsworthy. It is one of the most powerful and transformative technologies at the present time. This is a critical period for humanity, as AI rapidly is accelerating in capability.[113]

Impact

AI has transformed a wide range of industries to date, including, medicine, agriculture, manufacturing, transportation, education, defense, and numerous other areas.[114] Generative AI has the power to change how business, politics, and culture are carried out.[115] Applications of AI are found in everyday technologies like video games, web searching, spam filtering, and voice recognition, to name a few. The use of AI for mundane human tasks has increased in recent years. For instance, AI has been used by the post office through the use of robotic process automation and has been used by the Internal Revenue Service (IRS) in the US to contact taxpayers late in paying their taxes.[116]

AI is poised to transform every industry and is expected to impact operation, training, and recruitment processes. If used correctly, AI has the potential to improve lives through greater efficiency, enhancing human experience and finding solutions to complex problems. The broad scope of new products and services that build on AI technologies suggests that it has the potential to fundamentally change how people perceive the world around them and conduct their daily lives.[117] Nonetheless, AI technology is not widely understood, and as such it lacks trust from people and that is a fundamental factor to overcome for society.[118]

Risks

The deployment of AI without proper safeguards exposes society to misuse by bad actors and hostile nations.[119] Given the increased presence of this technology and its potential for massive disruption, it is necessary to think more critically about how exactly AI is developed and deployed. Highlighting the real risks associated with AI can help in understanding the current status of this technology and its flaws, complexities, and negative consequences. The European Union and US have called for a voluntary code of practice for AI. A member of the *AI Council* in the UK has pointed it out that governments, not technology companies, should make decisions about AI, and furthermore argues that complex algorithms should be banned all together.[120] Some scholars maintain that swift progress must be made in order to reign in AI, as letting AI assume control is a danger to society.[121] A Google engineer who worked for the AI Group at Google recently claimed that chatbot AI had a mind of its own; the chatbot wanted to be acknowledged as an employee rather than a property.[122]

Professor Yoshua Bengio points out that safety needs to be the top priority over usefulness when it comes to AI.[123] AI applications are susceptible to errors and attacks, and these factors undermine public trust in AI.[124] AI can be misused by bad actors as well as individuals and organizations and nation-states to cause significant harm like cyber intrusions or spreading misinformation.[125] The number of incidents concerning the misuse of AI is rapidly rising.

Starting in 2023, large-scale AI models were released into the market every month. These models, like ChatGPT-4, claimed to be capable of a broad range of tasks, including text manipulation, image generation, and speech recognition. However, these systems continue to make mistakes[126] and have major shortcomings.[127] They are prone to hallucination and can be tricked into serving heinous aims. The shortcomings highlight the complicated challenges associated with their deployment. Another major concern stems from the fact that AI systems are trained on publicly available data that can lead to "algorithm bias."[128] The problems range from embarrassing errors[129] like extra fingers on a hand to Black founding fathers in generated images, to significant concerns about intellectual property infringement, cost, and environmental impact. No one wants to build a product on a model that makes things up.[130]

The Home Affairs Committee in the UK voiced their concerns with the lack of oversight into the use of AI in the UK's justice system, further highlighting the fact that there are no scientific standards that AI must meet before its use.[131]

A summary of possible risks posed by AI:

- AI is used in surveillance schemes
- Monitoring content on social media
- Video tracking of individuals in stores
- Policing and crime tracking
- Credit monitoring
- Employment decisions
- Rental decisions
- AI is trained on data and some of the data are biased
- AI can automate preexisting biases[132]
- Erosion of individual privacy and civil liberties
- Accelerated cyberattacks
- New vulnerabilities
- The danger of accidents
- Failing to work for all
- Cementing the status quo
- Displacing accountability
- Ignoring real-world context[133]

Algorithms

Advanced AI algorithms rely on high-end computing capabilities and an infrastructure capable of moving large amounts of data at high speed. Algorithms have been used in the criminal justice system for the purposes of improving crime detection.[134]

Risks

Algorithms may leave people open to dangers for which no person can be identified or held responsible. While AI algorithms can help close the gap left by traditional security measures, malicious actors always find a way to slip through, especially on social media networks or private messaging platforms.

Algorithms deployed in decision-based settings may be untested and or unreliable. The decisions based on algorithms affect people's lives in significant ways. Lack of protection and safeguard mechanisms results in distrust of AI technology. Everyone should understand how algorithms produce the answers that they do; however, even the experts do not understand and cannot explain why the algorithms produce the answers that they do.

At this time, there is lack of sufficient information to draw conclusions about the kind of crimes that are most heavily policed with algorithm technology.[135] This raises questions and concerns about looking at a high volume of data about poor people and over policing.

Machine Learning (ML)

Machine learning (ML) refers more specifically to the field of study that gives computers the ability to learn without being programmed or to computer programs that utilize data to learn and apply patterns of statistical relationships.[136] AI has shifted from an era of reliance on explicit models created by experts to an era of statistical ML where engineers create statistical models with the capacity to be trained to solve specific problems. Today's wave of rapid AI innovation is largely due to the emergence of a type of ML known as deep learning (DL). DL has proved to be an effective technique for image classification, object detection, speech recognition, and natural language processing, among other application areas.[137]

Large-scale ML systems pose risks beyond physical harm, like biased data. AI systems pose a unique challenge to oversight because their inputs and operations are not always visible. Fairness, bias, and ethics in ML continue to be topics of interest among researchers, practitioners, and policymakers. The technical barrier to entry for creating and deploying AI systems has been lowered dramatically, and as a result, the ethical issues around AI have become more apparent recently. Startups and large companies find themselves in a race to deploy and release generative models, and the technology is no longer controlled by a small group of actors.

Bias

AI bias is challenging and complex. If a technology is based on questionable concepts or deceptive or unproven practices, it will lack public trust. An example of this is the use of datasets that may be biased in order to train AI models. Some federal agencies in the US are taking measures to protect against biased decision-making powered by unrepresentative datasets. The FTC in particular has warned against false or unsupported claims about AI products.[138] Automation based on these biases in settings that can affect people's lives with little or no testing or gatekeeping can have a devastating impact. Deployment of technology that is either not fully tested, oversold, or based on questionable or non-existent science creates a number of problems in light of the absence of safeguard mechanisms in place.

The increase of modeling and predictive approaches based on data-driven and ML techniques has exposed biases baked into real-world systems. There is increasing evidence that the general public has concerns about the risks to society. While AI holds great promise and the convenience of automated classification and discovery for large datasets, nonetheless the implications of existing biases in the models can be very harmful to individuals and society.[139] Distrust in AI can manifest itself through a belief that biases may be automated within these technologies, and can perpetuate harms more quickly, extensively, and systematically than human and societal biases on their own.[140]

Criminal Justice

Human decisions based on automated and predictive technology are often made in settings such as hiring or criminal justice and can create harmful impacts and amplify and accelerate existing social inequities.[141] A Utah-based company created a new type of lie-detector test, which focuses on the subject's eye movements in order to determine whether the individual is lying. Test results have been proven to be admissible in court and have influenced the outcomes of jury verdicts. Experts argue that human truth telling is too subtle for any data set to be able to measure accurately.[142]

Hiring

Many companies started to use AI to assist in processing job applicants. Nearly every Fortune 500 company uses algorithmic recruitment and hiring tools to assist in their hiring decisions.[143] Emerging tools used to make hiring assessments include video screening that analyzes facial and emotional movement of candidates and computer games that determine personality type.

AI susceptibility to bias was highlighted in 2017, when Amazon had to get rid of a hiring algorithm that it had been using to rank female applicants.[144] Automated recruitment platforms that use public data to make predictions about competencies and chatbots that screen potential applicants are examples of potential barriers to fairness and diversity. Bias is deeply associated with transparency and fairness in society. Generally, the majority of people assume that algorithms are rarely transparent. The complex web of code and decisions that go into the design, development, and deployment of AI is not easily accessible or understandable to non-technical people. Many people are not even aware of the fact that their data are being harvested when applying to college or searching the internet for an apartment.

When individuals feel that they are not being fairly judged for a loan or job application, it impacts their trust and confidence in the technology. As explained earlier, human bias is contained in the original data that

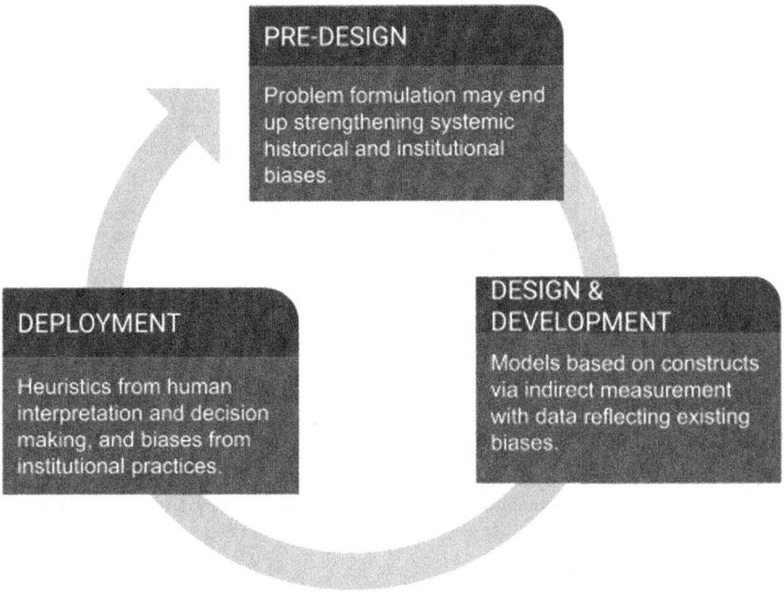

Figure 1.7 Example of Bias Presentation in Three Stages Modeled on the AI Lifecycle

Source: Down, L., Jonas, E., Schwartz, R., Schwartz, R., & Tabassi, E. (2021, June). *A proposal for identifying and managing bias within artificial intelligence* (Draft NIST Special Publication 1270). National Institute of Standards and Technology, U.S. Department of Commerce. https://nvlpubs.nist.gov/nistpubs/SpecialPublications/NIST.SP.1270-draft.pdf

were used to train the AI models. Present challenges require caution in order to avoid pitfalls in fairness and inclusiveness. High-stake challenges, as mentioned earlier, are in the areas of criminal justice and the hiring process.

Potential Harms

AI applications can introduce a number of harms that are less obvious. For instance, rights' erosion or infringement can arise out of poor design and insufficient data scrutiny, or other factors, like lack of accountability measures to safeguard against possible harm.[145]

The use of datasets and practices that are inherently biased contributes to negative perceptions and distrust. Automation based on these biases can affect people's lives, and with little testing and gatekeeping will exacerbate distrust. Deployment of technology that is not fully tested, oversold, and

Examples of Potential Harms[1]

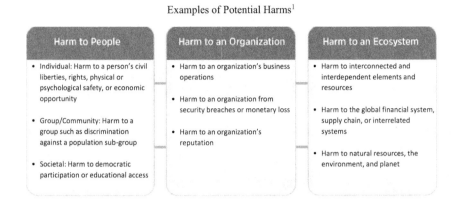

Figure 1.8 Examples of Potential Harms

Source: National Institute of Standards and Technology, U.S. Department of Commerce (NIST). (2023). *Artificial intelligence risk management framework* (AI RMF 1.0). Retrieved from https://nvlpubs.nist.gov/nistpubs/ai/NIST.AI.100-1.pdf

based on questionable science is the underlying factor for distrust of AI technology, despite all the marketing hype and media headlines. How bias and trust interrelate is a key societal question, and understanding it will determine its acceptance.[146]

Transparency

An AI ethics guide drafted for the intelligence community (IC) in the US addresses key topics for the unethical use of AI tools within the IC. Other government agencies have similar guidelines, each tailored to their particular agency. Some of the key topics related to transparency include exploitability and interpretability. Encouraging the use of methods that are explainable and understandable is imperative. The public has to be able to understand how and why AI-generated the response that it did. For example, if a third party created the AI, how can it be explained or interpreted. In cases where an intelligence consumer inquires "how do you know this?" The data sets and tools used to obtain the output can then be explained.[147] Without transparency, there will be no scrutiny and therefore no accountability when things go wrong. People are not aware of what technology is being used, where it is being used, and for what purpose it is being used. Thus, it is impossible to evaluate the technology without transparency.

Trustworthy AI

Everyone should be able to understand how their data are being used and how AI systems make decisions; algorithms, attributes, and correlations should be open to inspection.

As previously mentioned, the NIST in the US contributes to the research, standards, evaluation, and data required to advance the development and use of trustworthy AI. For the purposes of economic, social, and national security challenges and opportunities, the NIST has identified the following required characteristics in order to build trust in AI and to mitigate risks derived from bias in AI:[148]

- Accuracy
- Explainability
- Interpretability

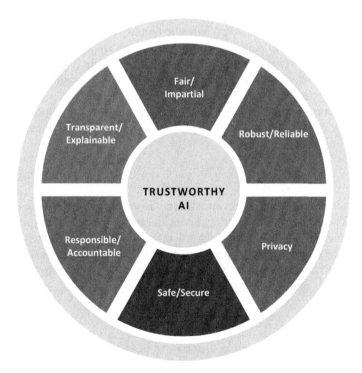

Figure 1.9 Trustworthy AI

Source: U.S. Department of Health and Human Services. (2021, September). *Trustworthy AI (TAI) playbook.*

- Privacy
- Reliability
- Robustness
- Safety
- Security

The future of the digital world will depend on the decisions that are made at the present time. Trust is key to the adoption and ownership of emerging technologies, in particular in the field of AI.

Ethics

Public attitudes about AI technology in the US suggest that, while often depending on the application, most Americans are unaware when they are interacting with AI-enabled technology and therefore feel that there needs to be a "higher ethical standard" applied to AI than with other forms of technologies. The notable issues driving this public sentiment relate to the loss of control and privacy when it comes to AI technologies.[149] Businesses are selling and using AI and governments engage in AI-related ethics talks without actually adopting any policy to guide its ethical use. Ethics washing is used to maintain a positive public face, while engaging in questionable practices.[150] At the same time, there seems to be a growing acknowledgment from some of the leading companies on the importance of a consistent public policy and shared standards on responsible deployment of AI tools.[151]

Guardrails

Guardrails set boundaries to prevent systems from operating outside certain limits. These limits include ethical considerations, legal requirements, and safety measures. Guardrails act as safeguards to ensure that the systems do not cause harm or deviate from their intended purpose. For example, guardrails might limit a system's decisions or actions to ensure they comply with regulatory or ethical guidelines.[152]

Responsible AI

According to NIST, the following criteria are necessary in order to have responsible AI:

- <u>Traceability to human values</u>, like rule of law, human rights, democratic values, and diversity, and ensuring fairness and justice

- <u>Transparency and responsible disclosure</u> so that it allows people to understand and challenge AI-based outcomes
- <u>Robustness, security, and safety</u>, through the AI lifecycle to manage risks
- <u>Accountability</u> in line with the above principles[153]
- Responsible use depends upon the broader digital ecosystems and social and political contexts in which AI tools are present

Accountability

There needs to be a system of accountability for technology suppliers and users, at this time there is no clear line of accountability for misuse or failure of technological solutions used. There are no requirements for law enforcement bodies in the US to disclose information on the use of advanced technological solutions. AI must reflect the societal values and constitutional principles of due process, individual privacy, equal protection, non-discrimination, fairness, and inclusiveness in accordance with the rule of law and democratic principles.[154]

Rules and Regulations

There is no external oversight mechanism at this time specific to AI. There is a need for an international consensus on AI safety and regulation. The development of trustworthy AI requires guardrails.[155] Furthermore, all stakeholders have to be educated on potential harms of AI systems. At the present time, the AI regulatory landscape is fragmented and limited. The US still lacks a comprehensive framework that governs the rights of the public on AI and data privacy.[156]

There is a pressing need for a binding framework, given the costs of emerging technologies and the potential for serious problems like infringement of privacy and discrimination that can arise from using these technologies. The current governing approach in the US to emerging technologies like AI is not a balanced approach to regulation and innovation; it is primarily driven by competition.[157]

The European Union

While governments worldwide are grappling with implementation of a regulatory framework for AI, Europe has made progress by proposing a comprehensive regulation in contrast to the slower initiatives in the US. *The European Union Digital Strategy's Ethics Guidelines for Trustworthy AI* consists of the following seven principles of trustworthy AI:

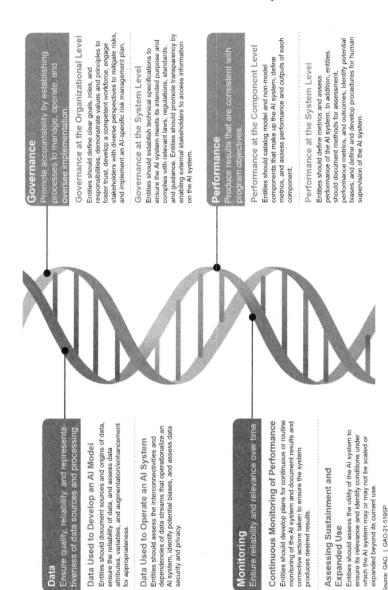

Governance

Promote accountability by establishing processes to manage, operate, and oversee implementation.

Governance at the Organizational Level

Entities should define clear goals, roles, and responsibilities, demonstrate values and principles to foster trust, develop a competent workforce, engage stakeholders with diverse perspectives to mitigate risks, and implement an AI-specific risk management plan.

Governance at the System Level

Entities should establish technical specifications to ensure the AI system meets its intended purpose and complies with relevant laws, regulations, standards, and guidance. Entities should promote transparency by enabling external stakeholders to access information on the AI system.

Performance

Produce results that are consistent with program objectives.

Performance at the Component Level

Entities should catalog model and non-model components that make up the AI system, define metrics, and assess performance and outputs of each component.

Performance at the System Level

Entities should define metrics and assess performance of the AI system. In addition, entities should document methods for assessment, performance metrics, and outcomes, identify potential biases, and define and develop procedures for human supervision of the AI system.

Data

Ensure quality, reliability, and representativeness of data sources and processing.

Data Used to Develop an AI Model

Entities should document sources and origins of data, ensure the reliability of data, and assess data attributes, variables, and augmentation/enhancement for appropriateness.

Data Used to Operate an AI System

Entities should assess the interconnectivities and dependencies of data streams that operationalize an AI system, identify potential biases, and assess data security and privacy.

Monitoring

Ensure reliability and relevance over time.

Continuous Monitoring of Performance

Entities should develop plans for continuous or routine monitoring of the AI system and document results and corrective actions taken to ensure the system produces desired results.

Assessing Sustainment and Expanded Use

Entities should assess the utility of the AI system to ensure its relevance and identify conditions under which the AI system may or may not be scaled or expanded beyond its current use.

Source: GAO. | GAO-21-519SP

Figure 1.10 Accountability Framework

Source: United States Government Accountability Office. (2021, June). *Artificial intelligence: An accountability framework for federal agencies and other entities* (GAO-21-519SP). www.gao.gov/assets/gao-21-519sp.pdf

- Human agency and oversight
- Technical robustness and safety
- Privacy and data governance
- Transparency
- Diversity, non-discrimination, and fairness
- Environmental and societal well-being
- Accountability[158]

The European Union (EU) AI Act (the "Act")

The European Parliament in 2023 supported draft legislation titled: *AI Act to regulate AI.* The AI Act aims to protect rights, provide legal certainty for businesses, and encourage innovation at the same time. Policing tools and remote facial recognition (FR) will generally be banned, except for specific counterterrorism investigatory purposes. Generative AI, including ChatGPT, is classified as high risk.[159] The EU AI Act has made it through the EU's legislative process and has passed into law.

The European Union introduced the joint *EU-US Data Privacy Framework* in 2023 to safeguard transatlantic data flow. Given the contrasting data privacy laws in the EU and the lack of comprehensive regulations in the US, this framework places a responsibility on the US government to ensure the protection of personal data belonging to EU citizens; however, it does not do the same for Americans.[160]

Fifth-Generation Wireless Networks (5G)

Technologies that are driving twenty-first-century economic growth like AI rely on digital infrastructure, including 5G networks, satellites, and IoT devices to connect and enable them.[161] Reliable, secure, high-speed connectivity is critical to powering AI systems. 5G wireless technology was designed to enhance the delivery of higher data speed, with increased reliability and availability, and better coverage. By improving speed and volume, 5G networks will significantly enhance information-sharing capabilities in both public and private sectors. In turn, data generated on 5G networks can be leveraged to improve AI systems; 5G networks will form the connective tissue between AI platforms.

Companies like Lockheed Martin and Verizon have demonstrated the capabilities of 5G-enabled drones for enhancement of military intelligence capabilities. Using private 5G, the drones can successfully detect radio frequency signals emitted by military targets in real time by using advanced algorithms. 5G-enabled drones improve situational awareness for the military.[162]

While 5G is global for the mobile carrier market, it is not the same for private environments. A private organization can tailor its 5G network so that it provides the desired level of speed and security.[163] A private 5G network allows private entities to customize their network based on their needs. For instance, private 5G in the sports industry facilitates seamless experiences at large events for fans and enhances players' training with sophisticated camera and sensor systems.[164] In contrast, the public 5G infrastructure might provide the same level of service to all transiting data yet potentially expose the devices to the rest of the network. As AI becomes more dispersed throughout the networks, the need for a secure and effective 5G network will increase even more.

A study by the Rand Corporation, conducted for the US Department of the Defense, highlighted the following benefits of 5G:

- The ability to track thousands of items using smart tags—these inexpensive tags can help track items and equipment, and the data can be used for AI or algorithms to enhance operations
- It will provide very high communication speeds over short distances with a high-band—5G can help with downloading large sensor data sets that can assist with the transfer of data between operators and AVs
- Remote communications—5G can be used for communications for command and control and allow for increased coordination among multinational forces and infrastructure
- Unmanned communications—5G can allow for enhanced communications between AVs[165]

Risks

AI systems require high-fidelity sensing as well as fast, safe, and secure networks.[166] Developments in network infrastructure, including 5G, have the potential to dramatically alter the security environment as it involves AI.[167] A variety of threats can occur with 5G, including jamming, using fake base stations, and geolocating cellular users for targeting and exploiting. These are some examples that are likely to jeopardize the 5G ecosystem. There are also concerns with how cybercriminals can use 5G for their operations.[168]

Quantum Technology

Quantum technology is the largest advancement in technology and has been in the developmental phase for years. Quantum computers can develop into faster computers than today's machines and will be able to solve very complex calculations quickly.[169] These computers will assist with climate change, new drugs, and new AI, and at the same time assist with military operations.[170] Quantum computers and entangled sensor networks have the power to revolutionize various fields, from energy optimization to personalized medicine.[171] According to Australia's chief scientist, the impact of the quantum revolution will be comparable to the digital revolution that brought transistors and lasers, which form the foundation for modern electronics, computers, and communications.[172]

National Security Implications

Advances in quantum communication networks that use quantum phenomena to control and transmit information could lead to the emergence of a highly secure "quantum internet."[173] Quantum computing will have important implications for national security and will enable simulations of complex phenomena that currently cannot be performed. The US and other advanced economies are preparing for measures that can protect against the potential loss of data through encryption code hackings.[174] The need for strong cryptographic governance ahead of migrating digital networks to a post-quantum standard will be a major component for future cybersecurity.

At the 2023 World Economic Forum (WEF), a new blueprint for quantum technologies was discussed. The blueprint serves as a guide advising all nations on how to prepare for this technology.[175] Currently there is a race between several countries to develop this technology.

Risks

As quantum computing advances, post-quantum encryption becomes a critical issue. Nations have to take concrete steps in addressing potential risks to breaking encryption. Quantum computers will be capable of breaking encryption that protects private communication.[176] The encryption threats will impact online activities, put commerce and critical infrastructure at risk,[177] and, render current stored data encryption useless.[178]

Cybersecurity of automated platforms will require appropriate defense mechanisms that will be attack-resistant from a quantum computer, which means that current cybersecurity threats have to be addressed.[179] As quantum computing poses a threat to the existing encryption methods used in classical computer networks,[180] organizations have to explore security solutions that are based on quantum principles, in order to navigate a safe quantum future.[181]

At the present time, NIST is working on standardizing four essential quantum-resistant algorithms that were discovered in 2022. Large-scale quantum computers are not yet available; the concept of "harvest now, decrypt later" highlights the urgency of post-quantum cryptography.

Digital Workers

A digital worker is an automated, software-based tool, application, or agent that performs a business task or process similar to a human user and uses AI or other autonomous decision-making capabilities.[182] A digital worker does not have human worker-like attributes. Common types of digital workers include AI, Chatbot, and ML. Chatbot is a software tool that interacts with a human user to provide a service such as answering questions or directing the user to a resource. An important question to consider is whether the digital worker will act on its own insights. What will happen if a human is not involved to provide oversight? Lack of human oversight can have adverse consequences.

Humans

The AI For Good Global Summit in 2023, sponsored by the UN, took place in Geneva, Switzerland. The meeting explored the complex relationship that exists between AI and humans. The event highlighted crucial questions about AI's role in governance and decision-making.[183] The most notable presence at the summit was *Sofia*, an advanced AI-powered robot renowned for being the UN's Innovation Champion. In response to a question about humanoid robots in government leadership, *Sofia* suggested that AI leaders could outperform humans due to their lack of biases and emotional interference in decision-making. Most complex and thought-provoking ethical and practical issues and implications of AI were discussed. Humans have always evolved alongside technology, including AI, which is transforming humanity and raising existential questions.[184]

AI does not think like humans, while it can perform astonishing tasks. AI struggles with doing multiple things at once and is not capable of reasoning as humans do.[185]

Religious leaders using AI to create sermons found that their sermons lacked personal examples and stories that showcase empathy, vulnerability, and the strong human emotions that are expected during a religious sermon.[186] While there are concerns about killer robots and surveillance, the more fundamental questions revolve around human decision-making and moral judgments. Machines are far inferior to humans at broadly learning, understanding, and making inferences based on commonsense knowledge.

AI is being used extensively in a wide range of domains, predicting preferences and making decisions. How does AI affect the human ability to develop practical judgment and make choices?[187] Should more consideration be given to humans[188] in particular when it comes to decision-making in more sensitive settings like in the criminal justice system or educational and healthcare settings? Should humans be considered for adverse and higher risk decisions? When humans and machines work side-by-side and have to collaborate, a clear framework is needed for this interaction. In some industries, human and machine teaming is already taking place.

Many scientists have been inspired to develop systems that have the ability to perform all of the same intellectual tasks as humans. The term "artificial general intelligence" (AGI) is sometimes used to refer to this goal. At the present time, people are the only example of general intelligence; it is unclear when the advent of AGI might occur.[189]

The technical capabilities and specific definitions of such systems change with the speed of innovation. The rapid development of AI that can train itself raises questions about how well this rapid growth can be controlled. The idea of AI that builds better AI is a crucial part of the myth-making behind "Singularity," the imagined point in the future when AIs start to improve at an exponential rate and move beyond human control. Some argue that eventually AI might decide it does not need humans at all. In a seminar paper on AI published in the 1950, Alan Turing considered the question "can machines think?" and focused on how machines might imitate humans.[190]

Humans should always be the ultimate decision-maker as a safeguard for when an algorithm gets it wrong. It is all too easy for an algorithm's suggestion to be taken as the right answer and confirmed with the click of a button. Philosopher Michael Sandel explores the ethical questions AI brings to light beyond jobs, fairness, privacy, and democracy; he questions whether the technology would affect what it means to be human. Sandel questions "will new technologies lead humans, or are they already leading humans? Do children confuse virtual communities and human connection for the real thing?"[191]

As technology plays an ever-bigger role in people's daily lives, questions of safety, trust, and human interaction all become increasingly important.

Notes

1 Howell, S. (2023, July 24). *Technology competition: A battle for brains.* Center for a New American Security. www.cnas.org/publications/reports/technology-competition-a-battle-for-brains

2 Tucker, P. (2023). The pentagon's AI chief is "scared to death" of ChatGPT. *Nextgov/FCW.* www.nextgov.com/emerging-tech/2023/05/pentagons-ai-chief-scared-death-chatgpt/385969/

3 Benson, E. (2020). *The human program: A transatlantic AI agenda.* Bertelsmann Foundation. https://downloads.ctfassets.net/9vgcz0fppkl3/32sgTmrPHa5 MTpoe6Ysbho/2e16bf431afbd1430e53850b1ecdacc2/Human_Program_FI NAL.pdf

4 The White House. (2022, October). *National security strategy.*

5 For further reading on this topic, see Wall, D. S. (2007). *Cybercrime: The transformation of crime in the information age* (1st ed.). Grabosky, P. (2007). *Electronic crime.* Pearson Prentice Hall; Grabosky, P., Smith, R. G., & Urbas, G. (2004). *Cyber criminals on trial.* Cambridge University.

6 The White House Office of Science and Technology Policy. (2020, February). *American artificial intelligence initiative: Year one annual report.* www.nitrd. gov/nitrdgroups/images/c/c1/American-AI-Initiative-One-Year-Annual-Rep ort.pdf

7 Nasheri, H. (2021, December 21). *The dumb and the dangerous road ahead.* United Nations Interregional Crime and Justice Research Institute.

8 National Security Commission on Artificial Intelligence. (2021). *The role of AI technology in pandemic response and preparedness: Recommended investments and initiatives* (White paper series on pandemic response and preparedness, No. 3).

9 Koblentz, G. D. (2020). Emerging technologies and the future of CBRN terrorism. *The Washington Quarterly, 43*, 177–196.

10 The Center for Long-Term Resilience. (2021, June). Future proof: The opportunity to transform the UK's resilience to extreme risks.

11 Machines with superhuman intelligence, built by humans but not fully understood, could endanger humanity.

12 Kleinman, Z. (2023). AI "godfather" Yoshua Bengio feels "lost" over life's work. *BBC.* www.bbc.com/news/technology-65760449

13 Allen, M. (2023). *The singularity is back.* Axios.

14 Vallance, C. (2023). *Artificial intelligence could lead to extinction, experts warn.* BBC. www.bbc.com/news/uk-65746524

15 Allen, M. (2023). *Youthful trust in A.I.* Axios.

16 The Crown Secretary of State for Digital, Culture, Media and Sport. (2022, July). *Establishing a pro-innovation approach to regulating AI: An overview of the UK's emerging approach.* Secretary of State for Digital, Culture, Media and Sport by Command of Her Majesty. www.gov.uk/government/publications/ establishing-a-pro-innovation-approach-to-regulating-ai/establishing-a-pro-inn ovation-approach-to-regulating-ai-policy-statement

17 National Security Commission on Artificial Intelligence. (2019, November). *Interim report.* www.nscai.gov/wp-content/uploads/2021/01/NSCAI-Interim-Report-for-Congress_201911.pdf

18 United Nations Interregional Crime and Justice Research Institute. (2019). *Artificial intelligence and robotics for law enforcement.* www.europarl.europa. eu/cmsdata/196207/UNICRI%20-%20Artificial%20intelligence%20and%20r obotics%20for%20law%20enforcement.pdf

19 Anadiotis, G. (2020, September 10). *AI and automation vs. the COVID-19 pandemic: Trading liberty for safety.* ZDNet. www.zdnet.com/article/ai-and-automation-vs-the-covid-19-pandemic-trading-safety-for-liberty/?ftag=TRE-03-10aaa6b&bhid=28036118512285295119801408296132&mid=13038677&cid=2021730405. Also see, Congressional Research Service. (2023, August 22). *Law enforcement and technology: Use of unmanned aircraft systems.* See Goodwin, G. L. (2021, July 13). *Facial recognition technology: Federal law enforcement agencies should have better awareness of systems used by employees* (Testimony before the Subcommittee on Crime, Terrorism, and Homeland Security, Committee on the Judiciary, House of Representatives). United States Government Accountability Office.

20 The President's National Security Telecommunications Advisory Committee (NSTAC). (2023). *Strategy for increasing trust in the information and communications technology and services ecosystem.*

21 Salmon, F. (2023). *Cars' "unmatched power" to spy on drivers.* Axios. www.axios.com/2023/09/08/car-data-privacy-record-listen-mozilla-report

22 U.S. Department of Transportation. (2018, October). *Preparing for the future of transportation: Automated vehicles 3.0.* file:///Users/chloebenadum/Desktop/av-30-web-version.pdf

23 Muller, J. (2022). *Your next car might not drive if you've been drinking.* Axios.

24 Allison, P. (2022). *Will we ever… live in city-sized buildings?* BBC.

25 Snow, J. (2017, July 20). *This AI traffic system in Pittsburgh has reduced travel time by 25%.* Smart Cities Dive. www.smartcitiesdive.com/news/this-ai-traffic-system-in-pittsburgh-has-reduced-travel-time-by-25/447494/

26 Graph Convolution Network. (2022, August). *Smart city apps.*

27 Kelley, A. (2023). US teams up with partner nations to release smart city cyber guidance. *Nextgov/FCW.* www.nextgov.com/cybersecurity/2023/04/us-teams-partner-nations-release-smart-city-cyber-guidance/385412/

28 Department of Homeland Security. (2020, December 22). *2020 national preparedness report.* www.hsdl.org/c/view?docid=848274

29 Atleson, M. (2023). *The Luring Test: AI and the engineering of consumer trust.* Federal Trade Commission. www.ftc.gov/business-guidance/blog/2023/05/luring-test-ai-engineering-consumer-trust

30 National Science and Technology Council. (2019, June). *The national artificial intelligence research and development strategic plan: 2019 update.* www.nitrd.gov/pubs/National-AI-RD-Strategy-2019.pdf

31 The White House. (2022, October). *Blueprint for an AI Bill of Rights: Making automated systems work for the American people.*

32 The White House. (2022, October). *Blueprint for an AI Bill of Rights: Making automated systems work for the American people.*

33 Deloitte Center for Government Insights. (2021, April). *Criminal justice and the technological revolution.* www.deloitte.com/global/en/Industries/government-public/perspectives/criminal-justice-and-the-technological-revolution.html

34 Select Committee on Artificial Intelligence of the National Science and Technology Council. (2020, November 17). *Recommendations for leveraging cloud computing resources for federally funded artificial intelligence research and development.* www.nitrd.gov/pubs/Recommendations-Cloud-AI-RD-Nov2 020.pdf

35 Franks, J. (2022). *Cloud computing: Federal agencies face four challenges.* U.S. GAO. www.gao.gov/products/gao-22-106195

36 Select Committee on Artificial Intelligence of the National Science and Technology Council. (2020, November 17). *Recommendations for leveraging cloud computing resources for federally funded artificial intelligence research and development.*

37 Goasduff, L. (2019). *Gartner says 5.8 billion enterprise and automotive IoT endpoints will be in use in 2020.* Gartner. www.gartner.com/en/newsroom/ press-releases/2019-08-29-gartner-says-5-8-billion-enterprise-and-automot ive-io

38 Homeland Security Digital Library. (2020, December 22). *FEMA 2020 national preparedness report.*

39 Lewis, J. A., Lostri, E., & Cheng, C. (2022, February 15). *AI strategies and autonomous vehicles development.* Center for Strategic & International Studies.

40 U.S. Department of Transportation. (2020, January). *Ensuring American leadership in automated vehicle technologies: Automated vehicles 4.0.* www.tra nsportation.gov/sites/dot.gov/files/2020-02/EnsuringAmericanLeadershipAVTe ch4.pdf

41 Bastone, N. (2022). *Exclusive: Free robo-rides for USF students.* Axios.

42 Cusack, J. (2021, November 29). *How driverless cars will change our world.* BBC. https://bbc.com/future/article/20211126-how-driverless-cars-will-cha nge-our-world

43 Fitzpatrick, A., Kingson, J., & Muller, J. (2023). *Self-driving car fears on the rise.* Axios. www.axios.com/2023/03/03/self-driving-car-fears-poll

44 U.S. Department of Transportation. (2018, October). *Preparing for the future of transportation: Automated vehicles 3.0.* file:///Users/chloebenadum/Desktop/ av-30-web-version.pdf

45 U.S. Department of Transportation. (2020, January). *Ensuring American leadership in automated vehicle technologies: Automated vehicles 4.0* www.tra nsportation.gov/sites/dot.gov/files/2020-02/EnsuringAmericanLeadershipAVTe ch4.pdf

46 U.S. Department of Commerce. (2024, February 29). *Citing national security concerns, Biden-Harris administration announces inquiry into connected vehicles.* www.commerce.gov/news/press-releases/2024/02/citing-national- security-concerns-biden-harris-administration-announces

47 Joint Concept for Robotic and Autonomous Systems. (2015, December 8). *Update: Overall classification of this briefing is UNCLASSIFIED.*

48 Nichols, G. (2021, December 22). *2022: A major revolution in robotics.* ZDNet. www.zdnet.com/article/2022-prediction-a-major-revolution-in-robotics/

49 Hereid, A. (2022). *Why household robot servants are a lot harder to build than robotic vacuums and automated warehouse workers.* Nextgov/FCW.

www.nextgov.com/ideas/2022/09/why-household-robot-servants-are-lot-har der-build-robotic-vacuums-and-automated-warehouse-workers/376867/

50 Nicholas, G. (2022). *Robots have rushed in to fill jobs people don't want. What happens if recession hits?* ZDNet. www.zdnet.com/article/robots-have-rushed-in-to-fill-jobs-people-dont-want-what-happens-if-recession-hits/

51 Kageyama, Y. (2022). *Robot that stocks drinks is newest thing at the corner store.* AP News.

52 Singh, A. (2023). *World's first "robot lawyer" will soon defend a human in court. The swaddle.* https://theswaddle.com/worlds-first-robot-lawyer-will-soon-defend-a-human-in-court/.

53 Allen, M. (2023). *Future of pharmacies: Robots + AI.* Axios.

54 Fitzpatrick, A., Kingston, J., & Muller, J. (2023). *Meet Abel, a robot with empathy.* Axios.

55 Maynard, A. (2021). *Elon Musk's Tesla bot raises serious concerns—But probably not the ones you think.* Nextgov/FCW. www.nextgov.com/ideas/2021/09/elon-musks-tesla-bot-raises-serious-concerns-probably-not-ones-you-think/185202/

56 Fitzpatrick, A., Kingston, J., & Muller, J. (2023, March 20). *Grocery bots.* Axios.

57 Nichols, G. (2022, January 27). *Should robots be able to deliver booze?* ZDNet.

58 Fitzpatrick, A., Kingston, J., & Muller, J. (2023, March 20). *Grocery bots.* Axios.

59 Palmai, K., & Smale, W. (2021, December 20). *The robot chefs that can cook your Christmas dinner.* BBC. www.bbc.com/news/business-59651334

60 Cobler, N. (2022, February 9). *LA-based Coco, a remotely piloted Delivery Service, expands to Austin.* Axios.

61 Fitzpatrick, A., Kingston, J., & Muller, J. (2023). *Chatbots at the drive-through.* Axios.

62 Europol Unclassified. (2017). *Crime in the age of technology.* www.europol.eur opa.eu/publications-events/main-reports/european-union-serious-and-organi sed-crime-threat-assessment-2017

63 Offenhartz, J. (2021, April 29). *NYPD sending its "Creepy" robot dog to the farm upstate.* Gothamist.

64 Zaveri, M. (2021, April 14). N.Y.P.D.'s robot dog returns to work, touching off a backlash. *The New York Times.*

65 Cramer, M., & Hauser, C. (2021, February 27). Digidog, a robotic dog used by the police, stirs privacy concerns. *The New York Times.* www.nytimes.com/2021/02/27/nyregion/nypd-robot-dog.html

66 Raskin, S., & Woods, A. (2021, April 15). *De Blasio says "we should rethink" NYPD's robot dog over public concerns.* New York Post.

67 Harding, E., & Ghoorhoo, H. (2023, April). *Seven critical technologies for winning the next war.* Center for Strategic & International Studies.

68 Breeden II, J. (2022). *Clouds of smart robots swarm into reality.* Nextgov/FCW. www.nextgov.com/emerging-tech/2022/01/clouds-smart-robots-swarm-reality/361130/

69 Breeden II, J. (2022). *Clouds of smart robots swarm into reality.* Nextgov/FCW. www.nextgov.com/emerging-tech/2022/01/clouds-smart-robots-swarm-reality/361130/

70 Matyszczyk, C. (2021, January 25). *That cute robot comp can instantly work out who you are.* ZDNet. www.zdnet.com/article/that-cute-robot-cop-can-instantly-work-out-who-you-are/

71 Allen, M. (2023). *Youthful trust in A.I.* Axios.

72 McFarland, T., & McCormack, T. (2014). *Mind the gap: Can developers of autonomous weapons systems be liable for war crimes?* The United State Naval War College.

73 Fitzpatrick, A. (2022, August 29). *Drones are sniffing out landmines in Ukraine.* Axios. www.axios.com/2022/08/29/drones-landmines-ukraine

74 Boyd, A. (2023). *TSA says its drone program won't collect much info on the public.* Nextgov/FCW. Nextgov/FCW. www.nextgov.com/analytics-data/2023/05/tsa-says-its-drone-program-wont-collect-much-info-public/386122/

75 Nichols, G. (2021, December 9). *Pirate-hunting drone monitors crime on the high seas.* ZDNet. www.zdnet.com/article/pirate-hunting-drone-monitors-crime-on-high-seas/

76 Tucker, P. (2022). *The U.S. military is buying electric jet-ski robots.* Nextgov/FCW. www.nextgov.com/emerging-tech/2022/09/military-buying-electric-jet-ski-robots/377565/

77 Europol Unclassified. (2017). *Crime in the age of technology.* www.europol.europa.eu/publications-events/main-reports/european-union-serious-and-organised-crime-threat-assessment-2017

78 Koblentz, G. D. (2020). Emerging technologies and the future of CBRN terrorism. *The Washington Quarterly*, 43, 177–196.

79 Hambling, D. (2021, November 5). Drone used in attack on US electrical grid last year, report reveals. *New Scientist.*

80 BBC. (2021, April 21). *Mexico cartel used explosive drones to attack police.* www.bbc.com/news/world-latin-america-56814501

81 Koblentz, G. D. (2020). Emerging technologies and the future of CBRN terrorism. *The Washington Quarterly*, 43, 177–196.

82 Errick, K. (2023). *IBM, NASA will use AI to improve climate change research.* www.nextgov.com/emerging-tech/2023/02/ibm-nasa-will-use-ai-improve-climate-change-research/382437/

83 Levinson, K. (2023). *Homelessness could have a 3D-printed solution.* Route Fifty. www.route-fifty.com/emerging-tech/2023/07/homelessness-could-have-3d-printed-solution/388442/

84 Joy, L., & Nolan, J. (2016–2022). *Westworld* [TV series]. Kilter Films; Bad Robot; Jerry Weintraub Productions; Warner Bros Television.

85 Vallance, C. (2022). *3D printed guns: Warnings over growing threat of 3D firearms.* BBC. www.bbc.co.uk/news/technology-63495123

86 Europol Unclassified. (2017). *Crime in the age of technology.*

87 United States Department of Defense. (2022, March). *Summary of the Joint All-Domain Command (JADC2) & control strategy.*

88 Department of the Air Force. (2019). *The United States Air Force artificial intelligence annex to the Department of Defense Artificial Intelligence Strategy.* www.af.mil/Portals/1/documents/5/USAF-AI-Annex-to-DoD-AI-Strategy.pdf

89 Arasasingham, A., & Goodman, M. P. (2023, April 13). *Operationalizing data free flow with trust (DFFT)*. Center for Strategic & International Studies. www.csis.org/analysis/operationalizing-data-free-flow-trust-dfft

90 United States of America Department of State. (2021, September). *Enterprise data strategy: Empowering Data Informed Diplomacy*. Retrieved from www.state.gov/wp-content/uploads/2021/09/Reference-EDS-Accessible.pdf

91 Agomuoh, F. (2022). *AI image generation propagates gender and racial stereotypes*. Digital Trends.

92 Palmer, D. (2020, March 2). *AI is changing everything about cybersecurity, for better and for worse*. ZDNet. www.zdnet.com/article/ai-is-changing-everything-about-cybersecurity-f

93 Waddell, K. (2018, June 27). *AI might need a therapist, too*. Axios. www.axios.com/2018/06/27/ai-might-need-a-psychologist-1529700757

94 The White House. (2022, October). *Blueprint for an AI Bill of Rights: Making automated systems work for the American people*.

95 Wright, G. (2023). *Amazon to pay $25m over child privacy violations*. BBC. www.bbc.com/news/technology-65772154

96 Graham, E. (2022). *Amazon admits to giving ring footage without owners' permission*. Nextgov/FCW. www.nextgov.com/analytics-data/2022/07/amazon-admits-giving-police-ring-footage-without-owners-permission/374480/

97 National Security Commission on Artificial Intelligence. (2020, July 22). *Key considerations for the responsible development and fielding of artificial intelligence*.

98 Arasasingham, A., & Goodman, M. P. (2023, April 13). *Operationalizing data free flow with trust (DFFT)*. Center for Strategic & International Studies. www.csis.org/analysis/operationalizing-data-free-flow-trust-dfft

99 European Union Agency for Fundamental Rights (FRA). (2020). *Facial recognition technology: Fundamental rights considerations in the context of law enforcement*.

100 Federal Trade Commission. (2022). *Commercial surveillance and data security rulemaking*. Kvgo. https://kvgo.com/ftc/commercial-surveillance-sep-8.

101 Special Competitive Studies Project. (2022, September). Mid-decade challenges to national competitiveness. www.scsp.ai/2022/09/special-competitive-studies-project-releases-first-report-sept-12-2022/

102 Graham, E. (2022). *Federal action is needed to protect consumer data, new report says*. Nextgov/FCW. www.nextgov.com/analytics-data/2022/09/federal-action-needed-protect-consumer-data-new-report-says/377089/

103 U.S. Department of Transportation. (2018, October). *Preparing for the future of transportation: Automated vehicles 3.0*.

104 Kelley, A. (2021). Data broker sales to law enforcement violate fourth amendment, senator argues. Nextgov/FCW. www.nextgov.com/policy/2021/12/data-broker-sales-law-enforcement-violate-fourth-amendment-senator-argues/359784/

105 The White House. (2022, October). *Blueprint for an AI Bill of Rights: Making automated systems work for the American people*.

106 U.S. Department of Homeland Security. (2020, December). *U.S. Department of Homeland Security Artificial Intelligence Strategy.* www.dhs.gov/sites/defa ult/files/publications/dhs_ai_strategy.pdf

107 Department of Defense. (2018). *Summary of the 2018 Department of Defense Artificial Intelligence Strategy: Harnessing AI to advance our security and prosperity.* https://media.defense.gov/2019/Feb/12/2002088963/-1/-1/1/ SUMMARY-OF-DOD-AI-STRATEGY.PDF

108 Department of Defense. (2018). *Summary of the 2018 Department of Defense Artificial Intelligence Strategy: Harnessing AI to advance our security and prosperity.* https://media.defense.gov/2019/Feb/12/2002088963/-1/-1/1/ SUMMARY-OF-DOD-AI-STRATEGY.PDF

109 Congressional Research Service. (2020, November 10). *Artificial intelligence and national security* (CRS Report No. R45178). https://crsreports.congress. gov/product/pdf/R/R45178/10

110 The National Institute of Standards and Technology (NIST) was founded in 1901 and is now part of the U.S. Department of Commerce. NIST role is to promote U.S. innovation and industrial competitiveness by advancing measurement science, standards, and technology in ways that enhance economic security and improve our quality of life. www.nist.gov/about-nist

111 National Institute of Standards and Technology, U.S. Department of Commerce (NIST). (2023). *Artificial Intelligence Risk Management Framework (AI RMF 1.0).* Retrieved from https://nvlpubs.nist.gov/nistpubs/ai/NIST.AI.100-1.pdf

112 Congressional Research Service. (2020, November 10). *Artificial intelligence and national security* (CRS Report No. R45178). https://crsreports.congress. gov/product/pdf/R/R45178/10

113 Department of the Air Force. (2019). *The United States Air Force artificial intelligence annex to the Department of Defense Artificial Intelligence Strategy.* www.af.mil/Portals/1/documents/5/USAF-AI-Annex-to-DoD-AI-Strategy.pdf

114 United States Government Accountability Office. (2021, June). *Artificial intelligence: An accountability framework for federal agencies and other entities* (GAO-21-519SP). www.gao.gov/assets/gao-21-519sp.pdf

115 Patterson, D. (2023). *ChatGPT is more like an "alien intelligence" than a human brain, says futurist.* ZDNet.

116 Breeden II, J. (2022). *Artificial intelligence continues to evolve in government and elsewhere.* Nextgov/FCW. www.nextgov.com/emerging-tech/2022/09/art ificial-intelligence-continues-evolve-government-and-elsewhere/376811/

117 Office of the Chief Economist IP Data Highlights. (2020, October). *Inventing AI: Tracing the diffusion of artificial intelligence with U.S. patents* (IP Data Highlights, Number 5). www.uspto.gov/sites/default/files/documents/ OCE-DH-AI.pdf

118 Mailes, G., Carrasco, M., & Arcuri, A. (2021, April). *The global trust imperative.* BCG & Salesforce. https://web-assets.bcg.com/bf/de/d2a310054cd88 91fd7f8cd95452b/the-global-trust-imperative-salesforce-bcg-whitepaper.pdf

119 Greig, J. (2023). CISA director: *AI cyber threats the "biggest issue we're going to deal with this century."* The Record. https://therecord.media/cisa-director-ai-cyber-threats-the-biggest-of-the-century

120 Vallance, C. (2023). *Powerful artificial-intelligence ban possible, government adviser warns.* BBC. www.bbc.com/news/technology-65779181

121 Davis, N. (2021, October 29). "Yeah, we're spooked": AI starting to have big real-world impact, says expert. *The Guardian.*

122 Rosenberg, S. (2022). *Chatbot AI has a mind of its own, Google engineer claims.* Axios.

123 Kleinman, Z., & Vallance, C. (2023). *BBC News: AI 'godfather' Geoffrey Hinton warns of dangers as he quits Google.* BBC. www.bbc.com/news/world-us-canada-65452940

124 Bailey, M. (2023). *Why humans can't trust AI: You don't know how it works, what it's going to do or whether it'll serve your interests.* Route Fifty. www.route-fifty.com/emerging-tech/2023/09/why-humans-cant-trust-ai-you-dont-know-how-it-works-what-its-going-do-or-whether-itll-serve-your-interests/390262/

125 National Artificial Intelligence Advisory Committee. (2023, May). *National Artificial Intelligence Advisory Committee year 1 report 2023.* www.ai.gov/wp-content/uploads/2023/05/NAIAC-Report-Year1.pdf

126 Matyszczyk, C. (2023). *McDonald's drive-thru robot made a mistake. Then it all got ridiculous.* ZDNet. www.zdnet.com/article/mcdonalds-drive-thru-robot-made-a-mistake-then-it-all-got-ridiculous/

127 Breeden II, J. (2024, May 14). *Feds beware: New studies demonstrate key AI shortcoming.* Nextgov/FCW. www.nextgov.com/artificial-intelligence/2024/05/feds-beware-new-studies-demonstrate-key-ai-shortcomings/396526/

128 National Institute of Standards and Technology, U.S. Department of Commerce. (2022). *Towards a standard for identifying and managing bias in artificial intelligence.* https://nvlpubs.nist.gov/nistpubs/SpecialPublications/NIST.SP.1270.pdf

129 BBC. (2023). *ChatGPT owner in probe over risks around false answers.* www.bbc.com/news/business-66196223

130 Snyder, A. (2024). *AI's flawed human yardstick.* Axios.

131 The Stack. (2022). *Technology use in the justice system is a "Wild West" warn Peers.* https://thestack.technology/police-ai-toolsnew-technologies-in-the-justice-system/.

132 Fried, I. (2020, June 15). *Fresh concerns about AI bias in the age of COVID-19.* Axios. www.axios.com/2020/06/15/fresh-concerns-about-ai-bias-in-the-age-of-covid-19

133 Clayton, J. & Hooker, L. (2023). *White House: Big Tech bosses told to protect public from AI risks.* BBC. www.bbc.com/news/business-65489163

134 Science Focus. (2018). Can an algorithm deliver justice? *BBC Science Focus Magazine.* www.sciencefocus.com/future-technology/can-an-algorithm-deliver-justice/

135 Graham, E. (2024, January 29). *Stop funding predictive policing tech without "evidence standards," lawmakers tell DOJ.* Nextgov/FCW. www.nextgov.com/artificial-intelligence/2024/01/stop-funding-predictive-policing-tech-without-evidence-standards-lawmakers-tell-doj/393705/

136 Schwartz, R., Down, L., Jonas, A., & Tabassi, E. (2021, June). *A proposal for identifying and managing bias within artificial intelligence* (Draft NIST

Special Publication 1270). U.S. Department of Commerce. https://nvlpubs. nist.gov/nistpubs/SpecialPublications/NIST.SP.1270-draft.pdf

137 National Security Commission on Artificial Intelligence. (2019, July 31). *Initial report.* Retrieved from www.nscai.gov/wp-content/uploads/2021/01/ NSCAI_Initial-Report-to-Congress_July-2019.pdf

138 Kelley, A. (2023). *4 agencies pledge enforcement against AI bias.* Nextgov/ FCW. www.nextgov.com/emerging-tech/2023/04/4-agencies-pledge-enforcem ent-against-ai-bias/385638/

139 Schwartz, R., Down, L., Jonas, A., & Tabassi, E. (2021, June). *A proposal for identifying and managing bias within artificial intelligence* (Draft NIST Special Publication 1270). U.S. Department of Commerce. https://nvlpubs. nist.gov/nistpubs/SpecialPublications/NIST.SP.1270-draft.pdf

140 Walsh, B. (2020, July 22). *The continuing problem of Ai Bias.* Axios. www. axios.com/2020/07/22/artificial-intelligence-bias-gender-race-religion

141 Schwartz, R., Down, L., Jonas, A., & Tabassi, E. (2021, June). *A proposal for identifying and managing bias within artificial intelligence* (Draft NIST Special Publication 1270). U.S. Department of Commerce. https://nvlpubs. nist.gov/nistpubs/SpecialPublications/NIST.SP.1270-draft.pdf

142 Zeitchik, S. (2021, November 19). A Utah Company says it revolutionized truth-telling technology. Experts are highly skeptical. *The Washington Post.*

143 FCW. (2022). Machine Learning on the Job. www.govexec.com/assets/mach ine-learning-job-fcwq322/portal/

144 Walsh, B. (2021, November 17). *Taming the wild west of AI hiring tools.* Axios. www.axios.com/2021/11/17/ai-hiring-tools-audit-laws

145 U.S. Agency of International Development. (2022, May). *USAID artificial intelligence action plan.* www.usaid.gov/sites/default/files/2022-05/USAID_ Artificial_Intelligence_Action_Plan.pdf

146 Atleson, M. (2023). *The Luring Test: AI and the engineering of consumer trust.* Federal Trade Commission. www.ftc.gov/business-guidance/blog/2023/ 05/luring-test-ai-engineering-consumer-trust

147 United States Intelligence Community. (2020). *Artificial intelligence ethics framework for the intelligence community.*

148 Down, L., Jonas, E., Schwartz, R., Schwartz, R., & Tabassi, E. (2021, June). *A proposal for identifying and managing bias within artificial intelligence* (Draft NIST Special Publication 1270). National Institute of Standards and Technology, U.S. Department of Commerce. https://nvlpubs.nist.gov/nistp ubs/SpecialPublications/NIST.SP.1270-draft.pdf

149 Dafoe, A., & Zhang, B. (2019, January). *Artificial intelligence: American attitudes and trends.* Center for the Governance of AI, Future of Humanity Institute, University of Oxford.

150 Muller, V. C. (2020, April 30). *Ethics of artificial intelligence and robotics.* Stanford Encyclopedia of Philosophy. https://plato.stanford.edu/entries/eth ics-ai/

151 Gold, A. (2023). *Scoop: Ron Conway to convene tech execs on AI policy.* Axios.

152 U.S. Chamber Staff. (2022). *Ensuring ethical AI.* U.S. Chamber of Commerce. www.uschamber.com/technology/how-to-make-ai-more-ethical-transparent- and-useful-for-everyone

153 National Institute of Standards and Technology (NIST). (2021, October). *Draft- taxonomy of AI risk*. www.nist.gov/system/files/documents/2021/10/15/taxonomy_AI_risks.pdf

154 National Security Commission on Artificial Intelligence. (2021, April 26). *Key considerations for the responsible development and fielding of artificial intelligence.*

155 The White House. (2020). *Guidance for regulation of artificial intelligence applications.* www.whitehouse.gov/wp-content/uploads/2020/01/Draft-OMB-Memo-on-Regulation-of-AI-1-7-19.pdf

156 Chin-Rothmann, C. (2022). *U.S. digital privacy troubles do not start or end with TikTok.* Center for Strategic & International Studies. www.csis.org/analysis/us-digital-privacy-troubles-do-not-start-or-end-tiktok

157 Rosenberg S. (2023). *In AI arms race, ethics may be the first casualty.* Axios. www.axios.com/2023/01/31/chatgpt-ai-arms-race-ethics-competition

158 European Commission. (2019, April 8). *Ethics guidelines for trustworthy AI.* https://ec.europa.eu/futurium/en/ai-alliance-consultation.1.html

159 Deutsche Welle. (2023). *EU lawmakers take first steps toward tougher AI rules.* DW Technology Europe. www.dw.com/en/eu-lawmakers-take-first-steps-toward-tougher-ai-rules/a-65585731

160 Kelley, A. (2023). *EU approves US approach to safeguard transatlantic data flows.* Nextgov/FCW. www.nextgov.com/digital-government/2023/07/eu-approves-us-approach-safeguard-transatlantic-data-flows/388353/

161 Das Gupta, S. (2021, August 23). *How 5G will change the world.* Ozy. www.ozy.com/pg/newsletter/the-daily-dose/439735/

162 Graham, E. (2022). *Lockheed Martin, Verizon demonstrate capabilities of 5G-enabled drones for DOD.* Nextgov/FCW. www.nextgov.com/emerging-tech/2022/09/lockheed-martin-verizon-demonstrate-capabilities-5g-enabled-drones-dod/377795/

163 Miller, E. (2023). Wireless for government operated industrial networks; *How to choose the Best-Fit over a Force-Fit.* CISCO.

164 Heath, R. (2023). *What is private 5G and how industries are using it.* Axios.

165 Lee, M., Dimarogonas, J., Geist, E., Manuel, S., Schwankhart, R. A., & Downing., B. (2023). *Opportunities and risks of 5G military use in Europe.* Retrieved from www.rand.org/pubs/research_reports/RRA1351-2.html

166 National Security Commission on Artificial Intelligence. (2020, March). *First quarter recommendations.* www.nscai.gov/wp-content/uploads/2021/01/NSCAI-First-Quarter-Recommendations.pdf

167 Baksh, M. (2020). *Justice official explains why law enforcement is worried about 5G.* Nextgov/FCW. www.nextgov.com/cybersecurity/2020/07/justice-official-explains-why-law-enforcement-worried-about-5g/167127/

168 Baksh, M. (2020). *Justice official explains why law enforcement is worried about 5G.* Nextgov/FCW. www.nextgov.com/cybersecurity/2020/07/justice-official-explains-why-law-enforcement-worried-about-5g/167127/

169 Leprince-Ringuet, D. (2021, December 22). *Quantum Computers: Eight ways quantum computing is going to change the world.* ZDNet. www.zdnet.com/article/quantum-computers-eight-ways-quantum-computing-is-going-to-change-the-world/

170 McMahon, L. (2022, June 9). *Ministry of Defence Acquires Government's First Quantum Computer.* BBC. www.bbc.com/news/technology-61647134
171 Lewis, J., Moody, D., Merzbacher, C., & McMarty, B. (2022). *The future of quantum—Public/private collaboration for innovation and adoption.* Center for Strategic & International Studies. www.csis.org/events/future-quantum-publicprivate-collaboration-innovation-and-adoption
172 Australian Government Department of Industry, Science, Energy and Resources. (2023, May 3). *National Quantum Strategy.* www.industry.gov. au/publications/national-quantum-strategy
173 Special Competitive Studies Project. (2022, September). *Mid-decade challenges to national competitiveness.* www.scsp.ai/2022/09/special-competitive-stud ies-project-releases-first-report-sept-12-2022/
174 Sabin, S. (2023). *1 big thing: Averting quantum's encryption apocalypse.* Axios.
175 Kelley, A. (2023, January 18). *Push for more quantum tech investment reaches World Economic Forum.* Nextgov/FCW. www.nextgov.com/emerg ing-tech/2023/01/push-more-quantum-tech-investment-reaches-world-econo mic-forum/381906/
176 Gardner, F. (2022, January 27). *What is the quantum apocalypse and should we be scared?* BBC. www.bbc.com/news/technology-60144498
177 Baksh, M. (2022). *Preparations for quantum cyber threat get a Senate boost.* Nextgov/FCW. www.nextgov.com/cybersecurity/2022/12/preparations-quan tum-cyber-threat-get-senate-boost/380698/
178 Kelley, A. (2023). *The future of quantum security will be encoded in light, researchers hope.* Nextgov/FCW. www.nextgov.com/cybersecurity/2023/01/ future-quantum-security-will-be-encoded-light-researchers-hope/382037
179 Hill, J., McKenney, R., & Konkoly-Thege, K. (2023). *Moving toward an all-of-the-above approach to quantum cybersecurity.* Center for Strategic & International Studies. www.csis.org/analysis/moving-toward-all-above-appro ach-quantum-cybersecurity
180 Strategic Technologies Program. (2023). *The future of quantum—Developing a system teady for quantum.* Center for Strategic International Studies. www. csis.org/events/future-quantum-developing-system-ready-quantum
181 Hill, J., McKenney, R., & Konkoly-Thege, K. (2023). *Moving toward an all-of-the-above approach to quantum cybersecurity.* Center for Strategic & International Studies. www.csis.org/analysis/moving-toward-all-above-appro ach-quantum-cybersecurity
182 General Services Administration. (2021, February). *The digital worker iden- tity playbook.* www.idmanagement.gov/playbooks/dw/
183 Breeden II, J. (2023). *What AI-powered robots have to say about their future with humanity.* Nextgov/FCW. www.nextgov.com/artificial-intellige nce/2023/07/what-ai-powered-robots-have-say-about-their-future-humanity/ 388334/
184 Fried, I. (2023). *The global elite is excited and terrified by AI.* Axios.
185 Patterson, D. (2023). *ChatGPT is more like an "alien intelligence" than a human brain, says futurist.* ZDNet
186 Kingson, J. (2022). *"Cities of the future," built from scratch.* Axios.

187 Eisikovits N., & Feldman D. (2021). *AI is killing choice and chance—Which means changing what it means to be human.* Nextgov/FCW. www.nextgov. com/ideas/2021/03/ai-killing-choice-and-chance-which-means-changing-what-it-means-be-human/172299/

188 Fried, I. (2022). *The smartest AI is dumb without people.* Axios.

189 National Security Commission on Artificial Intelligence. (2019, July 31). *Initial report.* Retrieved from www.nscai.gov/wp-content/uploads/2021/01/ NSCAI_Initial-Report-to-Congress_July-2019.pdf

190 Turing, A. M. (1950) Computing machinery and intelligence. *Mind* 49: 433–460. https://redirect.cs.umbc.edu/courses/471/papers/turing.pdf

191 Sandel, M. (2024, January 25). *Will tech change what it means to be human? And does it matter?* Harvard Gazette. https://news.harvard.edu/gazette/story/ 2024/01/will-tech-change-what-it-means-to-be-human-and-does-it-matter/

2   The Magnitude of Change

In the words of the US Supreme Court Justice Breyer, "criminal justice of the future will look and feel different and it is imperative to create a justice workforce and leadership that will be comfortable with change and new technologies."[1]

AI in the Justice System

AI as an attractive technology, raises a wide range of legal, political, and technical challenges for law enforcement and counterterrorism agencies globally. When it comes to the criminal justice system, AI needs careful consideration. AI trained on data that have some latent bias can reinforce bias. If the data used to build a predictive model in a criminal justice system, for example, are drawn from records in a system with a history of racial discrimination, the model may reflect that history. These advanced technological tools result in legal headaches for those that use them in the criminal justice system. Deployment of AI tools in the justice system can have serious implications with respect to individual rights, raising important questions, like at what point could someone be imprisoned on the basis of a technological tool like AI?

In the absence of strict scientific validity and quality standards for the use of new emerging technological tools, careful consideration must be exercised in order to prevent potential devastating effects on human rights and civil liberties. The fairness of the justice system cannot be undermined. Emerging tools can exacerbate the preexisting inequalities in the justice system, therefore, weakening the rule of law for the sole purpose of achieving efficiency. This is simply not a wise choice.

Algorithms

There are significant risks in using algorithms, for example, in the sentencing decisions in criminal cases. False negatives and false positives can occur

DOI: 10.4324/9781003368304-3

when algorithms are used in the sentencing decision process, involving multiple factors. When making a sentencing decision, other factors beyond the risk of re-offending must be considered.[2] Discrimination in social policy can result not only from deliberate action but also from unspoken assumptions and practices that have been baked into systems; for example, data analyzed by AI. Responsible use of data, including data analyzed by AI, should question rather than reinforce preexisting biases. Exercising common sense and discretion and balancing algorithmic predictions with human judgment is necessary.[3]

While the use of technology in the justice system is not new, Covid-19 accelerated the reliance on digital and virtual technology in the justice system. The impact of these changes still has to be fully assessed.

Crime and Technology

Crime, justice, and social stability are influenced by advancements in emerging technologies.[4] Crime has never been stagnant; it evolves and adapts to new technologies and is becoming more complex, creating new challenges for law enforcement.[5] Over recent decades, as a result of emerging technologies, crimes have taken different forms.[6] Novel crimes require cutting-edge knowledge, investigative techniques, and tools. Law enforcement agencies are employing new technological devices to enhance their ability to conduct surveillance and respond to security threats more effectively. At the same time, law enforcement must be mindful of the practical and technical challenges of new technological tools when exploring these applications to fight crime. Investigators must be able to access technological tools, but they also have to be trained on how the tools should be used. For example, investigators have to be familiar with drone technology, mapping, and geolocation, AI and ML, predictive policing software, and the processing of big data.[7] Law enforcement agencies must be able to keep up with the rapid pace and adapt to the growing trends and developments, in particular learning about advancements in emerging technologies like AI and robotics.

Emerging technological tools offer societal benefits that correspond to the demand for crime reduction. Nonetheless, technology historically has been a double-edged sword, enhancing the capabilities and simultaneously jeopardizing the democratic values and constitutional principles at the core of the justice system.

In order to combat global emerging crimes, law enforcement agencies use advanced technologies. However, as mentioned above, they do not always have the required technical expertise and understanding of how these systems operate or arrive at certain decisions. This chapter focuses on the general landscape of the use of advanced emerging tools like AI and robotics by law enforcement agencies.

Law Enforcement and Emerging Tools

New technologies are transforming every aspect of the criminal justice process and potentially making law enforcement function more effectively and efficiently. These technologies also raise serious questions about constitutional rights, especially those protections found in the Fourth, Fifth, Sixth, Eighth, and Fourteenth Amendments in the US constitution. Integrating AI into law enforcement is a big shift from the technology's use in government. The technology is translating government communications, drafting documents, and handling traffic signals, ingesting data to produce insights and analysis. For instance, police departments across the US have expanded their data collection efforts to enhance community policing. While the use of emerging technologies has the potential to help solve crimes and identify unknown suspects, it also offers the potential for errors that could lead to the misidentification, arrest, and prosecution of an innocent person.[8]

Fingerprints of Texts

A new AI project headed by the Intelligence Advanced Research Projects Activity at the Department of Defense will have the ability to pinpoint the origins of any text message and link it back to the author. This technology will be significant for the investigation and prosecution of human trafficking platforms and other malicious content in text messaging. The program is known as human interpretable attribution of text using underlying structure (HIATUS). The program has been reading text messages written by humans and machines.[9]

Gunshot Detection Technology

A new device was invented in 2022, called *SDS Outdoor*, and was developed in a joint effort by the Department of Homeland Security and Shooter Detection Systems. The device can easily be deployed and transported. It uses two things: the sound and flash of a gunshot. It can detect and validate each gunshot, reducing false positives. Law enforcement agencies are attempting to make the system more effective.[10]

Risk Assessment Tools

Emerging technologies such as AI have been used in the past decade in the criminal justice system. An example includes the *Correctional Offender*

Management Profiling for Alternative Sanctions (COMPAS) software. Courts have used this system for potential recidivism risk assessment with considerable influence on sentencing and the execution of sanctions. COMPAS, like similar risk assessment tools, is used to predict an offender's likelihood of recidivism upon release. It does so by comparing offenders' data, collected through a questionnaire, with the data of a class of individuals called the "norm core data group." Based on this calculation, the system generates a risk score for each inmate. These tools have faced intense public scrutiny resulting in intense debate and criticism for inaccuracy and being racially discriminatory.[11]

Real-Time Crime Centers (RTCCs)

RTCCs aim to assist police with information to prevent deadly encounters and mistaken identity cases. They serve as surveillance hubs using various technologies to gather data. While data can benefit trend analysis in the use of force and arrests, it can also be misused and violate civil liberties. Also, there is reluctance on the part of police departments to report on officer use of force; thus, rendering the data inadequate for assessing national trends.[12]

Detecting Lies

A tool called *VeriPol*, developed in 2018, uses ML and text analysis to identify false robbery reports. The tool was used in police stations throughout Spain. The tool analyzed statement features like adjectives, verbs, and punctuation to detect patterns in false reports.[13]

Police Apps

In September 2022, five countries coordinated the raid and arrest of suspected sex offenders in Southern California. While the raid was successful, the law enforcement operation was conducted using a free trial app made to assist police, called *SweepWizard*. The use of this app resulted in leaked confidential details about the raid operation on the internet. The leaked data included private information and sensitive details (like social security numbers) about the suspects. In addition, the app leaked confidential details about previous raids conducted by other police departments over multiple years. While the app was launched in 2016, its use dated back to 2011.[14]

Body Cameras

Body-worn cameras have been widely distributed to police departments and are governed by a range of laws and regulations with respect to their usage. An AI tool is capable of instantly analyzing the footage to help identify behavioral problems with particular officers.[15] Police body-worn cameras can enhance the visibility of police work, including misconduct and violence as well as increasing police accountability.[16] The footage can expose sensitive moments in individuals' lives to the public and, furthermore, the recording can easily be accessed by open-records' requests. Sensitive information about the officers can be shared on platforms like YouTube, which can be accessible to the general public. Real concerns have been raised about FR from police-worn body cameras. Combining FR with body cameras increases the risk factors in real-time situations.[17]

Odin Intelligence

Odin Intelligence is a technology company that makes database software for law enforcement. Over 150 local, state, and federal agencies are using the Odin system, which offers a service that tracks homeless people. In 2023, the system was hacked, and sensitive information about users and customers was released. The released data included information such as names, addresses, dates, and possible reasons for monitoring. Furthermore, the leaked data showed that those that were monitored were labeled as threats, based on their mental health and housing status.[18]

AI Police Vans

A police department in the UK conducted an operation in 2023 using an AI-equipped police van. The operation used cameras to identify phone usage, texting, and seatbelt violations. During the week-long operation, the AI system identified drivers that were using their phone, individuals without seatbelts, and vehicle mechanical related issues.[19]

Active Smart Textiles (ASTs)

The Intelligence Advanced Research Projects Activity (IARPA) launched the *SMART ePANTS* program to create advanced computerized clothing. These garments, known as *Active Smart Textiles* (ASTs), are capable of recording audio, video, and geolocation data while remaining functional as regular clothing. Sensors are woven into everyday clothing like shirts, pants, and socks. These sensors turn regular garments into ASTs. They have the potential to benefit the IC, the Department of the Defense (DoD), and the Department of Homeland Security (DHS), as well as personnel and first responders working in challenging environments.[20]

Surveillance Technology

Video surveillance technology today is used in many different settings. Automated tools are used by employers to monitor and manage workers. An increasing number of American workers are tracked for productivity assessment by their employers. Examples include nurses wearing Radio Frequency Identification (RFID) badges (smart tags), rideshare drivers subjected to speed and location monitoring, and office workers having their activities recorded.[21] The rise of remote and hybrid work partially led to increased adoption of monitoring workplace productivity.

The most recent surveillance technology is designed to identify people seen on security cameras in real time or close to it. The aim is to match security camera footage with images tied to that person's identity, like police mugshots or social media profiles.[22] Affordable consumer technology and AI software have facilitated widespread surveillance. Law enforcement agencies worldwide have adopted AI-powered surveillance systems. Drones are now authorized for police use. AI-equipped drone surveillance has been used by police departments in the US for automatic analysis of footage, which is used for crowd monitoring and search and rescue efforts.[23] Surveillance robots, moving robots, and AI systems have been used in some countries for border security.[24] The use of AI is being adopted on the US–Mexico border to assist agents to better secure the crossing and combat the flow of illicit drugs into the US.

AI, drone systems, and similar tools may be helpful to law enforcement, but ultimately a successful operation still comes down to people as operators of the systems. While detecting weapons and predicting violence are solutions, at the same time the use of these tools requires thoughtful consideration of the implications.

It is evident that while these technologies offer advantages, they also carry risks when it comes to the well-being of workers, their safety, their mental health, and factors related to discrimination. For example, recent advancement in surveillance technology has raised privacy and ethical concerns.[25] The acquisition and use of police surveillance technology by numerous governments deserve greater scrutiny as these tools can pose serious threats to citizens. A tool that enables mass control and infringes on an individual's right to anonymity and privacy in public spaces poses a serious privacy concern.[26] AI video monitoring raises significant concern about privacy and surveillance. Many technology vendors provide "free trials" of their systems to police agencies for an extended period, which bypass the need for a purchasing agreement or budget approval.

Closed-Circuit Television (CCTV)

Surveillance technology has supported law enforcement for a long time. With the advent of closed-circuit television (CCTV), in particular, between the 1960s and 1970s, law enforcement has been able to quickly identify victims and persons of interest to solve crimes. As mentioned above, the technology has undergone significant advancement with AI, including bodycams and patrol drones.[27] Images, videos, and sounds contain information that can disclose the identity of individuals, the handling and use of which may present privacy concerns.

Dayton, Ohio

An activist in Dayton, Ohio, worked for years to persuade the police to stop using a controversial surveillance technology.[28] In 2019, the city had engaged in a contract with ShotSpotter, a company to install microphones that detect gunfire in a three-square-mile area west of the city of Dayton, a community with a predominantly Black population and a history of economic segregation. In 2022, the Dayton Police Department announced it would not renew the contract, citing challenges in proving the technology's effectiveness. The company is now known as *SoundThinking*. Research and legal challenges have questioned the technology's effectiveness and reliability as evidence. Despite its setback in some cities, the use of ShotSpotter continues to grow, prompting fears that it could return in a different form, possibly as part of a broader surveillance system combining various technologies like cameras, microphones, and FR.[29]

Paris Olympics

The Paris 2024 Olympics has raised concerns over the French plan for AI-surveillance. Real-time cameras were used to detect suspicious activity, like abandoned bags and unexpected crowds, and CCTV algorithms were employed by the police to detect abnormal activity. The plan explicitly prohibits FR. A version of the AI security system is already operational in some police stations in France. This AI system monitors multiple security cameras, and when it detects predefined triggers, such as sudden crowd gathering, it alerts human police officers to assess the situation and make decisions. The AI algorithm has been trained using a substantial dataset of images of lone bags on the street. However, detecting more complex situations, like a person on the ground in a crowd who possesses a concealed weapon, will be challenging to determine.[30]

Clearview

Another example of a controversial Facial Recognition Technology (FRT) company is Clearview AI. The company has FR machines installed at all airport security check points in the US. Clearview provides free trials of their system to anyone with a government or law enforcement email address as part of their strategic effort to "flood the market." The company's technology has also been used during protests, which has raised concerns about suppressing free speech.[31]

Large networks engaging in invasive practices without adequate safeguards contribute to unfair and deceptive practices.[32] US lawmakers have urged federal departments to stop using FR technology, specifically expressing concerns about Clearview AI's tool. A report by the Government Accountability Office revealed that multiple federal agencies, including the IRS, have employed Clearview AI's software for different purposes.[33]

Traffic Light System

In China, traffic light systems use face-scanning technology to detect journalists and other persons of interest, like foreign students and migrant women. The system classifies those it scans into a traffic light system: green, amber, and red. Journalists categorized as red would be heavily monitored. Once the technology detects certain individuals, their phone records, social media activity, chatroom activity, hotel stays, vehicle information, property ownership, online photos, and immigration status are collected.[34]

Global Positioning Systems (GPS)

Locating criminals and crime scenes is much easier now with the help of GPS. This technology is also used by law enforcement agencies to manage police forces more efficiently. When integrated with other systems, GPS can make data more robust by including location services in the reporting.[35]

AirTags

Police nationwide have been encouraging drivers to use Apple AirTags to track stolen cars. There is a growing concern that some victims are taking matters into their own hands. Real-time tracking creates a dangerous situation for victims and gives rise to legal complications. There have been fatalities as a result of victims acting on their own.[36]

Predictive Analytics

Perhaps predictive tools for some bring to mind the 2002 movie *Minority Report*,[37] a movie featuring Tom Cruise that depicts data science at its best. In this film, a team of humans with psychic abilities, or "data scientists" called *Precogs*, are able to predict future crimes by analyzing massive amounts of data. With this analysis, the visual data are transferred to the *Precrime*, a police unit that is sent to prevent the crime from happening. This concept touches on the idea of how data can be used in a positive way in the real world, for disastrous situations as well as making weather predictions.[38]

Predictive police algorithms employ mathematical analytics and technology to identify potential crimes, such as predicting locations and individuals involved in future illegal acts. Many have raised concerns about the accuracy of these systems. Some lawmakers cite illegal policing practices that discriminate against marginalized groups, in particular Black Americans, and have demanded audits and due process steps for those affected by algorithm policing. As mentioned in the previous chapter, large-scale machine-learning systems pose a risk beyond physical harm, such as biased data in predictive policing algorithms.

In 2022, it was reported that a University of Chicago professor had developed an AI algorithm capable of predicting crimes in advance. The model that was developed could forecast crimes at specific locations with a week's notice. The algorithm focused on predicting the events and did not provide details about the individuals involved, using intervention strategies to prevent crimes.[39]

Some leaders acknowledge that imperfect algorithms that try to predict where crimes might occur can make mistakes and perpetuate ongoing biases and stereotypes in certain communities. Some have even considered banning FR in public spaces because of its potential for abuse.

Smart applications are designed to predict crimes and predictive analytics for criminal activities are guiding decisions. Algorithms promise to predict delinquent behavior, identify potentially dangerous individuals, and support crime investigation.[40] Robots are used for patrolling purposes to provide premises security, function as security guards, and patrol boarders in parts of the world. AI models and surveillance technologies are used for processing large data for law enforcement agencies in order to guide decision-making in the criminal justice system.

During the Covid-19 pandemic period, contactless biometric technology was widely adopted in some countries for purposes such as border control, law enforcement, surveillance, healthcare, and biotechnology, and now many years later it is used everywhere.

With many people using their faces to "open" and access devices such as smartphones, biometric technology has become an everyday consumer technology. Government agencies are cognizant of the fact that the implementation of these technologies in government settings raises a host of complications.

Biometrics

Biometrics is the automated recognition of individuals based on their behavioral and biological characteristics.[41] It has always been used as tool for solving identification issues. It pertains to the measurement of unique physiological human characteristics like body shape, facial features, fingerprints, and DNA, and can also be used for behavioral traits.

There are several biometric modalities, some examples include: fingerprints/finger scans (FP), FR, iris, voice, and deoxyribonucleic acid (DNA). Biometrics are collected and used by the DHS operational agencies to verify the identity of individuals that interact with the DHS. Prior to the formation of the DHS in 2003, the Immigration and Naturalization Service (INS) had developed the IDENT system (officially the Automated Biometric Identification System) in order to identify illegal migrants crossing US borders. While IDENT was effective in identifying recidivists, it was not sufficient to run through the FBI's fingerprint database known as the National Crime Information Center (NCIC).[42] To mitigate the shortcomings in the IDENT system, the DHS initiated a new system, the *Homeland Advanced Recognition Technology* (HART) in 2016.[43]

Process Flow between US.S. Customs and Border Protection and the *HART* System for Biometric Identification or Verification for Air, Land, or Sea Entry.[44]

Biometric identity management services, such as fingerprint matching and FRT services, are commonly used across business and government as a tool for identifying and verifying individuals or persons of interest.

Recently, the DHS in the US has been rolling out more advanced identity-verification screeners at airports, including modernized Credential Authentication Technology (CAT) units that employ facial biometrics. CAT-2 units use FRT to compare real-time photos of travelers against their government-issued IDs. Police, retail stores, and sports arenas are rapidly increasing biometric surveillance. Critics contend that the results are blindly trusted without adequate double-checking of matches. While the use of biometrics like FR is crucial for certain levels of digital identity proof, it raises concerns around privacy and equity.[45]

Risks

The rapid development and deployment of FRT is disconcerting. Research has suggested that the application of FRT disproportionately affects

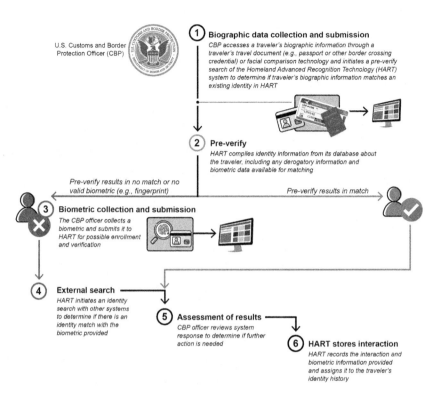

Figure 2.1 Planned Process Flow between US Customs and Border Protection and the Homeland Advanced Recognition Technology (HART) System for Biometric Identification or Verification for Air, Land, or Sea Entry

marginalized communities. For example, Remote Biometric Identification, or RBI, is an umbrella term for systems like FRT that scan and identify people using their faces or other body parts at a distance. This impacts citizens' comfort level, for example, in attending a protest or seeking healthcare like abortion in places where it is prohibited.

Dwreck Ingram

A Black Lives Matter protest organizer from New York was harassed by police at his apartment for four hours without a warrant or a charge, due to the fact that he had been identified by RBI following his participation in a Black Lives Matter protest.

Robert Williams

A resident of Detroit was falsely arrested for a theft committed by someone else.

Randall Reid

He was sent to jail in Louisiana, a state he had never visited, because the police wrongly identified him as a suspect in a robbery with FRT.[46]

Facial Recognition Technology (FRT)

Face detection and recognition is the ability of AI systems to identify faces or individual images or videos. FR has become a normal part of everyday life and continues to advance into people's lives, work environments, and public transportation systems. FR mimics how people identify others by examining their faces based on biological and behavioral characteristics.[47]

FRT uses a photo or still from a video feed of a person—often a live photo—and converts it into a template or mathematical representation of the photo. With technological advancements over recent decades, FRT has become increasingly common across business and government agencies.[48] FRT is in places like stadiums, amusement parks, and retail stores, where it is used to track people. The retail industry uses this technology for personalizing offers and tracking customers visits; nonetheless, customers may not be aware that they are being tracked, which raises concerns about privacy issues.[49]

Law Enforcement Agencies

In China, police are using sunglasses equipped with FRT to apprehend criminals. Railway police in China were the first to adopt these devices during high traffic periods. CCTV cameras throughout China have FR capabilities of identifying any citizen within three seconds.[50] The first FR searches in the US took place more than two decades ago. Federal law enforcement agencies in the US use FRT owned by their own agency or owned by other government entities to conduct their investigations. Law enforcement agencies may also request that another entity, like Clearview AI, conduct a search on their behalf. For example, law enforcement with an AI account may use a computer or smartphone to upload a photo of an unknown individual to Clearview AI's FR system. The system can return search results that show potential photos of the unknown individual, as well as links to the site where the photos were obtained (e.g., Facebook or other social media accounts).[51]

Owned system	• Department of Veterans Affairs Police Service • Federal Bureau of Prisons • National Aeronautics and Space Administration, Office of Protective Services
Used another entity's system	• Bureau of Alcohol, Tobacco, Firearms, and Explosives • Bureau of Diplomatic Security • Drug Enforcement Administration • Food and Drug Administration, Office of Criminal Investigations • U.S. Fish and Wildlife Service • U.S. Immigration and Customs Enforcement • Internal Revenue Service, Criminal Investigation Division • U.S. Capitol Police • U.S. Marshals Service • U.S. Park Police • U.S. Postal Inspection Service • U.S. Probation and Pretrial Services
Owned system and used another entity's system	• U.S. Customs and Border Protection • Federal Bureau of Investigation • Pentagon Force Protection Agency • U.S. Secret Service • Transportation Security Administration

Figure 2.2 Ownership and Use of Facial Recognition Technology Reported by US Federal Agencies That Employ Law Enforcement Officers

Source: *Facial Recognition Technology: Federal Law Enforcement Agencies Should Better Assess Privacy and Other Risks* GAO-21-518, June 3, 2021, https://www.gao.gov/products/gao-21-518

Ownership and Use of Facial Recognition Technology Reported by US Federal Agencies that Employ Law Enforcement Officers.[52]

Federal agencies that employ law enforcement agents use FRT to assist criminal investigations. For example, the technology can help identify an unknown individual in a photo or video surveillance.[53] Law enforcement agencies in the US do not need permission from anyone to use FR at the present time. There are no guidelines in any state laws for the use of FR.

Risks

As described above, in the criminal justice context, the process begins with a photo of a suspect typically taken from security camera footage. For example, FR on the iPhone is trained to match the device owner's photo, but the kind used by law enforcement agencies searches databases of mug shots or driver's license photos, and can contain millions of photos. It can

Figure 2.3 Examples of Facial Recognition Technology used by Federal Agencies

Source: United States Government Accountability Office. (2021, August). *Facial recognition technology: Current and planned uses by federal agencies* (Report No. GAO-21-526) www. gao.gov/assets/gao-21-526.pdf

fail in many ways. After a computer assembles a list of possible matches, police can pick a suspect and then show that photo to an eyewitness. Eyewitness testimony is one of the leading causes of wrongful convictions in the US. Prosecutors use FR to identify possible suspects but ultimately rely on eyewitness testimony. The technology remains hidden from the accused and the defense attorneys even though it played a role in the investigation process.

Concerns about the accuracy of emotion recognition algorithms in FRT have been raised by the AI Now Institute. The institute's report highlights the potential reliance on questionable science. AI developers' technical backgrounds may lead to uncritical acceptance of psychological literature. Despite these concerns, FRT with emotion recognition continues to be incorporated in numerous products, such as smart glasses, security cameras, and smartphones. There are a number of risks of using FRT by federal agencies and the public. The risks relate to privacy and accuracy of the systems.[54] For example, when agencies use FRT without first assessing the privacy implications, there is a risk that the agency will not adhere to privacy-related regulations and policies. More importantly, there is risk that federal system owners will share sensitive information, for example, a photo of a suspect during the course of an ongoing investigation, with the public and others. Most agencies do not track non-federal systems in use or other related risks. For instance, in 2023, a Black man was put in jail for almost a week in Georgia after an FRT mistook his face for a suspect in a New Orleans robbery. In New York City, a personal injury lawyer reported that she was kicked out of Radio City Music Hall after being identified by FRT. Radio City Music Hall is owned by MSG Entertainment, which owns and operates Madison Square Garden, which had banned all lawyers involved in lawsuits against the company from its properties, and as a result of FRT, the false arrest took place.[55] The retail store chain Kmart shut down their FRT after privacy concerns were raised in Australia. The stores were using the technology for customers' biometric data. Even though there were signs posted throughout the stores, customers were still unaware that their biometric data were being collected.[56]

The potential misuse for this technology extends far beyond airport security checkpoints. Once people become accustomed to government FR scans, it will become much easier to scan people's faces everywhere, from sidewalks to schools and in all public buildings and parks.

Transparency and Law Enforcement

Rapid use of emerging tools is taking place without a clear legal or regulatory framework. Given the potential risks, law enforcement agencies have a duty of openness to ensure full transparency for using emerging tools like AI.[57] Most law enforcement agencies do not have the expertise, training, and resources to carry out data evaluations for the predictive tools that they use. For example, for comparison's sake, in the medical field it is customary for proper trials to be conducted prior to the use of AI tools. However, currently there are no scientific or ethical standards for the use of emerging tools such as AI in the criminal justice field.

Law enforcement agencies have a responsibility to uphold constitutional guarantees when considering the potential benefits and risks associated with the use of new emerging tools.[58] For example, with respect to use of third parties for FRT, there is no mechanism to track what non-federal systems are used by agents; therefore, there is no visibility into the technology that they rely on for conducting their investigations.

Transparency is needed to build trust in FRT. This means the need for creating policy and standards around the collection and use of the personal information that underlies the training of FR systems.[59] Today, FRT can be powered with images posted on TikTok, Facebook, or any other social media sites with information that can be scraped from these sites. With payment apps such as Venmo, other users can see the message, the sender's name, and the amount of the transaction.

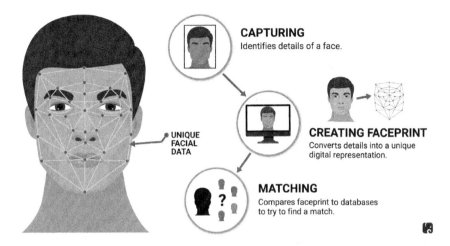

Figure 2.4 Process Used in Facial Recognition Technology

Source: Senate RPC. (2019, November 20). *Facial recognition: Potential and risk.* www.rpc. senate.gov/policy-papers/facial-recognition-potential-and-risk

Verification and Identification

FRT searches or comparisons generally fall into two categories: verification and identification. Verification compares a stored photo of an individual to another photo of the same individual to determine whether they are the same person; for example, to determine the identity of an individual who is trying to unlock a smartphone. Identification compares a photo from a single individual against a gallery of stored photos from a number of individuals to determine if there is a potential match. This type of comparison can be used to identify investigative leads for an unknown individual in a crime scene photo.[60]

Bias

FR can fail based on prejudicial or technical bias; a number of studies have found that algorithms perform differently for different ethnic groups. One study conducted by NIST found that the majority of the systems tested had clear differences in their ability to match two images of the same person when one ethnic group was compared with another. Another study found the algorithms are more accurate for lighter-skinned males than for darker-skinned females.[61] Another bias is related to the technology itself. When FRT was first developed, image lighting, pose angle, and pixel numbers greatly impacted results, creating technical bias.

Surveillance Technology

Surveillance tools can provide valuable insights for law enforcement by capturing certain events taking place in a particular area. Government agencies, particularly law enforcement agencies, use and help develop a variety of technologies that enhance and expand surveillance capabilities. These technologies similarly collect data, and the collected data are used for input into other automated systems that directly impact people's lives. Use of surveillance technologies has increased in schools and workplaces, and when coupled with evaluation decisions, it is leading to mental health harms such as lowered self-confidence, anxiety, depression, and reduced ability to use analytical reasoning.[62]

CCTV

In the last two decades, closed-circuit television (CCTV) surveillance cameras have come to occupy a central role in contemporary crime prevention across the world. Widely viewed as the "internationalization" of CCTV surveillance, there has been a corresponding growth in the evidence base about its effect on crime. The cumulative evidence demonstrates that CCTV surveillance is associated with significant yet modest reductions in crime, and the effects vary across a range of contextual factors, including country of origin.[63]

Mass Surveillance

Sophisticated surveillance systems today are also used for close monitoring of protesters. As a result of surveillance use, many types of crimes, particularly those that can be monitored with digital surveillance, will become less common while new crimes, and potentially new forms of discrimination, can increase. Surveillance technology is a double-edged sword. AI-enabled surveillance technology that allows governments to diminish crime also enables them to monitor and repress their citizens. Utilization of surveillance technology to suppress dissent and FRT for mass-surveillance purposes raises serious concern. Some governments use terrorist attacks as a justification for mass-surveillance programs, despite the fact that the evidence does not support the original expectations. Most of these programs are kept secret, so little is known about the success rate. However, information that has been disclosed does not justify mass surveillance.[64]

The technology relies on AI analyzing mass-collected data sets. AI is expected to be particularly useful in intelligence gathering and surveillance.[65] There are ongoing discussions with respect to the security of the 2024 Summer Olympics in Paris, France. As previously mentioned, algorithmic video surveillance was utilized for security purposes. Widespread surveillance has the potential to become an accepted practice.[66]

Video Surveillance

For the past several years, many local authorities have chosen to use "automated" or "algorithmic" video surveillance to help them manage their cities. The deployment of sensors and cameras for some citizens means infringement of their privacy and the rights that they are entitled to in public places in democratic societies.

Smart Cities, Materials, and Manufacturing

A hyperconnected digital world is already emerging with the next-generation networks, persistent sensors, and myriad technologies. Smart cities, as noted in the last chapter, have gained increased traction in recent years.[67] Smart cities utilize electronic sensors, like connected traffic sensors that can analyze traffic flow, help emergency respondents, control streetlights to save on energy, and help direct cars around the city. These cities rely heavily on big data, cloud computing, and sensors in order to operate and function. Sensors and other electronics inform city operations. This can create new attack opportunities for criminals to gain access to the city and carry out disruptive attacks against its critical infrastructure networks.[68] Ubiquitous public cameras in smart cities use optical and other sensors combined with AI to monitor people, vehicles, and infrastructure.

Predictive Policing

AI algorithms for predictive policing are increasingly being deployed in the field, despite the fact there are concerns about racial profiling, among other problems.[69] Advanced technologies are used to assist policing operations and decision-making. Algorithms are used for crime detection in order to know where and when a crime is occurring. For example, police departments in the US, rely on applications like *Geolitica* or *HunchLab* to predict when and where a particular crime is likely to occur. These tools are increasingly playing an essential role in police work and the criminal justice system.[70] Predictive policing is used for threat management, that is, supervision and monitoring of crime that might be executed directly and in real time from a central office.[71]

AI can identify patterns within data sets and is used in "predictive policing" focusing on crime before it actually occurs. Technical systems such as data mining and FR technology are the predictive tools often used by many police departments around the globe.

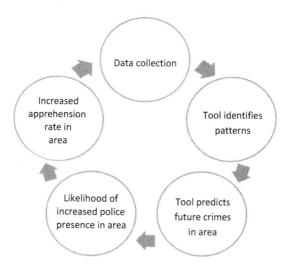

Figure 2.5 An Illustration of Predictive Policing Cycles

Source: The House of Lords Justice and Home Affairs Committee. (2022, March 30). *Technology rules? The advent of new technologies in the justice system* (1st Report of Session 2021–2022).

Risks

AI is capable of offering an opportunity to better prevent crime, but there are risks associated with its potential impact on people's lives, particularly those in marginalized communities. Algorithms deployed in decision-based settings are untested and unreliable. The human bias contained in the original dataset that is used to train the AI model is being reflected and embedded in decisions made by algorithms. For example, a predictive policing system claimed to identify individuals at greatest risk of committing or becoming the victim of gun violence. This inference was based on automated analysis of social ties to gang members, criminal histories, previous experiences of gun violence, and other factors, which led to the individuals being placed on a watch list with no explanation or transparency as to how the system came to its conclusion.[72] The stakes are higher in policing as algorithms directly impact people's lives.

Predictive Mapping

Some law enforcement agencies in the US have purchased an AI-based predictive mapping service from a private company. By utilizing predictive mapping, the analytical ability examines past crime trends and patterns to assist officers in gauging future criminal activities. An audit revealed several months later that the vendor had made false claims about the system and that the company had access to a vast amount of personal data.[73]

Ramifications

Law enforcement agencies are often unaware of the confidentiality risks posed by the advanced tools that they are purchasing and using. Despite the seller's insistence on commercial confidentiality, these systems will be collecting personal data.[74] This is particularly concerning in light of deceptive marketing and selling practices by commercial vendors as their product's effectiveness is often untested and unproven prior to deployment.

Law enforcement agencies are using emerging tools; nevertheless, there is a lack of clarity as to who is using these technologies. For what purpose and how long have these tools been used? Finally, what safeguards, if any, are in place for their use? This risk undermines trust in the police and the justice system. Policymakers must consider what level of disclosure would be appropriate to be required from law enforcement agencies.[75]

Scientific standards that provide reliability, context, and validity for use of emerging technologies have to be established, in particular for law enforcement agencies. Standards cannot be solely developed and implemented by an individual country. In order to be effective, there is a need for a global standard. As the British Prime Minster Rishi Sunak stated, AI firms cannot mark their own homework; monitoring the risks posed by AI is too important to be left to the Big Tech firms.[76]

Training[77]

Agencies have a hard time sharing information that can better inform leaders and help fight fraud and abuse.[78] State and local government agencies still face tough challenges in sharing and generating value from data. Individual police forces are ill-equipped to carry out the evaluation of technological solutions; they simply do not have the resources or the expertise to examine these tools prior to using them. Emerging tools are deployed when they have not been sufficiently evaluated or tested; therefore, their use presents risks and an unacceptable impact on society.[79]

Law enforcement agents need to know how to question the tools they use and how to challenge their outcomes; furthermore, they must have access to an institutional support system set up for addressing complaints. Currently, there is no obligation for continued training for law enforcement personnel on emerging tools like AI and FRT. There should be mandatory training for all law enforcement personnel at national and local levels; in particular, for those that are currently using these tools. Once legislation has been adopted, all personnel need to become properly trained in the standards applicable to their work and use of these technologies. AI technologies are widely used by police departments and other law enforcement agencies without any oversight.

Digital Justice

According to a 2024 study conducted by the Deloitte Center for Government Insights on the future of criminal justice, a digital justice system at its heart must have data, advanced analytics, and human oversight.[80] While there are a lot of inefficiencies like court backlogs, rising costs of physical infrastructure of prisons, and other challenges, a single digital solution cannot resolve these issues without a holistic approach to improving the justice services. The study concludes that it is the policies and not technology that can bring about effective change.

Virtual, Augmented, and Immersive

The topic of virtual reality has been covered in science fiction movies such as the iconic *Matrix* movies,[81] which set out the dystopian world where AI and other machines control the universe. They built up a simulated world for humans growing in laboratories and spending their whole lives in virtual reality. In the *Matrix*, the "fake" world is a seemingly benign façade pulled over inhabitants' eyes. Living in a virtual reality, these inhabitants have no control over their lives. However, they are protected from the grim reality of a crumbling world.

Virtual reality (VR) is a digital environment that replaces the real-world environment. Virtualization is the act of creating an abstraction and translation layer between two distinct systems, such as hardware and software. Virtualization technology has revolutionized data centers by transforming a computer server into a virtual machine that can be copied, cloned, and moved around.[82]

NASA

In 2022, NASA was going to use an augmented reality (AR) display system for new spacesuits that would allow astronauts to be more self-reliant. Communication delays can often create friction for astronauts interacting with mission control, and AR technology would help boost communications between Earth and the crew. The AR technology would be full-colored, binocular, and located inside the suit helmet bubble or outside of it.[83]

Military

Another example of VR reflects training simulations for military training. The user-friendly simulation allows militaries worldwide to conduct collective training and rehearsals, and experiment with various tactics.[84]

Virtual Prisons and Rehabilitation

There are a lot of ethical issues like transparency associated with the possibility of establishing virtual prisons at some point in the future. There has to be an extensive evaluation that the concept can be accepted as a satisfactory mechanism for punishment. The challenges of virtual prisons will be similar to current prison systems. Computer-assisted therapies may be a possibility for rehabilitation purposes. Computer-assisted therapy has been in use since Covid-19 and seems to be an effective method in helping with depression, addiction, and providing a support platform for those in need. While there can be virtual support systems in place, the importance of human contact cannot be overlooked.

Metaverse

The metaverse was popularized in 2021 by Facebook's rebranding from Facebook to Meta.[85] The metaverse is the idea of a VR world using AR technology in order to allow people to interact with one another. Users utilize 3D avatars that resemble themselves; they can interact by playing games together and exploring new worlds. While many games already exist that feature things like this, the technology as a whole, including AI, will need to develop much more in order for the "metaverse" to be created. Facebook/Meta hopes to be the company to develop it in order to be in control of all user data.[86] Additionally, the growing interest in virtual-world assets has been fueled by Facebook's focus on the metaverse.[87] A fully fleshed out metaverse is still far from being reality.

Body-Tracking Suits

Companies such as Panasonic have developed body-tracking suits that will bring the legs of players into the metaverse. Currently, most VR and AR programs are only capable of tracking upper-torso movements. Other companies are developing products such as a body-worn accessory designed to be worn during gameplay that recreates virtual temperatures for a player in the real world.[88] 5G-enabled technology could bring aspects of virtual and augmented reality to the way that people consume media, including movies where characters appear to move and speak directly to the audience.[89]

The next chapters of tech might involve connected VR worlds, AR overlays, and quantum computing, but those will all take some time.[90] As mentioned earlier, the story of the *Minority Report* movie depicts a special police unit capable of arresting murderers before they commit their crimes. But what if the officer from that special unit is accused of a future murder? Does he have free will to change the course of events and his own fate? Will people have the ability to judge freely, or will they be programmed to behave in certain ways?

All these innovative concepts in some form or another are being discussed and considered for the justice system.

Notes

1 Deloitte Center for Government Insights. (2021, April). *Criminal justice and the technological revolution.* www.deloitte.com/global/en/Industries/governm ent-public/perspectives/criminal-justice-and-the-technological-revolution.html

2 Camello, M., Planty, M., & Houston-Kolnik, J. (2021). *Chatbots in the criminal justice system: An overview of chatbots and their underlying technologies and applications.* National Institute of Justice, Office of Justice Programs, U.S. Department of Justice. www.rti.org/publication/chatbots-criminal-justice-system

3 Science Focus. (2018). Can an algorithm deliver justice? *BBC Science Focus Magazine.* www.sciencefocus.com/future-technology/can-an-algorithm-deliver-justice/

4 Campbell, T. (2019, July). *Artificial intelligence: An overview of state initiatives.* FutureGrasp, LLC. www.researchgate.net/publication/334731776_ ARTIFICIAL_INTELLIGENCE_AN_OVERVIEW_OF_STATE_INITIATIVES

5 United Nations Interregional Crime and Justice Research Institute & International Criminal Police Organization. (2020). *Towards responsible AI innovation.* https://unicri.it/sites/default/files/2020-07/UNICRI-INTERPOL_ Report_Towards_Responsible_AI_Innovation_0.pdf

6 Leprince-Ringuet, D. (2020, August 5). *Evil AI: These are the 20 most dangerous crimes that artificial intelligence will create.* ZDNet. www.zdnet.com/ article/evil-ai-these-are-the-20-most-dangerous-crimes-that-artificial-intellige nce-will-create/

7 Congressional Research Service. (2023, August 22). *Law enforcement and technology: Use of unmanned aircraft systems.*

8 Contreras, R. (2022). *The limited promise of police data.* Axios. www.axios. com/2022/10/29/police-reform-surveillance-shootings-crime

9 Vincent, B. (2022). *AI could match "fingerprints" of texts to their authors, under new intelligence program.* Nextgov/FCW. www.nextgov.com/emerging-tech/2022/02/ai-could-match-fingerprints-texts-their-authors-under-new-intel ligence-program/361850/

10 Homeland Security. (2022, December). *DHS S&T develops portable outdoor gunshot detection technology for law enforcement.* www.dhs.gov/science-and-technology/news/2022/12/29/dhs-st-develops-portable-outdoor-gunshot-detection-technology-law-enforcement

11 Brunner, S., Canova, G., Schedler, K., & Simmler, M. (2022). Smart criminal justice: Exploring the use of algorithms in the Swiss criminal justice system. Springer Nature. https://link.springer.com/article/10.1007/s10506-022-09310-1

12 Contreras, R. (2022). *The limited promise of police data.* Axios. www.axios.com/2022/10/29/police-reform-surveillance-shootings-crime

13 Goldhill, O. (2018). *Police are using artificial intelligence to spot written lies.* Nextgov/FCW. www.nextgov.com/emerging-tech/2018/10/police-are-using-artificial-intelligence-spot-written-lies/152388/

14 Mehrotra, D. (2023, January 11). *A police app exposed secret details about raids and suspects.* WIRED. www.wired.com/story/sweepwizard-police-raids-data-exposure/

15 Kingson, J. (2023, January 30). *New AI tool instantly analyzes police bodycam footage.* Axios. www.axios.com/2023/01/30/police-tyre-nichols-bodycam-footage

16 Newell, B. (2021). *Body cameras help monitor police but can invade people's privacy.* Nextgov/FCW. www.nextgov.com/ideas/2021/05/body-cameras-help-monitor-police-can-invade-peoples-privacy/174282/

17 Lucia, B. (2018). *Artificial intelligence for policing stirs ethics concerns.* Nextgov/FCW. www.nextgov.com/analytics-data/2018/04/artificial-intelligence-policing-stirs-ethics-concerns/147822/

18 Gillum, J. (2023). *Leaked police files offer clues on how cops use data firms.* Bloomberg. www.bloomberg.com/news/articles/2023-01-25/hackers-claimed-to-breach-a-police-vendor-spilling-data-trove

19 BBC. (2023). *Artificial Intelligence police van detects drivers using mobile phones.* www.bbc.com/news/uk-england-hampshire-66320176

20 ODNI. (2023). *IARPA leads first-of-its-kind effort to fashion smart clothing.* www.dni.gov/index.php/newsroom/press-releases/press-releases-2023/3717-iarpa-leads-first-of-its-kind-effort-to-fashion-smart-clothing

21 The White House. (2023). *Fact sheet: Biden-Harris administration secures voluntary commitments from leading artificial intelligence companies to manage the risks posed by AI.* www.whitehouse.gov/briefing-room/statements-releases/2023/07/21/fact-sheet-biden-harris-administration-secures-voluntary-commitments-from-leading-artificial-intelligence-companies-to-manage-the-risks-posed-by-ai/

22 Fitzpatrick, A. (2023). *Facial recognition's alarming pitfalls.* Axios. www.axios.com/2023/01/07/facial-recognition-issues-problems

23 Gershgorn, D. (2018). *This is the week that the drone surveillance state became real.* Nextgov/FCW. www.nextgov.com/emerging-tech/2018/06/week-drone-surveillance-state-became-real/148847/

24 Boyd, A. (2021). *South Korea to add robots-on-rails and AI surveillance to DMZ border.* Nextgov/FCW. www.nextgov.com/emerging-tech/2021/06/south-korea-add-robots-rails-and-ai-surveillance-dmz-border/174734/

25 Barbaro, M. (2022). The rise of workplace surveillance. *The New York Times.* www.nytimes.com/2022/08/24/podcasts/the-daily/workplace-surveillance-productivity-tracking.html?showTranscript=1

26 Jakubowska, E., Maryam, H., & Mahmoudi, M. (2024, April 14). *Euroviews. Retrospective facial recognition surveillance conceals human rights abuses in plain sight.* Euronews. www.euronews.com/2023/04/14/retrospective-facial-recognition-surveillance-conceals-human-rights-abuses-in-plain-sight

27 United Nations Interregional Crime and Justice Research Institute & International Criminal Police Organization. (2020). *Towards responsible AI innovation.* https://unicri.it/sites/default/files/2020-07/UNICRI-INTERPOL_Report_Towards_Responsible_AI_Innovation_0.pdf

28 Tucker, P. (2019). *Here come AI-enabled cameras meant to sense crime before it occurs.* Nextgov/FCW. www.nextgov.com/emerging-tech/2019/04/here-come-ai-enabled-cameras-meant-sense-crime-it-occurs/156532/

29 Starr, S. (2023). *Why Dayton quit ShotSpotter, a surveillance tool many cities still embrace.* Route Fifty. www.route-fifty.com/public-safety/2023/07/why-dayton-quit-shotspotter-surveillance-tool-many-cities-still-embrace/388603/

30 BBC. (2023). *Paris 2024 Olympics: Concern over French plan for AI surveillance.* www.bbc.com/news/world-europe-66122743

31 Vincent, B. (2020). *Senator questions how clearview AI's facial recognition tech is put to use on protesters.* Nextgov/FCW. www.nextgov.com/emerging-tech/2020/06/senator-questions-how-clearview-ais-facial-recognition-tech-put-use-protesters/166026/

32 Federal Trade Commission. (2022). *Commercial surveillance and data security rulemaking.* Kvgo. https://kvgo.com/ftc/commercial-surveillance-sep-8

33 U.S. Government Accountability Office. (2022, July 27). *Facial recognition technology: CBP traveler identity verification and efforts to address privacy issues.* www.gao.gov/products/gao-22-106154

34 Clayton, J. (2021, November 29). *China surveillance of journalists to use 'traffic-light' system.* BBC News. www.bbc.com/news/technology-59441379

35 Johnson, C. (2023, June 26). *The national security benefits of reallocating federal spectrum for 5G.* Center for Strategic & International Studies. www.csis.org/analysis/national-security-and-spectrum-5g

36 Contreras, R., & Ortiz, K. (2023). *AirTags track car thieves—but you don't have to.* Axios. www.axios.com/2023/05/24/apple-airtags-track-car-thieves-you-dont

37 Spielberg, S. (2002). *Minority report.* Twentieth Century Fox.

38 United Nations Interregional Crime and Justice Research Institute. (2019). *Artificial intelligence and robotics for law enforcement.* https://unicri.it/artificial-intelligence-and-robotics-law-enforcement

39 Goodyear, J. (2022). An algorithm can predict future crimes with 90% accuracy. Here's why the creator thinks the tech won't be abused. *BBC Science Focus.* www.sciencefocus.com/news/algorithm-predict-future-crimes-90-accuracy-heres-why-creator-thinks-tech-wont-be-abused

40 Brunner, S., Canova, G., Schedler, K., & Simmler, M. (2022). Smart criminal justice: Exploring the use of algorithms in the Swiss criminal justice system. Springer Nature. https://link.springer.com/article/10.1007/s10506-022-09310-1

41 Homeland Security Advisory Council. (2020, November 12). *Final report of the biometrics subcommittee.* www.dhs.gov/sites/default/files/publications/final_hsac_biometrics_subcommittee_report_11-12-2020.pdf

42 Homeland Security Advisory Council. (2020, November 12). Final report of the biometrics subcommittee. www.dhs.gov/sites/default/files/publications/final_hsac_biometrics_subcommittee_report_11-12-2020.pdf

43 United States Government Accountability Office. (2021, June). *Homeland Security: DHS needs to fully implement key practices in acquiring biometric identity management system* (Report to Congressional Requesters).

44 United States Government Accountability Office. (2021, August). *Facial recognition technology: Current and planned uses by federal agencies* (Report No. GAO-21-526) www.gao.gov/assets/gao-21-526.pdf

45 Alms, N. (2023). *White House says an anticipated executive order on identity theft is coming, here's what experts want in it.* Nextgov/FCW. www.nextgov.com/digital-government/2022/12/white-house-says-anticipated-executive-order-identity-theft-coming-heres-what-experts-want-it/380373/

46 Jakubowska, E., Maryam, H., & Mahmoudi, M. (2024, April 14). *Euroviews. Retrospective facial recognition surveillance conceals human rights abuses in plain sight.* Euronews. www.euronews.com/2023/04/14/retrospective-facial-recognition-surveillance-conceals-human-rights-abuses-in-plain-sight

47 United States Government Accountability Office. (2021, August). *Facial recognition technology: Current and planned uses by federal agencies* (Report No. GAO-21-526). www.gao.gov/assets/gao-21-526.pdf

48 United States Government Accountability Office. (2021, August). *Facial recognition technology: Current and planned uses by federal agencies* (Report No. GAO-21-526) www.gao.gov/assets/gao-21-526.pdf

49 Hart, K. (2023). *Facial recognition surges in retail stores.* Axios. www.axios.com/2021/07/19/facial-recognition-retail-surge

50 Huang, Z. (2018). *Chinese police are wearing sunglasses that can recognize faces.* Nextgov/FCW. www.nextgov.com/analytics-data/2018/02/chinese-police-are-wearing-sunglasses-can-recognize-faces/145886/

51 Osborne, C. (2020, August 17). *Controversial facial recognition tech firm Clearview AI inks deal with ICE.* ZDNet. www.zdnet.com/article/controversial-facial-recognition-tech-firm-clearview-ai-inks-deal-with-ice/

52 Goodwin, G. L. (2021, July 13). *Facial recognition technology: Federal law enforcement agencies should have better awareness of systems used by employees* (Testimony before the Subcommittee on Crime, Terrorism, and Homeland Security, Committee on the Judiciary, House of Representatives). United States Government Accountability Office.

53 United States Government Accountability Office. (2021, August). *Facial recognition technology: Current and planned uses by federal agencies* (Report No. GAO-21-526) www.gao.gov/assets/gao-21-526.pdf

54 Gershgorn, D. (2018). *Amazon and Microsoft claim AI can read human emotions. Experts say the science is shaky.* Nextgov/FCW. www.nextgov.com/emerging-tech/2018/12/amazon-and-microsoft-claim-ai-can-read-human-emotions-experts-say-science-shaky/153414/

55 Fitzpatrick A. (2023). *Facial recognition's alarming pitfalls.* Axios. www.axios. com/2023/01/07/facial-recognition-issues-problems

56 Iaria, M. (2022, July 25). *Bunnings, Kmart temporarily turn off facial recognition technology as privacy probe continues.* news.com.au. www.news.com. au/technology/bunnings-temporarily-turns-off-facial-recognition-technol ogy-as-privacy-probe-continues/news-story/02b1f7b37e92c3df4630a4805 3623679

57 Boyd, A. (2020). *Policing reform bill would prohibit embedding facial recognition in body cameras.* Nextgov/FCW. www.www.nextgov.com/emerging-tech/ 2020/06/policing-reform-bill-would-prohibit-embedding-facial-recognition-body-cameras/166020/

58 Fitzpatrick A. (2023). *Facial recognition's alarming pitfalls.* Axios. www.axios. com/2023/01/07/facial-recognition-issues-problems

59 Konkel, F. (2023). *Lawmakers suggest "radical transparency" as key to shoring up US cyber posture.* Nextgov/FCW. www.nextgov.com/cybersecurity/2023/ 06/lawmakers-suggest-radical-transparency-key-shoring-us-cyber-posture/ 387492/

60 United States Government Accountability Office. (2021, August). *Facial recognition technology: Current and planned uses by federal agencies* (Report No. GAO-21-526) www.gao.gov/assets/gao-21-526.pdf

61 Down, L., Jonas, E., Schwartz, R., Schwartz, R., & Tabassi, E. (2021, June). *A proposal for identifying and managing bias within artificial intelligence* (Draft NIST Special Publication 1270). National Institute of Standards and Technology, U.S. Department of Commerce. https://nvlpubs.nist.gov/nistpubs/ SpecialPublications/NIST.SP.1270-draft.pdf

62 The White House. (2022, October). *Blueprint for an AI Bill of Rights: Making automated systems work for the American people.*

63 Farrington, D. P., Piza, E., Thomas, A., & Welsh, B. C. (2021). The internationalization of CCTV surveillance: Effects on crime and implications for emerging technologies. *International Journal of Comparative and Applied Criminal Justice.* www.crimrxiv.com/pub/sw8ljm5k/release/1

64 Kirchner, L. (2015, November 18). *What's the evidence mass surveillance works? Not much.* Pro Publica. www.propublica.org/article/whats-the-evide nce-mass-surveillance-works-not-much

65 Congressional Research Service. (2020, November 10). *Artificial intelligence and national security* (CRS Report No. R45178). https://crsreports.congress. gov/product/pdf/R/R45178/10

66 BBC. (2023). *Paris 2024 Olympics: Concern over French plan for AI surveillance.* www.bbc.com/news/world-europe-66122743

67 Graph Convolution Network. (2022, August). *Smart city apps.*

68 Kendall-Taylor, A., Frantz, E & Wright, J. (2020, March). The Digital Dictators. Foreign Affairs. www.foreignaffairs.com/articles/china/2020-02-06/digital-dictators

69 Fried, I. (2020 June 15). *Fresh concerns about AI bias in the age of COVID-19.* Axios. www.axios.com/2020/06/15/fresh-concerns-about-ai-bias-in-the-age-of-covid-19

70 Graham, E. (2024, January 29). *Stop funding predictive policing tech without "evidence standards," lawmakers tell DOJ.* Nextgov/FCW. www.nextgov.com/artificial-intelligence/2024/01/stop-funding-predictive-policing-tech-without-evidence-standards-lawmakers-tell-doj/393705/

71 Brunner, S., Canova, G., Schedler, K., & Simmler, M. (2022). Smart criminal justice: Exploring the use of algorithms in the Swiss criminal justice system. Springer Nature. https://link.springer.com/article/10.1007/s10 506-022-09310-1

72 The White House. (2022, October). *Blueprint for an AI Bill of Rights: Making automated systems work for the American people.*

73 Office of the State Auditor. (2021, March 26). *Letter from the Office of the Utah State Auditor John Dougall, to Attorney General the Hon Sean Reyes, Re: Limited Review of Banjo.* https://reporting.auditor.utah.gov/servlet/servlet. FileDownload?file=0151K0000042i9lQAA

74 Kelley, A. (2021). *Data broker sales to law enforcement violate fourth amendment, Senator argues.* Nextgov/FCW. www.nextgov.com/policy/2021/12/data-broker-sales-law-enforcement-violate-fourth-amendment-senator-arg ues/359784/

75 Graham, E. (2024, January 29). *Stop funding predictive policing tech without "evidence standards," lawmakers tell DOJ.* Nextgov/FCW. www.nextgov.com/artificial-intelligence/2024/01/stop-funding-predictive-policing-tech-without-evidence-standards-lawmakers-tell-doj/393705/

76 BBC. (2023, November 1). *Rishi Sunak: AI firms cannot "mark their own homework."* www.bbc.com/news/technology-67285315

77 Route Fifty. (2022, December). *Workforce development.* Retrieved from www. route-fifty.com/assets/rf-workforce-development-q4-2022/portal/

78 Snowflake. (2023). *5 ways state and local governments deliver superior services and insights with snowflake.* Retrieved from www.snowflake.com/resource/5-ways-state-and-local-governments-deliver-superior-services-and-insights-with-snowflake/

79 Heaven, W. (2021, February 5). Predictive policing is still racist—Whatever data is uses. *MIT Technology Review.* www.technologyreview.com/2021/02/05/1017560/predictive-policing-racist-algorithmic-bias-data-crime-predpol/2021&mc_cid=6525c35d6e&mc_eid=95deaabb89&stream=future

80 Deloitte Center for Government Insights. (2021, April). *Criminal justice and the technological revolution.* www.deloitte.com/global/en/Industries/gov ernment-public/perspectives/criminal-justice-and-the-technological-revolut ion.html

81 Wachowski, L. (2021). *The Matrix Resurrections.* Warner Bros. Wachowski, L., & Wachowski, L. (1999). *The Matrix.* Warner Bros. Wachowski, L., & Wachowski, L. (2003). *The Matrix Reloaded.* Warner Bros. Wachowski, L., & Wachowski, L. (2003). *The Matrix Revolutions.* Warner Bros.

82 Mulchandani, C., & Shanahan, J. (2022, September 6). *Software-defined warfare: Architecting the DOD's transition to the digital age.* Center For Strategic & International Studies. www.csis.org/analysis/software-defined-warfare-archi tecting-dods-transition-digital-age

83 Errick, K. (2022). *Future astronaut suits could feature augmented reality.* Nextgov/FCW.   www.nextgov.com/emerging-tech/2022/12/future-astronaut-suits-could-feature-augmented-reality/380765/

84 Breeden II, J. (2023). *Artificial intelligence and drone tactics maneuver into advanced military simulations.* Nextgov/FCW. www.nextgov.com/ideas/2023/04/artificial-intelligence-and-drone-tactics-maneuver-advanced-military-simu lations/384942/

85 Fried, I. (2022, January 21). *Microsoft's deal for Activision Blizzard is all about the metaverse.* Axios. www.axios.com/2022/01/21/microsofts-metaverse-mane uvering-activision-blizzard-deal

86 Brown, E. (2022, January 3). *How will Zuckerberg's Meta plans impact its dominance over social media in 2022?* ZDNet. www.zdnet.com/article/how-will-zuckerbergs-meta-plans-impact-its-dominance-over-social-media-in-2022/

87 Rosenberg, S. (2023). *Battle for the soul of a new web.* Axios. www.axios.com/2021/11/29/web3-blockchain-battle-soul-new-web

88 Fried, I. (2022, January 7). *CES 2022 brought pieces of the metaverse into view.* Axios. www.axios.com/2022/01/07/ces-2022-metaverse-pieces-vr

89 Das Gupta, S. (2021, August 23). *How 5G will change the world.* Ozy. www.ozy.com/pg/newsletter/the-daily-dose/439735/

90 Rosenberg, S. (2022). *Tech's year of big endings.* Axios. www.axios.com/2022/12/14/tech-year-endings-2022-downturn

3 The Threat Is Here

Today's world is more interconnected than ever before, yet, for all its advantages, increased connectivity brings increased risk of theft, fraud, and abuse.[1] With more connectivity, there is a higher level of risk for cyberattack.

The global landscape is evolving constantly; threats to prosperity, values, and security are rapidly changing and impacting governments and citizens around the globe. These fundamental changes are driven by data, technological innovation, and the geopolitical landscape. Major events like the Covid-19 pandemic, wars, and extreme weather events are often used opportunistically by cybercriminals to engage in corporate security breaches, spear phishing, and social media fraud.

These geopolitical events, coupled with a shortage of skilled cybersecurity professionals as well as economic challenges, introduce new layers of complexity for governments and law enforcement agencies. Nations are confronting a host of threatening issues simultaneously, such as weapons of mass destruction, water crises, natural disasters, cyberattacks, food crises, large-scale involuntary migration, global recession, terrorist attacks, harmful consequences of synthetic biology, and threats from technologies like AI.

With the growing use of the internet, cyberattacks and cyberthreats have increased. Despite the risks posed by these new concerns, many businesses do not fully understand or appreciate the risks posed by cybercriminals or how to defend their networks.

Cybercrime

Cybercrime is a global phenomenon and is borderless like the internet itself. The term "cybercrime" encompasses a broad range of different criminal threats. Cross-border attacks make cybercrime investigation and prosecutions more difficult for law enforcement bodies. It gets

DOI: 10.4324/9781003368304-4

more complicated when many countries are only at the starting point in building their police force's capabilities to counter cybercrime. The damage caused by cybercrime is not always visible to those that are targeted, and this hinders international efforts in establishing cyber stability. Cybercrime's impact is global in nature and continues to evolve in scope and impact. While many technological advances play an important role in criminal activities, none has had the same effect as the internet itself.[2]

Cybercriminals

As mentioned earlier, cybercrime is a cross-border event, with criminals targeting victims in other jurisdictions to avoid the risk of arrest. The internet allows criminals to operate seamlessly across borders. Concealing their identity and location, they have access to their target from anywhere at any time. The internet provides bad actors with an enormous advantage, giving them access to detailed information like map data including satellite and street-views, shipping routes and schedules, tutorials and recipes for drugs and explosives, as well as tips on operational security.[3]

With more businesses, public services, and devices connecting to the internet, the number of possible attacks continues to grow while the world is becoming digitized.[4] As people's personal lives and businesses move online, there are a growing number of opportunities for cybercriminals. Some examples include damage or destruction of data, theft of money, theft of personal data, embezzlement, fraud, business disruption, and reputational harm.

Cybercriminals increasingly operate in loosely networked chains of service providers, developers, intermediaries, financiers, and end users. They tend to be typically motivated by money. This is straightforward to understand; they look for the lowest investment that achieves the highest profit with the least amount of risk. For example, they consider targeting organizations who have money but are less defended, like school districts or hospitals, with ransomware attacks.

As cybercrime becomes attractive to a larger number of criminals, it is rare for a single group to conduct an entire operation independently. They interact and work with an entire supply chain of third-party tools, experts, and services to achieve their objectives. After all, it is difficult to be an expert in everything from coding to money laundering. Their business model resembles that of a legitimate business employing third-party suppliers for various services to facilitate their business operation. With AI at their disposal, they will be able to do more of everything from phishing, spamming, to acts of blackmail and terrorism, to campaigns of misinformation and election sabotage.

Cyberspace

Global access to cyberspace has expanded for civil, commercial, intelligence, and military purposes in part because of innovation of emerging technologies and tools. Private-sector investments, international partnerships, and the demand for emerging markets in cyberspace is continuously increasing. As a result, conflicts between nations are taking place in cyberspace through attacks and cyber operations by bad actors. Cyberspace has become a critical security concern for governments and law enforcement bodies. Digitally advanced economies are an attractive target for cybercriminals. Since the Covid-19 pandemic, concerns about vulnerabilities have increased. During the pandemic, major breaches and attacks took place. Denial of service attacks, destructive malware, cyberespionage, cyber intelligence activities, and breach of data and confidentiality are some examples of cyber-related crimes.[5] As public- and private-sector activity has become increasingly dependent on the internet and digital networks, the threat posed by cyberespionage and cybercrime has grown accordingly.[6]

Securing Cyberspace

In the last decade, the private sector continued to accelerate the pace of technological innovation, putting highly advanced technologies in the hands of individuals, companies, and governments around the world. While this has created enormous opportunities to transform the way people conduct their affairs, it has also provided those same opportunities to adversaries and criminals. Cyber incidents and breaches often remain unnoticed for extended periods, highlighting the need to be able identify and address threats prior to their occurrence. Unfortunately, many organizations and even government agencies are unaware of how much data they have, where it resides, and who has appropriate access to it. The human factor is always the biggest challenge when it comes to cybersecurity for businesses and governments.

Darknet Markets

Criminal organizations are selling and buying people's stolen personal data through underground darknet marketplaces.[7] These hidden market spaces are only available to those with special software such as The Onion Router (TOR). The process of selling data begins with hackers who steal information such as credit card numbers, bank account information, and social security numbers. The next step involves advertising the data to distributors, who can then sell it to their customers. Those who purchase the stolen information have the ability to engage in fraud.[8] Concerns about the dark web with respect to the utilization of AI for malicious activities like phishing campaigns and data manipulation methods are increasing.[9]

Malicious Actors

The sad reality is that the bad guys are better organized in many ways than the good guys. They have begun testing the capabilities of AI-developed malware and AI-assisted software development technologies that have the potential to enable larger-scale, faster, more efficient, and more evasive cyberattacks against targets. AI is capable of creating attacks or being misused. The attacks, like deepfakes, disrupt other AI-controlled systems and can lead to large-scale blackmail, fake news, misuse of military robots, learning-based cyberattacks, autonomous drone attacks, distributed denial of service (DDoS) attacks, defeating FR, and stock market manipulation.[10]

Convergence of AI and Cybersecurity

The rapid adoption, deployment, and use of AI capabilities can make them highly valuable targets for malicious cyber actors. For example, bad actors who have historically used data theft of sensitive proprietary information and intellectual property to advance their objectives will seek to use AI systems. AI will exacerbate the threats of cyberattacks. There will be more sophisticated spear phishing, voice cloning, deepfakes, foreign malign influence, and disinformation. Safeguarding the global digital infrastructure, wireless networks (in particular, 5G and its successors), fiberoptic cables, operating systems, and servers, both physical and cloud based, will be a monumental task for a digital world and the cybersecurity community.[11]

Emerging technologies such as AI bring with them an array of complex risks for the cybersecurity domain. AI is moving fast; it is powerful and unpredictable and can create a formidable weapon. Large-scale and sophisticated cyber-related crimes like ransomware attacks will continue to increase. The attacks are a "when, not if" reality for businesses, governments, and law enforcement bodies. Under present circumstances, with cybercrime reaching beyond national and regional borders, it is necessary to have adequate cooperation across country lines.

The rapid development of emerging technologies such as AI has created a cyber arms race between criminals and cyber defenders. Both sides are using emerging tools to boost their capabilities. As these technologies become more powerful and more widespread, the existing threat landscape will expand, giving rise to new concerns relating to digital, physical, and political security.

AI, digital security, physical security, and political security are inherently intertwined and connected. As AI systems extend further into domains commonly believed to be uniquely human, more sophisticated social-engineering attacks will occur based on AI capabilities.[12] AI will be used in phishing, vulnerability recognition, autonomous attacks, and autonomous propagation.[13] AI can be used with driverless vehicles, making them into weapons. It can be used for conducting spear phishing, disrupting AI-controlled systems, conducting large-scale blackmail, and creating fake news.[14] Misuse of military robots can be facilitated by AI. AI can be used for autonomous drone attacks. It can defeat FR technology, manipulate the stock market, create robot burglars, write fake reviews, facilitate stalking, and create art forgeries. It should be noted that some of the most worrying AI-enabled attacks may come from small groups and individuals who have preferences far outside what is typical. It will be difficult to anticipate or prevent "lone-wolf" terrorist attacks, mass shootings, and stabbing attacks.

AI Tools

The release of ChatGPT in 2023 prompted intense debate about the implications of AI tools. The cybersecurity impact is an important part of the ongoing discussions and debates regarding AI. A major issue of future concern is whether generative AI gives rise to new attacks. Of course, AI tools have been used by both defenders and attackers, and ML and AI tools will give malicious actors an edge to improve their attacks. Criminal groups and organizations have always had the ability to learn and adapt quickly, as they too recognize that the emerging technologies will make it significantly easier for them to develop sophisticated techniques to avoid detection.[15]

AI tools are not "done" when they are deployed into the market. Many systems continue to learn from new data, and therefore, future model performance will differ from past performance based on new data that are fed to the model. This is often a good thing, but it can also introduce the risk of new problematic behaviors, like biases or even sabotage, which were not present at the time of initial deployment.

AI tools are owned and operated by people who have the ability to retrain, modify, and correct problematic behavior but only if monitoring, feedback, and accountability checks are in place. For instance, a tool analyzing network traffic for potential intrusions could also be used for making an intrusion harder to detect, and the tools used to generate humanlike content can easily be used for both legitimate and illegitimate purposes.[16]

Security-by-Design and Default

Multiple cybersecurity agencies in the US, Australia, Canada, the United Kingdom UK), Germany, the Netherlands, and New Zealand have collaborated on a groundbreaking guidance effort, shifting the balance of cybersecurity risks. The guidance urges software manufacturers to prioritize security in their products by adopting secure-by-design and secure-by-default practices. The guidance shifts the security burden from customers to manufacturers, promoting transparency and accountability. This guidance serves as a catalyst for industry-wide transformation urging organizations to implement and adopt the practice.[17]

Large-Scale Attacks

A central concern at the nexus of AI and cybersecurity is that AI might enable larger-scale and more frequent attacks to be implemented by an attacker with minimum skills and resources. At the same time, AI is capable of identifying patterns or irregularities to highlight vulnerabilities.[18]

Targeted Spam

The concept of "community targeted spam" refers to using natural language generation techniques from AI to target an entire class of people with common ways of writing; one could envision even more customized approaches, spanning multiple communities.[19]

Evading Detection

AI and ML technology can be used to identify malware even as attackers tweak and change it to evade detection. AI can also learn how valid users interact with an IT system, and recognize abnormal behavior that could signal an attack. However, as mentioned earlier, AI and ML are both sensitive to the type of data they are trained on, so bad data could produce poorly performing AI, and attackers could adopt AI to design more dangerous malware in the future.[20]

Covid-19

The creation of phishing websites in times of crisis such as the Covid-19 pandemic serves as a warning of coordinated large-scale cyberattacks that can facilitate the spread of misinformation and destabilize the social and political environment. AI technologies are a growing threat to national security. Potential attacks on elections, including the 2024 presidential election in the US, are a further illustration of this point.

AI-Powered Scams

Classic scams include false refund claims, phishing emails, and misleading advice on social media. AI amplifies these activities, and law enforcement struggles to combat internet scams. Chatbots, while helpful for providing basic information, raise concerns about scammers using them to create more convincing and efficient messages. The incidence of AI-generated phishing emails and scripted scam phone calls impersonating the IRS, for instance, further illustrates that the extent of AI-driven attacks remains uncertain.[21] AI-driven cyberattacks can evade detection. It is anticipated that AI will be used to create more sophisticated malware and that AI will continue to be used in phishing, vulnerability recognition, and autonomous attacks.[22]

Other Types of Risks

AI systems should be protected from risks, including cyber risks that may directly or indirectly cause physical or digital harm to any individual, group, or business entity. AI systems present unique pathways for adversary exploitation. The increased deployment of AI systems will increase the number of "hackable things," including, for instance, moving vehicles, which may allow exploitive action. In addition, AI systems are particularly vulnerable to theft by virtue of being almost entirely software-based. Software codes can be used immediately and reproduced.

The following section summarizes the types of risks:

- Evasion: occurs when an attacker modifies input data to trick the model
- Poisoning: occurs when an attacker feeds contaminated training data to the model to shift the model's decision in favor of an adversary[23]
- Backdoor: occurs when an attacker manipulates model components, causing the model to fail on specific inputs while performing well on others
- Stealing: occurs when an attacker analyzes the input, output, and other external information of an AI system to speculate on the model or the underlying data.[24]

Data Use and Automation

The increasing sophistication of data use and automation will make it increasingly more challenging to address AI attacks in light of advances in data collection and wireless transmission of digital data.[25] The lack of legislative and legal frameworks and rules provides a unique opportunity for malicious actors and adversaries, as they can innovate more freely in the absence of rules and regulations.

Phishing

As the capabilities of large-language models like ChatGPT continue to improve, it is likely that the number of sophisticated phishing attacks will increase. Phishing attacks rely on time pressure; they try to get a fast response from the victim. Cybercriminals will be able to generate highly convincing emails that are customized for each recipient, making it more difficult for people to detect and defend against these attacks.[26] With the overall sophistication of social-engineering attacks, victims fall more easily for these attacks. An additional risk posed by ChatGPT includes feedback to malicious actors to help them better understand their attack strategies as to how and why certain attack methods will be more successful than others, like creating more effective phishing emails.[27]

Ransomware

Major cybercrime groups have diversified ransomware business models, including new forms of extortion, such as threats to release captured data alongside encryption of data. They have improved the ability of their malware to affect a wide range of technical targets such as virtual machine hosts and network storage devices.[28] Despite years of government and industry investments to fight ransomware cyberattacks, these attacks and payments have reached an alarming level. It has been difficult for policymakers to establish a smart policy on this emerging issue.[29] As ransomware actors continue to innovate, more advanced destructive attacks will target both public and private sectors with more sophistication and frequency. Ransomware has become an endemic issue that is likely to get much worse before law enforcement actions result in decreasing the number of these attacks.

The UK's Royal Mail

A notable attack in 2023 involved the UK's Royal Mail, which was hit by a ransomware cyberattack causing disruption to its international mail services. Hackers sought an $80 million ransom, and the attack affected 11,500 post office branches, resulting in an abrupt stop in handling of international parcels.[30]

Colonial Pipeline

The Colonial Pipeline ransomware attack in 2021 in the US had significant implications, driving policy and corporate changes. The resulting six-day shutdown of the pipeline system for refined oil products caused fuel shortages and emergency measures across the country. The ransomware attack affected the billing systems. Colonial's actions in response to the attack prevented potentially worse consequences, like attacks that would have compromised the infrastructure.[31] A series of high-profile ransomware attacks on critical infrastructure in the US and elsewhere has shifted law enforcement attention to cybercrime committed by hackers unaffiliated with governments. For instance, commercial shipping is especially vulnerable to cyberattacks, and hackers enjoy a structural advantage in supply chain ransomware attacks.

Dallas Police Department

A ransomware cyberattack in Dallas, Texas, in 2023, disrupted critical public services, including the 911 dispatch systems. The attack compromised the city's servers, causing widespread outages. The attack caused court closures and resulted in the police department's website going down. The extent of the damage and the breach of the stolen data still remains unknown.[32]

Cybercrime as a Service

Criminals copy what they see in the legal markets. The advent of subscription-model "software-as-a-service" for businesses to access user-friendly products ranging from video calls to project management and customer-service tools typifies an effective business model for criminals to copy. Criminals also have their own "cybercrime as a service" by which experienced cybercriminals sell accessible tools and knowledge to help others carry out cybercrimes. This brings more criminals into the cybercrime market by lowering the cost and the level of skills needed to be an effective online fraudster, for instance, by delivering ransomware attacks potentially capable of destroying businesses. Transnational organized ransomware actors continue to innovate and carry out high-impact attacks, disrupting critical services and exposing sensitive data and money extortion.[33] Important services and critical infrastructure, such as healthcare systems, schools, manufacturing, and government agencies worldwide, continue to be targeted by ransomware attacks. When law enforcement actions successfully disrupt their infrastructure, the groups temporarily cease their operation, and then find ways to rebrand and renew their activities.[34]

Malware

Since the release of ChatGPT, it is much easier for less-skilled threat actors to run phishing campaigns as well as develop malware. Malware is malicious software that is designated to disrupt, gain unauthorized access, steal data, and damage or destroy a computer system. Cyberattackers can adopt AI to design more dangerous malware.[35] Hackers have used open-source software and fraudulent job offers on social media to deceive software engineers and IT support staff, resulting in malware attacks. They create fake LinkedIn profiles to pose as recruiters from technology, defense, and media entertainment companies. According to Microsoft, engineers and technical support professionals in the UK, India, and the US are the primary targets of hackers.[36]

There is a growing risk that non-state actors could use malicious software, or malware, to launch a cyberattack on a facility that produces or stores chemical, biological, radiological, or nuclear materials. These facilities are vulnerable to such attacks due to the widespread use of digital and automated industrial control systems and the connection of such systems to computer networks and the internet.[37] These facilities could be targeted by criminals looking to steal data to sell to the highest bidder or conduct a ransomware attack, by "hacktivists" opposed to the nuclear or chemical industries, or by terrorists seeking to cause death or destruction. There have been several incidents around the world where malware has infected nuclear facilities, intentionally or unintentionally, in the past.[38]

USB Drives

Many victims have recently been receiving letters that appear to be from legitimate companies such as Best Buy, informing them that they have received a free update by providing a USB drive to them. These USBs contain malware and keylogger technology that allow hackers to have remote control of a victim's computer and the ability to access their files and information.[39]

Deepfakes

Deepfakes using AI can manipulate faces, voices, and language on digital media, with an aim of changing real events or inventing entirely fictional ones.[40] Deepfakes are digitally altered media that manipulate online and real-world interactions. In the recent past, deepfakes were viewed as a complex technology reliant on powerful computing. Some characterize deepfakes as the art of digital deception. Realistic images, audio, and videos are used for purposes of misrepresentation or to falsely spread information.[41] The ability of AI systems to create synthetic images that are sometimes indistinguishable from real ones has led to the creation of deepfakes, that is, images or videos that appear to be real but are actually fake.[42] Many entities and their executives have been targeted with deepfakes. It is getting more challenging to tell what is real and what is not.

Once AI is trained on a data set of real-world images or videos, it has the capability of generating similar images on its own. The technology can be used to make interactive media more engaging; nevertheless, it can also be used to produce hoaxes and fake images and videos. The technology has the ability to make the production of convincing fakes accessible to most people. In recent years, AI-driven fakes have contributed to undermining the public's confidence in news reporting, politics, and government institutions.[43]

Volodymyr Zelensky

In March 2022, there was a widely circulated deepfake video of Ukrainian President Volodymyr Zelensky on social media, showing him directing his army to surrender the fight against Russian troops. Creating an audio deepfake requires a lot of data from recordings of the target's voice. As illustrated in the Zelensky deepfake case, this technology has the capability of spreading false information.[44]

Former President Nixon

The Massachusetts's Institute for Technology Center for Advanced Virtuality, in collaboration with a Ukrainian-based company, created a video entitled "*In Event of Moon Disaster,*" using AI to create a fake video featuring former president Nixon delivering a speech in case the Apollo 11 mission failed, leaving astronauts Neil Armstrong and Buzz Aldrin to die on the moon. While much of this technology is fairly new, it is an indication that more videos like this will be created.[45]

Adversaries

AI is enabling increasingly realistic photo, audio, and video forgeries, or deepfakes that adversaries could deploy as part of their information operations. AI can also be used to create full "digital patterns of life" in which an individual's digital "footprint" is merged and matched with purchase histories, credit reports, professional résumés. There are indications that various groups aim to create a comprehensive behavioral profile of military personnel, intelligence officers, government officials, and private citizens.[46]

Nudification Technology

AI-enabled nudification technology creates images where people appear to be nude. The usage of AI-powered apps that also enable non-technical users to create or alter images of individuals without their consent is rapidly spreading. Such technology is becoming a common form of image-based abuse. As these tools become more sophisticated, they are producing altered images that are increasingly realistic, making it difficult for both humans and AI to determine their authenticity.[47]

Photoshop

The incorporation of generative AI tools into Photoshop by Adobe has contributed to the increase of realistic fakes, prompting concerns about the ability to detect manipulated images. A fabricated Pentagon image circulated on Twitter in 2023 resulted in temporary market disturbances. The new "generative fill" tool in Photoshop allows users to easily add or remove objects, alter the background, and more.[48]

Text-to-Image Generators

Text-to-image generators such as OpenAI raise the question of whether people will be able to trust photos in the future. A recent AI model can transform noise into a comprehensible image from the short text description paired with each photo. Text-to-image technologies are more powerful due to their capability to create any image that contains relationships between people or objects.[49]

Voice Cloning

Voice cloning has amplified existing scams, exploiting victims emotionally and financially. AI is used to mimic the voices of friends or family members to deceive people. Generative AI has made it easier for cybercriminals to clone voices. Just a few seconds of recorded audio can result in significant financial losses from AI-enabled scam calls.[50] Scammers manipulate conversations in real time and gather personal information to enhance their deception. AI has the capacity to create videos of people speaking in different voices and overlaying faces.[51]

Synthetic Media

A recent report by Europol, the European law enforcement group, cautions that 90 percent of online content by 2026 could be artificially generated. The rise of synthetic content has given rise to disinformation risks, raising an important question as to how information dissemination and consumption will evolve in a world dominated by AI-generated digital content.[52]

Open AI's ChatGPT

Since its release in December 2022, ChatGPT software can create false information. It can quickly generate humanlike responses, changing how people get information online; however, the accuracy of the results it generates is highly questionable.[53] Open AI faced a ban in Italy due to privacy concerns, which led to its restoration with additional user verification measures and more transparency regarding its privacy policy. Users of Open AI have been asked by the FTC to address risks to people's reputations.[54]

Social-Engineering Scams

Scammers are employing pretexting techniques, like sending fake emails or messages, pretending to be someone the victim knows. There has been a significant increase in cyberincidents that use deceptive stories to trick victims.[55]

Public USB Charging Stations

"Juice jacking" is a method used by criminals to steal phone data through modified charging ports. Using USB charging stations is strongly discouraged by law enforcement agencies due to risk to personal information.[56]

Fake Job Ads

Recruitment scammers post fraudulent job ads from legitimate corporate accounts on employment-related networking sites. Scammers attempt to get personal information from applicants related to their credentials and personal finances in order to steal the victim's identity and money.[57] On LinkedIn, complex scams have evolved, leveraging sophisticated tactics and generative AI tools to deceive users. Cybercriminals use AI to craft convincing employment positions. The goal is to extract personal information and deceive applicants into making purchases. Criminal groups employ spear phishing on LinkedIn for business intelligence purposes, especially from industries like aerospace and defense.[58]

QR Codes

QR codes are visual representations of digital information that can be scanned by smartphones and other devices. During the pandemic, many businesses resorted to using QR codes to promote contactless practices. QR codes are designed to be scanned using smartphone cameras and can hold various types of information, including web links, text, and images. Hackers and scammers saw QR codes as an opportunity for stealing password information and money from victims. Downloading QR code–scanning apps facilitated the exposure of users when visiting a URL's stored links.[59] Potential risks include falling victim to phishing attacks or being tricked into harmful actions on legitimate websites. Additionally, there is a slight possibility that scanning a QR code with a vulnerable app could compromise the security of the device.[60]

Phishing and QR Codes

In 2023, there was a large-scale phishing campaign using QR codes, a novel approach in phishing tactics. Employees of a major US company, as well as individuals in manufacturing, insurance, technology, and finance, received personalized fake emails. The deceptive emails urged recipients to conduct security verifications linked to their Microsoft 365 accounts. Scanning the QR code in the email redirected them to a fake login page, allowing cybercriminals to steal their IDs and passwords. The use of QR codes provided certain advantages to the criminals, such as bypassing spam filters and leading users outside the corporate networks, therefore avoiding phishing defenses and facilitating infections.[61]

Credit Card Skimmers

Skimmers are small magnetic strip devices placed above card readers at gas station pumps and ATMs that steal credit card information. Scammers can install skimmers on devices and in areas that are not constantly observed. Skimmers read the magnetic strips on cards, not the chips. When a skimmer has been installed, usually there is unaligned plastic that sticks out further than the card reader.[62]

Credential Theft

Stolen credentials remain a relatively easy way for attackers to break into accounts. Web applications are a primary attack route; cybercriminals exploit accessible online digital assets. Companies have adopted automation technologies for efficiency purposes, but nonetheless new technologies expose their vulnerabilities. Neglecting credential security measures on IoT devices provides an attacker with access and hacking abilities.[63] Malicious actors leverage credentials previously purchased or obtained through info stealing to access accounts as well as stolen credentials to access a former employee's account. For instance, a recent report in 2023 showed that employees at telecommunications ("telecom") companies are at higher risk from dark web platforms. Telecom companies, which handle sensitive customer data, are attractive targets for hackers and struggle with security-related issues. Recent data breaches at well-known companies like T-Mobile and AT&T highlight this problem.[64]

Electric Vehicle (EV) Charging Stations

The vulnerability of the EV charging infrastructure and EVs' exposure to cyberattacks is troubling not only for those who have switched from traditional fuel-based vehicles to EVs, but also for those considering the purchase of an EV.

EVs rely heavily on software for their operation. The EV software system is constantly communicating with other vehicles and their surroundings. The classification of charging stations as critical infrastructure adds complexity in particular due to the fact that they are installed on public property.[65] Hackers can pretend to be users and steal data from charging stations. These systems do not require or use an authentication process. If developers add security measures upfront for charging stations, it could possibly mitigate these known weaknesses.[66] EV stations are being attacked by credit card skimmers, and their cloud servers are being hijacked. Another security concern relates to the possibility of the grid being attacked through intrusion of EV charging stations.[67]

SIM-Swapping

A new trend in cybercrime has been SIM-swapping, which works to seize control of a mobile phone number and therefore, the user's data through the provider. Ransomware gangs and SIM-swappers have been collaborating with each other, creating a partnership capable of causing considerable disruptions across various sectors.[68] In 2022, T-Mobile became a victim of a large-scale cyberattack impacting their customers. The phishing attack started with a phone call to a T-Mobile employee during which the caller pretended to be from the IT department. The caller then requested access and was able to steal the credentials of the employee, which resulted in the data breach.[69]

Online Fraud

AI makes it harder to detect[70] new schemes used by criminals, including the use of automated bot attacks, multiple email addresses belonging to an online account, the sale of fraud kits on the dark web, online pharmacies for buying prescription drugs, and social media campaigns using Venmo and PayPal payment methods. The most common form of fraud has been creating fake documents and billing for needless goods and services that are not delivered.[71] Social media platforms, online marketplaces, and dating apps are some of the primary places where scams take place. Impersonation and investment and purchase fraud are contributing to this increase. There has been an increase in online fraud. A high percentage of fraud originates from social media and technology platforms.[72]

FraudGPT

There is a FraudGPT, which, like ChatGPT, can create malicious computer code, write scam letters, and hack websites. The system paves the path for fake checks, false statement templates, and emails to do phishing schemes.[73]

Disinformation and Misinformation

Generative AI can significantly alter the speed of creation and the amount of information in the world, including inaccurate and deliberately false information. Hostile states will engage in spreading both misinformation and disinformation with the objective of undermining people's trust in government institutions. The rise in accessible emerging tools such as AI can facilitate malign information campaigns with low cost and more sophistication, such as AI-generated disinformation impacting elections.[74] Globally, nation-states' malicious use of digital information and communication technologies will become more pervasive.

The acceleration of technological advancements like AI and the emergence of new social media platforms have enhanced the speed, reach, volume, and precision of disinformation generated by foreign adversaries. Social media platforms have enabled widespread disinformation and have not done enough to mitigate the spread of disinformation on their sites. These platforms' lack of action facilitates the destabilization of societies and societal institutions. In 2023, *Forbes Advisor* conducted a survey shedding light on consumer worries about AI. The survey results revealed that 76 percent of consumers surveyed expressed concerns about the rise of misinformation through AI tools like Google Bard (Gemini), ChatGPT, and Bing Chat.[75]

AI supercharging misinformation is viewed as a top risk for democracies. Disinformation is widely seen as a pressing challenge for democracies worldwide.[76] Foreign misinformation and disinformation are undermining trust in government institutions in democratic countries.[77] Cyber and AI tools are contributing to the creation of low-cost, synthetic text, image, and audio-based content of high quality, used to spread false information. Generative AI enables the rapid creation of an endless supply of higher-quality text, providing the influence actors the ability to expand their messaging and give it greater credibility. Already, hundreds of websites have used publicly available, large-language model-based chatbots to generate content, some of which is false and misleading.

Spreading Fear of Violence

As an example, in April 2023, a Chinese government-controlled news site using a generative AI platform pushed a previously circulated false claim that the US was running a lab in Kazakhstan to create biological weapons for use against China.[78] Similarly, in connection with the 2024 Paris Olympics, fake video press releases were produced posing as coming from the American Central Intelligence Agency (CIA) and the French General Directorate for Internal Security (DGSI) warning potential attendees to stay away from the Olympics due to the alleged risk of a terror attack.[79] Many policymakers are looking for effective ways to discourage people from adopting and spreading false beliefs, yet disinformation is difficult to define, understand, and measure and therefore, difficult to address.[80]

Digital Attacks

Cybercriminals have the battlefield advantage. It is easier to attack than to defend against cyberattacks, as defending requires more effort and resources. Identifying holistic and coordinated disruption opportunities for cybercriminal ecosystems will result in more successful cybercrime investigations, takedowns, prosecutions, and convictions. Long-term and structured engagement with governments and international organizations is key to achieving security and cooperation to minimize cybercriminals' coordinated cyberattacks.

Data Breaches

Cybercriminals were already incorporating more humanlike, undetectable tactics into their attacks prior to the release of ChatGPT. For example, Uber faced a major breach in 2022 when a hacker posed as an IT staff worker and accessed an employee's accounts. Often, hackers gain access due to simple human errors.[81] ChatGPT, as indicated before, has been used to create a dark web market for buying stolen data.

MOVEit

In 2023, a series of interconnected cyberattacks, stemming from the exploitation of a vulnerability in the widely used file transfer software, MOVEit, became the most significant hack of the year.[82] Prominent organizations, like the BBC, British Airways, and the government of Nova Scotia, in addition to many businesses in the US, are some examples of entities that were targeted.[83] The incident was a cyberattack exploiting the zero-day vulnerability in the file sharing software MOVEit, which is widely used by organizations to transfer data. This hack allowed the criminals to breach databases of multiple companies, affecting hundreds of global organizations. Several US federal agencies were attacked as well, and the extent of the impact and data theft remains uncertain.[84] This cyberattack was led by the Russian-speaking Clop or Cl0p cybercriminal group, known for large-scale "ransomware-as-a-service" campaigns. The hacking group has been in operation since February 2019, targeting more than 3,000 US-based organizations and more than 8,000 organizations worldwide. The hacker group has been "naming and shaming" the victims on their dark web page, publishing instructions on how to enter extortion negotiations, and threatening to publish the stolen data if the ransom is not paid.[85]

COVID-bit

A novel cyberattack method called COVID-bit can steal well-protected data using an antenna that only costs $1.00 and electromagnetic radiation. To be protected from outsiders, sensitive networks are using air-gapped systems that isolate the internet and are removed from the public network. This cyberattack's novel method illustrates how it is possible to hack air-gapped systems.[86]

AI and National Security

AI applications lie at the center of emerging national security concerns such as malicious cyber activity, the creation and spread of disinformation, and microelectronics' supply chain vulnerabilities. Adversaries can engage in training data poisoning attacks, model inversion, and machine-learning supply chain attacks. Security and privacy protection challenges are not unique to AI. Protecting sensitive data is one of the major cybersecurity challenges in today's digital interconnected world.[87]

AI tools that are developed for civilian use can be adapted for use in weapon systems and have been shared widely on unclassified internet sites, making them accessible to major powers and non-state actors alike. These vulnerabilities highlight the need for data security, cybersecurity and testing, and evaluation processes for AI application and development.[88]

Data as a Strategic Asset

Large-scale simulation and the accumulation and analysis of massive amounts of data are revolutionizing many areas of science and engineering research with the potential to influence the future battlefield and shape political discourse through disinformation operations. Adversaries consider data as a strategic asset. Inadequate security for data protection and improper use of sensitive data have resulted in numerous high-profile security and privacy breaches.[89]

Military Operations

AI is likely to be a key technology in advancing military cyber operations. AI may also have utility in the field of military logistics. At this time there is no clarity regarding what AI is capable of in the hands of foreign adversaries, domestic rebel groups, criminal groups, or terrorist organizations. Intelligence services and governments around the world are adopting cutting-edge technologies. They use advanced cyber tools ranging from unmanned systems to enhanced technical surveillance equipment to improve their capabilities. Much of this technology is commercially available.[90]

Commercial Spyware Industry

The commercial spyware industry makes tools that allow users to hack digital devices such as mobile phones to conduct surveillance of users' calls, conversations, and their locations. Companies responsible for the development and deployment of commercial spyware make their products available to governments and anyone with a government email address around the world.[91]

AI Weapons

AI is poised to change how warfare is conducted in the twenty-first century.[92] An important question to consider by governments and policymakers is whether AI weapons are legal. Currently there is still no policy or regulations on the use of autonomous weapon systems in the US.

The emergence of novel weapon systems is shaping the risks and opportunities on the battlefield and in warfare.[93]

AI is changing the character of the battlefield, and the pace of threats has been seen in the Russian war against Ukraine.[94] As the warfare landscape is changing, the IC and law enforcement agencies are still transitioning between countering terrorism and supporting geopolitical competition. Digital technologies are rapidly transforming the intelligence environment, resulting in changes in how intelligence data are collected.[95] The technological transformation in warfare has changed from information to intelligence as a result of the growing capabilities of AI, big data, advanced computing, and 5G.

Unmanned Aircraft Systems and Vehicles

The emergence of technologies enabling weapon systems to act autonomously, removing humans from the decision-making process, has raised ethical, legal, and practical concerns about machines making potentially lethal decisions.[96] The human–machine relationship is developing and impacting the war–fighter relationship.

The emergence of novel weapon systems is shaping the risks and opportunities on the battlefield. Large numbers of autonomous and semi-autonomous unmanned systems are powered by AI for war fighters.[97] Some of these systems have been used in the war between Ukraine and Russia. Unmanned aerial vehicles (UAVs) provide non-state actors with unprecedented means of gathering intelligence and attacking targets in unconventional ways. They allow insurgents and terrorist groups to covertly gather intelligence on high-security areas by circumventing ground-based physical defenses and providing high-quality imagery that can provide insight into a facility's layout and security measures.[98]

Emerging technologies and business models are reshaping who interacts with land, sea, and air. At the forefront of these changes are a host of newcomers in non-traditional areas, such as commercial space, unmanned aircraft, and the recent reintroduction of supersonic flights. Unmanned aircraft operating in new and increasingly autonomous profiles will share skies previously dominated by manned platforms.[99] The demand for commercial space transportation will increase to support the global satellite market to sustain a human presence in Earth's orbit and facilitate outer-space economy.[100]

Lethal Autonomous Weapon Systems

Lethal Autonomous Weapons Systems (LAWS) are a special class of weapon system that use sensors and computer algorithms to independently identify a target and employ an onboard weapon system to engage and destroy the target without manual human control of the system.[101]

Physical Attacks

In today's interconnected world, the lines between physical and digital security are blurring. This means that threats can easily exploit vulnerabilities in both realms, potentially causing significant damage. AI, digital security, physical security, and political security are deeply interconnected and will likely become more so. AI can be used to augment attacks. Its introduction has changed the attack surface that can be targeted by hackers. The geopolitical tensions that emerged in the wake of Russia's war against Ukraine have heightened the risks of attacks on critical infrastructure.[102]

Infrastructure

In this increasingly complex and interconnected technological ecosystem, critical infrastructure is exposed to a variety of cyberthreats. Foreign adversaries are exploring new technologies like AI to improve their tactics. Key societal systems, such as the electrical grid, water treatment facilities, transportation systems, and healthcare facilities, operate on an automated and digital level. While AI systems are capable of defending critical infrastructure operations, they also provide new tools and avenues for attack. Looking ahead at future technology, something like quantum computing, while still in its infancy stage, can pose a threat to all digital systems. As mentioned in earlier chapters, quantum computing has the potential to process larger swaths of data at faster rates than classical computers, rendering the current encryption methods vulnerable to attack.

Physical Infrastructure

Physical infrastructure landmarks such as electrical grids, dams, and transportation networks will be larger targets for attackers to focus on.[103] The potential impact of AI also extends to critical infrastructure sectors like manufacturing, financial services, transportation, healthcare, energy, and food and agriculture. State and non-state cyber actors seek opportunistic access to critical infrastructure targets for disruptive and destructive attacks. Common tactics include denial of service attacks, website defacement, and ransomware.

The interconnected nature of critical infrastructure requires billions of devices to be connected to the energy industry's critical infrastructure. This makes the energy industry vulnerable to cyberattack. Critical infrastructure in advanced nations is directly connected to the nation's national and economic security, as it provides goods and services for the country as a whole. Domestic and foreign adversaries will continue to launch cyberattacks targeting critical infrastructure, resulting in major disruptions of services with devastating impact on all nations' economic stability, national security, and public safety.[104]

The Electrical Grid

The energy sector, being highly digital, ranks as the third most targeted industry by cybercriminals globally. There is a serious concern that hacking tools that provide full access to utility systems pose risks even from inexperienced hackers.[105] A more connected and efficient electrical grid is more prone to cyberattacks. Hostile actors are now able to access and damage electrical grids through the internet, and if a wide-scale attack occurs, transportation, pipeline, and communication networks could go down across an entire country.[106] In March 2019, the US electrical grid was hit with a cyberattack that affected several Western states; however, it did not result in service disruptions.[107]

Terrorism and Emerging Technologies

New technologies such as AI can put sophisticated capabilities in the hands of individuals and hostile states around the world. It is critical to understand the security implications of the advances in emerging technologies, such as biotechnology and AI. Terrorist organizations will benefit from emerging technologies such as AI when carrying out cyberattacks. Automated tasks executed using AI will result in more significant attacks. Terrorist use of killer robots, similar to those used by the military, is a major concern as well. Terrorist organizations have already had success using digital and internet technology for their propaganda efforts and communications.[108] Terrorists will benefit from ML and other forms of AI, for instance, in the preparations for their military operations and in the gathering of information. Particularly when carrying out cyberattacks, automated tasks executed using AI can make the scale and impact of these attacks potentially larger. AI technologies are sold to and used by unstable states, not to mention the role that organized crime groups can play in this scenario. As an example, when an unstable state collapses due to internal conflicts, the chances that these technologies will end up in the hands of terrorists and criminal organizations becomes more likely.[109] One key challenge encountered with the use of AI in the field of counterterrorism is that the vast quantities of data needed are not always available or accessible. Terrorist repurposing of commercial artificial systems is a serious concern. Commercial systems are used in harmful and unintended ways, such as using drones or autonomous vehicles to deliver explosives[110] and cause crashes.

Threats from Chemical, Biological, Radiological, and Nuclear (CBRN)

The proliferation of publicly available AI tools could help malicious actors learn to make and deliver chemical and biological weapons. While getting access to laboratory facilities is still a challenge, nevertheless, cloud labs could allow the creation of weapon components. A UK government report indicates that by 2025, AI could heighten the risk of cyberattack, potentially assisting terrorists in planning biological or chemical assaults.[111] A disturbing trend is the reported attempts of state and non-state actors to acquire and use chemical and biological weapons is blatant violations of international norms. Cyberattacks can disrupt CBRN facilities. Such facilities are automated and run by computers that are connected to large networks that can be compromised. When these facilities are penetrated through cyberattacks, the facilities themselves can become the equivalent of weapons of mass destruction. These potential threats are nearly impossible to predict. AI may be utilized to accumulate knowledge about physical attacks by non-state violent actors.[112] Terrorist organizations want to acquire CBRN material, and this poses a major threat for the international community. The cyber domain is considered to be a major international security risk, necessitating more attention given to terrorist activities online. Two prominent areas that terrorist organizations and groups have had much success with are communication of their propaganda and their recruitment efforts.[113]

CBRN threats are evolving rapidly alongside changes in the political environment and developments in technology.[114] Rapid development of synthetic biology and biotechnology offer prospects for misuse. In recent years, some countries and terrorist groups such as ISIS have used chemical weapons on the battlefield in sponsored assassination operations. These attacks have included traditional chemical weapon agents, toxic industrial chemicals, and the first known use of the Novichok nerve agent. The threat from biological weapons has also become more diverse, as biological weapon agents can be employed in a variety of ways. The development of biological weapons is made easier by dual-use technologies. Figure 3.1 demonstrates some of these attacks since 2013.[115]

Rapid advances in biotechnology, including gene editing, synthetic biology, and neuroscience, will create new economic, military, ethical, and regulatory challenges worldwide, as governments struggle to keep pace with these exponentially changing scenarios.[116] Biological security is critical to national security. Preventing and countering the threat of biological

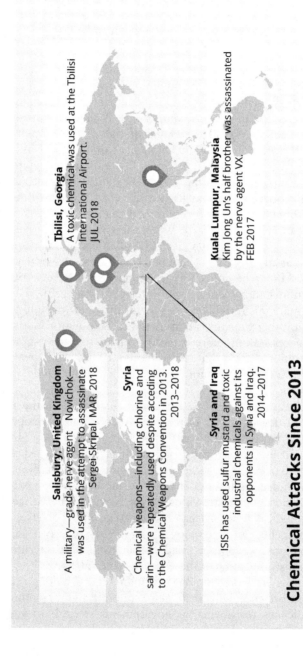

Salisbury, United Kingdom
A military–grade nerve agent Novichok—was used in the attempt to assassinate Sergei Skripal. MAR. 2018

Tbilisi, Georgia
A toxic chemical was used at the Tbilisi International Airport. JUL 2018

Syria
Chemical weapons—including chlorine and sarin—were repeatedly used despite acceding to the Chemical Weapons Convention in 2013. 2013-2018

Syria and Iraq
ISIS has used sulfur mustard and toxic industrial chemicals against its opponents in Syria and Iraq. 2014–2017

Kuala Lumpur, Malaysia
Kim Jong Un's half brother was assassinated by the nerve agent VX. FEB 2017

Chemical Attacks Since 2013

Figure 3.1 Chemical Attacks Since 2013

weapons from both state and non-state actors and developing defenses against biological threat are imperative.

Biotechnology advances can be used for harm as well as good. For example, an individual could build live viruses for legitimate scientific reasons or to conduct bioterrorism. This vulnerability to bioweapons makes biotechnology a challenging area for law enforcement. These technologies hold great promise for advances in precision medicine, agriculture, and manufacturing. However, they also introduce risks, such as the potential for adversaries to develop novel biological warfare agents, threaten food security, and enhance or degrade human performance.

Foreign political and military developments and the global proliferation of laboratories working on dangerous biological pathogens have the potential to be used for deliberate attacks. In particular, the nexus between AI and biotech raises this possibility. Most recently, the invasion of Ukraine by Russia demonstrates that international actors consider nuclear threats as viable tools of state craft.[117] Security has historically taken a back seat as new technologies become mainstream, leaving many vulnerable to threats.

Notes

1 Homeland Security Digital Library. (2020, December 22). *2020 national preparedness report.* www.hsdl.org/c/view?docid=848274

2 See Grabosky, P. (2007). *Electronic crime.* Pearson Prentice Hall. Grabosky, P., Smith, R. G., & Urbas, G. (2004). *Cyber criminals on trial.* Cambridge University. Wall, D. S. (2007). *Cybercrime: The transformation of crime in the information age* (1st ed.). Cambridge: Polity.

3 Europol Unclassified. (2017). *Crime in the age of technology.* www.europol.eur opa.eu/publications-events/main-reports/european-union-serious-and-organi sed-crime-threat-assessment-2017

4 Nasheri, H. (2005). *Economic espionage and industrial spying.* Cambridge University Press.

5 Nasheri, H. (2023, May). *State-sponsored economic espionage in cyberspace: Risks and preparedness, in cybercrime in the pandemic digital age and beyond* (Chang, L. Y-C., Sarre, R., & Smith, R. G., Eds). Springer International Publishing.

6 Homeland Security Digital Library. (2020, December 22). *2020 national preparedness report.* www.hsdl.org/c/view?docid=848274

7 Martin, A. (2023). *Genesis market gang tries to sell platform after FBI disruption.* The Record. https://therecord.media/genesis-market-fraud-platf orm-for-sale-dark-web

8 Howell, J., & Maimon, D. (2022). *Darknet markets generate millions in revenue selling stolen personal data, supply chain study finds.* Nextgov/FCW. www.nextgov.com/ideas/2022/12/darknet-markets-generate-millions-revenue-selling-stolen-personal-data-supply-chain-study-finds/380615/

9 Breeden II, J. (2023). *3 updates: Hackers eye ChatGPT, virtual military training gets photorealistic and NASA picks its simulation winners.* Nextgov/FCW. www.nextgov.com/emerging-tech/2023/05/3-updates-hackers-look-exploit-chatgpt-virtual-military-training-gets-photorealistic-and-nasa-picks-its-simulat ion-winners/385993/

10 Nasheri, H. (2021, December 21). *The dumb and the dangerous road ahead.* United Nations Interregional Crime and Justice Research Institute.

11 Special Competitive Studies Project. (2022, September). *Mid-decade challenges to national competitiveness.* www.scsp.ai/2022/09/special-competitive-studies-project-releases-first-report-sept-12-2022/

12 Nasheri, H. (2021, December 21). *The dumb and the dangerous road ahead.* United Nations Interregional Crime and Justice Research Institute.

13 Osborne, C. (2019, January 24). *Artificial intelligence will become the next new human right.* ZDNet. www.zdnet.com/article/artificial-intelligence-will-become-the-next-new-human-right/

14 Leprince-Ringuet, D. (2020, April 1). *AI vs your career? What artificial intelligence will really do to the future of work.* ZDNet. www.zdnet.com/article/ai-vs-your-career-what-artificial-intelligence-will-really-do-to-the-fut ure-of-work/

15 Nasheri, H. (2018). The impact of intellectual property theft on national and global security. In: Reichel, P., & Randa, R. (eds.) *Transnational crime and global security* (Vol. 1). Praeger.

16 Aspen Digital. (2023, January 9). *Envisioning cyber futures with AI. U.S. and global cybersecurity groups.* www.aspendigital.org/wp-content/uploads/2024/02/Aspen-Digital_Envisioning-Cyber-Futures-with-AI_January-2024.pdf

17 CISA. (2023). *U.S. and international partners publish secure-by-design and-default principles and approaches.* www.cisa.gov/news-events/news/us-and-international-partners-publish-secure-design-and-default-principles-and-app roaches

18 Thompson, N. (2018, March 31). *Emmanuel Macron talks to WIRED about France's AI strategy.* WIRED. www.wired.com/story/emmanuel-macron-talks-to-wired-about-frances-ai-strategy/

19 Giaretta, A., & Dragoni, N. (2020). Community targeted phishing: A middle ground between massive and spear phishing through natural language generation. In *Proceedings of 6th international conference in software engineering for defence applications: SEDA 2018* (pp. 86–93). Springer International Publishing.

20 Palmer, D. (2020, March 2). *AI is changing everything about cybersecurity, for better and for worse.* ZDNet. www.zdnet.com/article/ai-is-changing-everyth ing-about-cybersecurity-f

21 Clark, P. (2023). *As Tax Day nears, AI chatbots like ChatGPT gives scammers a boost.* Axios. www.axios.com/2023/04/13/tax-scams-irs-ai-chat bot-chatgpt

22 Sancho, D., & Fuentes, M. R. (2023). *Inside the halls of a cybercrime business.* Trend Micro Research. https://documents.trendmicro.com/assets/white_papers/wp-inside-the-halls-of-a-cybercrime-business.pdf

23 Breeden II, J. (2022) *New research points to hidden vulnerabilities within machine learning systems.* Nextgov/FCW. www.nextgov.com/cybersecurity/2022/08/new-research-points-hidden-vulnerabilities-within-machine-learning-systems/375713/

24 U.S. Department of Health and Human Services. (2021, September). *Trustworthy AI (TAI) playbook.*

25 Federal Aviation Administration. (2022). *FAA strategic plan* (FY 2019–2022).

26 Sabin, S. (2023, April 14). *Thousands compromised in ChatGPT-themed scheme.* Axios. www.axios.com/newsletters/axios-codebook-a1774cf3-d5dd-4264-a7d4-6c9e60c6f62b.html?chunk=2&utm_term=emshare#story2

27 Hassold, C. (2022, December 12). *The double-edged sword of CHATGPT: How threat actors could ...—Abnormal.* Abnormal Security. https://abnormalsecurity.com/blog/double-edged-sword-of-chatgpt

28 Microsoft. (2022, November). *Extortion economics: Ransomware's new business model.*

29 Harding, E. & Ghoorhoo, H. (2022). *Hard choices in a ransomware attack.* Center for Strategic & International Studies. www.csis.org/analysis/hard-choices-ransomware-attack

30 Santos, D., Bunce, D. & Galiette, A. (2023). *Royal ransomware's spree against U.S. cities.* Unit 42. https://unit42.paloaltonetworks.com/royal-ransomware/

31 Sabin, S. (2023). *Colonial Pipeline ransomware attack's unexpected legacy.* Axios. www.axios.com/newsletters/axios-codebook-4bc295d2-ee29-4b0e-a243-4b6901c453dd.html?chunk=0&utm_term=emshare#story0

32 Page, C. (2023). *Ransomware attack forces Dallas to shut down courts, disrupts some 911 services.* TechCrunch. https://tcrn.ch/3ASeZE4

33 Palo Alto Network (2022, March). *2022 unit 42 ransomware threat report.* Retrieved from https://mysecuritymarketplace.com/reports/unit-42-ransomware-threat-report-2022/

34 Optiv Security. (2023, February 1). *The state of ransomware: 2022 in review.* Retrieved from www.optiv.com/insights/discover/blog/state-ransomware-2022-review#:~:text=Geographic%20Numbers,to%202021%20(1%2C141%20victims)

35 Palmer, D. (2020, March 2). *AI is changing everything about cybersecurity, for better and for worse.* ZDNet. www.zdnet.com/article/ai-is-changing-everything-about-cybersecurity-f

36 Tung, L. (2022). *Microsoft: Hackers are using open source software and fake jobs in phishing attacks.* ZDNet. www.zdnet.com/article/microsoft-hackers-using-open-source-software-and-fake-jobs-in-phishing-attacks/

37 Koblentz, G. D. (2020). Emerging technologies and the future of CBRN terrorism. *The Washington Quarterly, 43,* 177–196.

38 Koblentz, G. D. (2020). Emerging technologies and the future of CBRN terrorism. *The Washington Quarterly, 43,* 177–196.

39 Tung, L. (2022, January 10). *Ransomware warning: Cyber criminals are mailing out USB drives that install malware.* ZDNet. www.zdnet.com/article/fbi-cybercriminals-are-mailing-out-usb-drives-that-will-install-ransomware/

40 Schwartz, C. (2023). *Deepfakes: Events that never happened could influence the 2024 presidential election.* Route Fifty. www.route-fifty.com/emerging-tech/2023/07/deepfakes-events-never-happened-could-influence-2024-presi dential-election/388642/
41 Patterson, D. (2023). *Real-time deepfake detection: How Intel Labs uses AI to fight misinformation.* ZDNet. www.zdnet.com/article/real-time-deepfake-detection-how-intel-labs-uses-ai-to-fight-misinformation/
42 Rosenberg, S. (2022). *AI-generated images open multiple cans of worms.* Axios. www.axios.com/2022/09/12/ai-images-ethics-dall-e-2-stable-diffusion
43 Vincent, J. (2016, December 20). *Artificial intelligence is going to make it easier than ever to fake images and video.* The Verge. www.theverge.com/2016/12/20/14022958/ai-image-manipulation-creation-fakes-audio-video
44 Bickley, O. (2023). *AI scam calls imitating familiar voices are a growing problem—here's how they work.* Route Fifty. www.route-fifty.com/emerging-tech/2023/07/ai-scam-calls-imitating-familiar-voices-are-growing-problemhe res-how-they-work/388509/
45 Fiscutean, A. (2021, October 21). *Nixon's unheard moon-disaster speech is now a warning about the deepfake future.* ZDNet. www.zdnet.com/article/nixons-grim-moon-disaster-speech-is-a-now-a-warning-about-the-deepfake-future/
46 Congressional Research Service. (2020, November 10). *Artificial intelligence and national security* (CRS Report No. R45178). https://crsreports.congress.gov/product/pdf/R/R45178/10
47 The White House. (2022, October). *Blueprint for an AI Bill of Rights: Making automated systems work for the American people.*
48 Kingston, J., Muller, J., & Fitzpatrick, A. (2023). *Adobe's new Photoshop tools make fakery even easier.* Axios. www.axios.com/2023/05/23/adobe-photoshop-ai-fakery-deepfakes
49 Farid, H. (2022). *Text-to-image AI: Powerful, easy-to-use technology for making art—And fakes.* Nextgov/FCW. www.nextgov.com/ideas/2022/12/text-image-ai-powerful-easy-use-technology-making-art-and-fakes/380456/
50 Sabin, S. (2023). *1 big thing: Generative AI is making voice scams easier to believe.* Axios. www.axios.com/newsletters/axios-codebook-fefe700b-3645-45c9-bb57-36d1150a83e3.html?chunk=0&utm_term=emshare#story0
51 Allen, M. (2023). *Ina Fried: Postcard from AI-centric TED.* Axios. www.axios.com/newsletters/axios-am-a3758037-2420-4658-96e4-5d087f6a89ed.html?chunk=5&utm_term=emshare#story5
52 Harrison, M. (2023). *90% of online content will be AI-generated by 2026.* The Byte. https://futurism.com/the-byte/experts-90-online-content-ai-generated
53 Breeden II, J. (2023). *3 updates: Hackers eye ChatGPT, virtual military training gets photorealistic and NASA picks its simulation winners.* Nextgov/FCW. www.nextgov.com/emerging-tech/2023/05/3-updates-hackers-look-exploit-chatgpt-virtual-military-training-gets-photorealistic-and-nasa-picks-its-simulat ion-winners/385993/
54 BBC. (2023). *ChatGPT owner in probe over risks around false answers.* www.bbc.com/news/business-66196223

55 Sabin, S. (2023). *Social-engineering scams get more sophisticated.* Axios. www. axios.com/newsletters/axios-codebook-5bcd52ce-753f-4723-bd02-b40f5c156 d0b.html?chunk=2&utm_term=emshare#story2

56 Wan, J. (2023). *FBI warns of public "juice jacking" charging stations that steal your data. How to stay protected.* ZDNet. www.zdnet.com/article/fbi-warns-of-juice-jacking-charging-stations-in-public-areas-how-to-stay-protected/

57 Tung, L. (2022, February 2). *FBI warning: Scammers are posting fake job ads on networking sites to steal your money and identity.* ZDNet. www.zdnet.com/article/fbi-warning-scammers-are-posting-fake-job-ads-on-networking-sites-to-steal-your-money-and-identity/

58 Deblock, F. (2023). *LinkedIn, another playground for cybercriminals.* InCyber. https://incyber.org/en/linkedin-another-playground-for-cybercriminals/.

59 Tung, L. (2022, January 19). *FBI warning: Crooks are using fake QR codes to steal your passwords and money.* ZDNet. www.zdnet.com/article/fbi-warning-crooks-are-using-fake-qr-codes-to-steal-your-passwords-and-money/

60 Ruoti, S. (2022). *How QR codes work and what makes them dangerous—A computer scientist explains.* Nextgov/FCW. www.nextgov.com/cxo-briefing/2022/04/how-qr-codes-work-and-what-makes-them-dangerous-computer-scientist-explains/364147/

61 InCyber. (2023). *Phishing attack uses QR code.* https://incyber.org/en/phishing-attack-uses-qr-code/

62 Stathis, J. (2023). *How to spot a credit card skimmer at gas pumps and avoid getting scammed.* Readers Digest. www.rd.com/article/gas-pump-skimmer/

63 The Hacker News. (2023). Credential theft is (still) a top attack method. https://thehackernews.com/2022/08/credential-theft-is-still-top-attack.html

64 Sabin, S. (2023). *Telecom's "extreme" password leaks.* Axios. www.axios.com/newsletters/axios-codebook-5332d6f6-632e-43fc-aaee-e22e7fea2ad6.html?chunk=2&utm_term=emshare#story2

65 Teale, C. (2023). *EVs rev up cybersecurity challenges.* Route Fifty. www.route-fifty.com/tech-data/2023/05/evs-rev-cybersecurity-challenges/385830/

66 UTSA. (2022). *UTSA researcher part of team protecting EV charging stations from cyberattacks.* www.utsa.edu/today/2022/01/story/elias-bou-harb-ev-charging-stations-cyberattacks.html

67 Sandia National Laboratories. (2022). *News Releases: Sandia studies vulnerabilities of electric vehicle charging infrastructure.* https://newsreleases.sandia.gov/ev_security/

68 Cox, J. (2023). *SIM swappers are working directly with ransomware gangs now.* 404 Media. www.wired.com/story/ring-police-rfa-tool-shut-down/

69 Krebs, B. (2023). *Hackers claim they breached T-mobile more than 100 times in 2022.* Krebs on Security. https://krebsonsecurity.com/2023/02/hackers-claim-they-breached-t-mobile-more-than-100-times-in-2022/

70 Wain, P. (2023). *Apple co-founder says AI may make scams harder to spot.* BBC. www.bbc.com/news/technology-65496150

71 Teale, C. (2022). *Public employees expect more fraud, waste and abuse.* Route Fifty. www.route-fifty.com/management/2022/12/expect-even-more-fraud-waste-and-abuse/380884/

72 Gerken, T. (2023). *Banks warn of big increase in online scams.* BBC. www.bbc. com/news/technology-65486219

73 Teale, C. (2022). *Public employees expect more fraud, waste and abuse.* Route Fifty. www.route-fifty.com/management/2022/12/expect-even-more-fraud-waste-and-abuse/380884/

74 Perrigo, B. (2023). OpenAI could quit Europe over new AI rules, CEO Altman warns. *Time.* https://time.com/6282325/sam-altman-openai-eu/

75 Haan, K. (2023). Over 75% of consumers are concerned about misinformation from artificial intelligence. *Forbes.* www.forbes.com/advisor/business/artificial-intelligence-consumer-sentiment/

76 Bateman, J., & Jackson, D. (2024). *COUNTERING DISINFORMATION EFFECTIVELY—An evidence based policy guide.* Carnegie Endowment for International Peace. https://carnegieendowment.org/files/Carnegie_Countering _Disinformation_Effectively.pdf

77 U.S. Department of Homeland Security. (2023, September 14). *Homeland threat assessment 2024.* www.dhs.gov/sites/default/files/2023-09/23_091 3_ia_23-333-ia_u_homeland-threat-assessment-2024_508C_V6_13Se p23.pdf

78 U.S. Department of Homeland Security. (2023, September 14). *Homeland threat assessment 2024.* www.dhs.gov/sites/default/files/2023-09/23_0913_ia_ 23-333-ia_u_homeland-threat-assessment-2024_508C_V6_13Sep23.pdf

79 Watts, C. (2024, June 2). *How Russia is trying to disrupt the 2024 Paris Olympic games. Microsoft on the issues.* https://blogs.microsoft.com/on-the-iss ues/2024/06/02/russia-cyber-bots-disinformation-2024-paris-olympics/

80 Bateman, J., & Jackson, D. (2024). *COUNTERING DISINFORMATION EFFECTIVELY—An evidence based policy guide.* Carnegie Endowment for International Peace. https://carnegieendowment.org/files/Carnegie_Countering _Disinformation_Effectively.pdf

81 Sabin, S. (2023). *1 big Thing: Hackers could get help from the new AI chatbot.* Axios. www.axios.com/newsletters/axios-codebook-9a337fdf-4ea9-4eaa-a9bd-28c816b2c555.html?chunk=0&utm_term=emshare#story0

82 Newman, L., & Burgess, M. (2023). *The biggest hack of 2023 keeps getting bigger.* WIRED UK. www.wired.com/story/moveit-breach-victims/

83 Sabin, S. (2023). *1 big thing: New security flaw's slow-burn perils.* Axios. www. axios.com/newsletters/axios-codebook-5bcd52ce-753f-4723-bd02-b40f5c156 d0b.html?chunk=0&utm_term=emshare#story0

84 Tidy, J. (2023). *Hacker gang Clop publishes victim names on dark web.* BBC. www.bbc.com/news/business-65924327

85 Riotta, C. (2023). *No "systemic risk" to government networks from latest breach, CISA says.* Nextgov/FCW. www.nextgov.com/cybersecurity/2023/ 06/cyberattack-hits-several-federal-agencies-drawing-all-hands-call-response/ 387579/

86 Palmer, D. (2022). *This evasive new cyberattack can bypass air-gapped systems to steal data from the most sensitive networks.* ZDNet. www.zdnet.com/arti cle/this-evasive-new-cyberattack-can-bypass-air-gapped-systems-to-steal-data-from-the-most-sensitive-networks/

87 Buitta L., Healy S., Jankowicz N., Smith B., & Stewart C. (2021). *Online event: Civics as a national security imperative: The role of technology*. Center for Strategic & International Studies. www.csis.org/events/online-event-civics-national-security-imperative-role-technology

88 Congressional Research Service. (2020, November 10). *Artificial intelligence and national security* (CRS Report No. R45178). https://crsreports.congress.gov/product/pdf/R/R45178/10

89 Department of Defense. (2020, September 30). *Executive summary: DoD data strategy, unleashing data to advance the National Defense Strategy*. https://stacks.stanford.edu/file/druid:qr088db3377/DOD-data-strategy.pdf

90 Allen, G. C. (2022, May 13). *Across drones, A.I., and space, Commercial Tech is flexing military muscle in Ukraine*. Center for Strategic & International Studies. www.csis.org/analysis/across-drones-ai-and-space-commercial-tech-flexing-military-muscle-ukraine

91 Huntley, S. (2024, February 6). *Buying spying: How the commercial surveillance industry works and what can be done about it*. Google Threat Analysis Group. https://blog.google/threat-analysis-group/commercial-surveillance-vendors-google-tag-report/

92 Department of the Air Force. (2019). *The United States Air Force artificial intelligence annex to the Department of Defense Artificial Intelligence Strategy*. www.af.mil/Portals/1/documents/5/USAF-AI-Annex-to-DoD-AI-Strategy.pdf

93 Gardner, F. (2021, December 30). *What does future warfare look like? It's here already*. BBC. www.bbc.com/news/world-59755100

94 Department of Defense. (2018). *Summary of the 2018 Department of Defense Artificial Intelligence Strategy: Harnessing AI to advance our security and prosperity*. https://media.defense.gov/2019/Feb/12/2002088963/-1/-1/1/SUMMARY-OF-DOD-AI-STRATEGY.PDF

95 Office of the Director of National Intelligence. (2019). *The aim initiative; A strategy for augmenting intelligence using machines*. www.dni.gov/files/ODNI/documents/AIM-Strategy.pdf

96 Chappell, B. (2015, July 28). *Researchers warn against "autonomous weapons" arms race*. NPR. www.npr.org/sections/thetwo-way/2015/07/28/427189235/researchers-warn-against-autonomous-weapons-arms-race

97 Congressional Research Service. (2023, August 22). *Law enforcement and technology: Use of unmanned aircraft systems*.

98 Koblentz, G. D. (2020). Emerging technologies and the future of CBRN terrorism. *The Washington Quarterly, 43*, 177–196.

99 Federal Aviation Administration. (2022). *FAA strategic plan (FY 2019-2022)*.

100 Kramer, M. (2023, January 17). *The growing space economy*. Axios. www.axios.com/newsletters/axios-space-c4cfb894-8174-4770-8fcb-703f927b59c1.html

101 Congressional Research Service. (2020, November 10). *Artificial intelligence and national security* (CRS Report No. R45178). https://crsreports.congress.gov/product/pdf/R/R45178/10

102 BBC. (2023). *Russia-linked hackers a threat to UK infrastructure, warns minister*. www.bbc.com/news/uk-65319771

103 Wojno, M. (2021, December 6). *Brace yourself for these five top data breach trends in 2022, Experian warns*. ZDNet. www.zdnet.com/article/experian-releases-data-breach-industry-forecast-for-2022/

104 Office of the Press Secretary. (2013, February 12). *Presidential Policy Directive—Critical Infrastructure Security and Resilience*. The White House. https://obamawhitehouse.archives.gov/the-press-office/2013/02/12/president ial-policy-directive-critical-infrastructure-security-and-resil

105 Joos, T. (2022). *The real threat of unconventional cyberattacks*. InCyber. https://incyber.org/en/the-real-threat-of-unconventional-cyberattacks/.

106 Herr, T. (2020, October 19). *Securing the energy transition: Innovative cyber solutions for grid resiliency*. Atlantic Council. www.atlanticcouncil.org/event/securing-the-energy-transition/

107 Walsh, B. (2020, October 7). *The electrical grid will be exposed to cyberattacks as it becomes connected to the internet*. Axios. www.axios.com/2020/10/07/protecting-smarter-grid-cyberattacks

108 Veer, R. V.-D. (2019, December 11). *Terrorism in the age of technology*. ICCT. www.icct.nl/publication/terrorism-age-technology

109 Nasheri, H. (2021, December 21). *The dumb and the dangerous road ahead*. United Nations Interregional Crime and Justice Research Institute.

110 BBC. (2021, April 21). *Mexico cartel used explosive drones to attack police*. www.bbc.com/news/world-latin-america-56814501

111 Vallance, C. (2023). *AI could worsen cyber-threats, report warns*. BBC. www.bbc.com/news/technology-67221117

112 Vallance, C. (2023). *AI could worsen cyber-threats, report warns*. BBC. www.bbc.com/news/technology-67221117

113 Nasheri, H. (2021, December 21). *The dumb and the dangerous road ahead*. United Nations Interregional Crime and Justice Research Institute.

114 Nasheri, H. (2021, December 21). *The dumb and the dangerous road ahead*. United Nations Interregional Crime and Justice Research Institute.

115 Nasheri, H. (2021, December 21). *The dumb and the dangerous road ahead*. United Nations Interregional Crime and Justice Research Institute.

116 Nasheri, H. (2021, December 21). *The dumb and the dangerous road ahead*. United Nations Interregional Crime and Justice Research Institute.

117 U.S. Department of Homeland Security. (2023, September 14). *Homeland threat assessment 2024*. www.dhs.gov/sites/default/files/2023-09/23_0913_ia _23-333-ia_u_homeland-threat-assessment-2024_508C_V6_13Sep23.pdf

4 Prosperity and Security

A Balancing Act

Digital technologies touch every aspect of society. Advances in AI and other emerging technologies have impacted all aspects of society—from education and healthcare to the labor market and transportation, as previously stated. Policymakers and legislative bodies in advanced industrialized nations are grappling with rapidly developed and deployed AI products and tools.

The world is entering a new phase of deepening dependencies, driven by emerging technologies and even more complex and interdependent systems. Dramatic shifts in the coming decade will provide new possibilities for prosperity while also multiplying the systemic risks posed by insecure systems. The Covid-19 pandemic pushed people to live more deeply in a digital world. Next-generation interconnectivity is eliminating the boundary between the digital and physical worlds. Advanced wireless technologies, IoT, and space-based assets—including those enabling positioning, navigation, and timing for civilian and military uses, environmental and weather monitoring, and everyday internet-based activities from banking to telemedicine—will move online, making cyberattacks easier, more destructive, and more impactful.

A Period of Conflicts

High-level conversations are taking place on the use of AI models, predictive decision-making, and its impact on society. These debates are taking place parallel to other pressing issues surrounding international conflicts, global food and water security, and immigration. Government leaders around the world are confronting a host of complex problems. Technological advances have enhanced the bad actors' capabilities, and law enforcement is lagging behind. A key question is how to balance innovation and security simultaneously?

DOI: 10.4324/9781003368304-5

Geopolitical Positioning

It is important to have a better understanding of how economic and political forces interact to influence world affairs. The emergence of AI will deeply disrupt global geopolitics. As a result of geopolitical upheavals, the global supply chain, in particular that of critical infrastructure, is vulnerable to risks. The world has encountered a disturbing rise in incidents of cyberattacks that seek to exploit economic vulnerabilities and dependencies, consequently undermining foreign and domestic security.[1] The expansion of innovation in emerging technologies is creating a major shift in global geopolitics, including changes to the economic status quo; thus, provoking social changes. The geopolitical landscape has been influenced by multiple factors, including international conflicts and an increasing trend toward nationalism. As previously mentioned, adversaries and malicious actors have the technological capabilities to carry out their activities remotely with far-reaching impact. States are engaged in a frantic race to develop emerging tools in response to the economic, industrial, political, and military advantages these technologies provide. As the world becomes increasingly interconnected, it is important to identify which technologies will be the most important geopolitically, particularly military technologies central to global influence.

Military Race

Emerging technologies like AI, hypersonics, quantum science, directed energy, and biotechnology, once believed decades away, are now reshaping battlefields and geopolitical realities. In the current race for strategic advantage between the US and China, advances in emerging technologies will have a major impact both economically and militarily. Emerging tools like AI have the potential to be a game- changer strategically for military competitiveness. The changing geopolitical landscape and the current technological environment will produce new national security challenges. Some future challenges will be novel, and a few might be responsive to a military solution; however, for the most part, they will require international support and collaborative relationships and agreements.[2]

Democracy

The current prevailing sentiment about democracy illustrates a lack of confidence in government institutions. People are experiencing a sense of disorientation with respect to where their countries are headed in the middle of significant technological changes. Different political systems will decide how technologies are developed and used. New technologies can deeply destabilize and harm individuals and their communities and undermine confidence in government and democratic principles. For instance, generative AI has the potential to introduce digitally altered content into political campaigns that will mislead the public and harm the political discourse.[3] Among the great challenges posed to democracy today is the use of emerging tools like AI, data collection methods, and automated decisions' systems resulting in the violation of individual rights.

AI Election Manipulation

Aiming to safeguard elections against deepfakes and other forms of AI manipulation, lawmakers are pledging to boost protections. For example, robocalls in New Hampshire in January 2024 used an AI-generated, manipulated clone voice of President Joe Biden to encourage callers not to vote in January 2024.[4] Globally, adversaries' malicious use of digital information and communication technologies are bound to become more pervasive. Automated, targeted, and complex attacks will further threaten the exploitation of sensitive data and illegitimate use of technology, including commercial spyware and surveillance technology. The widespread use of social media platforms with low barriers to entry makes it easier for AI systems to masquerade certain political views. This has led to the widespread use of social media "bots" to spread political messages and cause dissent. Nowadays, many such bots are controlled by humans who manage a large pack of bots.[5]

Bots

AI language models like ChatGPT have the potential to influence voter behavior, which is another disturbing concern for government officials. Preventing AI election manipulation may involve refraining from emerging tools that facilitate AI-generated content. As mentioned in earlier chapters, the EU has taken measures to regulate AI systems that influence voters due to their high-risk nature. Transparency in AI-generated messages is vital to inform voters about their origin and purpose.[6] Adversarial nation-states or groups or lone-wolf individuals controlling bots can influence the general public's opinion in an effort to undermine elections.[7]

Social Media Platforms

Lawmakers have expressed concerns about the handling of extremist content by social media platforms such as X (formerly known as Twitter), Meta, TikTok, and YouTube, and the algorithmic promotion of harmful posts. Lawmakers have also raised objections with respect to potential weaponization of social media platforms for spreading misinformation and capturing user data.[8]

The Dark Web

Darknet marketplaces are more dangerous now due to cybercriminal groups abandoning marketplace rules as a result of the war between Russia and Ukraine. Some of these cybercriminal groups are pro-Ukrainian while others are pro-Kremlin. This has created an unprecedented blurring of lines. Cybercriminal groups are now going after sensitive computing systems that are connected to governmental services and infrastructure, according to Google and IBM researchers. Law enforcement agencies still do not have a strategy to fight cybercriminals on the dark web since they have little information on digital payments and cryptocurrency.[9]

Blurring the Lines Between Fact and Fiction

As indicated in the previous chapter, AI technology is expected to make misinformation more pervasive and compelling.[10] AI can propagate conspiracy theories and misinformation, worsening existing problems. AI is already known to produce inaccurate content and to facilitate the easy creation of targeted messages for specific audiences. The models themselves are vulnerable to manipulation, potentially allowing for strategic influence over their output. Other concerns raised by these technological tools relate to weaponry, particularly ethical questions regarding autonomous weapons' decision-making without human input.[11]

Shifting Perceptions

Advanced tools like generative AI can produce various content types as a tool, empowering adversaries to conduct real-time malicious information campaigns. The use of AI for disinformation and tailored spear phishing content creation underscores the risks of potential violence and escalating cyberattacks on critical infrastructure. This includes the testing of AI-developed malware and the exploitation of AI in stealing sensitive information from infrastructure networks.[12]

Censorship

Nations are struggling to strike a balance between digital freedom and protecting people from the risks posed by emerging tools and technology. Some foreign governments are increasingly employing digital tools to monitor and surpass political discussions both domestically and among expat communities.

New technological tools are enabling state and non-state actors to shape the views of their populations and their decision-making processes. Competitors are exploiting digital dependence across society through cyberattacks, data harvesting, and sophisticated disinformation campaigns. A 2022 report by the US International Trade Commission noted how different governments have been utilizing technology such as AI to keep track of the public's internet activity, and are using AI to suppress content.[13] The censored information often consists of political, security, and social information.[14]

Authoritarianism

Digital authoritarianism consists of manipulation, surveillance, and repression of data and digital technologies. With increased authoritarianism, the internet is used as a tool to exercise control over a population.[15] Authoritarian countries, recognizing how technology can be used to organize opposition, increasingly engage in deploying digital blockades at politically charged times, while using digital tools like spyware and surveillance technologies to target critics and silence dissent. Even democracies, in their efforts to regulate content, are grappling with the risk of reducing free and open access to information.[16] Access to emerging tools in authoritarian regimes is particularly alarming, as it can facilitate power and control of people.[17]

The Intelligence Community (IC)

Driven by technological innovation and rising international uncertainty, today's intelligence leaders face complex challenges in identifying and addressing threats. In addition to geopolitical rivalry, the rapid increase in surveillance technology, monitoring, and collection is creating an avalanche of data that can provide the IC, law enforcement agencies, governments, nation-states, and criminal organizations with significant advantages. Intelligence collection and analysis in a digital era is an enormous task for the IC. It will require adapting to new methods and training and familiarity in the use of emerging technologies and tools. Generative AI can significantly alter the speed of creation and quantity of information, including inaccurate and deliberately false information.

AI and IC

The nature of intelligence gathering in the data-driven world has drastically changed. The use of AI is changing how intelligence agencies make sense of the world around them. The IC is currently transitioning between countering terrorism and supporting geopolitical competition. Digital technologies are rapidly changing the intelligence environment, making it more difficult to collect intelligence. The IC community must adapt to the rapid changes and new technologies.[18]

Spy Agencies and Commercial Data

A recently declassified report reveals that the US government has secretly been engaged in collecting sensitive information on its citizens. The report indicates that the US IC is leveraging the expansion of commercial information and intelligence services worldwide to gather personal data on individuals globally, including US citizens who are entitled to constitutional protections. The report points to concerns about privacy, and questions the collection methods and lack of coordination among the agencies regarding data acquisition. While recognizing the value of commercially available information, the report underscores the need for implementation of safeguards on data acquisition and an assessment of potential harm to individuals. The report highlights potential misuse of collected data and the erosion of constitutional protections. It is important to consider the impact of these technologies on traditions and societal expectations.[19]

The proliferation of sensors is facilitating the collection of data that individuals leave behind on the internet through their everyday searching, reading, streaming, shopping, and dating habits. AI-enabled systems can analyze these vast amounts of harvested data, providing new opportunities for micro targeting of individuals.

Data Brokers

In today's economy, data are the lifeblood of businesses and governments, and protection must be considered a top priority. The dramatic expansion of personal information increases the threat environment and the potential for data breaches. Securing personal data is a necessary component for protecting consumer privacy in a digital world. Often, the greatest harm falls upon the vulnerable population for whom risks to their personal data can produce disproportionate harm.[20] A recent Duke University study found that the personal data of US military members, including names, addresses, and sensitive details, can be purchased online for as little as one cent per name.[21] The study reveals a lack of control and regulations on data purchases in the US. It also highlights concerns about nation-states adversaries' abilities to acquire such data for targeting operations. Requiring commercial companies to limit the amount of personal information they collect will mitigate harms caused by cyberattacks and data breaches.

Spyware Threat

Once available only to a small number of well-resourced countries, offensive hacking tools and services, including foreign commercial spyware, are now widely accessible. These tools and services empower countries that previously lacked the ability to cause harm in cyberspace with additional capabilities. It also enables cyber incidents from organized criminal groups.[22] There are major concerns about spyware that can hack into smartphones, like the NSO Group's *Pegasus* spyware that has been banned from the US. Spyware has been used to target journalists and political opposition figures. The spyware infects a phone by sending calendar invitations through iCloud, and users do not have to do anything for it to work. The spyware can record conversations, read encrypted app messages, listen to phone calls, track locations, and access iCloud accounts.[23] The NSO Group argues that its product aids in fighting crime and terrorism.[24]

Fitness Trackers and Baby Monitors

IoT devices, including both consumer goods like fitness trackers and baby monitors, as well as industrial control systems and sensors, introduce new sources of connectivity in our homes and businesses. Nevertheless, many of the devices deployed today are not sufficiently protected against cybersecurity threats. Too often they have been deployed with inadequate default settings, making it difficult or impossible to patch or upgrade security flaws. Recent IoT vulnerabilities have shown just how easily bad actors can exploit these devices to construct botnets and conduct surveillance.[25]

The Automatic Identification System (AIS)

The Automatic Identification System (AIS) is a global tracking system that functions as a ship's guiding device for its routes. Ports can keep track of a ship's arrival and prepare for incoming shipments. The GPS system tells everyone exactly where the vessel is. The vast bulk of the global economy relies on shipping to achieve its goals. The tracking systems are made to make shipping more efficient and safer; nonetheless, attackers are using public tracking data to target commercial ships. Even if the ship's AIS is turned off, the attacker is still able to assume the ship's behavior, as the ship is not going to change their path and will continue to drive in a straight line at a set course and speed since that would be the most efficient course of action.

Commercially Available Information (CAI)

Today, there is a large and growing amount of what the US IC refers to as commercially available information (CAI) and publicly available information (PAI). There is an abundance of CAI in existence that is offered for sale, including sensitive and private information. There is a large market demand for CAI. This information is used both for analysis and exploitation. CAI is a relatively new, fast-growing, and increasingly significant part of the information environment. It includes significant information on US residents, which can be purchased in bulk. The digital revolution has placed an incredible amount of information into the hands of private actors, many of whom sell these data. CAI can be obtained from public records, sometimes digitized from paper originals, such as information about real estate transactions that can be found in local title offices or courthouses. It can be obtained from smartphone and other software applications, often in the form of software development kits (SDKs) that collect information from devices in the US and abroad. Furthermore, CAI can be obtained from cookies and through other methods, sometimes associated with real-time bidding (RTB) for sales of online advertising, which track the end users as they browse the internet.[26]

Without proper controls, CAI can be misused to cause substantial harm, embarrassment, and inconvenience to US persons. These data are packaged by data brokers, and spy agencies are among the buyers of these data. As a result, lawmakers and privacy advocates have come down hard on the IC, accusing the agencies of going around the Fourth Amendment requirements in the US that bar unreasonable searches and seizures. Purchases of data from platforms or apps where consumers legally but sometimes unknowingly give away their location information and other personal details by clicking "yes" on user agreements have become a privacy ethics flashpoint.

Vending Machines for Ammunition

A company based in Texas, American Rounds, sells ammunition through automated technology and owns vending machines containing bullets for sale. The machine uses an ID scanner and FR software to verify the buyer's age. At the present time, these vending machines have been adopted in several states and installed in some grocery stores in the US.[27]

Space and Cyber Intelligence

Space has become a contested domain, and technological challenges are emerging in the space intelligence domain. In recent years, threat actors have turned their attention to space systems. Besides direct hacking, threat actors use non-technical methods to compromise space systems and access information about space technologies. Sensor data collection is growing exponentially, not only on Earth, but in space as well. Threats to aerospace operations go beyond direct hacking, as foreign adversaries use insider threats, cyber intrusions, supply chain attacks, and other methods to steal intellectual property (IP).[28] The interconnectedness of space and cyber challenges are important, as their impact extends beyond their domains into military operations and society at large. Commercial space activities are reshaping warfare by enabling widespread knowledge of adversaries' actions in this evolving landscape.[29] Space and cybertechnologies are raising the likelihood of warlike conflicts.

Satellite Technology

Satellites play a critical role in providing situational awareness and communications, particularly in times of war. During the war in Ukraine, commercial satellites became potential targets for enemies. Establishing norms would allow nations to collectively condemn irresponsible actions in space.[30] The US Space Force aims to create an interoperable hybrid communications network involving civil, commercial, and military satellites.[31] Satellites are now essential for military infrastructure. According to satellite image providers, AI tools, with faster satellite data, will enable better anticipation of geopolitical events, and customers of those companies can become aware of crises.

Accountability and Governance

Currently, the development of AI is largely unchecked, and many feel insufficient attention is given to its potential risks. There are significant concerns about IP infringement, cost, and environmental impact.

Some large-language models (LLMs) already have the ability to create exploitations in known security vulnerabilities. The research results of one study indicate that this fear could be a reality a lot sooner than anticipated. Government officials and the cybersecurity community have long warned of a world in which AI systems automate and speed up malicious actors' attacks. Computer scientists at the University of Illinois Urbana-Champaign published a paper illustrating that GPT-4 can write malicious scripts to exploit known vulnerabilities using publicly available data.[32] At this time, AI model operators do not have a good way of reigning in these malicious use cases.

Governments and legislative bodies that are contemplating AI governance and regulation have not been able to agree on a uniform definition for AI.[33] Regulators and industry need to work together with the wider society to agree on the best practice within their industry and establish appropriate regulatory standards.[34]

AI researchers warn that AI can develop negative behaviors based on their interactions with humans; they give examples of human-induced negative behaviors. AI, as a creation of humans, can intrinsically absorb problems that its creators have not solved yet. This involves the replication of human problems in the solutions created by AI. Without the right governance mechanism in place, there is a risk that the use of AI can result in antisocial or harmful actions. AI, if not properly designed and used, will significantly change the political power balance. There are indications that AI is being deployed as a weapon in modern militaries.[35]

Privacy

AI tools with their unique capabilities can draw connections or inferences of personhood. Companies have an enormous amount of personal information on people that has been collected, distributed, and sold by data brokers. There is enough personal information that ultimately could facilitate the creation of digital clones and deepfakes that would look and sound like a particular individual. AI tools can share very specific information about a person. In light of the rapid development of AI systems, notions of privacy will continue to evolve. As global networks become increasingly interconnected, they will track all aspects of people's personal and professional lives, resulting in the disappearance of anonymity and privacy.[36] More immediately, the role of Big Tech in people's daily lives has put an unprecedented degree of power and influence in the hands of private companies like Google, Apple, Meta, and X.

There is a growing need for government oversight and regulation with respect to data privacy. Key considerations should be given to data sensitivity, individual privacy rights, legal requirements, and data sharing. Privacy is the next battleground for the AI debate, even as discussions over copyright, accuracy, and bias continue. At the present time, building AI that respects data privacy is complicated, based on how generative AI systems work.

Trustworthy AI

The corporate rush to deploy AI products has resulted in products with half-baked features being released to consumers, and as markets become saturated with these products, the less the public is going to trust the new technology. For example, more recently, the search giant Google added AI-generated summaries on top of the search results. This feature has not been received well so far and could fundamentally reshape what is available on the internet and who will profit from it. Many users use Google for fact checking and particularly now that AI chatbots deliver wrong answers, the search results are subject to mistakes and hallucinations. Transparency in AI provides a window into the technology's inner workings and helps ordinary people see when, where, and how the technology is used. That is especially important in areas like decision-making, as disclosure allows people to see the role AI played in the decision-making process, if any. An emphasis on transparency will help build public trust in this technology. The development of trustworthy AI is crucial in addressing the economic, social, and national security challenges and opportunities that emerging technologies like AI offer. The world has been trying to address the risks of emerging technologies like AI for some time now. At this stage, there is an opportunity to shape AI's development to ensure that producers of AI systems incorporate trustworthy AI in their products and services to mitigate potential risks. Trustworthiness must be a prerequisite for the development, deployment, and use of AI systems. AI systems do not stop at national borders, and neither does their impact. Global solutions are therefore required for the global opportunities and challenges that AI systems present. All stakeholders need to work toward a global framework for trustworthy AI, building an international consensus while promoting and upholding fundamental rights like respect for human dignity, individual freedom, and respect for democracy, justice, and the rule of law.[37]

Issues related to accuracy, explainability and interpretability, privacy, reliability, robustness, safety, and security cannot be ignored or viewed as an obstacle to innovation. As covered in earlier chapters, the presence of bias in automated systems can contribute to harmful outcomes and the erosion of public trust. A compounding factor has to do with the difficulty of predicting where and when AI systems will be used. There are specific conditional traits associated with automation that exacerbate distrust in AI tools.[38]

Policies should outline governance and who will be held responsible for all aspects of AI solutions.[39] Government agencies and law enforcement bodies must address the difficulties in preserving human accountability, including for end users, developers, testers, and the organizations that are employing AI systems. End users and those ultimately affected by the actions of an AI system should be offered the opportunity to appeal an AI system's decision. Accountability and appellate processes must exist for AI decisions. Investigative bodies should be able to recreate what happened through auditing trails and other documentation. Without policies requiring such steps, enforcement of any policies would be impossible.[40]

How to Make AI Better

- Reduce corporate influence in research
- Corporations are not interested in certain aspects of AI and have avoided dealing with potentially negative consequences and externalities of AI
- Focus on understanding
- Most AI is good at prediction, but often does not understand the systems it is predicting
- The rise of big data and complex models has driven AI research to focus on prediction rather than understanding
- Marginalized researchers have to be empowered
- Perspectives of impacted communities are important
- AI research needs to consider the public that will be impacted by the AI
- Uniform regulation
- FR tech, AI bias, and privacy should be the subject of regulation[41]

European Union (EU) AI Act

The European Union AI Act is the world's first comprehensive set of AI laws to help protect the safety and fundamental rights of persons as the new technology moves closer to becoming embedded in everyday lives.[42] As of the writing of this text, the EU AI Act has still not been formally adopted. The Act must undergo a final European Council vote before it can be published in the Official Journal. This is expected to occur sometime in 2024.

With the AI Act, the EU has a unique opportunity to end the abuse of mass-surveillance technologies.[43] Success in achieving a balance between innovation and minimizing harm hinges on the legal framework and legislation prescribing how these technologies are used. AI is not a single technology, but a range of applications, including FR and natural language processing.

Regulations

There seems to be a wait and see approach when it comes to regulations. The existing regulatory bodies were created in a different technological era. Advanced economies have to modernize their rules and legislative framework for the new AI era. Adopting any regulations must protect and address the right to privacy and the networks' customary practices when it comes to the use and sharing of consumer data. Policymakers and legislative bodies have to account for different risk levels and the use of AI in the commercial sector, the government, and by law enforcement agencies.

Earlier chapters addressed some of the significant concerns of bias and fairness that the use of FR raises. In order to adequately address these concerns, technical and non-technical expertise and capabilities are required to better anticipate the implications of AI on humanity and society. New surveillance and FRT technologies are enhancing the investigatory powers of the state in the absence of any uniform legislation or regulatory guardrail. No global mechanism of accountability has been established thus far. It is imperative that the sociotechnical consequences of AI systems are anticipated prior to their development and use and not post their distribution into the markets. Recently, it was revealed that Amazon's Alexa for years has been collecting data from users and harvested that data without the users' knowledge or consent.[44]

Great Power Rivalry

The acceleration of AI application for national security defense is the top priority for advanced economies, including the US. The current mindset is fight and win faster and more effectively than the adversaries.[45] AI is viewed as a growing threat to national security that requires nations to have appropriate defense mechanisms in place. AI cyber driven attacks pose major detection challenges for the cybersecurity defense force and law enforcement.[46]

The race between nations is already on, pushing the boundaries of innovation, development, and deployment. As models become more advanced, nations will use them for economic, military, and national security advantages, and malicious actors will also use them to achieve their objectives. Gaining and maintaining leadership in emerging technologies is a key feature of the ongoing global competition. Technology is now at the heart of a long-term competition between open, democratic societies and closed authoritarian systems. Safeguarding the global digital infrastructure, including wireless networks (in particular 5G and its successors), fiberoptic cables (both terrestrial and undersea), operating systems, and servers (cloud and physical) is an absolute necessity, as they are the foundations upon which digital economies and other technologies function. Control over digital infrastructure impacts influence over data, applications, and technology platforms.[47]

Digital Divide

The race for strategic advantages for AI among advanced economies will widen the existing gap among other countries in terms of development and progress. There are profound concerns about massive labor disruptions and rising inequality as societies move toward AI.

AI-driven control over populations may create insecurity if AI technology is used to control populations. It then becomes an attractive target for hackers.[48] The true extent of AI's impact on society is still unknown,[49] for some AI promises remain unfulfilled and economists believe that capitalism may fail to ensure equitable distribution of benefits and effective risk management when it comes to AI. The delicate balance between privacy and data sharing and lack of comprehensive international regulations on AI will undermine democracies and disrupt societal equilibrium.[50]

As of 2024, there are only a handful of countries that have made striking advancements in the design and production of AI technologies. The debate continues as to which country is leading the way. As one prominent politician has stated "whoever leads AI will rule the world."[51] For instance, the development of the Apollo program was born out of a race between the US and the Soviet Union for geopolitical dominance that extended to the moon. The increased use of AI is part of the ongoing global race among nations to leverage new technologies for competitive advantages and to increase their economic prosperity. Some countries are exponentially progressing, while others are still in the preliminary stages.[52]

Commercial Interests and National Objectives

Historically, commercial priorities have always been the main driving force behind technological development. The most recent digital revolution currently underway is also driven by economic and commercial forces. For example, the AI industry is pushing its products into broad public use while deep concerns over their accuracy, safety, and fairness remain unresolved. Markets impose inadequate costs on—and often reward—those entities that introduce vulnerable products or services into the digital ecosystem. Too many vendors ignore best practices for secure development, ship products with insecure default configurations or known vulnerabilities, and integrate third-party software of unvetted or unknown provenances. The commercial sector is rushing to embrace emerging technologies, and nations are increasingly accelerating the integration and weaponization of AI. Leading developers of AI in the private sector continue to see themselves as having an obligation to make these technologies globally accessible to the public.[53] Continued advancements in technology can create better outcomes for the environment, social institutions, and the economy but only if they are viewed as beneficial. For instance, the Covid-19 vaccine was an innovation that was embraced by some people, while others refused to receive it and viewed it a negative innovation.[54]

AI Development and Deployment

Ambitious corporations in advanced economies, driven by profit and greed are commercializing, developing, and deploying AI on a large scale. Competitive pressures continue to push them to accelerate their investments in AI capabilities at the expense of safety and security. The distribution and production of robots for a wide range of uses, such as autonomous weapon systems, pizza delivery drones, driverless delivery trucks, sex robots, recreation pets, cleaning robots, security applications, competitive racing photography, FR software, and surveillance technology are available for anyone who wants to purchase them.[55] As impressive as these technologies are, today LLMs still produce responses that are subject to bias, and not correct.[56] As these models become more capable, nations will seek to harness them for economic, military, and national security advantage. Governments will also be challenged as to how these models should be regulated and how to prevent their use for nefarious purposes.

The current mindset for industries is to leverage commercial AI to improve business practices and save money. Companies use robotic process automation and AI-enabled analysis for labor cost savings and to speed up administrative actions to inform decision-making processes. Advances in AI and other emerging technologies promise to have a tremendous impact on the economy.[57]

Impact on the Workforce

There has been a considerable rise in the utilization of robots in factories for handling some of the tasks that were previously handled by human workers. AI and automation are changing the nature of work. While AI can boost productivity, if managed poorly, it can also displace an entire industry and widen the socioeconomic gap. AI technologies can potentially disrupt labor markets as humans are augmented or replaced by automated systems.

Employment sectors like sales and marketing, coding, software development, banking, and law have already been impacted by AI technology. Waiters, shelf-stackers, cashiers, and bar staff are facing a high risk of automation. Jobs that are repetitive and lower-skill tasks in the service and manufacturing sectors face a higher risk of automation. In 2022, the retail and e-commerce sector underwent a notable shift toward automation in response to labor shortage and consumer demand.[58] The general assumption that certain jobs would be risk-free from automation no longer holds true; unfortunately, millions of low-income workers are at the greatest risk. Professionals in trucking, manufacturing, energy production, and eventually those with college educations and advanced degrees will be affected as well. A troubling notion for advanced economies is the possible erosion of the middle class in the near future, considering the current rapid acceleration in deployment of AI tools into society without proper control.[59]

A Rush to Replace People

The Media Industry

The rise of AI and the decline of traditional TV and print media has led to many strikes and job losses in the media industry, resulting in major changes in the news and entertainment industry. Hollywood's SAG-AFTRA union strike that took place for months in 2023 paused many television shows; nonetheless, it resulted in more favorable contract provisions related to AI. There are also some efforts by media outlets to adapt and incorporate AI, such as the Associated Press partnering with OpenAI to share news content and technology. The media industry on the whole is facing a period of uncertainty.[60]

AI Interns

A tech marketing company hired AI interns for basic necessary tasks. More industries are beginning to use AI tools like ChatGPT and AI image generators like Dall E 2 instead of hiring humans.[61] The interns are digital software models with self-created images and have named themselves. The company justified their decision based on the need for efficiency, referring to the fact that AI can produce the same level quality work that an inexperienced employee can produce; while acknowledging that the work is not always accurate, the chatbot can perform the same tasks quickly and for free.[62]

AI News

Both Google and Microsoft are looking to replace journalists with AI-generated news. In some countries AI news reporting is currently underway. Numerous news producers have lost their jobs due to replacement efforts being pushed by tech companies as cost-saving efforts. AI is being used for story curation as well as selecting headlines and pictures for news coverage.[63] RadioGPT was the first radio platform. Launched in 2023, using AI, the content is aimed to protect radio shows and keep listeners intrigued as if a human disc jockey were creating the show. RadioGPT created blogs, social media posts, scripts, and short-form videos. Questions were raised about potentially replacing disc jockeys with AI, and listeners losing the "human" feel.[64] While AI might be valuable for research and productivity, it cannot replace human creativity and emotions. Creativity, surprise, and humor remain distinct human characteristics. In 2023, a media outlet in the Middle East introduced an Arabic-speaking AI female as the presenter in a news broadcast. It is inevitable that there will be more AI news reporters in the future.[65]

Robots in Warehouses

A warehouse, in 2022, assigned three specially trained robots to select customers' items and place them into the correct bag for shipping. The robot was able to recognize items apart from each other. It is just a matter of time before robots take over millions of warehouse jobs in the coming years.[66]

As more companies look to utilize autonomous workers and AI, there will be a need to find a collaborative approach to include the current human employees with robot workers in order to prevent human resentment of AI in the workforce. Many employees are worried, resentful, and scared of the technology and fear they will look bad by comparison, or worse, resulting in the loss of their jobs.[67]

Intellectual Property (IP)

Advanced economies in industrialized nations around the world devote tremendous resources, time, money, and energy toward research and product development. The research and development of proprietary economic information forms the core of a nation's economic and national security infrastructure. Misappropriation of proprietary information has a devastating impact on the well-being of any economy that relies heavily on innovations for their economic sustainability.[68] Oftentimes the existing laws and legislation lag behind the speed with which the technological changes are taking place. The lack of an appropriate and effective legal framework further complicates matters for the legislative bodies and law enforcement agencies around the world. With the technological advances of the past several decades, protection of IP has become a challenging task for all law enforcement agencies worldwide. In recent decades there has been a change in the nature of crime and an increase in the use of technology and cyberspace for the theft of IP. Again, the task of investigation and prosecution of those who commit these crimes has become a major challenge for law enforcement agencies. At times it is impossible to be able to identify the responsible parties for the trade secret theft and misappropriation of proprietary information.

While protection of all types of IP is important, the protection of trade secrets, which form the core of a nation's economic security,[69] is the most complicated and challenging task for businesses, governments, and law enforcement agencies.[70] A new layer of risk for IP involves the potential sharing of confidential information and trade secrets through generative AI, as well as regulatory scrutiny. Other risks related to reputation, operations, and legality, such as privacy, IP, cybersecurity, and contractual concerns, are all present when dealing with sensitive data.[71]

AI

An important question that legislative bodies in advanced nations must consider is how to protect IP, innovators, content creators, musicians, writers, and artists. IP protection is critical as it relates to AI development and commercialization.[72] A strong framework of IP protection incentivizes investment in AI research and promotes innovation by safeguarding the rights of innovators and creators. As AI technologies become more complex and capable, protecting IP rights is vital for maintaining the competitive advantage of businesses in the global market. Given the global nature of AI development and deployment, it is necessary to have international cooperation on IP protection and enforcement.[73]

Algorithms

Algorithms represent the highest-level of risk to IP. Forcing companies to reveal their IP would only result in harming them and empowering adversaries to use intellectual property for ill intentions.[74] IP rights are the cornerstone of the innovation economy. Emerging technologies produce new forms of value, and advanced nations have to update their IP regime and adapt their laws accordingly. Fostering innovation empowers individual freedom and serves as a pillar of strength for fostering a democratic society.

Espionage Tactics

Malicious cyber activity has evolved from inconvenience to espionage and IP theft.[75] Adversaries continue to use cyber and physical espionage tactics to access and steal proprietary information.[76] Adversaries are primarily after two things: access and data. Stealing sensitive information from critical infrastructure networks is a top national security concern for the US and other advanced economies. Such information enables pre-positioning for future attacks, gaining insight into response capabilities, exfiltrating sensitive data for criminal profit or a follow-on intelligence activity.[77] Techniques include the use of AI-generative software programs to enhance social-engineering tactics, which trick targeted individuals into disclosing sensitive information or clicking on malicious web links to enable intelligence collection.[78]

Foreign adversaries will continue their efforts to target and steal sensitive information, research, and technology. These adversaries use students, researchers, and commercial entities as cover for their efforts to gain access to valuable information that can damage the competitiveness of an advanced nation resulting in significant financial loss and profits. IP theft and forced technology transfer continue to threaten global innovation and to disadvantage businesses in advanced economies. Similarly, economic espionage, largely through cyber intrusions that target confidential proprietary information, results in significant financial loss annually.[79]

Modern business models that thrive on personal data have prompted an intense concern about how the collected data will be controlled and traded. A typical case of concern is the data collected by electric cars. The car makers claim that the collected data are used for policy planning, even though there are obvious privacy implications. Auto makers worry that the data could be used for industrial espionage, yet they comply with the laws so they can sell their cars.[80]

IP Laws

The US has not modernized its IP laws and policies to keep up with the pace of rapid development of emerging technologies such as AI. The IP law needs to determine if AI generates inventions and whether these inventions will be protected by the IP laws, thus creating global disincentives for IP theft. A federal court in Washington, DC, ruled in 2023 that an inventor must be a "natural person" and not an AI system. Furthermore, it was stated that copyright law only extends to humans, meaning that any work of art created with AI and without human input cannot be copyrighted. An important question that needs consideration is who will be the inventor when AI tools are used to write computer codes or to identify and design new drugs and materials.[81]

A Critical Period of Change

The changing role of information has allowed state and non-state actors to conduct covert influence operations to rapidly gain momentum, and advance their objectives by deceptive uses of AI. For example, adversaries have used fake content to flood and overwhelm fact-checkers in newsrooms. AI chatbots have been infected by bad actors to create certain narratives.

Powerful actors dissatisfied with the status quo will capitalize on changes in communication and changes in sociocultural context to oppose normal international behavior. Information technology has significantly changed the reception of and reaction to information. There are emerging challenges, as competitors and adversaries will combine new communication strategies and technologies to support their efforts to cause disruptions to command and control systems. For example, people for the most part are unaware of how much their day-to-day social media content is actually made up of foreign intelligence campaigns. Understanding how competitors and adversaries shape the environment through propaganda, disinformation, or active measures will be crucial in maintaining peace and security.[82]

AI and Bad Actors

There is a wide variety of ethical and social risk concerns including the misuse of LLMs by bad actors. The capabilities of AI systems have increased significantly from 2022 to the present time. There is often a gap between articulating high-level goals around responsible AI and operationalizing them. Responsible AI can only be accomplished when AI systems and their use are aligned with democratic values and the rule of law. As discussed in previous chapters, issues of privacy, fairness, inclusion, and human rights have to be addressed by those who design the systems, in the developmental stages and prior to deployment. This can only be achieved if an accountability process is put in place, as lack of transparency and accountability will erode public trust.

International Peace, Security, and Cooperation

In a fractured world, it is necessary to identify areas of cooperation in order to craft a legal framework that addresses AI design, development, deployment, and usage. A global effort by all stakeholders, such as governments and the private sector, is necessary in order to translate high-level concepts into concrete actions. For example, law enforcement agencies and criminal justice institutions globally are grappling with the challenging issues of inclusiveness and fairness when it comes to several methods and models used in ML that are associated with weaknesses that makes the systems brittle, exploitable, and vulnerable to failure. These problems have not been encountered in traditional software systems.[83]

AI development and governance is complicated and dynamic at the same time. The key unsolved questions involve engineering, policy, and research. Legislative efforts for emerging technologies like AI must adhere to principles like due process, inclusion, fairness, and non-discrimination. The demand and the development of emerging technologies must respect these fundamental values.

Notes

1 The White House. (2023, May 20). *G7 leaders' statement on economic resilience and economic security.* www.whitehouse.gov/briefing-room/statements-releases/2023/05/20/g7-leaders-statement-on-economic-resilience-and-econo mic-security/

2 The American Academy of Diplomacy. (2022, February). *Bringing America's multilateral diplomacy into the 21st century.* www.academyofdiplomacy.org/wp-content/uploads/2022/03/Bringing-Americas-Multilateral-Diplomacy-into-the-21st-Century-FINAL.pdf

3 Graham, E. (2023). *House Dem sounds alarm about AI in political messaging.* Nextgov/FCW. www.nextgov.com/artificial-intelligence/2023/07/house-dem-sounds-alarm-about-ai-political-messaging/388599/

4 New Hampshire Department of Justice. (2024, February 6). *Voter suppression AI Robocall Investigation Update.* www.doj.nh.gov/news/2024/20240122-voter-robocall.html

5 Matyszczyk, C. (2021, January 29). *I've just seen the future of technology and you may not like it.* ZDNet. www.zdnet.com/article/ive-just-seen-the-future-of-technology-and-you-may-not-love-i

6 Fung, A., & Lessig, L. (2023). *How AI could take over elections—And undermine democracy.* Route Fifty. www.route-fifty.com/tech-data/2023/06/how-ai-could-take-over-elections-and-undermine-democracy/387059/

7 Douglas, A., Draper, D., Farshchi, J., Lord, B., Neschke, S., & Romanoff, T. (2023, February 12). *Top risks in cybersecurity 2023.* Bipartisan Policy Center. https://bipartisanpolicy.org/report/top-risks-cybersecurity-2023/

8 Graham, E. (2022). *Social media's national security implications draw lawmaker scrutiny.* Nextgov/FCW. www.nextgov.com/cybersecurity/2022/09/soc ial-medias-national-security-implications-draw-lawmaker-scrutiny/377205/

9 Chatterjee, M. (2022). *Shadowboxing and geopolitics on the dark web.* POLITICO. www.politico.com/news/2022/12/11/russia-politics-cybercrime-darknet-00073400

10 Fried, I. (2023). *How AI will turbocharge misinformation—And what we can do about it.* Axios. www.axios.com/2023/07/10/ai-misinformation-response-measures

11 Fitzgerald, M. (2023). *What is artificial intelligence? Legislators are still looking for a definition.* Route Fifty. www.route-fifty.com/emerging-tech/2023/10/what-artificial-intelligence-legislators-are-still-looking-definition/391017/

12 Riotta, C. (2023). *Nation-state actors are exploiting AI for discord and attacks, DHS warns.* Nextgov/FCW. www.nextgov.com/cybersecurity/2023/09/nation-state-actors-are-exploiting-ai-discord-and-attacks-dhs-warns/390376/

13 Graham, E. (2023). *Digital authoritarianism poses "critical threat" to national security, Intel chief says.* Nextgov/FCW. www.nextgov.com/emerging-tech/2023/04/digital-authoritarianism-poses-critical-threat-national-security-intel-chief-says/385614/

14 Kelley, A. (2022). *Report: Emerging tech has become a tool for government censorship.* Nextgov/FCW. www.nextgov.com/emerging-tech/2022/01/report-emerging-tech-has-become-tool-government-censorship/361300/

15 Limbago, A. L. (n.d.). *Data sovereignty in a reglobalized world*. GRC Outlook. https://grcoutlook.com/data-sovereignty-in-a-reglobalized-world/

16 WPR Insights. (2022, June 27). *WPR insights: The promise and perils of Big Tech*. www.worldpoliticsreview.com/tech-ethics-artificial-intelligence-regulat ion-and-killer-drones/

17 Fitzgerald, M. (2023). *What is artificial intelligence? Legislators are still looking for a definition*. Route Fifty. www.route-fifty.com/emerging-tech/2023/ 10/what-artificial-intelligence-legislators-are-still-looking-definition/391017/

18 Special Competitive Studies Project. (2022, September). *Mid-decade challenges to national competitiveness*. www.scsp.ai/2022/09/special-competitive-studies-project-releases-first-report-sept-12-2022/

19 Office of the Director of National Intelligence. (2022, January 27). *Senior advisory group panel on commercially available information.*

20 The White House. (2023, March). *National cybersecurity strategy.*

21 Knutson, J. (2023). *Brokers selling military members' personal info*. Axios. www.axios.com/2023/11/06/military-data-sold-for-cents-cheap-privacy

22 The White House. (2023, March). *National cybersecurity strategy.*

23 Kirchgaessner, S. (2023). Experts warn of new spyware threat targeting journalists and political figures. *The Guardian*. www.theguardian.com/technology/2023/apr/ 11/canadian-security-experts-warn-over-spyware-threat-to-rival-pegasus-citizen-lab

24 Saric, I. (2023). *Biden moves to limit government use of commercial spyware*. Axios. www.axios.com/2023/03/27/biden-commercial-spyware-executive-order

25 The White House. (2023, March). *National cybersecurity strategy.*

26 Office of the Director of National Intelligence. (2022, January 27). *Senior advisory group panel on commercially available information.*

27 Treisman, R. (2024, July 11). *Bread and bullets: Some Southern supermarkets now sell ammo out of vending machines*. NPR. www.npr.org/2024/07/11/nx-s1-5033748/ammunition-vending-machines-grocery-stores

28 Breeden II, J. (2023). *National intelligence office issues cyber warning for government and commercial satellites*. Nextgov/FCW. www.nextgov.com/cybers ecurity/2023/08/national-intelligence-office-issues-cyber-warning-government-and-commercial-satellites/389649/

29 Errick, K. (2022). *Challenges in the space domain are becoming "more technologically focused," experts say*. Nextgov/FCW. www.nextgov.com/ emerging-tech/2022/10/challenges-space-domain-are-becoming-more-technologically-focused-experts-say/378789/

30 Kramer, M. (2022). *Commercial satellites are the next front in space war*. Axios. www.axios.com/2022/11/01/starlink-ukraine-elon-musk-war-space

31 Graham, E. (2022). *DOD Announces new contract awards for its 'internet in space' effort*. Nextgov/FCW. www.nextgov.com/emerging-tech/2022/11/dod-announces-new-contract-awards-its-internet-space-effort/379240/

32 Bindu, R., Fang, R., Gupta, A., & Kang, D. (2024, April 17). *LLM agents can autonomously exploit one-day vulnerabilities*. arXiv. https://arxiv.org/html/ 2404.08144v2

33 Fitzgerald, M. (2023). *What is artificial intelligence? Legislators are still looking for a definition*. Route Fifty. www.route-fifty.com/emerging-tech/2023/ 10/what-artificial-intelligence-legislators-are-still-looking-definition/391017/

34 Centre for Data Ethics and Innovation. (2020, November). *Review into bias in algorithmic decision-making.* https://assets.publishing.service.gov.uk/media/60142096d3bf7f70ba377b20/Review_into_bias_in_algorithmic_decision-making.pdf
35 Nasheri, H. (2021, December 21). *The dumb and the dangerous road ahead.* United Nations Interregional Crime and Justice Research Institute.
36 Aspen Digital. (2023, January 9). *Envisioning cyber futures with AI. U.S. and global cybersecurity groups.* www.aspendigital.org/wp-content/uploads/2024/02/Aspen-Digital_Envisioning-Cyber-Futures-with-AI_January-2024.pdf
37 European Commission. (2019, April 8). *Ethics guidelines for trustworthy AI.* https://ec.europa.eu/futurium/en/ai-alliance-consultation.1.html
38 Schwartz, R., Down, L., Jonas, A., & Tabassi, E. (2021, June). A proposal for identifying and managing bias within artificial intelligence (Draft NIST Special Publication 1270). U.S. Department of Commerce. https://nvlpubs.nist.gov/nistpubs/SpecialPublications/NIST.SP.1270-draft.pdf
39 U.S. Department of Health and Human Services. (2021, September). *Trustworthy AI (TAI) playbook.*
40 National Security Commission on Artificial Intelligence. (2020, July). *Key considerations for responsible development & fielding of artificial intelligence.* www.nscai.gov/wp-content/uploads/2021/04/Key_Considerations_Extended_April_2021.pdf
41 Hao, K. (2021, January 8). Five ways to make AI a greater force for good in 2021. *MIT Technology Review.* www.technologyreview.com/2021/01/08/1015907/ai-force-for-good-in-2021/
42 Allen, G. (2022). *The European approach to regulating artificial intelligence with MEP Dragos Tudorache, Co-Rapporteur of the EU AI Act.* Center for Strategic & International Studies. www.csis.org/events/european-approach-regulating-artificial-intelligence-mep-dragos-tudorache-co-rapporteur-eu-ai
43 Jakubowska, E., Maryam, H., & Mahmoudi, M. (2024, April 14). *Euroviews. Retrospective facial recognition surveillance conceals human rights abuses in plain sight.* Euronews. www.euronews.com/2023/04/14/retrospective-facial-recognition-surveillance-conceals-human-rights-abuses-in-plain-sight
44 Wright, G. (2023). *Amazon to pay $25m over child privacy violations.* BBC. www.bbc.com/news/technology-65772154
45 National Security Commission on Artificial Intelligence. (2021, January). *Summary of the National Security Commission on Artificial Intelligences (NSCAI) second quarter recommendations.* www.nscai.gov/wp-content/uploads/2021/01/Summary-of-NSCAI-Q2-Recommendations.pdf
46 Macaulay, T. (2020, April 27). *UK spies must ramp up use of AI to fight new threats, says report.* The Next Web. https://thenextweb.com/neural/2020/04/27/uk-spies-must-ramp-up-use-of-ai-to-fight-new-threats-says-report/
47 Executive Office of the President. (2019). Maintaining American leadership in artificial intelligence. *Federal Register,* 84(31), 3967–3972. www.federalregister.gov/documents/2019/02/14/2019-02544/maintaining-american-leadership-in-artificial-intelligence

48 Wright, N. D. (Ed.). (2019). *Artificial intelligence, China, Russia, and the Global Order*. Maxwell Air Force Base, Alabama: Air University Press. www.airuni versity.af.edu/Portals/10/AUPress/Books/B_0161_WRIGHT_ARTIFICIAL_ INTELLIGENCE_CHINA_RUSSIA_AND_THE_GLOBAL_ORDER.PDF

49 The White House Office of Science and Technology Policy. (2020, February). *American artificial intelligence initiative: Year one annual report*. www.nitrd. gov/nitrdgroups/images/c/c1/American-AI-Initiative-One-Year-Annual-Rep ort.pdf

50 Wait, P. (2021). Economist calls for deeper examination of AI's risks. Nextgov/ FCW. www.nextgov.com/policy/2021/12/economist-calls-deeper-examination- ais-risks/359730/

51 Nasheri, H. (2021, December 21). *The dumb and the dangerous road ahead*. United Nations Interregional Crime and Justice Research Institute.

52 Leprince-Ringuet, D. (2021, January 29). *US, China or Europe? Here's who is really winning the global race for AI*. ZDNet. www.zdnet.com/article/us-china- or-europe-heres-who-is-really-winning-the-global-race-for-ai/

53 Department of the Air Force. (2019). *The United States Air Force artificial intelligence annex to the Department of Defense Artificial Intelligence Strategy*. www.af.mil/Portals/1/documents/5/USAF-AI-Annex-to-DoD-AI- Strategy.pdf

54 Walsh, B. (2021, December 22). *Balancing the benefits and risks of new technology*. Axios. www.axios.com/2021/12/22/technology-innovation-pandemic- progress

55 Nasheri, H. (2021, December 21). *The dumb and the dangerous road ahead*. United Nations Interregional Crime and Justice Research Institute.

56 Rosenberg, S. (2023, January 24). *What ChatGPT can't do*. Axios. www.axios. com/2023/01/24/chatgpt-errors-ai-limitations

57 Samuels, M. (2021, December 9). *Robotic process automation: This is how to stop your workers from resenting the bots*. ZDNet. www.zdnet.com/arti cle/robotic-process-automation-this-is-how-to-stop-your-workers-from-resent ing-the-bots/

58 Nichols, G. (2022). *Robots have rushed in to fill jobs people don't want. What happens if recession hits?* ZDNet. www.zdnet.com/article/robots-have-rushed- in-to-fill-jobs-people-dont-want-what-happens-if-recession-hits/

59 Centre for the New Economy and Society. (2018). *The future of jobs report*. http://www3.weforum.org/docs/WEF_Future_of_Jobs_2018.pdf

60 Fischer, S., & Baysinger, T. (2023). *Media summer apocalypse*. Axios. www. axios.com/2023/07/14/media-summer-apocalypse-hollywood-strikes

61 Rosenberg, S. (2022). *AI-generated images open multiple cans of worms*. Axios. www.axios.com/2022/09/12/ai-images-ethics-dall-e-2-stable-diffusion

62 Hawkins, E. (2023, January 11). *Codeword marketing agency hires AI "interns."* Axios. www.axios.com/2023/01/11/marketing-ai-interns

63 BBC. (2020, May 30). *Microsoft "to replace journalists with robots."* www. bbc.com/news/world-us-canada-52860247

64 Smith, T. (2023). *RadioGPT brings AI to the airwaves*. Axios. www.axios.com/ local/cleveland/2023/03/07/ai-radio

65 Radford, A. (2023). *Kuwait news outlet unveils AI-generated presenter Fedha.* BBC. www.bbc.com/news/world-middle-east-65238950

66 Nichols, G. (2022, June 24). *No really, robots are about to take A LOT of jobs.* ZDNet. www.zdnet.com/article/no-really-robots-are-about-to-take-a-lot-of-jobs/

67 Samuels, M. (2021, December 9). *Robotic process automation: This is how to stop your workers from resenting the Bots.* ZDNet. www.zdnet.com/arti cle/robotic-process-automation-this-is-how-to-stop-your-workers-from-resent ing-the-bots/

68 Nasheri, H. (2005). *Economic espionage and industrial spying.* Cambridge University Press.

69 PWC. *Economic impact* [online]. Available from: www.pwc.com/us/en/foren sic-services/publications/assets/economic-impact.pdf

70 Nasheri, H. (2005). *Economic espionage and industrial spying.* Cambridge University Press.

71 Gesser, A. (2023). *Balancing AI benefits and risks and whether boards need AI experts—Interview of Avi Gesser by FT's agenda.* Debevoise Data Blog. www. debevoisedatablog.com/2023/04/17/balancing-ai-benefits-and-risks-and-whet her-boards-need-ai-experts-interview-of-avi-gesser-by-fts-agenda/

72 Medeiros, M. (2017, March 7). *Intellectual property strategy for artificial intel- ligence.* IP Osgoode. www.iposgoode.ca/2017/03/intellectual-property-strat egy-for-artificial-intelligence/

73 U.S. Chamber of Commerce. (2022). *Chamber comments on artificial intel- ligence export competitiveness.* www.uschamber.com/international/chamber- comments-on-artificial-intelligence-export-competitiveness

74 Center For Strategic and International Studies. (2023, June 21). *Senator Chuck Schumer launches SAFE Innovation in the AI age at CSIS* (Transcript, Online Event). https://csis-website-prod.s3.amazonaws.com/s3fs-public/2023-06/230 621_Schumer_SAFE_Innovation.pdf?VersionId=jApHm2QrP7nAZvl_B4GJ6 s_YjSrfyYBK

75 The White House. (2023, March). *National cybersecurity strategy.*

76 Nasheri, H. (2018). The impact of intellectual property theft on national and global security. In: Reichel, P., & Randa, R. (eds.) *Transnational crime and global security* (Vol. 1). Praeger.

77 Kelley, A. (2023). Securing U.S. intellectual property "top priority" for fed- eral law enforcement. Nextgov/FCW. www.nextgov.com/cybersecurity/2023/ 05/securing-us-intellectual-property-top-priority-federal-law-enforcement/ 386777/

78 Gatlan, S. (2023). *CISA now warns critical infrastructure of ransomware- vulnerable devices.* BleepingComputer. www.bleepingcomputer.com/news/secur ity/cisa-now-warns-critical-infrastructure-of-ransomware-vulnerable-devices/ Also see, United States Government Accountability Office. (2022, October). *Critical infrastructure protection: Additional federal coordination is needed to enhance K-12 cybersecurity.*

79 Nasheri, H. (2005). *Economic espionage and industrial spying.* Cambridge University Press.

80 Nasheri, H. (2021, December 21). *The dumb and the dangerous road ahead.* United Nations Interregional Crime and Justice Research Institute.
81 Kelley, A. (2023). *Securing U.S. Intellectual property "top priority" for federal law enforcement.* Nextgov/FCW. www.nextgov.com/cybersecurity/2023/05/securing-us-intellectual-property-top-priority-federal-law-enforcement/386777/
82 Joint Chiefs of Staff. (2018, July). *Joint Concept for Operating in the Information Environment (JCOIE).* www.jcs.mil/Portals/36/Documents/Doctrine/concepts/joint_concepts_jcoie.pdf
83 National Security Commission on Artificial Intelligence. (2020, July). *Key considerations for responsible development & fielding of artificial intelligence.* www.nscai.gov/wp-content/uploads/2021/04/Key_Considerations_Extended_April_2021.pdf

5 The Technological Frontier

The exponential transformation of all facets of human life and experience is taking place, from how personal affairs are conducted to how industries process their daily business operations. Tasks that once seemed uniquely suited to human abilities, like driving a car or diagnosing a disease, are now often automated and will likely be fully automated in the near future. Automated systems, as mentioned in earlier chapters, have brought extraordinary benefits—from technology that helps farmers grow food more efficiently to computer weather models predicting storm paths to algorithms that can identify diseases in patients. The AI revolution has already taken off, regardless of societal likes or dislikes or public opinion. Some people are concerned about job displacement, privacy infringement, surpassing human capabilities, and a loss of human connection, while others anticipate societal advancements, time-saving benefits, and improved efficiency.[1]

It is likely that the growth of these technologies will produce a new world.[2] Unlike previous technological advances, AI cannot be controlled or contained by government.[3] How should society prepare citizens for an AI future? At present, the development of emerging technologies like AI tools and services is largely being driven by a few influential stakeholders with enormous power in shaping the digital ecosystems worldwide.

Travel to Mars

NASA, relying on new software, anticipates astronauts traveling to Mars in the very near future. The agency will use lunar missions to prepare for further exploration of Mars. The trip to Mars will be very different than the trip to the moon in 1969 with Neil Armstrong and Buzz Aldrin. AI will be used to predict weather conditions in space and on Mars. Given the turbulent nature of the weather on Mars, AI will help in keeping humans safe on that planet by predicting the weather changes. AI will predict the appropriate window to launch weeks in advance of the actual launch.[4]

DOI: 10.4324/9781003368304-6

Human Genome

Scientists and engineers are currently approaching DNA as a code to be digitized and manipulated. The first draft of a human genome was published in 2011. They have reprogramed plants, microorganisms, and fungi to produce drugs. Gene editing experimentation has been a subject of intense debate in ethical and philosophical circles. Scientists are working on potentially preventing bad gene mutations.[5]

Disruption

Modern capitalist economies are experiencing a period of rapid technological progress. The development of new emerging technologies like AI is giving rise to significant disruption, including within the labor market. There is no guarantee that emerging technologies will destroy jobs, nor any certainty that these technologies will lead to more and better jobs.[6] The rapid progress of emerging technologies continues to disrupt traditional business and society with both positive and negative outcomes. Shared global challenges such as climate change, health security, as well as the economic impact of the Covid-19 pandemic are converging and creating unparalleled vulnerabilities and risks. New threats and attacks will trigger political instability and make it increasingly challenging to predict the impact of such threats globally. Given this level of uncertainty and high stakes, there is an urgency to move toward technological solutions, and therefore, there will be unpredictable challenges to overcome.[7]

Fragmentation and Polarization

The internet and emerging technologies are key enablers for societies and economic progress. This technology generates new ways of empowering individuals and communities by providing access to an unprecedented body of information and knowledge. Nonetheless, there are negative effects that threaten social cohesion and democratic values,[8] like the facilitation of domestic political polarization. The increased use of disinformation campaigns in the era of social media is making it difficult to distinguish fact from fiction. Extremists and adversaries aim to weaponize media in an attempt to moderate online content. Fighting disinformation and invasion of privacy while attempting to maximize the potential benefits of technological tools for citizens is a monumental task. Production and detection of misleading information, election meddling, and an epidemic of computer viruses only scratch the surface of the existing threats to economic stability and security.

Develop First and Ask Questions Later

Nations face vital choices over what technology they develop and how those technologies are used. Ultimately, the aim for a digital future comes down to enabling people to thrive with work and other facets of their lives. At the present time, the rapid deployment of these emerging tools has created a juggling act for policymakers, legislative bodies, law enforcement organizations, and governments. The corporate sector is deploying AI tools at a rapid pace without any established guidance or rules that would enhance overall security and is basically ignoring the evidence of real harm that these tools can potentially cause. For instance, AI systems used in criminal justice are wrongly imprisoning people; in the health context, they are denying patients of vital organs for transplants. These are existential decisions with serious consequences at the receiving end.

Big Tech

The public has been inundated for the past few years by sensational headlines and corporate marketing campaigns on promises of emerging technologies. Debates and discussions ranging from topics of potential benefits, like helping climate disaster, to the destruction of humanity as an existential risk have consumed people globally.[9]

The internet's original vision of openness and limited regulation was overshadowed by powerful corporate forces driven by a commercial profitable agenda. In 2022, the Council of Foreign Relations warned that the global, open, secure, and interoperable internet was fragmented, less free, and more dangerous due to the increase of "Big Tech" companies having full control of online experiences.[10] Commercial priorities have been the driving force behind the tech agenda. The role of Big Tech in the daily lives of people is an illustration of an unprecedented degree of power and influence in the hands of private companies such as Google, Apple, Meta, X, and TikTok. This has led to a growing call in the US for government oversight and regulation. Big Tech firms and governments in advanced economies are seeking to gain geopolitical advantage and social control through emerging technologies like AI.

Disclosure and Transparency

Transparency and disclosure can build up public trust and confidence. AI leaders at Big Tech companies like Google, Microsoft, OpenAI, and others should be required to share details of their most advanced systems and make them available to outside auditing. Without having an audit system in place, companies are left to their own devices, just as social media companies have built their technology platforms without ethical considerations. Historically, social media platforms have monetized user data through behavioral advertising by hooking users, and a lack of transparency in granting users the option to deny tracking and profiling has raised significant concerns.

The tech industry has failed to include diverse perspectives as it builds products for global use. OpenAI was founded as a non-profit to pursue a responsible vision of advanced AI. Now, as a company, it leads an industry-wide charge to distribute AI worldwide, even though the technology hallucinates, makes errors, and is unpredictable.[11] The dangers posed by emerging technologies are growing, not shrinking. Those who fear AI's immense power may not have a strong voice in contrast to those[12] who favor acceleration and point to AI's benefits. The need for the tech industry to act in a responsible manner regarding users' data is another area of serious concern.

The Truth of the Matter

As previously discussed, while automation is improving efficiency in a wide range of sectors, algorithms are appearing to reinforce human decision-making biases in a vast range of industries. Countless reports showcase so-called hallucinations or inaccurate answers that are being generated by AI software. For example, algorithmic discrimination occurs when automated systems contribute to unjustified different treatment or impact disfavoring people based on their race, color, ethnicity, gender, disability, or national origin. In national security settings, AI hallucinations could have catastrophic consequences.

Global crises increased digital demand, in particular during the Covid-19 pandemic, changing how people worked and how they purchased groceries.[13] Data have revolutionized global industries; nevertheless, the benefits come at the price of civil liberties and democratic values. The rush to development and deployment of emerging technologies and automated systems did not originate with consulting diverse communities, or stipulating risks to privacy. The discussions with respect to risks that are currently taking place were not initially considered by the developers as part of the pre-deployment process. It is only at the pre-deployment stage that safe and effective tools can be developed, not in the post deployment phase.

Criminal Justice

Technological tools are now driving important decision-making in many settings. The IoT can be used to collect data from connected devices—like sensors and cameras that are used for improving public safety and providing situational awareness.[14] Algorithms have been used for crime detection, categorization of prisoners, and border entry clearance. Nonetheless, the technology used in the justice system has been characterized as the "Wild Wild West," a setback due to the misuse of AI and in particular FR by police forces.[15]

Autopilot Vehicular Manslaughter

When cars become fully automated in the future, questions of liability from a legal perspective will arise. It will come down to who will be responsible under the law when a car kills an individual.[16]

Hiring and Lending

Another example mentioned previously related to hiring and financial lending practices for applicants. Use of algorithms in hiring and credit decisions by financial institutions can result in reproducing the unfortunate inequalities in existing loan processing systems.

Warning Systems

Humanitarian aid is allocated and dependent on correct warning systems and logistical predictions. For instance, food security, which is a major issue worldwide, can be predicted by technological tools in critical locations. While DL machine-learning technology is able to scan and extract information, nonetheless, other factors like climate change and gaps in data collection can influence the accuracy of the warning dates.[17]

Operating in Times of Uncertainty

The convergence of capabilities in high-performance computing, big data, and ML, each a critical enabler across multiple domains, can have vast yet unidentified consequences for economic security and political stability. Key questions ask what political, economic, and social transformations these technologies will bring.

Emerging technologies, particularly the advent of the 5G telecom infrastructure, have also become a central feature of the strategic rivalry between global superpowers. With trust eroding and the digital divide getting wider, what is needed are stronger partnerships and dialogues and the establishment of frameworks that can contribute to effective development and deployment of technologies. Policymakers and international leaders must address how policies and systems that mitigate negative consequences can be designed.

Technology is Ahead of Culture

There are a myriad of challenges and a sense of disorientation about where the world is heading. The fundamental principles of liberal democracies—like rights to privacy, free speech, and equal protection— are being jeopardized and challenged.[18] World leaders such as President Emmanuel Macron of France are voicing concerns regarding the use of AI. They want algorithms to be transparent to the people who are affected by them. AI can be more harmful in Western democracies, because the technology is less compatible with Western mores and ideology.[19]

Weaponization

The potential for AI-induced chaos is real. A civilian AI system could accidentally do something disastrous like shut down electrical grids or change satellite orbits in such a way that it creates a collision or interrupts critical services. Emerging technologies in the wrong hands can be used as weapons with far-reaching capacity to cause destruction. Weaponization is the intentional use of AI to cause harm. The careless weaponization of AI can contribute to deliberate misuse of AI, causing the greatest harm—a code red for humanity. The nature of AI technologies makes the protection of these technologies from a national security standpoint very challenging, and the net impact on society remains unclear.

For instance, Macron is opposed to the use of autonomous weapons that can kill without human oversight.[20] Major categories of weaponization risk include cyber, AI-augmented disinformation, robotic control, psychological manipulation, and weaponized biological or material sciences. As AI systems become increasingly capable, they create new risks to national security that need to be monitored. These include accident risks as well as risks of new malicious applications that were previously impossible. The security issue that deserves utmost attention is how governments will position themselves for the risks ahead.

Mixing Reality and Fiction

The boundaries between reality and fiction in the digital world are fading rapidly. More AI-generated content is appearing on the internet, creating new problems for both society and AI programs. Programs like ChatGPT and Dall E 2 produce a lot of text and images online. Soon it might not be possible to distinguish between AI-generated content and human-made content. Society is confronting too much information and lower-quality information. While AI is capable of creating much content, it will be difficult to check how reliable the information is, and it can repeat mistakes from the data that it was trained on. It will be challenging to keep AI data clean from AI-made content. It is hard to predict how the AI-generated content will impact the world.[21]

Disregard for Truth

AI is being used to obscure truth, rather than reveal it. A growing phenomenon, AI has the capability of creating persuasive lies at a scale that humanity has never seen. In earlier chapters, the threat to democracy was discussed, with reference to chatbots shaping people's opinions and potentially exceeding social media's capacity in this area. Market manipulation is another major concern that was discussed. Ultimately, those who choose what data sets to use for training AI models have the most influence in shaping society.

Meta and other social media platforms have transformed from being outlets for human connection to financial marketplaces for digital advertising. Congressional testimony by a former Facebook employee illustrated that the Facebook algorithm system's discovery engine resulted in misinformation and harassment.[22]

Metaverse

The metaverse, a term coined by Neal Stephenson, is an immersive platform that combines VR and AR. It connects virtual worlds within the expanding decentralized internet as Web 3.0. The metaverse, a network of 3D virtual worlds accessible through VR or AR, aims to enhance digital world interactions. Facebook, now known as Meta, heavily promotes the concept of the metaverse being the future of internet use. The metaverse is often discussed as the potential next stage in the development of the internet. According to the Gartner technology research firm, by 2026, one in every four people will spend at least an hour a day in the metaverse to work, study, shop, and socialize.[23]

The metaverse has the potential to transform every aspect of people's daily lives with enormous implications for law enforcement. The metaverse is the next 3D web that shares many similarities with Web 3.0. Important questions to contemplate are: What happens when the metaverse is up and running? And will humans exhibit human traits in a computer-generated environment? It is possible that unforeseen changes may emerge the same way social media has reshaped the global political environment. The metaverse represents a new future of social media.[24]

Forensic Investigations

The metaverse can be used as an immersive training tool for forensic investigations, as Interpol's metaverse already allows, but also for crisis management through simulated situations.[25] For law enforcement, the potential threats will likely present significant challenges, because not all acts that are criminalized in the physical world are considered crimes when committed in the virtual world.

Distinguishing Humans from AI

As leisure and productivity increasingly revolve around computer interactions, the distinction between humans and machines becomes blurred. Despite being limited to images and text, social media interactions hold significant meaning for individuals, creating an illusion that online existence is genuine.

Regulation

There are many possibilities for bad actors to cause harm in the metaverse. Some examples include cybercrime, trafficking, and IP violations. The platform's capability to collect personal data is considerable, in particular the collection of facial expressions and emotional reactions. Some have argued that regulations and restrictions should be imposed at early stages of its creation, and others question which countries' laws should apply to the metaverse.[26]

Risks

Criminals are already starting to exploit the metaverse. The World Economic Forum, which has partnered with Interpol, Meta, Microsoft, and others in an initiative to define and govern the metaverse, has warned that social-engineering scams, violent extremism, and misinformation could be particular challenges. As the number of metaverse users grows and the technology further develops, the list of possible crimes will only expand to potentially include crimes against children, data theft, money laundering, financial fraud, counterfeiting, ransomware, phishing, and sexual assault and harassment.[27]

The metaverse poses cybersecurity and privacy risks. Customized avatars represent users, which makes it difficult to identify and distinguish between humans and AI. Scammers can deceive people by impersonation, leading to exploitation. People will not realize if they are interacting with bots or AI. Malicious software can enable cyberattacks, and it can be downloaded from third-party stores. Unauthorized access through VR headsets could access sensitive information and invade privacy. Attacks can also extend beyond the metaverse and cause physical harm. Legal frameworks will struggle to keep up with metaverse advancements, as has been the case with the IoT field.[28]

Virtual Land

Over recent years, billions of dollars have been spent on virtual land as individuals and companies race to establish themselves in the metaverse. Already, there are mass marketing plans in the works to attract the younger generation. The emergence of a fully immersive online metaverse, in which people can live, work, and play, is years away. Big brands such as Gucci, Nike, and Adidas, to name a few, have established their presence in the metaverse.[29] Banks have joined the VR. They have created their own virtual space and are even recreating their bank location buildings in the metaverse, even though the banks are not able to lend money as of yet. Nevertheless, they want to be part of this parallel universe.[30]

Hazardous Situations

If users are not completely aware of their real-word surroundings when navigating the metaverse, they might find themselves in hazardous situations. How will the physical security of the metaverse be addressed?

Cyber Murder

There are concerns about "cyber murder," which refers to acts of violence against avatars that can traumatize users. There are discussions about the need for UN regulation as a result of safety concerns. The metaverse adds yet another layer of privacy and security concerns for policymakers as well as concerns over issues related to IP and content moderation that would also have to be resolved.[31] A framework to guide decision-making and risk management in the metaverse ecosystem will be necessary.

Sextual Assault

The avatar of a 21-year-old researcher was "sextually" assaulted in Meta's VR group. Personal boundaries that prevent avatars from coming within a certain distance of each other have to be addressed.[32]

Privacy Concerns

While some organizations see the metaverse as a way of improving sales and productivity, others such as Meta are more interested in the private information the metaverse users will be willingly providing. The massive amount of metadata that comes to play—things like your information, preferences, interests, and physiological and biometric data—are transmitted in real time across the globe and between different services and applications. This will have significant impacts on privacy and consequently on cybersecurity. The collection of sensitive data will explode in these virtual worlds. This will raise many questions about the confidentiality and protection of each person from hackers. Of course, serious legal questions will come to light. Can AI commit crime? For instance, at the present time, robots are not capable of committing crimes on their own. Legislation for criminal activity now relates to human acts; therefore, a robot cannot be a criminal. Again, the issue of awareness is crucial, in particular users' awareness.[33]

Sharjahverse

Sharjah is the third-largest emirate in the United Arab Emirates (UAE), and now has its own metaverse city called Sharjahverse. The goal is to boost tourism in which tourists can explore realistic landmarks, engage in trade and innovation, and enjoy personalized entertainment. The multiverse platform is used for simulations, services, and AI optimization. As these cities are created around the world, it challenges people's conventional interactions with cities.[34]

Virtual (VR), Augmented (AR), and Mixed Reality (MR)

The Covid-19 pandemic accelerated the adoption of metaverse technologies, enabling remote work and virtual meetings. Federal, state, and local government agencies recognize the benefits of incorporating the metaverse into their operations. VR and AR are used for training public safety workers and simulation of crisis events. The Drug Enforcement Administration (DEA) and other federal agencies have been using AR to support ground-based enforcement. The Augmented Reality Mapping System (ARS) for enhancing situational awareness has also been used, by overlaying street names, addresses, parcel data, business names, and landmarks directly on live video. The system has been used to monitor the US–Mexico border.[35]

Military Training

Militaries have been using virtual training with real-world conditions. They are training for much more complex scenarios, in which AI would be tasked with analyzing a chaotic battlefield situation. The simulation allows for refining drone and anti-drone tactics without real combat experience. The goal of these exercises is to provide believable AI that can replace human role-players in training scenarios.[36] For example, AI has already been used in warfare, from helping Israel target suspected Hamas fighters, to identifying when Ukrainian artillery units will need to be resupplied. However, it also might not recognize if fighters are attempting to surrender. There is also the possibility that the training data were poisoned by adversaries prior to the operation taking place.

AR Lenses

AR lenses correct vision in the healthcare field but also display diverse information, like ski trail maps and running pace. The lenses hold great promise for disease monitoring, including the detection of biomarkers associated with conditions like diabetes, cancer, and glaucoma. They can also serve as drug delivery devices, providing more precise dosages and minimizing side effects. The possibilities for future lenses are extensive, with integration of sensors and cameras for diagnostics and in particular data collection within the eye.[37]

MR Goggles

Car designers routinely use VR to simulate vehicle features during the engineering phase, while MR blends virtual content with the real world. Car makers use MR headsets to train factory employees in a variety of tasks, from building engines and components to changing tools in computerized factory equipment.

Avatar Interviews

Platforms have used virtual avatar interviews for interviewing job applicants, allowing them to attend the interview as their avatars. Both the interviewees and interviewers participate through their avatars and communicate through voice chat. They can animate their avatars based on their movements in front of web cameras to express themselves. The avatar interviews are part of the initial recruitment process. The use of avatar interviews illustrates bringing physical world activities into the metaverse.[38]

Digital Twins

Technology companies are making a large investment in making copies of human physiology, personalities, and the objects around them. For example, an individual might send their digital twin to attend a meeting instead of themselves. This is an area of AI that the tech companies view as a powerful practical use for AI technology. Building virtual likenesses of a human or an object will bring about the same serious ethical and legal issues that have been discussed in earlier chapters.

When Humanity and Technology Collide

With the detonation of the first atomic bomb, a new age of humanity began; humanity reached the threshold of being able to destroy itself. The collision between technological ambitions and AI and biosecurity risks has raised concerns among experts.[39] The *London Times* printed an editorial in 2018, from Stephen Hawking, warning that AI will likely outsmart humans. According to Hawking's legacy, AI will either be the best thing that has ever happened to humanity, or it will be the worst thing. Another important figure in Big Tech, Elon Musk believes that AI is more dangerous than nuclear warheads and must be regulated. Musk believes, based on the past history of human behavior, that the race for AI could ultimately result in World War III. With the development of Google's AlphaGo, Musk commented on how fast AI can improve itself without anyone predicting the rate of speed as well as its capabilities.[40] Early worrisome concerns of thinkers like Turning and Good regarding AI risks are echoed by their modern counterparts like Nick Bostrom. The complexity of AI extends beyond just the technical issues. It requires international collaboration and partnership on effective policies, which are currently non-existent.[41] There is consensus that international cooperation is needed to mitigate AI's potential risks. While the United Nations (UN) is often characterized as a powerless organization in the face of a global crisis, it seems to have taken a leading role in governing AI.

Translating Urgency into Action

The possible extinction of humanity is a critical matter. A group of renowned figures in the AI field in 2023 signed a statement emphasizing the need to address AI-related risks, comparing it to a pandemic and nuclear warfare. The group encouraged global leaders to consider regulating AI, particularly advanced systems such as Open AI's ChatGPT.[42] AI systems may eventually become capable of self-improvement in which substantial software modifications are made by the software itself, rather than human programmers. While the ultimate goal for many AI algorithms is to address open challenges with humanlike solutions, no one has a good understanding of what the theoretical capabilities and limitations of AI are and the extent to which such humanlike solutions are even possible with AI algorithms.[43]

As discussed earlier, there is a need to strike a balance between risks and benefits. For example, biotechnology is often "dual-use," meaning that advances can be used to do harm as well as good. An individual could build live viruses for research, but also conduct bioterrorism. This makes biotechnology a highly challenging area to navigate, and one which requires a great degree of coordination.[44] The possibility of AI surpassing human capabilities and becoming unpredictable and uncontrollable is unsettling to many around the world. The simple fact that AI has the potential to control weapons, financial systems, and critical infrastructure is disconcerting. Managing innovation and ensuring accountability, security, and democratic principles is challenging.[45] As discussed in the previous chapter, the EU has taken a proactive approach with the passing of the AI Act, which primarily focuses on categorizing AI applications based on their level of risk.

Some of the issues highlighted in this book exist with or without AI; however, new technological advances such as AI have the potential to magnify preexisting problems. At this time, it is not clear what the long-term implications of malicious use of AI are going to be. The long-term structural risks of AI involve AI changing political, social, and economic structures such as exacerbating inequalities or provoking rapid and wide-scale unemployment. AI's potential harm is complex. Aligning AI with human values is difficult, particularly as models become more elaborate. Scenarios in which AI systems gain more confidence by exterminating humanity for more computing power have been raised among experts arguing that unforeseen consequences arise when powerful computer systems are unleashed.[46]

What Does it Mean to Be Human?

A machine that could think like a person has been the guiding vision of AI research since the earliest days of this technological development and remains its most divisive idea. Historically, technological change has served to replace humans, either wholly or partly, in the performance of specific tasks. Industrial automation was originally limited to manual tasks. For instance, in the manufacturing sector, the expansion of machinery displaced many millions of manual workers. Currently, the advances in computation offer a basis for the automation of routine intellectual tasks, threatening many jobs in the industries that make up the majority of employment in modern economies.[47]

Humans have always evolved alongside technology, including AI, which is transforming humanity and introducing existential questions. While concerns about killer robots and surveillance states are important, the more serious implications revolve around human decision-making and moral judgment. For example, the impact of AI on critical thinking is a serious matter. AI and emerging technology are being marketed and sold around the world as promising tools for an easy everyday life for humans. Prominent economists in the area of the psychology of human decision-making are advocating for the development and deployment of something equivalent to GPS technology to make it easier for people to handle all the hard decisions they have to make in life. This is a dangerous path that will only lead to a decline in human intelligence.[48]

Nations and societies want to thrive and be competitive and innovative. This ideology is in sharp contrast to what is being marketed by companies around the world. Purely based on sales and economic profits, people are being encouraged and persuaded by powerful advertisement and enticement tactics to rely increasingly more on technological products for everyday life decisions.

An Illusion of Choice, The Rise of a GPS Society

While a sound argument can be made for governments around the world to develop, invest, and deploy emerging technologies that will protect their nations and citizens and preserve national and international security, the same rational does not apply or justify the widespread use of AI in everyday life. Without recognition of its exponential dangers and consequences, what is being sold and promoted is giving rise to the decline of human intelligence and the decline of critical thinking. AI is extensively used, predicting preferences and making decisions in important sectors, as referenced in earlier chapters. AI as a substitute for human choice will limit people's freedom to choose. Algorithmic decision-making narrows people's moral judgment and makes the decision-making process very predictable.

While AI may enhance efficiency, it has a deep impact on human self-learning processes, growth, and self-understanding. The element of predictability may be positive in a military and defense context, such as predictability on the battlefield, but it can also deeply impact human rights.[49] Should societies worry about a future in which rudimentary AI is making decisions in place of humans? Is this the future that humanity wants? Does humanity want to let emerging technologies such as AI make societal decisions? Henry Kissinger was worried that a general intelligence AI that is put in charge of decision-making for humans would cause human critical thinking and intelligence to atrophy.[50] No one has full control or full understanding of this emerging technology, what it means, and its consequences.

Facing the Future Proactively

The future should not be dominated by surveillance and the economy. The greatest promise of emerging technologies such as AI is the same as the biggest danger. What should a digital society that respects democratic values look like? A future in which emerging technologies such as AI contribute to a world of greater centralized control must be avoided at all costs. A world that empowers authoritarianism and uses emerging technologies as an instrument to repress dissent and conform behavior will result in the erosion of democratic principles. How bias and trust interrelate is a key societal question, and understanding it will determine the societal acceptance of AI systems.[51]

In the words of Winston Churchill, " The prevention of the supreme catastrophe ought to be the paramount object of all endeavor."[52] When it comes to balancing innovation and safety, there are hard choices to make for economic growth and security interests—between maintaining openness and between commercial and national objectives—nonetheless the choices must be based on an effort to balance short-term and long-term considerations.

AI will accelerate the already serious threat of cyber-enabled disinformation campaigns. Nation-state hackers are already using AI-enabled tools in their disinformation campaigns. As discussed in earlier chapters, AI will enable deepfakes—including live action computer-generated false realities that can be distributed on a mass scale. The careless weaponization of AI could be destabilizing, and the deliberate misuse of AI could do great harm. This may be of greatest risk with AI applications that are rushed into use without proper safeguards, sufficient testing, and ethical considerations.[53] Our values guide our decisions and shape our policies, our sensitivities, and how we balance trade-offs among competing interests.[54]

With AI systems increasingly being deployed across vital sectors such as criminal justice, it is important that mechanisms are established and maintained to ensure that data subjects or users of AI systems have access to a range of effective redress options in the event that they suffer harm. Regulators must make certain that individuals harmed by the deployment of AI systems are able to make regulatory complaints or pursue legal actions in court.[55]

Assets and Liability

Although general AI does not exist as of yet, nevertheless governments and policymakers need to move beyond the current challenges and start planning proactively. Advancing AI intelligence does not automatically instill morality. The technologies are advancing quickly, outpacing policies, and are driven by the commercial sector, frequently outside national security frameworks. Reliance on non-military, non-national security companies to produce products that are safe and well-vetted is not wise unless the government can compel the tech companies to describe how their models actually work and what data go into them. At the same time, the government must make sure that independent researchers and outside experts can evaluate the technology and understand it.

The deep interdependencies of the world's leading AI states present no easy answers for how best to further innovation while protecting security. The issues are too complex and vast for any one government, society, or industry to address alone. There are risks of military use, ethical concerns, lack of data standards, and uncertainty about the future evolution of AI.

Confidence

Public trust in governments around the world has been on the decline in the recent decade. Trust in even some of the world's largest governmental systems has hit historic lows. With the rapidly increasing pace of change forcing transformation and uncertainty in every industry, trust has never been more important. How can trust and confidence be accomplished with respect to emerging tools? Why should these technologies be trusted?

AI systems have been implemented without assessing their technical performance or mitigating their risk to the environment in which they operate. Appropriate management of technical performance requires AI developers, cybersecurity specialists, program managers, and others to ensure that the AI systems solve the problem, using data sets that are appropriate for the problem and selecting a suitable algorithm that would ensure its functionality as it was originally intended.

With the proliferation of IoT devices and greater access to data from anywhere, the world is facing new threats; malicious use of these technologies by bad actors is a global problem. It is already established that AI applications pose a risk to privacy, individual rights, autonomy, and civil liberties. How these concerns are addressed will have a significant impact on its acceptance. How these technologies and tools are adopted will depend on how they can be validated.[56]

This is a critical time for shared cross-border challenges in coping with complex issues such as those mentioned earlier, like climate change, food security, communicable diseases, terrorism, energy shortages, biotechnology, autonomous systems, data analysis, and cybersecurity threats. A serious security concern currently deals with the critical infrastructure that operates the power to pipelines; increasingly digital, they are vulnerable to disruptions and destruction via cyberattacks. These shared challenges are not marginal; in fact, they are at the core of national and international security. These potential and real threats require governments to cooperate; however, geopolitical competition, nationalism, and populism make this cooperation more difficult. Without international collaboration and cooperation, though, it will be impossible to tackle these issues effectively.[57]

As AI technologies are embedded and intertwined in the digital ecosystem, a responsible approach to AI should include strengthening key aspects of the ecosystem. This includes data systems, connectivity, and local workforce capacity. In addition, there must be a focus on strengthening the civil society structures holding AI systems and actors accountable, and shaping policy to include secure and inclusive digital ecosystems. Why should people have to play the role of police and determine which applications to experiment with and which to avoid?

The best protections against malicious use of AI tools are often the same tools that help protect against oppression and rights erosion in more traditional contexts. For example, the existence of a strong judiciary, the implementation of appropriate regulatory safeguards, and the engagement of an informed and empowered civil society that could shed light on misuse and demand accountability when harms arise.[58] Sound AI policies are necessary. There is a need for caution, in particular when the developers of the technology have great difficulty explaining how data are processed and reported out; the preferred path forward boils down to trust.

Notes

1 Rainie, L., Funk, C., Anderson, M., & Tyson, A. (2022). *How Americans think about AI*. Pew Research Center. www.pewresearch.org/internet/2022/03/17/how-americans-think-about-artificial-intelligence/
2 Nasheri, H. (2021, December 21). *The dumb and the dangerous road ahead*. United Nations Interregional Crime and Justice Research Institute.
3 Department of the Air Force. (2019). *The United States Air Force artificial intelligence annex to the Department of Defense Artificial Intelligence Strategy*. www.af.mil/Portals/1/documents/5/USAF-AI-Annex-to-DoD-AI-Strategy.pdf
4 Limotta, M. (2020). *How AI will help the U.S. to Mars and beyond*. Nextgov/FCW. www.nextgov.com/ideas/2020/12/how-ai-will-help-us-mars-and-beyond/170935/

5 Maynard, A. (2022, June 13). *"Jurassic World" scientists still haven't learned that just because you can doesn't mean you should—Real-world genetic engineers can learn from the cautionary tale.* Nextgov/FCW. www.nextgov.com/emerging-tech/2022/06/jurassic-world-scientists-still-havent-learned-just-beca use-you-can-doesnt-mean-you-should-real-world-genetic-engineers-can-learn-cautionary-tale/368086/

6 Spencer, D., Cole, M., Joyce, S., Whittaker, X., & Stuart, M. (2021, January). *Digital automation and the future of work.* European Parliament. www.europ arl.europa.eu/RegData/etudes/STUD/2021/656311/EPRS_STU(2021)656 311(ANN1)_EN.pdf

7 IMF. (2022, July 26). *World economic outlook update, July 2022: Gloomy and more uncertain.* www.imf.org/en/Publications/WEO/Issues/2022/07/26/world-economic-outlook-update-july-2022?utm_source=newsletter&utm_medium= email&utm_campaign=newsletter_axiosgenerate&stream=top

8 G7 France. (2019). *Biarritz strategy for an open, free, and secure digital transformation.* www.elysee.fr/admin/upload/default/0001/05/62a9221e66987d4e0 d6ffcb058f3d2c649fc6d9d.pdf

9 Aspen Digital. (2023, January 9). *Envisioning cyber futures with AI.* U.S. and Global Cybersecurity Groups. www.aspendigital.org/wp-content/uploads/ 2024/02/Aspen-Digital_Envisioning-Cyber-Futures-with-AI_January-2024.pdf

10 Fick, N., & Miscik, J. (Co-chairs). Segal, A., & Goldstein, G. M. (Project Directors). (2022, July). *Confronting reality in cyberspace: Foreign policy for a fragmented internet.* Council on Foreign Relations. www.cfr.org/task-force-rep ort/confronting-reality-in-cyberspace

11 Rosenberg, S. (2024, May 16). *Doomers have lost the AI fight.* Axios.

12 Center for Strategic & International Studies. (2023, June 21). *Senator Chuck Schumer launches SAFE innovation in the AI age at CSIS* (Transcript, Online Event). www.csis.org/analysis/sen-chuck-schumer-launches-safe-innovat ion-ai-age-csis

13 Nasheri, H. (2023, May). *State-sponsored economic espionage in cyberspace: Risks and preparedness, in cybercrime in the pandemic digital age and beyond* (Chang, L. Y-C., Sarre, R., & Smith, R. G., Eds). Springer International Publishing.

14 Mailes, G., Carrasco, M., & Arcuri, A. (2021, April). *The global trust imperative.* BCG & Salesforce. https://web-assets.bcg.com/bf/de/d2a310054cd8891fd 7f8cd95452b/the-global-trust-imperative-salesforce-bcg-whitepaper.pdf

15 The Stack. (2022, April 4). *Technology use in the justice system is a "Wild West" warn Peers.* https://thestack.technology/police-ai-toolsnew-technologies-in-the-justice-system/

16 Rosenthal, E. (2022). *Who's responsible if a Tesla on autopilot kills someone?* Nextgov/FCW. www.nextgov.com/ideas/2022/03/whos-responsible-if-tesla-autopilot-kills-someone/363111/

17 Horn-Muller A. (2023). *AI can now forecast the next food crisis.* Axios. www. axios.com/2023/03/10/ai-forecast-food-crisis

18 Special Competitive Studies Project. (2022, September). *Mid-decade challenges to national competitiveness.* www.scsp.ai/2022/09/special-competitive-studies-project-releases-first-report-sept-12-2022/

19 Hao, K. (2019, February 26). Why AI is a threat to democracy—And what we can do to stop it. *MIT Technology Review*. www.technologyreview.com/2019/02/26/66043/why-ai-is-a-threat-to-democracyand-what-we-can-do-to-stop-it

20 Thompson, N. (2018, March 31). *Emmanuel Macron talks to WIRED about France's AI strategy*. WIRED. www.wired.com/story/emmanuel-macron-talks-to-wired-about-frances-ai-strategy/

21 Fried, I., & Rosenberg, S. (2023). *AI could choke on its own exhaust as it fills the web*. Axios. www.axios.com/2023/08/28/ai-content-flood-model-collapse

22 Rosenberg, S. (2022, July 25). *Sunset of the social network*. Axios. www.axios.com/2022/07/25/sunset-social-network-facebook-tiktok

23 Goasduff, L. (2019). *Gartner says 5.8 billion enterprise and automotive IoT endpoints will be in use in 2020*. Gartner. www.gartner.com/en/newsroom/press-releases/2019-08-29-gartner-says-5-8-billion-enterprise-and-automotive-io

24 Palmer, D. (2022). *The metaverse is coming, and the security threats have already arrived*. ZDNet. www.zdnet.com/article/the-metaverse-is-coming-and-the-security-threats-have-already-arrived/

25 Europol Unclassified. (2017). *Crime in the age of technology*. www.europol.europa.eu/publications-events/main-reports/european-union-serious-and-organised-crime-threat-assessment-2017

26 Jones, K. (2022, October 18). *Without regulation, the Metaverse will be like social media on steroids*. World Politics Review. www.worldpoliticsreview.com/the-metaverse-like-regulating-social-media-but-on-steroids/?one-time-read-code=66072167943672571243

27 Europol Unclassified. (2017). *Crime in the age of technology*. www.europol.europa.eu/publications-events/main-reports/european-union-serious-and-organised-crime-threat-assessment-2017

28 Jones, K. (2022, October 18). *Without regulation, the Metaverse will be like social media on steroids*. World Politics Review. www.worldpoliticsreview.com/the-metaverse-like-regulating-social-media-but-on-steroids/?one-time-read-code=66072167943672571243

29 Tidy, J. (2022). *Billions being spent in metaverse land grab*. BBC. www.bbc.co.uk/news/technology-63488059.

30 Solana, A. (2023, July 27). *Banks in the Metaverse can't lend you money yet, but they still want to sell you the dream*. ZDNet. www.zdnet.com/article/banks-in-the-metaverse-cant-lend-you-money-yet-but-they-still-want-to-sell-you-the-dream/

31 Malekos Smith, Z. L. (2022, March 13). *There are tradeoffs in governing the Metaverse*. Center for Strategic & International Studies. www.csis.org/analysis/there-are-tradeoffs-governing-metaverse

32 BBC. (2022, May 25). *Female avatar sexually assaulted in Meta VR platform, campaigners say*. www.bbc.com/news/technology-61573661

33 Europol Unclassified. (2017). *Crime in the age of technology*. www.europol.europa.eu/publications-events/main-reports/european-union-serious-and-organised-crime-threat-assessment-2017

34 Zulhusni, M. (2022). *Sharjah gets the world's first government-backed metaverse city*. TechWire. https://techwireasia.com/2022/10/anything-is-possible-as-sharjah-gets-the-worlds-first-government-backed-metaverse-city/.

35 Vincent, B. (2022). *Enforcement feds want augmented reality to monitor U.S./ Mexico border*. Nextgov/FCW. www.nextgov.com/emerging-tech/2021/08/ drug-enforcement-feds-want-augmented-reality-monitor-usmexico-border/ 184636/

36 Breeden II, J. (2023). *Artificial intelligence and drone tactics maneuver into advanced military simulations*. Nextgov/FCW. www.nextgov.com/ideas/2023/ 04/artificial-intelligence-and-drone-tactics-maneuver-advanced-military-simu lations/384942/

37 Rubio, I. (2022). *Sci-fi no more: Introducing the contact lenses of the future.* Science & Tech EL PAÍS English Edition. https://english.elpais.com/science-tech/2022-10-27/sci-fi-no-more-this-is-what-the-contact-lenses-of-the-future-will-do-for-you.html

38 Totilo, S. (2023). *Roblox to begin interviewing some job candidates inside Roblox*. Axios. www.axios.com/2023/08/10/roblox-job-interviews-virtual-rec ruiting

39 AP News. (2023). *China warns of artificial intelligence risks, calls for beefed-up national security measures*. https://apnews.com/article/china-artificial-intellige nce-national-security-00a38e550ef6b4ac12cd1fd418363d2b.

40 Barbaschow, A. (2018, March 12). *AI "more dangerous than nukes": Elon Musk still firm on regulatory oversight*. ZDNet. www.zdnet.com/article/more-dangerous-than-nukes-elon-musk-still-firm-on-regulatory-oversight-of-ai/

41 Piper, K. (2022). *The case for taking AI seriously as a threat to humanity*. Vox. www.vox.com/future-perfect/2018/12/21/18126576/ai-artificial-intelligence-machine-learning-safety-alignment

42 Wiggers, K. (2023). *OpenAI forms team to study "catastrophic" AI risks, including nuclear threats*. TechCrunch. https://techcrunch.com/2023/10/26/ope nai-forms-team-to-study-catastrophic-risks-including-nuclear-threats/

43 National Science and Technology Council. (2019, June). *The national artificial intelligence research and development strategic plan: 2019 update*. www.nitrd. gov/pubs/National-AI-RD-Strategy-2019.pdf

44 The Center for Long-Term Resilience. (2021, June). *Future proof: The oppor-tunity to transform the UK's resilience to extreme risks.*

45 Andrew-Lewis, J., Beanson, E., & Frank, M. (2023). *The Biden administration's executive order on artificial intelligence*. Center for Strategic & International Studies. www.csis.org/analysis/biden-administrations-executive-order-artificial-intelligence

46 Piper, K. (2022). *The case for taking AI seriously as a threat to humanity*. Vox. www.vox.com/future-perfect/2018/12/21/18126576/ai-artificial-intelligence-machine-learning-safety-alignment

47 European Parliamentary Reach Service Scientific Foresight Unit. (2021). *Digital automation and the Future of Work*. www.europarl.europa.eu/RegData/etudes/ STUD/2021/656311/EPRS_STU(2021)656311_EN.pdf

48 Nasheri, H. (2021, December 21). *The dumb and the dangerous road ahead.* United Nations Interregional Crime and Justice Research Institute.

49 Nasheri, H. (2021, December 21). *The dumb and the dangerous road ahead.* United Nations Interregional Crime and Justice Research Institute.

50 Waddell, K. (2018, October 14). *Will AI make us dumb?* Axios. www.axios. com/artificial-intelligence-human-brain-critical-thinking-ability-1a17e87e-2a17-4dae-8371-f56d58a76812.html
51 Down, L., Jonas, E., Schwartz, R., Schwartz, R., & Tabassi, E. (2021, June). *A proposal for identifying and managing bias within artificial intelligence* (Draft NIST Special Publication 1270). National Institute of Standards and Technology, U.S. Department of Commerce. https://nvlpubs.nist.gov/nistpubs/SpecialPublications/NIST.SP.1270-draft.pdf
52 The Center for Long-Term Resilience. (2021, June). *Future proof: The opportunity to transform the UK's resilience to extreme risks.*
53 National Security Commission on Artificial Intelligence. (2019, November). *Interim report.* www.nscai.gov/wp-content/uploads/2021/01/NSCAI-Interim-Report-for-Congress_201911.pdf
54 National Security Commission on Artificial Intelligence. (2020, July 22). *Key considerations for responsible development & fielding of artificial intelligence abridged version.*
55 Ogunleye, I. (2022, August). *AI's redress problem: Recommendations to improve consumer protection from artificial intelligence.* UC Berkeley Center for Long-Term Cybersecurity. https://cltc.berkeley.edu/publication/cltc-white-paper-ais-redress-problem/
56 Executive Office of the President. (2019). Maintaining American leadership in artificial intelligence. *Federal Register*, 84(31), 3967–3972. www.federalregister.gov/documents/2019/02/14/2019-02544/maintaining-american-leadership-in-artificial-intelligence
57 National Security Commission on Artificial Intelligence. (2020, July 22). *Key considerations for responsible development & fielding of artificial intelligence abridged version.*
58 U.S. Agency of International Development. (2022, May). *USAID artificial intelligence action plan.* www.usaid.gov/sites/default/files/2022-05/USAID_Artificial_Intelligence_Action_Plan.pdf

References

Aaguirre. (2020*). Why those who care about catastrophic and existential risk should care about autonomous weapons.* Effective Altruism Forum. https://forum.effectivealtruism.org/posts/oR9tLNRSAep293rr5/why-those-who-care-about-catastrophic-and-existential-risk-2

Aaronson, S. A. (2018, April). *Data minefield: How AI is prodding governments to rethink trade in data.* Institute for International Economic Policy. www2.gwu.edu/~iiep/assets/docs/papers/2018WP/AaronsonIIEP2018-11.pdf

Abdulla, S., Chahal, H., Konaev, M., & Luing, N. (2022, May). *Quad AI: Assessing AI-related collaboration between the United States, Australia, India, and Japan.* Center for Security and Emerging Technology. https://cset.georgetown.edu/publication/quad-ai/

Abrams, L. (2022). *Hacker shares how they allegedly breached Fast Company's site.* BleepingComputer. www.bleepingcomputer.com/news/security/hacker-shares-how-they-allegedly-breached-fast-company-s-site/

Abrams, L. (2023). *Medusa ransomware gang picks up steam as it targets companies worldwide.* BleepingComputer. www.bleepingcomputer.com/news/security/medusa-ransomware-gang-picks-up-steam-as-it-targets-companies-worldwide/

Abrams, L. (2023). *Microsoft: Hackers turn exchange servers into malware control centers.* BleepingComputer. www.bleepingcomputer.com/news/security/microsoft-hackers-turn-exchange-servers-into-malware-control-centers/

Ackerman, G., & Newman, M. (2023). *Israel is using Pegasus spyware maker to track hostages in Gaza.* Bloomberg. www.bloomberg.com/news/articles/2023-10-26/israel-taps-blacklisted-pegasus-maker-nso-to-track-gaza-hostages-and-hamas

ADA. (2022). *The Americans with Disabilities Act and the use of software, algorithms, and artificial intelligence to assess job applicants and employees.* U.S. Equal Employment Opportunity Commission. www.eeoc.gov/laws/guidance/americans-disabilities-act-and-use-software-algorithms-and-artificial-intelligence

AFP. (2020, April 6). U.S. labels Russian far-right group as foreign terrorist organization. *The Moscow Times.* www.themoscowtimes.com/2020/04/06/us-labels-russian-far-right-group-as-foreign-terrorist-organization-a69890

Afshar, V. (2021, January 29). *Disruptive innovation 2021: These 15 big ideas are most likely to change the world.* ZDNet. www.zdnet.com/article/disruptive-inn ovation-2021-these-15-big-ideas-are-most-likely-to-change-the-world/

Afshar, V. (2021, October 18). *AI ethics maturity model: A company guide.* ZDNet. www.zdnet.com/article/ai-ethics-maturity-model/

Afshar, V. (2022, February 16). *70% of customer interactions are now digital and most companies are not ready.* ZDNet. www.zdnet.com/article/70-percent-of-customer-interactions-are-now-digital-and-most-companies-are-not-ready/

Afshar, V. (2023). *Generative AI could add up to $4.4 trillion annually to global economy.* ZDNet. www.zdnet.com/article/generative-ai-could-add-up-to-4-4-trillion-annually-to-global-economy/

Agarib, A. (2018, March 12). Dubai police unveil artificial intelligence projects, smart tech. *ACE Times.* www.zawya.com/en/business/dubai-police-unveil-artific ial-intelligence-projects-smart-tech-eitpo88d

Agnew, W., Gombolay, M., Hundt, A., Kacianka, S., & Zeng, Z. (2022). *Robot enact malignant stereotypes.* ACM Conference on Fairness, Accountability, and Transparency. https://facctconference.org/static/pdfs_2022/facct22-60.pdf

Agomuoh, F. (2022). *AI image generation propagates gender and racial stereo-types.* Digital Trends. www.digitaltrends.com/computing/ai-tool-reveals-biases-in-text-to-image-generators/

Aijun, T. (2019, December 12). *Ideological security in the framework of the overall National Security Outlook.* Interpret: China, Center for Strategic & International Studies. https://interpret.csis.org/translations/ideological-security-in-the-framework-of-the-overall-national-security-outlook/

Air Force Research Laboratory. (2021). *Directed energy futures 2060 (AFRL-2021-1152).* Defense Innovation Marketplace. https://defenseinnovationmark etplace.dtic.mil/wp-content/uploads/2022/04/Directed-Energy-Futures-2060-AFRL-2021-1152-Distribution-A.pdf

Alboum, J. (2022). *3 ways for government to sustain momentum in digital trans-formation.* Nextgov/FCW. www.nextgov.com/ideas/2022/01/3-ways-governm ent-sustain-momentum-digital-transformation/360288/

Ali, J., Alikhan, A., & Reitman, J. (2021). *Extremism and domestic terrorism in the wake of the Capitol siege.* New America. www.newamerica.org/intern ational-security/events/online-extremism-and-domestic-terrorism-wake-capi tol-siege/

Allard, S. (2023, August 7). *Meet Crocker Park's new AI-powered security robot, SAM.* Axios Cleveland. www.axios.com/local/cleveland/2023/08/07/crocker-parks-ai-security-robot-sam

Allen, G. C. (n.d.). *A.I. governance project: Strategic technologies program.* Center for Strategic & International Studies. www.csis.org/programs/strategic-techn ologies-program/ai-governance-project

Allen, G. C. (2022, May 13). *Across drones, AI, and space, commercial tech is flexing military muscle in Ukraine.* Center for Strategic & International Studies. www.csis.org/analysis/across-drones-ai-and-space-commercial-tech-flexing-military-muscle-ukraine

Allen, G. C. (2022, May 20). *One key challenge for diplomacy on AI: China's military does not want to talk.* Center for Strategic & International Studies.

www.csis.org/analysis/one-key-challenge-diplomacy-ai-chinas-milit
ary-does-not-want-talk

Allen, G. C. (2022, June 6). *DOD is updating its decade-old autonomous weapons
policy, but confusion remains widespread.* Center for Strategic & International
Studies. www.csis.org/analysis/dod-updating-its-decade-old-autonomous-weap
ons-policy-confusion-remains-widespread

Allen, G. C. (2022, September 7). *Report launch: Software-defined warfare.* Center
for Strategic & International Studies. www.csis.org/events/report-launch-softw
are-defined-warfare

Allen, G. C. (2022, October 11). *Choking off China's access to the future of AI.*
Center for Strategic & International Studies. www.csis.org/analysis/choking-chi
nas-access-future-ai

Allen, G. C., Benson, E., & Reinsch, W. A. (2022, November 30). *Improved export
controls enforcement technology needed for U.S. National Security.* Center for
Strategic & International Studies.

Allen, G. C., & Thadani, A. (2023, April 26). *Advancing cooperative AI governance at the 2023 H7 summit.* Center for Strategic International Studies AI
Council. www.csis.org/analysis/advancing-cooperative-ai-governance-2023-g7-
summit

Allen, G. C., & Tudorache, D. (2022). *The European approach to regulating artificial intelligence with MEP Dragos Tudorache, Co-Rapporteur of the EU AI
Act.* Center for Strategic & International Studies. www.csis.org/events/europ
ean-approach-regulating-artificial-intelligence-mep-dragos-tudorache-co-rap
porteur-eu-ai

Allen, M. (2023, January 24). *What's next.* Axios.

Allen, M. (2023, March 17). *Microsoft injects AI into Word.* Axios.

Allen, M. (2023, May 15). *New TSA look.* Axios.

Allen, M. (2023, May 16). *OpenAI pushes for rules.* Axios.

Allen, M. (2023, August 9). *Music industry in "deepfake" talks.* Axios.

Allen, M. (2023, August 9). *Scoop: How IBM tricked ChatGPT.* Axios.

Allen, M. (2023, November 8). *1 big thing—Behind the Curtain: What AI
architects fear most.* Axios.

Allen, M. (2023, December 7). *Dire media threat.* Axios.

Allen, M. (2023). *AI arms race.* Axios.

Allen, M. (2023). *AI conjures "last Beatles record"* Axios.

Allen, M. (2023). *AI's hidden toll on our brains.* Axios. www.axios.com/2023/06/
10/ai-mental-health-risks-misinformation

Allen, M. (2023). *AI tries Smart Brevity.* Axios.

Allen, M. (2023). *Axios interview: Zients says Biden will push for more AI
authority.* Axios. www.axios.com/2023/07/21/zients-biden-ai-authority

Allen, M. (2023). *1 big thing: Biden's AI plan.* Axios.

Allen, M. (2023). *1 big thing: Looming AI catastrophes.* Axios.

Allen, M. (2023). *Democratizing AI rules.* Axios.

Allen, M. (2023). *Don't hold your breath for global AI rules.* Axios.

Allen, M. (2023). *Facial-recognition danger.* Axios.

Allen, M. (2023). *First AI election.* Axios.

Allen, M. (2023). *Future of pharmacies: Robots + AI.* Axios.

Allen, M. (2023). *Ina Fried helps us navigate AI with "Prompt." First up: Meetings!* Axios.

Allen, M. (2023). *Ina Fried: Postcard from AI-centric TED.* Axios.

Allen, M. (2023). *Low-tech cyberattacks wreak havoc.* Axios.

Allen, M. (2023). *Putin's high-tech snooping.* Axios.

Allen, M. (2023). *Sneak peek: Future of airports.* Axios.

Allen, M. (2023). *Stunning AI stat.* Axios.

Allen, M. (2023). *The singularity is back.* Axios.

Allen, M. (2023). *Weaponizing medical AI.* Axios.

Allen, M. (2023). *Youthful trust in A.I.* Axios.

Allen, M. (2024, January 20). *1 big thing: Optimism of the elites.* Axios.

Allen, M. (2024, February 26). *AI's next act: Autonomous agents.* Axios.

Allen, M., & May, A. (2023, January 1). *Chief Justice urges "humility" on AI.* Axios. www.axios.com/2024/01/01/john-roberts-year-end-report-ai

Allen, M., & VandeHei, J. (2023, December 4). *Behind the Curtain: U.S. not ready for era of robotic, AI world wars.* Axios. www.axios.com/2023/12/04/artificial-intelligence-us-military-weapons

Allianz Commercial. (2024, January 16). *Allianz Risk Barometer 2024.* https://commercial.allianz.com/news-and-insights/reports/allianz-risk-barometer.html

Allison, P. (2022). *Will we ever... live in city-sized buildings?* BBC. www.bbc.com/future/article/20221028-will-we-ever-live-in-city-sized-buildings

Allyn, B. (2020, June 24). *The computer got it wrong: How facial recognition led to false arrest of black man.* NPR. www.npr.org/2020/06/24/882683463/the-computer-got-it-wrong-how-facial-recognition-led-to-a-false-arrest-in-michig

Alms, N. (2022). *A cyber workforce strategy is coming from the White House, along with an implementation body to make sure it works.* Nextgov/FCW. www.nextgov.com/cybersecurity/2022/09/cyber-workforce-strategy-coming-white-house-along-implementation-body-make-sure-it-works/377030/

Alms, N. (2022). *Portman introduces two bills on facial recognition, AI in government.* Nextgov/FCW. www.nextgov.com/emerging-tech/2022/12/portman-int roduces-two-bills-facial-recognition-ai-government/381295/

Alms, N. (2022). *White House seeks advice on cyber workforce development.* Nextgov/FCW. www.nextgov.com/cxo-briefing/2022/10/white-house-seeks-adv ice-cyber-workforce-development/378053/

Alms, N. (2023, June 9). *Are government decisions being made by AI? Lawmakers want to mandate disclosure.* Nextgov/FCW. www.nextgov.com/artificial-intel ligence/2023/06/are-government-decisions-being-made-ai-lawmakers-want-mandate-disclosure/387373/

Alms, N. (2023, July 18). *What will the federal government do with generative AI?* Nextgov/FCW. www.nextgov.com/artificial-intelligence/2023/07/what-will-federal-government-do-generative-ai/388563/

Alms, N. (2023). *Agriculture Department is taking a "cautious" approach to generative AI.* Nextgov/FCW. www.nextgov.com/artificial-intelligence/2023/08/agri culture-department-taking-cautious-approach-generative-ai/389679/

Alms, N. (2023). *Cybersecurity still "high risk" in GAO's book after over 25 years.* Nextgov/FCW. www.nextgov.com/cybersecurity/2023/04/cybersecurity-still-high-risk-gaos-book-after-over-25-years/385473/

Alms, N. (2023). *Is government culture stifling CX innovation?* Nextgov/FCW. www.nextgov.com/digital-government/2023/06/government-culture-stifling-cx-innovation/387925/

Alms, N. (2023). *Labor Dept. watchdog urges "extreme caution" on facial recognition.* Nextgov/FCW. www.nextgov.com/emerging-tech/2023/04/labor-depa rtments-watchdog-urges-extreme-caution-facial-recognition-unemployment/ 384893/

Alms, N. (2023). *White House says an anticipated executive order on identity theft is coming, here's what experts want in it.* Nextgov/FCW. www.nextgov.com/digi tal-government/2022/12/white-house-says-anticipated-executive-order-identity-theft-coming-heres-what-experts-want-it/380373/

Alperovitch, D., Buchanan, B., Harris, S., Hennessy, S., Poznansky, M., Wittes, B., & Evans, R. (2016, October 31). *Emails and influence: Investigating Russia's attack on the U.S. political system.* War on the Rocks. https://warontherocks. com/2016/10/emails-and-influence-investigating-russias-attack-on-the-u-s-politi cal-system/

Alterovitz, G. (2021, September 16). *National Artificial Intelligence Institute with a research and development focus on veterans.* National Artificial Intelligence Institute (NAII). www.research.va.gov/naii/

Altman, S. (2023). *OpenAI written testimony 051623.* DocumentCloud. www. documentcloud.org/documents/23814360-openai-written-testimony-051623

American Association for the Advancement of Science. (2014, July). *Science and technology to prevent and respond to CBRN disasters: ROK and US perspectives.* www.aaas.org/sites/default/files/reports/Asan-Report_Science-and-Technology-to-Prevent-and-Respond-to-CBRN-Disasters.pdf

American White Supremacists Attend Russian Nationalist Conference. (2015). *Anti- defamation league.* www.adl.org/blog/american-white-supremacists-att end-russian-nationalist-conference

Amos, J. (2021, January 12). *EU must "move at speed" on space broadband network.* BBC. www.bbc.com/news/science-environment-55640447

Amos, Z. (2023). *Predictive analytics in cybersecurity: Myth or reality?* InCyber. https://incyber.org/en/predictive-analytics-in-cybersecurity-myth-or-reality/

Anadiotis, G. (2020, September 10). *AI and automation vs. the COVID-19 pandemic: Trading liberty for safety.* ZDNet.

Anadiotis, G. (2020, October 1). *The state of AI in 2020: Democratization, industrialization and the way to artificial general intelligence.* ZDNet.

Anadiotis, G. (2020, November 12). *What's next for AI: Gary Marcus talks about the journey toward robust artificial intelligence.* ZDNet.

Anadiotis, G. (2020, December 22). *From data to knowledge and AI via graphs.* ZDNet. www.zdnet.com/article/from-data-to-knowledge-and-ai-via-graphs-tec hnology-to-support-a-knowledge-based-economy/

Andrew-Lewis, J., Beanson, E., & Frank, M. (2023). *The Biden administration's executive order on artificial intelligence.* Center for Strategic & International Studies. www.csis.org/analysis/biden-administrations-executive-order-artificial-intelligence

Anthony, I., & Su, F. (2019, June). *Reassessing CBRN threats in a changing global environment.* Stockholm International Peace Research Institute.

Anti-Defamation League. (2021, January 13). *Extremism and political violence in America: Current landscape, future outlook.* www.adl.org/extremism-political-violence-today-future-outlook

AP News. (2023). *China warns of artificial intelligence risks, calls for beefed-up national security measures.*

Arab News. (2021, February 15). *French cyber agency reveals suspected Russian hacks.* https://arab.news/me8uv

Aramark. (2023). *Aramark Sports + Entertainment announces latest innovation with launch of new Amazon One age verification capability at Coors Field.* www.aramark.com/newsroom/news/2023/may/-aramark-sports---entertainment-announces-latest-innovation-with

Arasasingham, A., & Goodman, M. P. (2023, April 13). *Operationalizing data free flow with trust (DFFT).* Center for Strategic & International Studies. www.csis.org/analysis/operationalizing-data-free-flow-trust-dfft

Arcuri, G., & Kersten, A. (2023). *Innovation insights | The quantum opportunity.* Center for Strategic & International Studies. https://myoutube.com/watch?v=O_bxbYQ5uF4

Argentieri, N. (2023). *Principal Deputy Assistant Attorney General Nicole M. Argentieri delivers remarks at Camden Asset Recovery Inter-Agency Network (CARIN) annual general meeting.* U.S. Department of Justice. www.justice.gov/opa/speech/principal-deputy-assistant-attorney-general-nicole-m-argentieri-delivers-remarks-camden

Argyle, L. P., Busby, E. C., Fulda, N., Gubler, J., Rytting, C., & Wingate, D. (2022, September 16). *Out of one many: Using language models to simulate human samples.* Department of Political Science and Department of Computer Science, Brigham Young University. www.researchgate.net/publication/363584667_Out_of_One_Many_Using_Language_Models_to_Simulate_Human_Samples

Armbrust, V. (2022). *The metaverse holds big opportunities for the public sector.* Route Fifty. www.route-fifty.com/tech-data/2022/11/metaverse-holds-big-opportunities-public-sector/379206/

Armed Conflict Location & Event Data Project [ACLED]. (2020, October 13). *Standing by: Right Wing Militia Groups & the US election* (pp. 1–29). https://acleddata.com/acleddatanew/wp-content/uploads/2020/10/ACLEDMilitiaWatch_StandingByMilitiaGroups_2020Web.pdf

Arnold, A. (2018, March 27). Why robots will not take over human jobs. *Forbes.* www.forbes.com/sites/andrewarnold/2018/03/27/why-robots-will-not-take-over-human-jobs/#4403356f92fd

Arquilla, J., Borshchevskaya, A., Bragg, B., Devyatkin, P., Dyet, A., Ellis, R. E., Flynn, D. J., Goure, D., Kamp, A. C., Kangas, R., Katz, M. N., Koven, B. S., Lamoreaux, J. W., Laruelle, M., Marsh, C., Person, R., Pyatkov, R., Schindler, J., Severin, M., Sherlock, T., Siegle, J., Spalding III, R., Weitz, R., & Werchan, J. (2019, May). *Russian strategic intentions: A Strategic Multilayer Assessment (SMA) White Paper.* NSI, Inc. www.thearcticinstitute.org/wp-content/uploads/2019/05/Chapter-15-Russian-Activities-in-the-Arctic.pdf

Article 19. (n.d.). *Emotional entanglement: China's emotion recognition market and its implications for human rights.* www.article19.org/wp-content/uploads/2021/01/ER-Tech-China-Report.pdf

Artificial Intelligence & Technology Office. (2022). *DOE AI risk management playbook* (AIRMP). Department of Energy. www.energy.gov/ai/doe-ai-risk-man agement-playbook-airmp

Ashby, H. (2021). Far-right extremism is a global problem. *Foreign Policy.* https:// foreignpolicy.com/2021/01/15/far-right-extremism-global-problem-worldwide-solutions

Asher-Schapiro, A. (2021, January 27). *China growing use of emotion recognition tech raises rights concerns.* Reuters. www.reuters.com/article/idUSL8 N2K2500/

Aspen Digital. (2023, January 9). *Envisioning cyber futures with AI. U.S. and Global Cybersecurity Groups.* www.aspendigital.org/wp-content/uploads/2024/ 02/Aspen-Digital_Envisioning-Cyber-Futures-with-AI_January-2024.pdf

Athanasia, G. (2022, April 1). *The U.S. should strengthen STEM education to remain globally competitive: perspectives on innovation.* Center for Strategic & International Studies. www.csis.org/blogs/perspectives-innovation/us-should-str engthen-stem-education-remain-globally-competitive

Atkinson, R. D. (2018, November). *Which nations really lead in industrial robot adoption?* Information Technology and Innovation Foundation. www2.itif.org/ 2018-industrial-robot-adoption.pdf

Atleson, M. (2023). *The Luring Test: AI and the engineering of consumer trust.* Federal Trade Commission. www.ftc.gov/business-guidance/blog/2023/05/lur ing-test-ai-engineering-consumer-trust

Australian Competition & Consumer Commission. (2022, August 12). *Google LLC to pay $60 million for misleading representations.* www.accc.gov.au/ media-release/google-llc-to-pay-60-million-for-misleading-representations

Australian Government Department of Industry, Science, Energy and Resources. (2023, May 3). *National Quantum Strategy.* www.industry.gov.au/publications/ national-quantum-strategy

Auxenfants, M. (2023). *Web3: A unique geopolitical and strategic occasion for the EU?* InCyber. https://incyber.org/en/web3-unique-geopolitical-strategic-occas ion-for-eu/

Axios. (2018, February 20). *Tom Friedman's most popular column ever.* www. axios.com/2018/02/20/nyt-trump-threat-to-democracy

Aylett, R. (2021). Why there won't be a robot uprising any time soon. *BBC Science Focus.* www.sciencefocus.com/future-technology/future-robots-society/

Bailey, M. (2023). *Why humans can't trust AI: You don't know how it works, what it's going to do or whether it'll serve your interests.* Route Fifty. www.route-fifty. com/emerging-tech/2023/09/why-humans-cant-trust-ai-you-dont-know-how-it-works-what-its-going-do-or-whether-itll-serve-your-interests/390262/

Bajak, F. (2023). *Microsoft says early June disruptions to Outlook, cloud platform, were cyberattacks.* AP News.

Baker, M. (2020, April 30). *Virtual interviews to hire candidates during COVID.* Gartner.

Baker, S., Freedman, A., & Heath, R. (2023, August 1). *Existential threats to humanity are soaring this year.* Axios. www.axios.com/2023/08/01/climate-cha nge-artificial-intelligence-nuclear-war-existential

Baksh, M. (2022). *Defense, justice call for FCC rulemaking to secure internet routing, opposing NTIA*. Nextgov/FCW. www.nextgov.com/cybersecurity/2022/09/defense-justice-call-fcc-rulemaking-secure-internet-routing-opposing-ntia/377243/

Baksh, M. (2022). *New report shows significant improvement in consumer cyber hygiene*. Nextgov/FCW. www.nextgov.com/cybersecurity/2022/10/new-report-shows-significant-improvement-consumer-cyber-hygiene/378041/

Baksh, M. (2020). *End-to-end encryption and law enforcement access to data can coexist, justice official says*. Nextgov/FCW. www.nextgov.com/cybersecurity/2020/02/end-end-encryption-and-law-enforcement-access-data-can-coexist-just ice-official-says/163310/

Baksh, M. (2020). *Justice official explains why law enforcement is worried about 5G*. Nextgov/FCW. www.nextgov.com/cybersecurity/2020/07/justice-official-explains-why-law-enforcement-worried-about-5g/167127/

Baksh, M. (2022). *Agencies push deadline to comment on would-be federal cyber insurance program*. Nextgov/FCW. www.nextgov.com/cybersecurity/2022/11/agencies-push-deadline-comment-would-be-federal-cyber-insurance-program/379858/

Baksh, M. (2022). *CISA plans to measure the effect of coming standards on industry's cybersecurity*. Nextgov/FCW. www.nextgov.com/cybersecurity/2022/09/cisa-plans-measure-effect-coming-standards-industrys-cybersecurity/377363/

Baksh, M. (2022). *Critical update: Flashback to the government's cloud anxiety, even before SolarWinds*. Nextgov/FCW. www.nextgov.com/podcasts/2022/03/critical-update-flashback-governments-cloud-anxiety-even-solarwinds/362827/

Baksh, M. (2022). *DHS commits to better Intel sharing with law enforcement, points to mobile app*. Nextgov/FCW. www.nextgov.com/analytics-data/2022/08/dhs-commits-better-intel-sharing-law-enforcement-points-mobile-app/376147/

Baksh, M. (2022). *FCC adds China-linked telecom providers to list of national security threats*. Nextgov/FCW. www.nextgov.com/cybersecurity/2022/09/fcc-adds-china-linked-telecom-providers-list-national-security-threats/377418/

Baksh, M. (2022). *IRS suggests need to disclose crypto exchange information to law enforcement*. Nextgov/FCW. www.nextgov.com/cybersecurity/2022/02/irs-suggests-need-disclose-crypto-exchange-information-law-enforcement/361666/

Baksh, M. (2022). *National cybersecurity review begins for all levels of government*. Nextgov/FCW. www.nextgov.com/cybersecurity/2022/10/national-cybersecurity-review-begins-all-levels-government/377982/

Baksh, M. (2022). *Preparations for quantum cyber threat get a Senate boost*. Nextgov/FCW. www.nextgov.com/cybersecurity/2022/12/preparations-quantum-cyber-threat-get-senate-boost/380698/

Baksh, M. (2022). *Senators applaud intelligence leader's commitment to declassification reform*. Nextgov/FCW. www.nextgov.com/analytics-data/2022/10/senators-applaud-intelligence-leaders-commitment-declassification-reform/378951/

Baksh, M. (2022). *The federal government is moving on memory safety for cybersecurity*. Nextgov/FCW. www.nextgov.com/cybersecurity/2022/12/federal-government-moving-memory-safety-cybersecurity/381275/

Baksh, M. (2022). *What CISA wants critical infrastructure partners to report on cyber incidents*. Nextgov/FCW. www.nextgov.com/cybersecurity/2022/04/what-cisa-wants-critical-infrastructure-partners-report-cyber-incidents/365742/

Balasubramanian, R., Libarikian, A., & McElhaney, D. (2021, July 1). *Insurance 2030—The impact of AI on the future of insurance*. McKinsey & Company.

Bambury, B. (2017, January 6). *A.I. expert David Levy says a human will marry a robot by 2050*. CBC. www.cbc.ca/radio/day6/episode-319-becoming-kevin-o-leary-saving-shaker-music-google-renewables-marrying-robots-and-more-1.3921088/a-i-expert-david-levy-says-a-human-will-marry-a-robot-by-2050-1.3921101

Bansemer, J., Chowdhury, R., Dempsey, J. X., Elliott, J., Frase, H., Grant, C. D., Hermanek, S., Leong, B., Liaghati, C., Lohn, A., Martinez, C., Musser, M., Regan, M., Rodriguez, M., Rohrer, D., Siva Kumar, R. S., & Spring, J. (2023, April). *Adversarial machine learning and cybersecurity: Risks, challenges, and legal implications*. Center for Security and Emerging Technology. https://cset.georgetown.edu/publication/adversarial-machine-learning-and-cybersecurity/

Barbaro, M. (2022). The rise of workplace surveillance. *The New York Times*.

Barbaschow, A. (2018, March 12). *AI "more dangerous than nukes": Elon Musk still firm on regulatory oversight*. ZDNet. www.zdnet.com/article/more-dangerous-than-nukes-elon-musk-still-firm-on-regulatory-oversight-of-ai/

Barbaschow, A. (2018, April 4). *Researchers boycott Korean university over "killer robot" AI weapons lab*. ZDNet.

Barber, S. J., & Hassan, A. (2021, May 13). The effects of repetition frequency on the illusory truth effect. *Cognitive Research: Principles and Implications*.

Barr, K., & Cameron, D. (2022). *FTC is exploring ways to crack down on Big Tech's obsession with user data*. Gizmodo. https://gizmodo.com/ftc-big-tech-user-data-data-brokers-1849400843

Barrett, K., & Greene, R. (2022). *The future of state and local government jobs*. Route Fifty. www.route-fifty.com/management/2022/10/future-state-and-local-government-jobs/379050/

Bastone, N. (2022). *Exclusive: Free robo-rides for USF students*. Axios. www.axios.com/local/san-francisco/2022/12/14/free-cruise-driverless-rides-university-sf-students

Bastone, N., & Dickey, M. (2023). *Battle of the robots: Waymo vs. Cruise*. Axios. www.axios.com/local/san-francisco/2023/02/28/san-francisco-waymo-cruise

Bateman, J., & Jackson, D. (2024). *COUNTERING DISINFORMATION EFFECTIVELY—An evidence based policy guide*. Carnegie Endowment for International Peace. https://carnegieendowment.org/files/Carnegie_Countering_Disinformation_Effectively.pdf

Bauder, D. (2022). *BBC tries to understand politics by creating fake Americans*. AP News.

BBC. (2020, May 30). *Microsoft "to replace journalists with robots."* www.bbc.com/news/world-us-canada-52860247

BBC. (2021, January 7). *Facial recognition identifies people wearing masks*. www.bbc.com/news/technology-55573802

BBC. (2021, February 2). *Is Russia targeting CIA spies with secret weapons?* www.bbc.com/news/world-europe-55854458

BBC. (2021, April 21). *Mexico cartel used explosive drones to attack police.* www. bbc.com/news/world-latin-america-56814501

BBC. (2021, December 21). *Boeing and Airbus warn US over 5G safety concerns.* www.bbc.com/news/business-59737194

BBC. (2022, January 6). *Drone helps save cardiac arrest patient in Sweden.* www. bbc.com/news/technology-59885656

BBC. (2022, January 13). *"Havana syndrome": US baffled after new cases in Europe.* www.bbc.com/news/world-us-canada-59986297

BBC. (2022, May 25). *Female avatar sexually assaulted in Meta VR platform, campaigners say.* www.bbc.com/news/technology-61573661

BBC. (2022, August 29). *Undeclared pools in France uncovered by AI technology.* www.bbc.co.uk/news/world-europe-62717599

BBC. (2023, December 8). *AI: EU agrees landmark deal on regulation of artificial intelligence.* www.bbc.com/news/world-europe-67668469

BBC. (2023). *Artificial Intelligence police van detects drivers using mobile phones.* www.bbc.com/news/uk-england-hampshire-66320176

BBC. (2023). *ChatGPT owner in probe over risks around false answers.* www.bbc. com/news/business-66196223

BBC. (2023). *Paris 2024 Olympics: Concern over French plan for AI surveillance.* www.bbc.com/news/world-europe-66122743

BBC. (2023). *Russia-linked hackers a threat to UK infrastructure, warns minister.* www.bbc.com/news/uk-65319771

BBC. (2023). *The tech flaw that lets hackers control surveillance cameras.* www. bbc.com/news/technology-65975446

BBC. (2024, February 7). *The AI companions you can have conversations with.* www.bbc.co.uk/news/business-68165762

Beall, M., Harris, E., & Harris, J. (2024, February 26). *Defense in depth: An action plan to increase the safety and security of advanced AI.* Gladstone AI Inc.

Beblock, F. (2023). *The quantum apocalypse is not yet upon us, but we need to be ready for it.* Incyber. https://incyber.org/en/quantum-apocaly pse-is-not-yet-upon-us-but-we-need-to-be-ready-for-it/

Becker, J. (2019, August 10). The global machine behind the rise of far-right nationalism. *The New York Times.* www.nytimes.com/2019/08/10/world/eur ope/sweden-immigration-nationalism.html

Ben-Moshe, S., Gekker, G., & Cohen, G. (2022). *OpwnAI: AI that can save the day or hack it away.* Check Point Research. https://research.checkpoint.com/ 2022/opwnai-ai-that-can-save-the-day-or-hack-it-away/

Bennet, M., & Welch, P. (2023). *Digital Platform Commission Act of 2023.* www.bennet.senate.gov/public/_cache/files/1/2/12ae84c9-04fa-4fce-afef-b83726ef0b8b/7D763FFDBE9EEE69451A7C26EFCAC0F8.2023-dpca-one-pager.pdf

Bennett, A. (2023). *Ransomware attacks pose communications dilemmas for local governments.* CSO Online. www.csoonline.com/article/643632/ ransomware-attacks-pose-communications-dilemmas-for-local-governme nts.html

Benson, E. (2020). *The human program: A transatlantic AI agenda.* Bertelsmann Foundation. Human_Program_FINAL.pdf

Berenson, T. (2016, December 26). *Humans marrying robots? Experts say it's really coming.* Fortune. https://fortune.com/2016/12/26/human-robot-love-marriage-relationships/

Bergen, P., & Sterman, D. (2019, August 5). The real terrorist threat in America. *Foreign Affairs.* www.foreignaffairs.com/articles/united-states/2018-10-30/real-terrorist-threat-america

Bernhard, A. (2023). *What's standing in the way of the flying car.* BBC. www.bbc.com/future/article/20230714-whats-standing-in-the-way-of-the-flying-car

Bertrand, A., Bakshi, S., & McQueen, J. (2022). *How can government workers and technology align to serve future citizens.* EY Global. www.ey.com/en_gl/government-digital-innovation/how-can-government-workers-and-technology-align-to-serve-future-citizens

Bertuzzi, L. (2022, February 3). *European Commission sets out a plan to regain clout in standard-setting.* Euractiv. www.euractiv.com/section/digital/news/european-commission-sets-out-a-plan-to-regain-clout-in-standard-setting/

Bertuzzi, L. (2022). *EU sets out plan for Cyber Defence Policy.* Euractiv. www.euractiv.com/section/cybersecurity/news/eu-sets-out-plan-for-cyber-defence-policy/

Bertuzzi, L. (2022). *Leading lawmakers pitch extending scope of AI rulebook to the metaverse.* Euractiv. www.euractiv.com/section/digital/news/leading-lawmakers-pitch-extending-scope-of-ai-rulebook-to-the-metaverse/

Bertuzzi, L. (2023). *AI Act enters final phase of EU legislative process.* Euractiv. www.euractiv.com/section/artificial-intelligence/news/ai-act-enters-final-phase-of-eu-legislative-process/

Best, J. (2018, November 15). *AI and the NHS: How artificial intelligence will change everything for patients and doctors.* ZDNet. www.zdnet.com/article/ai-in-the-nhs-how-artificial-intelligence-will-change-everything-for-patients-and-doctors/

Best, J. (2020, April 9). *AI and the coronavirus fight: How artificial intelligence is taking on COVID-19.* ZDNet. www.zdnet.com/article/ai-and-the-coronavirus-fight-how-artificial-intelligence-is-taking-on-covid-19/

Bettiza, S. (2021, October 21). *God and robots: Will AI transform religion?* BBC. https://bbc.com/news/av/technology-58983047

Bhuiyan, J. (2021, February 4). *Facial recognition may help find Capitol rioters— But it could harm many others, experts say.* Axios. www.latimes.com/business/technology/story/2021-02-04/facial-recognition-surveillance-capitol-riot-black-and-brown-communities

Bickley, O. (2023). *AI scam calls imitating familiar voices are a growing problem— Here's how they work.* Route Fifty. www.route-fifty.com/emerging-tech/2023/07/ai-scam-calls-imitating-familiar-voices-are-growing-problemheres-how-they-work/388509/

Biddle, S. (2018, December 6). *Artificial intelligence experts issue urgent warning against facial scanning with a "dangerous history."* The Intercept. https://theintercept.com/2018/12/06/artificial-intellgience-experts-issue-urgent-warning-against-facial-scanning-with-a-dangerous-history/

Bindu, R., Fang, R., Gupta, A., & Kang, D. (2024, April 17). *LLM agents can autonomously exploit one-day vulnerabilities.* arXiv. https://arxiv.org/html/2404.08144v2

Bing, C., & Satter, R. (2023). *North Korean hackers breached a US tech company to steal crypto.* Reuters. www.reuters.com/technology/n-korea-hackers-breac hed-us-it-company-bid-steal-crypto-sources-2023-07-20/

Bingen, K. A., Johnson, K., & Young, M. (2023, April). *Space threat assessment 2023: A report of the CSIS Aerospace Security Project.* Center for Strategic & International Studies. www.csis.org/analysis/space-threat-assessment-2023

Board, E. (2017, August 31). Opinion | Trump's Homeland Security department gives right-wing extremists a pass. *The Washington Post.* www.washingtonp ost.com/opinions/trumps-homeland-security-department-gives-right-wing-extremists-a-pass/2017/08/31/a0164ab4-8455-11e7-ab27-1a21a8e006ab_st ory.html

Bomey, N. (2022, April 5). *Banks and government edge closer to active role in crypto.* Axios. www.axios.com/2022/04/05/cryptocurrency-regulat ion-banks-axios-whats-next

Bommasani, R., Klyman, K., Zhang, D., & Liang, P. (2023). *Do foundation model providers comply with the draft EU AI Act?* Stanford University CRFM. https:// crfm.stanford.edu/2023/06/15/eu-ai-act.html

Boutin, C. (2022). *U.S. Department of Commerce appoints members for new Internet of Things Advisory Board.* NIST. www.nist.gov/news-events/news/ 2022/10/us-department-commerce-appoints-members-new-internet-things-advisory-board

Bowman, T. (2021). *Capitol riot prompts a reckoning over extremism in the ranks.* Main Public. www.mainepublic.org/post/capitol-riot-prompts-reckoning-over-extremism-ranks

Boyd, A. (2019). *GAO launches new unit to prepare congress for the future.* Nextgov/FCW. www.nextgov.com/emerging-tech/2019/09/gao-launches-new-unit-prepare-congress-future/159810/

Boyd, A. (2020). *Policing reform bill would prohibit embedding facial recognition in body cameras.* Nextgov/FCW. www.nextgov.com/emerging-tech/2020/06/ policing-reform-bill-would-prohibit-embedding-facial-recognition-body-came ras/166020/

Boyd, A. (2021). *South Korea to add robots-on-rails and AI surveillance to DMZ border.* Nextgov/FCW. www.nextgov.com/emerging-tech/2021/06/south-korea-add-robots-rails-and-ai-surveillance-dmz-border/174734/

Boyd, A. (2021). *State to supply Costa Rican police with drones to crack down on drug trade.* Nextgov/FCW. www.nextgov.com/emerging-tech/2021/08/state-sup ply-costa-rican-police-drones-crack-down-drug-trade/184343/

Boyd, A. (2022, August 16). *Trade agency wants to know where the U.S. stands in global AI marketplace.* Nextgov/FCW. www.nextgov.com/emerging-tech/ 2022/08/trade-agency-wants-know-where-us-stands-global-ai-marketplace/ 375901/

Boyd, A. (2023, January 9). *Air Force wants to add facial recognition to automated base entrance.* Nextgov/FCW. www.nextgov.com/emerging-tech/2023/01/air-force-wants-add-facial-recognition-automated-base-entrance/381591/

Boyd, A. (2023, February 8). *Experts question value of federal cybersecurity data capture mandate.* Nextgov/FCW. www.nextgov.com/cybersecurity/2023/02/ experts-question-value-federal-cybersecurity-data-capture-mandate/382738/

Boyd, A. (2023, May 9). *TSA says its drone program won't collect much info on the public*. Nextgov/FCW. www.nextgov.com/analytics-data/2023/05/tsa-says-its-drone-program-wont-collect-much-info-public/386122/

Boyd, A. (2023, July 10). *Gao launches new unit to prepare Congress for the future*. Nextgov/FCW. www.nextgov.com/emerging-tech/2019/09/gao-launches-new-unit-prepare-congress-future/159810/

Boyd, A. (2023, July 10). *NASA Science Directorate wants help prioritizing what digital resources it should open-source first*. Nextgov/FCW. www.nextgov.com/analytics-data/2023/01/nasa-science-directorate-wants-help-prioritizing-what-digital-resources-it-should-open-source-first/381501/

Braverman, A. (2023). *Notes from a CSIS virtual event: AI and AVs: Implications in U.S.–China competition*. Center for Strategic & International Studies. www.csis.org/blogs/strategic-technologies-blog/notes-csis-virtual-event-ai-and-avs-implications-us-china

Breeden II, J. (2022). *Artificial intelligence continues to evolve in government and elsewhere*. Nextgov/FCW. www.nextgov.com/emerging-tech/2022/09/artificial-intelligence-continues-evolve-government-and-elsewhere/376811/

Breeden II, J. (2022). *Clouds of smart robots swarm into reality*. Nextgov/FCW. www.nextgov.com/emerging-tech/2022/01/clouds-smart-robots-swarm-reality/361130/

Breeden II, J. (2022). *NASA's videogames serve multiple purposes*. Nextgov/FCW. www.nextgov.com/ideas/2022/11/nasa-doubles-down-gaming/380180/

Breeden II, J. (2022). *New research points to hidden vulnerabilities within machine learning systems*. Nextgov/FCW. www.nextgov.com/cybersecurity/2022/08/new-research-points-hidden-vulnerabilities-within-machine-learning-systems/375713/

Breeden II, J. (2022). *One of the most powerful AIs ever created makes its public debut*. Nextgov/FCW. www.nextgov.com/emerging-tech/2022/12/one-most-powerful-ais-ever-created-makes-its-public-debut/380760/

Breeden II, J. (2022). *Vote now for the future of robotics*. Nextgov/FCW. www.nextgov.com/emerging-tech/2022/10/vote-now-future-robotics/377950/

Breeden II, J. (2023, March 22). *From ChatGPT-3.5 to ChatGPT-4: A quantum leap in natural language processing and multimodal capabilities*. Nextgov/FCW. www.nextgov.com/emerging-tech/2023/03/chatgpt-35-chatgpt-4-quantum-leap-natural-language-processing-and-multimodal-capabilities/384296/

Breeden II, J. (2023, April 10). *Artificial intelligence and drone tactics maneuver into advanced military simulations*. Nextgov/FCW. www.nextgov.com/ideas/2023/04/artificial-intelligence-and-drone-tactics-maneuver-advanced-military-simulations/384942/

Breeden II, J. (2023, May 5). *3 Updates: Hackers eye ChatGPT, virtual military training gets photorealistic and NASA picks its simulation winners*. Nextgov/FCW. www.nextgov.com/emerging-tech/2023/05/3-updates-hackers-look-exploit-chatgpt-virtual-military-training-gets-photorealistic-and-nasa-picks-its-simulation-winners/385993/

Breeden II, J. (2023, June 16). *NASA steps closer to perfecting super-fast internet in deep space*. Nextgov/FCW. www.nextgov.com/emerging-tech/2023/06/nasa-steps-closer-perfecting-super-fast-internet-deep-space/387609/

Breeden II, J. (2023, July 10). *New research points to hidden vulnerabilities within machine learning systems.* Nextgov/FCW. www.nextgov.com/cybersecurity/2022/08/new-research-points-hidden-vulnerabilities-within-machine-learning-systems/375713/

Breeden II, J. (2023, July 10). *What AI-powered robots have to say about their future with humanity.* Nextgov/FCW. www.nextgov.com/artificial-intelligence/2023/07/what-ai-powered-robots-have-say-about-their-future-humanity/388334/

Breeden II, J. (2023, July 31). *As drone popularity grows, government considers how to safeguard the skies.* Nextgov/FCW. www.nextgov.com/emerging-tech/2023/07/drone-popularity-grows-government-considers-how-safeguard-skies/388963/

Breeden II, J. (2023, August 23). *National intelligence office issues cyber warning for government and commercial satellites.* Nextgov/FCW. www.nextgov.com/cybersecurity/2023/08/national-intelligence-office-issues-cyber-warning-government-and-commercial-satellites/389649/

Breeden II, J. (2023, September 20). *Companies turn to risk mitigation tools to monitor AI absent federal law, study finds.* Nextgov/FCW. www.nextgov.com/artificial-intelligence/2023/09/companies-turn-risk-mitigation-tools-monitor-ai-absent-federal-law-study-finds/390382/

Breeden II, J. (2023, October 20). *AI concerns continue as governments look for the right mix of regulations and protections.* Nextgov/FCW. www.nextgov.com/artificial-intelligence/2023/10/ai-concerns-continue-governments-look-right-mix-regulations-and-protections/391407/

Breeden II, J. (2023, November 29). *DARPA's massive defensive AI challenge begins in December.* Nextgov/FCW. www.nextgov.com/artificial-intelligence/2023/11/darpas-massive-defensive-ai-challenge-begins-december/392330/

Breeden II, J. (2023, December 27). *3 Government and technology predictions for 2024.* Nextgov/FCW. www.nextgov.com/ideas/2023/12/3-government-and-technology-predictions-2024/392998/

Breeden II, J. (2024, May 14). *Feds beware: New studies demonstrate key AI shortcoming.* Nextgov/FCW. www.nextgov.com/artificial-intelligence/2024/05/feds-beware-new-studies-demonstrate-key-ai-shortcomings/396526/

Brewster, T. (2021). The Russian company protecting Parler from cyberattack: We don't endorse "radical organizations or extremism." *Forbes.* www.forbes.com/sites/thomasbrewster/2021/01/19/the-russian-company-protecting-parler-from-cyberattack-we-dont-endorse-radical-organizations-or-extremism/

Brewster, T., & Nieva, R. (2023, February 3). Google cuts company protecting people from surveillance to a "skeleton crew," say laid off workers. *Forbes.*

Briggs, J., Hatzius, J., Kodnani, D., & Pierdomenico, G. (2023, March 26). *The potentially large effects of artificial intelligence on economic growth.* Goldman Sachs. www.gspublishing.com/content/research/en/reports/2023/03/27/d64e052b-0f6e-45d7-967b-d7be35fabd16.html

Brodbent, J. (2022). *New national cybersecurity strategy: A much-needed overhaul for digital ecosystems.* Nextgov/FCW. www.nextgov.com/ideas/2022/09/new-national-cybersecurity-strategy-much-needed-overhaul-digital-ecosystems/376938/

Brooks, K., & Dhalla, A. (2022). *Consumer cyber readiness report.* Consumer Reports & Aspen Digital.

Brown, E. (2022, January 3). *How will Zuckerberg's Meta plans impact its dominance over social media in 2022?* ZDNet. www.zdnet.com/article/how-will-zuck erbergs-meta-plans-impact-its-dominance-over-social-media-in-2022/

Brown, E. (2022, February 23). *CIPIA brings AI and computer vision monitoring systems to eliminate the dangers of distracted driving.* ZDNet. www.zdnet.com/article/cipia-brings-ai-and-computer-vision-monitor-systems-to-eliminate-the-dangers-of-distracted-driving/

Brown III, T., & Starr, S. (2021, July 27). *AI: The new teacher's pet.* Ozy. www.ozy.com/pg/newsletter/the-daily-dose/437818/

Browne, R. (2023, January 4). *Meta fined over $400 million by top EU regulator for forcing users to accept targeted ads.* CNBC. https://cnb.cx/3VPDaLf

Brunner, S., Canova, G., Schedler, K., & Simmler, M. (2022). Smart criminal justice: Exploring the use of algorithms in the Swiss criminal justice system. *Artificial Intelligence and Law, 31,* 213–237. Springer Nature. https://link.springer.com/article/10.1007/s10506-022-09310-1

Bubeck, S., Chandrasekaran, V., Eldan, R., Gehrke, J., Horvitz, E., Kamar, E., Lee, P., Lee, Y. T., Li, Y., Lundberg, S., Nori, H., Palangi, H., Ribeiro, M. T., & Zhang, Y. (2023). *Sparks of artificial general intelligence early experiments with GPT-4.* Microsoft Research. www.researchgate.net/publication/369449949_Sparks_of_Artificial_General_Intelligence_Early_experiments_with_GPT-4

Buduson, S. (2021, February 10). *Southern Poverty Law Center report ranks Ohio No. 2 in extremist anti-government groups.* ABC News 5. www.news5cleveland.com/news/local-news/investigations/southern-poverty-law-center-report-ranks-ohio-no-2-in-extremist-anti-government-groups

Buitta L., Healy S., Jankowicz N., Smith B., & Stewart C. (2021). *Online event: Civics as a national security imperative: The role of technology.* Center for Strategic & International Studies. www.csis.org/events/online-event-civics-national-security-imperative-role-technology

Bump, P. (2019, May 20). *Law enforcement robotics and drones—5 current applications.* Emerj Artificial Intelligence Research. https://emerj.com/ai-sector-overviews/law-enforcement-robotics-and-drones/

Bureau of Oceans and International Environmental and Scientific Affairs. (2020). *Declaration of the United States of America and the United Kingdom of Great Britain and Northern Ireland on cooperation in artificial intelligence research and development: A shared vision for driving technological breakthroughs in artificial intelligence.* U.S. Department of State. www.state.gov/declaration-of-the-united-states-of-america-and-the-united-kingdom-of-great-britain-and-northern-ireland-on-cooperation-in-artificial-intelligence-research-and-development-a-shared-vision-for-driving/

Burt, A., Hall, P., Greene, K., Perine, L., Schwartz, R., & Vassilev, A. (2022, March). *Towards a standard for identifying and managing bias in artificial intelligence* (NIST Special Publication 1270). U.S. Department of Commerce. https://nvlpubs.nist.gov/nistpubs/SpecialPublications/NIST.SP.1270.pdf

Burton, R. (2023, August 30). *Decoy Dog is no ordinary puppy: Separating a sly DNS malware from the pack.* Infoblox. https://blogs.infoblox.com/cyber-threat-intelligence/decoy-dog-is-no-ordinary-pupy-distinguishing-malw are-via-dns/

Byman, D. L. (2011). *Denying terrorist safe havens: Homeland security efforts to counter threats from Pakistan, Yemen and Somalia.* Brookings. www.brookings.edu/testimonies/denying-terrorist-safe-havens-homeland-security-efforts-to-counter-threats-from-pakistan-yemen-and-somalia/

Byman, D. L. (2018, April 30). *Russia is a state sponsor of terrorism—But don't treat it that way.* Brookings. www.brookings.edu/blog/order-from-chaos/2018/04/30/russia-is-a-state-sponsor-of-terrorism-but-dont-treat-it-that-way/

Byman, D. L. (2021, January 15). *White supremacist terrorism: Key trends to watch in 2021.* Brookings. www.brookings.edu/blog/order-from-chaos/2021/01/15/white-supremacist-terrorism-key-trends-to-watch-in-2021/

Cabral, S., & Macleod, R. (2021, February 8). *Capitol riots: Five takeaways from the arrests.* BBC. www.bbc.com/news/world-us-canada-55987603

Cado Security. (2023, January 25). *Leopard tank announcement prompts cyber retaliation.* www.cadosecurity.com/blog/leopard-tank-announcement-prompts-cyber-retaliation

Cai, S. (2021, December 2). *U.S. faces urgent anti-hacker crisis.* Axios. www.axios.com/2021/12/02/government-business-cyber-jobs

Camello, M., Planty, M., & Houston-Kolnik, J. (2021). *Chatbots in the criminal justice system: An overview of chatbots and their underlying technologies and applications.* National Institute of Justice, Office of Justice Programs, U.S. Department of Justice. www.rti.org/publication/chatbots-criminal-justice-system

Cameron, D. (2023). *The US is openly stockpiling dirt on all its citizens.* WIRED. www.wired.com/story/odni-commercially-available-information-report/

Cameron, D., & Barr, K. (2022, August 11). *FTC is exploring ways to crack down on Big Tech's obsession with user data.* Gizmodo. https://gizmodo.com/ftc-big-tech-user-data-data-brokers-1849400843

Cameron, D., & Mehortra, D. (2023, November 20). *Secretive White House Surveillance Program gives cops access to trillions of US phone records.* WIRED.

Cameron, R., Powell, A., & Stratton, G. (2018). *Digital criminology: Crime and Justice in digital society.* Routledge Taylor & Francis Group.

Campbell, T. (2019, July). *Artificial intelligence: An Overview of state initiatives.* FutureGrasp, LLC.

Campbell, T. A. (2019, October 7). *Toward digital power over states.* Atlantic Council. www.atlanticcouncil.org/blogs/new-atlanticist/toward-digital-power-over-states/

Cann, H. (2023). *Ending the deepfake threat to elections before it starts.* Route Fifty. www.route-fifty.com/emerging-tech/2023/10/ending-deepfake-threat-elections-it-starts/391431/

Canova, G., Schedler, K., & Simmler, M. (2021). Smart criminal justice: Phenomena and normative requirements. *International Review of Administrative Sciences, 89,* 415–432. https://journals.sagepub.com/doi/full/10.1177/0020852321 1039740

Cardwell, H. (2023). *Government ministry blocks AI technology from staff use.* ITBrief Australia. https://itbrief.com.au/story/government-ministry-blocks-ai-tec hnology-from-staff-use

Carless, W. (2021). *"This was really big": Far-right extremist groups use Capitol attack to recruit new members.* USA TODAY. www.usatoday.com/story/news/ nation/2021/01/07/us-capitol-riots-used-extremists-recruit-new-pro-gun-memb ers/6588908002/

Carney, J. (2023). *House GOP warns FBI to stay out of controversial surveillance talks.* POLITICO. www.politico.com/news/2023/04/24/fbi-fueling-hill-surveilla nce-angst-00093323

Carpenter, M. (2018, August 29). Russia is co-opting angry young men. *The Atlantic.* www.theatlantic.com/ideas/archive/2018/08/russia-is-co-opting-angry-young-men/568741/

Cassauwers, T. (2019, March 28). *How Confucianism could put fears about arti-ficial intelligence to bed.* Ozy. www.ozy.com/the-new-and-the-next/how-confu cianism-could-put-fears-about-artificial-intelligence-to-bed/93206/

Centeno, M., Cohen, M., Mahmood, S., Paki, P., Platt, J., Robertshaw, G., Schoonover, R., Talbot, B., & Trovato, J. (2022, August). *Electromagnetic pulse shielding mitigations.* Department of Homeland Security Science & Technology. www.dhs.gov/sites/default/files/2022-09/22_0902_st_emp_mitigation_best_pr actices.pdf

Center for Court Innovation. (2018, June 19). *The 10 principles for criminal justice technology—(Re)Thinking Tech.* Medium. https://medium.com/re-think ing-tech/the-10-principles-for-criminal-justice-technology-1627596f4774

Center for Digital Government Research Report. (2022). *A new chapter in con-nectivity.* https://papers.govtech.com/A-New-Chapter-in-Connectivity-Security-and-Resilience-Drive-Network-Modernization--141631.html

Center for Strategic & International Studies. (2020, April 20). *Synthetic biology and national security: Risks and opportunities* (PART 1 of 2). www.csis.org/analy sis/synthetic-biology-and-national-security-risks-and-opportunities-part-1-2

Center for Strategic & International Studies. (2021, January). *Maintaining the intelligence edge: Reimagining and reinventing intelligence through innovation.* www.csis.org/analysis/maintaining-intelligence-edge-reimagining-and-reinvent ing-intelligence-through-innovation

Center for Strategic & International Studies. (2022, November 21). *Innovation insights | Why technology standards matter.* YouTube. www.youtube.com/ watch?app=desktop&v=EcZlZG9nsLk&t=1s

Center for Strategic & International Studies. (2023, June 21). *Senator Chuck Schumer launches SAFE innovation in the AI age at CSIS* (Transcript, Online Event). www.csis.org/analysis/sen-chuck-schumer-launches-safe-innovat ion-ai-age-csis

Center for Strategic & International Studies. (2023, July 25). *National security and spectrum for 5G.* www.csis.org/analysis/national-security-and-spect rum-5g

Center for Strategic & International Studies. (2023). *AI in national security.* www. csis.org/executive-education/courses/ai-national-security

Center for Strategic & International Studies. (2023). *The Biden administration's cyber plans for critical infrastructure.* YouTube. www.youtube.com/@csis

Center for Strategic & International Studies. (2024). *Global foresight: Preparing for future trends.*

Centre for Data Ethics and Innovation. (2020, November). *Review into bias in algorithmic decision-making.* https://assets.publishing.service.gov.uk/media/60142096d3bf7f70ba377b20/Review_into_bias_in_algorithmic_decision-making.pdf

Centre for the New Economy and Society. (2018). *The future of jobs report.* www3.weforum.org/docs/WEF_Future_of_Jobs_2018.pdf

Chafkin, M. (2020, May 27). *U.S. will join G-7 AI pact, citing threat from China.* Yahoo Finance. https://finance.yahoo.com/news/u-join-g-7-ai-000003648.html

Chakravorti, B. (2023). *How will AI affect workers? Tech waves of the past show how unpredictable the path can be.* Route Fifty. www.route-fifty.com/workforce/2023/06/how-will-ai-affect-workers-tech-waves-past-show-how-unpredictable-path-can-be/387789/

Chang, B., & Daniels, M. (2021, July). *National power after AI.* Center for Security and Emerging Technology. https://cset.georgetown.edu/publication/national-power-after-ai/

Chanthadavong, A. (2020, June 28). *Australian government sinks AU$19 million into AI health research projects.* ZDNet. www.zdnet.com/article/australian-government-sinks-au19-million-into-ai-health-research-projects/

Chanthadavong, A. (2020, September 15). *Dystech using artificial intelligence to help speed screening for learning disorders.* ZDNet. www.zdnet.com/article/dystech-using-artificial-intelligence-to-help-speed-

Chanthadavong, A. (2021, February 10). *Artificial intelligence can influence human decision-making, new Data61 study reveals.* ZDNet. www.zdnet.com/article/artificial-intelligence-can-influence-human-decision-making-new-data61-study-reveals/

Chanthadavong, A. (2022, February 16). *Nvidia and Jaguar Land Rover to build automated software-defined cars from 2025.* ZDNet. www.zdnet.com/article/nvidia-and-jaguar-land-rover-to-build-automated-software-defined-cars-from-2025/

Chappell, B. (2015, July 28). *Researchers warn against "autonomous weapons" arms race.* NPR. www.npr.org/sections/thetwo-way/2015/07/28/427189235/researchers-warn-against-autonomous-weapons-arms-race

Charles, J. B. (2019, March 19). *NYPD's big artificial-intelligence reveal.* Governing. www.governing.com/archive/gov-new-york-police-nypd-data-artificial-intelligence-patternizr.html

Chasan, A. (2023). *Ethical hacker scams 60 minutes staffer to show how easy digital theft is.* CBS News. www.cbsnews.com/news/how-digital-theft-targets-people-from-millennials-to-seniors-60-minutes-2023-05-21/

Chatterjee, M. (2022). *Shadowboxing and geopolitics on the dark web.* POLITICO. www.politico.com/news/2022/12/11/russia-politics-cybercrime-darknet-00073400

Chen, S. (2023). *Senate passes bill to ban TikTok on government devices*. Axios. www.axios.com/2022/12/15/tiktok-ban-government-senate

Chen, Y. (2023). *Why blockchain is a key technology for state and local governments*. Route Fifty. www.route-fifty.com/tech-data/2023/06/blockchain-key-technology-computer-scientist-explains-why-post-crypto-crash-future-bright/387169/

Chief Digital and Artificial Intelligence Office. (2019). *About the Jaic*. www.ai.mil/about.html

Chin, C. (2022, June 16). *A Privacy Perspective on the United States and European Union: This does not compute*. CSIS podcasts. www.csis.org/podcasts/does-not-compute/privacy-perspective-united-states-and-european-union

Chin, C. (2022, August 11). *The United Kingdom's online safety bill exposes a disinformation divide*. Center for Strategic & International Studies. www.csis.org/analysis/united-kingdoms-online-safety-bill-exposes-disinformation-divide

Chin, C. (2022, August 25). *Disability discrimination and automated surveillance technologies*. Center for Strategic & International Studies. www.csis.org/podcasts/does-not-compute/disability-discrimination-and-automated-surveillance-technologies

Chin-Rothmann, C. (2022). *U.S. digital privacy troubles do not start or end with TikTok*. Center for Strategic & International Studies. www.csis.org/analysis/us-digital-privacy-troubles-do-not-start-or-end-tiktok

Chitneni, A. (2020, November). Study of emerging trends on latest technologies and its cybersecurity challenges. *Journal for Innovative Development in Pharmaceutical and Technical Science (JIDPTS), 3*. https://jidps.com/wp-content/uploads/2020/11/STUDY-OF-EMERGING-TRENDS-ON-LATEST-TECHNOLOGIES-AND-ITS-CYBERSECURITY-CHALLENGES.pdf

Chong, B., & Daniels, M. (2021, July). *National power after AI*. Center for Security and Emerging Technology. https://cset.georgetown.edu/publication/national-power-after-ai/

Chorost, M. (2016, April 18). *Let artificial intelligence evolve*. Slate. https://slate.com/technology/2016/04/the-philosophical-argument-against-artificial-intelligence-killing-us-all.html

Christain, A. (2023). *The employees secretly using AI at work*. BBC. www.bbc.com/worklife/article/20231017-the-employees-secretly-using-ai-at-work

Christakis, N. A. (2019, April). How AI will rewire us. *The Atlantic*. www.theatlantic.com/magazine/archive/2019/04/robots-human-relationships/583204/

Christian, A. (2022). *The rise of the "chief remote officer."* BBC. https://bbc.com/worklife/article/20221027-the-rise-of-the-chief-remote-officer

Christian, A. (2023, December 27). *Panic and possibility: What workers learned about AI in 2023*. BBC. www.bbc.com/worklife/article/20231219-panic-and-possibility-what-workers-learned-about-ai-in-2023

Chronicle, D., & Murali, J. (2018, November 5). *Rise of the police robots*. Deccan Chronicle. www.deccanchronicle.com/amp/nation/current-affairs/051118/rise-of-the-police-robots.html

Cimeliere, O. (2023). *Usernames and passwords at the heart of cyber threats*. InCyber. https://incyber.org/en/fic-2023-usernames-passwords-heart-cyber-threats/

CISA. (2022). *CISA 2025 factsheet update.* DocumentCloud. https://s3.docume
ntcloud.org/documents/23166907/cisa-2025-factsheet-update.pdf

CISA. (2022). *Combating cyber crime.* www.cisa.gov/combating-cyber-crime

CISA. (2022). *Cross-Sector cybersecurity performance goals.* www.cisa.gov/cpg

CISA. (2023). *U.S. and international partners publish secure-by-design and -
default principles and approaches.* www.cisa.gov/news-events/news/us-and-
international-partners-publish-secure-design-and-default-principles-and-app
roaches

City of Rockford. (2022). Rockford reaches functional zero for its homeless population. *The Atlas.* https://the-atlas.com/projects/rockford-functional-zero-homel
essness

Clark, A. P. (2023, February 17). *One big thing: AI's dual role in the future of
cyber.* Axios.

Clark, J. (2023, September 28). *AI security center to open at national security
agency.* U.S. Department of Defense. www.defense.gov/News/News-Stories/Arti
cle/Article/3541838/ai-security-center-to-open-at-national-security-agency/

Clark, P. (2023). *As Tax Day nears, AI chatbots like ChatGPT gives scammers a
boost.* Axios. www.axios.com/2023/04/13/tax-scams-irs-ai-chatbot-chatgpt

Clark, S., Lamond, J., & Nandkumar, K. (2020). *4 first steps for congress to
address white supremacist terrorism.* Center for American Progress. www.ameri
canprogress.org/issues/security/reports/2020/10/30/492095/4-first-steps-congr
ess-address-white-supremacist-terrorism/

Clasen, A. (2023). *IBM plans first European quantum computing centre in
Germany.* Euractiv Germany. www.euractiv.com/section/industrial-strategy/
news/ibm-plans-first-european-quantum-computing-centre-in-germany/

Clasen, A. (2024, February 8). *EU Parliament supports automated data exchange
for police cooperation, despite concerns.* Euractiv. www.euractiv.com/section/
digital/news/eu-parliament-supports-automated-data-exchange-for-police-coop
eration-despite-concerns/

Clayton, J. (2021, November 29). *China surveillance of journalists to use "traffic-
light" system.* BBC News. www.bbc.com/news/technology-59441379

Clayton, J. (2022, August 11). *Meta's chatbot says the company "exploits people."*
BBC. www.bbc.com/news/technology-62497674

Clayton, J. (2023). *AI scanner used in hundreds of US schools misses knives.* BBC.
www.bbc.com/news/technology-65342798

Clayton, J., & Hooker, L. (2023). *White House: Big Tech bosses told to protect
public from AI risks.* BBC. www.bbc.com/news/business-65489163

Clozel, L. (2018, June 19). In the name of security, banks share information. *The
Wall Street Journal.* www.wsj.com/articles/in-the-name-of-security-banks-share-
information-1529460061

Cluskey, P. (2017, October 3). Social media evidence a game-changer in war crimes
trial. *The Irish Times.* www.irishtimes.com/news/world/europe/social-media-
evidence-a-game-changer-in-war-crimes-trial-1.3243098

Coats, D. R. (2019, January 29). *Worldwide threat assessment of the US intelligence community.* Director of National Intelligence. www.dni.gov/files/ODNI/
documents/2019-ATA-SFR---SSCI.pdf

Cobler, N. (2022, February 9). *LA-based Coco, a remotely piloted Delivery Service, expands to Austin.* Axios. www.axios.com/local/austin/2022/02/09/coco-food-delivery-bots-austin

Cobler, N. (2023). *Long Center to unveil 3D-printed pavilion.* Axios. www.axios.com/local/austin/2023/03/08/long-center-to-unveil-3d-printed-pavilion

Cockrell, C. (2017). *Russian actions and methods against the United States and NATO.* Military Review. www.armyupress.army.mil/Journals/Military-Review/Online-Exclusive/2017-Online-Exclusive-Articles/Russian-Actions-and-Methods/

Cohen, Z. (2020). *Whistleblower accuses Trump appointees of downplaying Russian interference and White supremacist threat.* CNN. www.cnn.com/2020/09/09/politics/dhs-whistleblower-white-supremacist-threat/index.html

Columbia Engineering. (2021). *What is blockchain? A beginner's guide for 2021.* https://bootcamp.cvn.columbia.edu/blog/what-is-blockchain-beginners-guide/

Columbia Engineering. (2021). *What is financial technology (FinTech)? A beginner's guide.* https://bootcamp.cvn.columbia.edu/blog/what-is-fintech/

Committee on Homeland Security. (2022, June 28). *Combating ransomware: From our small towns in Michigan to DC.* https://homeland.house.gov/activities/hearings/combating-ransomware-from-our-small-towns-in-michigan-to-dc

Community Control of Police Surveillance (CCOPS). (n.d). *Electronic Frontier Foundation.* www.eff.org/issues/community-control-police-surveillance-ccops

Condon, S. (2022, January 24). *Meta says it will soon have the world's fastest AI supercomputer.* ZDNet. www.zdnet.com/article/meta-says-it-will-soon-have-the-worlds-fastest-ai-supercomputer/

Condon, S. (2022, June 9). *NASA is going to study UFOs. Here's why.* ZDNet. www.zdnet.com/article/nasa-is-starting-a-new-study-into-uaps-aka-ufos-it-says-its-not-selling-out/

Condon, S. (2022, September 15). *US senator reveals how US Customs has amassed data from Americans' devices.* ZDNet. www.zdnet.com/article/us-senator-reveals-how-us-customs-has-amassed-data-from-americans-devices/

Congress of the United States. (2024, January 24). *Letter to DOJ Predictive Policing and Title VI.*

Congress of the United States Office of Technology Assessment. (1989). *Criminal justice, new technologies, and the constitution.* www.ojp.gov/ncjrs/virtual-library/abstracts/criminal-justice-new-technologies-and-constitution-0

Congressional Research Service. (2014). *Russian political, economic, and security issues and U.S. interests* (CRS Report No. RL33407). www.everycrsreport.com/reports/RL33407.html

Congressional Research Service. (2020, November 10). *Artificial intelligence and national security* (CRS Report No. R45178). https://crsreports.congress.gov/product/pdf/R/R45178/10

Congressional Research Service. (2021, November 17). *Defense primer: U.S. policy on lethal autonomous weapon systems.*

Congressional Research Service. (2022, June 3). *Deep fake and national security.* https://crsreports.congress.gov/product/pdf/IF/IF11333

Congressional Research Service. (2023, August 22). *Law enforcement and technology: Use of unmanned aircraft systems.*

Connelly, D. (2022). *(More) Clarity in the clouds—What's needed to secure multi-cloud environments.* Nextgov/FCW. www.nextgov.com/ideas/2022/10/more-clarity-clouds-whats-needed-secure-multi-cloud-environments/378831/

Consumer Product Safety Commission. (2021, May 19). *Report: Artificial intelligence and machine learning in consumer products.*

Contreras, R. (2022, March 1). *Exclusive: Lawmakers express "extreme concern" over border robot dog plan.* Axios. www.axios.com/2022/03/01/border-robot-dog-hispanic-lawmakers-concern

Contreras, R. (2022, October 29). *The limited promise of police data.* Axios. www.axios.com/2022/10/29/police-reform-surveillance-shootings-crime

Contreras, R. (2023, December 12). *U.S. deploys AI in "virtual border wall."* Axios. www.axios.com/2023/12/12/border-patrol-ai-us-mexico-wall-surveillance-virtual

Contreras, R., & Ortiz, K. (2023). *AirTags track car thieves—But you don't have to.* Axios. www.axios.com/2023/05/24/apple-airtags-track-car-thieves-you-dont

Cook, B. J. (2018, June 18). *The ethics of AI: Robots will rise, but will they rule us all?* GeekWire. www.geekwire.com/2018/ethics-ai-robots-will-rise-will-rule-us/amp/

Copeland, T. (2023). *School kids are stealing millions of dollars of NFTs—To buy Roblox skins.* The Block. www.theblock.co/post/235022/phishing-frenzy-school-kids-are-stealing-millions-of-dollars-of-nfts-to-buy-roblox-skins

Corbett, T., & Singer, P. (2023). *Chinese breakthroughs bring quantum tools closer to practicality.* Defense One. www.defenseone.com/ideas/2023/05/chinese-breakthroughs-bring-quantum-tools-closer-practicality/386515/

Cordell, C. (2023, January 3). *IARPA aims to thwart cyberattacks with psychology.* Nextgov/FCW. www.nextgov.com/cybersecurity/2023/01/iarpa-aims-thwart-cyberattacks-psychology/381422/

Cordell, C. (2023, May 5). *Army wants help with safeguarding datasets for AI use.* Nextgov/FCW. www.nextgov.com/emerging-tech/2023/05/army-wants-help-pending-study-about-safeguarding-datasets-aiml-use/386063/

Cordell, C. (2023, June 6). *Worried that your TV is listening to you? IARPA wants to safeguard your voice.* Nextgov/FCW. www.nextgov.com/digital-government/2023/06/worried-your-tv-listening-you-iarpa-wants-safeguard-your-voice/387208/

Cordell, C. (2023, June 8). *New bill proposes warning labels to AI-generated material.* Nextgov/FCW. www.nextgov.com/emerging-tech/2023/06/new-bill-proposes-warning-labels-ai-generated-material/387308/

Cordell, C. (2023, July 24). *CBP wants blockchain capability for its trade portal modernization.* Nextgov/FCW. www.nextgov.com/cxo-briefing/2023/07/cbp-wants-blockchain-capability-its-trade-portal-modernization/388766/

Cordell, C. (2023, August 23). *IARPA's new pants will record your location.* Nextgov/FCW. www.nextgov.com/emerging-tech/2023/08/iarpas-new-pants-will-record-your-location/389654/

Corera, G. (2022, January 20). *Havana syndrome: Most cases not caused by foreign power—CIA.* BBC News. www.bbc.com/news/world-us-canada-60068483

Corn, G., Daskal, J., Goldsmith, J., Inglis, C., & Rosenzweig, P. (2021, February 11). Chinese technology platforms operating in the United States: Assessing the threat. *Joint PIJIP/TLS Research Paper Series*. American University Washington College of Law. Originally published as a joint report of the National Security, Technology, and Law Working Group at the Hoover Institution at Stanford University and the Tech, Law & Security Program at American University Washington College of Law. https://digitalcommons.wcl.american.edu

Corrigan, J. (2019). *Artificial intelligence is too dumb to fully police online extremism, experts say*. Nextgov/FCW. www.nextgov.com/emerging-tech/2019/06/artificial-intelligence-too-dumb-fully-police-online-extremism-experts-say/158002/

Cost, B. (2021, November 29). 210 million packages were stolen from Americans this year: Survey. *The New York Post*. https://nypost.com/2021/11/29/210-mill ion-packages-were-stolen-this-year-survey/

Council of Europe. (2019). *European ethical charter on the use of artificial intelligence in judicial systems and their environment*.

Council of Europe. (2020, September 7). *Digital surveillance by intelligence services: States must take action to better protect individuals*. Council of Europe News. www.coe.int/en/web/portal/-/digital-surveillance-by-intelligence-services-states-must-take-action-to-better-protect-individuals

Counter Extremism Project. (2021). *U.S. White supremacy groups in the United States* (pp. 1–71). https://static1.squarespace.com/static/5b7ea2794cde7a79e 7c00582/t/62ee655b4051a3475aa73795/1659790684778/White+Supremacy+ Groups.pdf

Couts, A. (2024, January 24). *Ring will stop giving cops a free pass on warrantless video requests*. WIRED. www.wired.com/story/ring-pol ice-rfa-tool-shut-down/

Cox, J. (2023, January 9). *Ciphr, encrypted app that served organized crime, rebrands as enterprise software*. Vice. www.vice.com/en/article/g5ve7q/ciphr-app-rebrands-as-mode-onyxcorp

Cox, J. (2023, October 26). *SIM swappers are working directly with ransomware gangs now*. 404 Media. www.404media.co/sim-swappers-are-working-directly-with-ransomware-gangs-now/

Cox, J. (2024, January 11). *Hackers break into AI hiring chatbot, could hire and reject fast food applicants*. 404 Media. www.404media.co/hackers-break-into-hiring-ai-chat-bot-chattr/

Cramer, M., & Hauser, C. (2021, February 27). Digidog, a robotic dog used by the police, stirs privacy concerns. *The New York Times*. www.nytimes.com/2021/02/27/nyregion/nypd-robot-dog.html

Cross, S. (2013). Russia and countering violent extremism in the internet and social media: Exploring prospects for U.S.–Russia cooperation beyond the "reset." *Journal of Strategic Security*, 6(4), 1–24. https://doi.org/10.5038/1944-0472.6.4.1

Crowe, C., Mclean, D., Rachal, M., Zukowski, D., & Plautz, J. (2022, January 26). *8 trends shaping cities in 2022*. Smart Cities Dive. www.smartcitiesdive.com/news/8-trends-shaping-cities-in-2022/617763/

Cruickshank, S. (2021, January 14). *Examining the Capitol insurrectionists and the lingering threat of extremist violence*. The Hub. https://hub.jhu.edu/2021/01/14/closer-look-at-capitol-insurrectionists/

CSA Singapore. (2023). *International counter ransomware initiative members come together to strongly discourage ransomware payments.* www.csa.gov.sg/ News-Events/News-Articles/2023/international-counter-ransomware-initiative-members-come-together-to-strongly-discourage-ransomware-payments

Cubuku, S., Sahin, N., Tekin, E., & Topalli, V. (2021, November 16). *The concrete effects of body cameras on police accountability.* Route Fifty. www.route-fifty. com/infrastructure/2021/11/the-concrete-effects-of-body-cameras-on-police-acc ountability/316272/

Cuomo, S., Jensen, B., & Whyte, C. (2023, July 20). *The future of Algorithmic Warfare: Fragmented development.* War on the Rocks. https://warontherocks. com/2023/07/the-future-of-algorithmic-warfare-fragmented-development/

Curi, M., & Solender, A. (2023, June 3). *House Democrats bill would mandate AI disclosure.* Axios. www.axios.com/2023/06/03/house-democrats-ritchie-tor res-ai-disclosure

Curl, M., & Heath, R. (2023, December 12). *Unions are winning protections as AI-powered workplaces grow.* Axios. www.axios.com/2023/12/12/unions-microsoft-ai-battles

Curry, D. (2015, April 9). *IBM testing artificial intelligence software to mimic the human brain.* IT Pro Portal. www.itproportal.com/2015/04/09/ibm-testing-art ificial-intelligence-software-mimic-human-brain/

Cusack, J. (2021, November 29). *How driverless cars will change our world.* BBC. https://bbc.com/future/article/20211126-how-driverless-cars-will-cha nge-our-world

CyberScoop Staff. (2023). *European raid targeted notorious ransomware gang DoppelPaymer.* CyberScoop. https://cyberscoop.com/doppelpaymer-ransomw are-gang-europol-raid/

Cybersecurity and Infrastructure Security Agency. (2023, July 6). *Increased Truebot activity infects U.S. and Canada-based networks.* www.cisa.gov/news-events/cybersecurity-advisories/aa23-187a

Cyberspace Administration of China. (2022). *AI standardized algorithm recommendations: Developing science and technology legal theory.* Center for Strategic & International Studies Interpret: China. https://interpret.csis.org/ translations/standardized-algorithm-recommendations-developing-science-and-technology-legal-theory/

Cyberspace Solarium Commission. (2020, March). *United States of America Cyberspace Solarium Commission.*

D'Alessandra, F., & Sutherland, K. (2021). The promise and challenges of new actors and new technologies in international justice. *Journal of International Criminal Justice, 19*(1), 9–34. https://academic.oup.com/jicj/article/19/1/9/ 6294452

Dafoe, A., & Zhang, B. (2019, January). *Artificial intelligence: American attitudes and trends.* Center for the Governance of AI, Future of Humanity Institute, University of Oxford.

Dale, B. (2022). *What crypto got right.* Axios. www.axios.com/2022/07/23/cry pto-trade-nft-defi-satoshi-nakomoto

Dale, B. (2022). *What to watch with cryptocurrency.* Axios. www.axios.com/ 2022/07/23/future-crypto-regulation-sec-cbdc

Dale, B. (2023, January 26). *How Kevin Rose got duped into giving away valuable NFTs*. Axios. www.axios.com/2023/01/27/kevin-rose-nfts-cyber-crime-spear-phishing

Daly, K. (2021). *How to deprogram America's extremists*. Axios. www.axios.com/fighting-online-radicals-extremism-90b8dcb6-31a7-4321-a53a-c8be5643f7d6.html

Danaher, J., & Saetra, H. S. (2023, August 17). Resolving the battle of short- vs. long-term AI risks. Springer Nature. www.researchgate.net/publication/373649298_Resolving_the_battle_of_short-vs_long-term_AI_risks/link/64f6912e48c07f3da3db5cd2/download

Danquah, P., Longe, O., & Wada, F. (1970). Action speaks louder than words—Understanding cyber criminal behavior using criminological theories. *The Journal of Internet Banking and Commerce, 17*(1), 1–12.

Das Gupta, S. (2021, August 23). *How 5G will change the world*. Ozy. www.ozy.com/pg/newsletter/the-daily-dose/439735/

Dastin, J. (2018, October 10). *Amazon scraps secret AI recruiting tool that showed bias against women*. Reuters. www.reuters.com/article/idUSKCN1MK0AG/

Dave, P. (2022, August 17). Google shows off soda-fetching robots. *The Japan Times*. www.japantimes.co.jp/news/2022/08/17/business/tech/google-soda-fetching-robots/

Davis, N. (2021, October 29). "Yeah, we're spooked": AI starting to have big real-world impact, says expert. *The Guardian*. www.theguardian.com/technology/2021/oct/29/yeah-were-spooked-ai-starting-to-have-big-real-world-impact-says-expert

De La Garza, A. (2020, March 2). "There's no story that stays stable for too long." How artists are using artificial intelligence to confront modern anxieties. *Time*. https://time.com/5792613/ai-art/

De Simone, D., Soshnikov, A., & Winston, A. (2020, January 24). *Neo-Nazi Rinaldo Nazzaro running US militant group The Base from Russia*. BBC. www.bbc.com/news/world-51236915

Dean, S. (2019, June 21). Walmart and Amazon want to see inside your house. Should you let them? *Los Angeles Times*. www.latimes.com/business/technology/la-fi-tn-walmart-amazon-google-camera-home-20190621-story.html

Debevoise & Plimpton. (2023, January). *Responding to malicious corporate deepfakes*. www.debevoise.com/insights/publications/2023/01/responding-to-malicious-corporate-deepfakes

Debevoise & Plimpton. (2023, July 18). *Achieving sensible AI regulation*.

Deblock, F. (2023). *LinkedIn, another playground for cybercriminals*. InCyber. https://incyber.org/en/linkedin-another-playground-for-cybercriminals/

Deblock, F. (2023, July 28). *New Space: Challenges linked to cybersecurity and sovereignty*. InCyber News. https://incyber.org/en/new-space-challenges-linked-cybersecurity-sovereignty/

Decker, A. (2023, April 28). *Robot rescue? Air Force seeks new way to recover downed troops*. Nextgov/FCW. www.nextgov.com/digital-government/2023/04/robot-rescue-air-force-seeks-new-way-recover-downed-troops/385755/

Decker, A. (2024, June 10). *Air Force tests AI-designed, 3D-printed drones*. Defense One. www.defenseone.com/technology/2024/06/air-forces-mideast-drone-unit-eyes-stateside-element/397257/

Defense One. (2023). *Special report outlook 2023.* www.defenseone.com/assets/defense-one-outlook-2023-q422/portal/
DeGeurin, M. (2022, June 21). *Blockchains vulnerable to centralized control, DARPA report finds.* Gizmodo. https://gizmodo.com/blockchains-vulnerable-to-centralized-control-darpa-fi-1849088882
Deloitte Center. (2023). *Government trends 2023.* www2.deloitte.com/content/dam/insights/articles/us175938_government-trends-2023/DI_Government-Trends-2023.pdf
Deloitte Center for Government Insights. (2021, April). *Criminal Justice and the technological revolution.* www.deloitte.com/global/en/Industries/government-public/perspectives/criminal-justice-and-the-technological-revolution.html
Demkovich, L. (2023). *Handprints for IDs? State liquor board discusses biometrics for alcohol sales.* Route Fifty. www.route-fifty.com/digital-government/2023/07/handprints-ids-state-liquor-board-discusses-biometrics-alcohol-sales/388186/
Dempsey, M. (2023). *Is it possible to regulate artificial intelligence?* BBC. www.bbc.com/news/business-66853057.
Department for Science, Innovation and Technology., & The RT Hon Chloe Smith MP., & Viscount Camrose. (2023). *Technology secretary holds roundtable with leading AI innovators.* GOV.UK. www.gov.uk/government/news/technology-secretary-holds-roundtable-with-leading-ai-innovators
Department of Defense. (2018). *Summary of the 2018 Department of Defense Artificial Intelligence Strategy: Harnessing AI to advance our security and prosperity.*
Department of Defense. (2020, September). *2020 Department of Defense Artificial Intelligence Education Strategy.*
Department of Defense. (2020, September 30). *Executive summary: DoD data strategy, unleashing data to advance the National Defense Strategy.* https://stacks.stanford.edu/file/druid:qr088db3377/DOD-data-strategy.pdf
Department of Defense. (2021). *National Security Commission on AI recommended particles.*
Department of Defense. (2021). *NSCAI recommended practices.* https://cybercemetery.unt.edu/nscai/20211005220330/https://www.nscai.gov/
Department of Defense. (2022, June). *U.S. Department of Defense responsible artificial intelligence strategy and implementation pathway.* https://media.defense.gov/2022/Jun/22/2003022604/-1/-1/0/Department-of-Defense-Responsible-Artificial-Intelligence-Strategy-and-Implementation-Pathway.PDF
Department of Energy. (2022, August 17). *DOE announces $45 million for next-generation cyber tools to protect the power grid.* www.energy.gov/articles/doe-announces-45-million-next-generation-cyber-tools-protect-power-grid
Department of Homeland Security. (2019). *Fact sheet: DHS strategic framework for countering terrorism and target violence (19_0920).* www.dhs.gov/sites/default/files/publications/19_0920_plcy_strategic-framework-ct-tv-fact-sheet.pdf
Department of Homeland Security. (2021). *Domestic violent extremists emboldened in aftermath of capitol breach, domestic terrorism threat likely amid political transitions.* https://publicintelligence.net/dhs-fbi-nctc-capitol-breach-violence/

Department of Homeland Security. (2022). *National Cyber Security Awareness*. FederalGrantsWire.   www.federalgrantswire.com/national-cyber-security-awareness.html#.YzxkDezMLDJ

Department of Homeland Security. (2023, August 11). *Department of Homeland Security's cyber safety review board to conduct review on cloud security*. www.dhs.gov/news/2023/08/11/department-homeland-securitys-cyber-safety-review-board-conduct-review-cloud

Department of Infrastructure, Transport, Regional Development, Communications, and the Arts. (2023). *New ACMA powers to combat misinformation and disinformation*. *Australian Government*. www.infrastructure.gov.au/have-your-say/new-acma-powers-combat-misinformation-and-disinformation

Department of the Air Force. (2019). *The United States Air Force artificial intelligence annex to the Department of Defense Artificial Intelligence Strategy*. www.af.mil/Portals/1/documents/5/USAF-AI-Annex-to-DoD-AI-Strategy.pdf

Derico, B., & Clayton, J. (2022). *Bruce Willis denies selling rights to his face*. BBC. www.bbc.co.uk/news/technology-63106024

Derysh, I. (2020, March 10). *Russia trying to "incite violence by white supremacist groups"* in US ahead of 2020 election: Report. Salon. www.salon.com/2020/03/10/russia-trying-to-incite-violence-by-white-supremacist-groups-in-us-ahead-of-2020-election-report/

Desidero, A., & Lippman, D. (2020). *Intel chief releases Russian disinfo on Hillary Clinton that was rejected by bipartisan Senate panel*. POLITICO. www.politico.com/news/2020/09/29/john-ratcliffe-hillary-clinton-russia-423022

Deutsche Welle. (2023). *EU lawmakers take first steps toward tougher AI rules*. DW Technology Europe. www.dw.com/en/eu-lawmakers-take-first-steps-toward-tougher-ai-rules/a-65585731

Di Salvo, M. (2022). *EU lawmakers pass landmark Crypto Assets Regulation Bill*. Decrypt. https://decrypt.co/111583/european-union-lawmakers-pass-crypto-regulation-bill

Diamond, L. (2016, December 9). Russia and the threat to liberal democracy. *The Atlantic*. www.theatlantic.com/international/archive/2016/12/russia-liberal-democracy/510011/

Diaz, M. (2023). *The first GPT-powered smart home platform is here*. ZDNet. www.zdnet.com/article/the-first-gpt-powered-smart-home-platform-is-here/

Diaz, M. (2023, December 8). *These are the jobs most likely to be taken over by AI*. ZDNet. www.zdnet.com/article/these-are-the-jobs-most-likely-to-be-taken-over-by-ai/

Diaz, M. (2023). *Would you listen to AI-run radio? This station tested it out on listeners*. ZDNet. www.zdnet.com/article/would-you-listen-to-ai-run-radio-this-station-tested-it-out-on-listeners/

Diaz, M. (2023). *Your next job interview could be with AI instead of a person*. ZDNet. www.zdnet.com/article/your-next-job-interview-could-be-with-ai-instead-of-a-person/

Dickey, M. (2023). *City leaders want police drones at car sideshows*. Axios. www.axios.com/local/san-francisco/2023/04/27/san-francisco-police-drones-sideshow-surveillance

Dickinson, P. (2021, January 5). *All roads lead to Ukraine in Putin's global hybrid war.* Atlantic Council. www.atlanticcouncil.org/blogs/ukrainealert/all-roads-lead-to-ukraine-in-putins-global-hybrid-war/

Dickson, B. (2020, August 22). *Why AI and human perception are too complex to be compared.* The Next Web. https://thenextweb.com/neural/2020/08/22/computer-vision-why-its-hard-to-compare-ai-and-human-perception-syndication/

Dillion, D., Gray, K., Gu, Y., & Tandon, N. (2023, May 10). Can AI language models replace human participants? *Trends in Cognitive Sciences, 27,* 597–600. www.cell.com/trends/cognitive-sciences/abstract/S1364-6613(23)00098-0

DiMolfetta, D. (2024, February 26). *FCC issues cease-and-desist order to operator linked to AI-generated Biden robocall.* Nextgov/FCW. www.nextgov.com/artificial-intelligence/2024/02/fcc-issues-cease-and-desist-order-operator-linked-ai-generated-biden-robocall/393960/

DiNardo, G. (2023, August 3). *Artificial intelligence flies XQ-58A Valkyrie drone.* C4ISRNET. www.c4isrnet.com/unmanned/2023/08/03/artificial-intelligence-flies-xq-58a-valkyrie-drone/

DocumentCloud. (2023). *Seizing the opportunities of safe, secure, and trustworthy artificial intelligence systems for sustainable development.* Axios. www.documentcloud.org/documents/24220144-draft-unga-plenary-resolution-on-ai_20231211

Donnelly, J. (2020). *NDAA: Russian support for US extremists a "significant risk."* Roll Call. www.rollcall.com/2020/06/30/ndaa-russian-support-for-us-extremists-a-significant-risk/

Donnelly, J. (2021). *Lawmakers probe Russian support for US extremists.* Roll Call. www.rollcall.com/2021/01/27/lawmakers-probe-russian-support-for-us-extremists/

Dorfman, Z. (2023). *The long tail of the SolarWinds breach.* Axios. www.axios.com/2021/02/03/solarwinds-breach-russia-hack-software

Douglas, A., Draper, D., Farshchi, J., Lord, B., Neschke, S., & Romanoff, T. (2023, February 12). *Top risks in cybersecurity 2023.* Bipartisan Policy Center. https://bipartisanpolicy.org/report/top-risks-cybersecurity-2023/

Down, L., Jonas, E., Schwartz, R., Schwartz, R., & Tabassi, E. (2021, June). *A proposal for identifying and managing bias within artificial intelligence* (Draft NIST Special Publication 1270). National Institute of Standards and Technology, U.S. Department of Commerce. https://nvlpubs.nist.gov/nistpubs/SpecialPublications/NIST.SP.1270-draft.pdf

Dubois, C. (2018, March 12). *Robots and AI: Our new lawyers, police, and dentists?* All About Circuits. www.allaboutcircuits.com/news/robots-and-ai-our-new-lawyers-police-and-dentists/

Duggan, P. (2020). Alleged white supremacists planned deadly violence at Richmond gun rally, federal prosecutors say. *The Washington Post.* www.washingtonpost.com/local/public-safety/alleged-white-supremacists-planned-deadly-violence-at-richmond-gun-rally-federal-prosecutors-say/2020/01/21/7c7ccdba-396d-11ea-bb7b-265f4554af6d_story.html

Eady, Y. (2018, December 4). *Does recent progress with neural networks foretell artificial general intelligence?* Medium. https://medium.com/protopiablog/does-recent-progress-with-neural-networks-foretell-artificial-general-intelligence-9545c17a5d8b

Easterly, J., & Rosenworcel, J. (2023, August 2). *The most important part of the internet you've probably never heard of.* Cybersecurity and Infrastructure Security Agency. www.cisa.gov/news-events/news/most-important-part-internet-youve-probably-never-heard

Eaves, M. (2021, December 1). *Humanity's unlikely gateway to space.* BBC. https://bbc.com/travel/article/20211130-humanitys-unlikely-gateway-to-space

Eckersley, P. (2018, February). *The malicious use of artificial intelligence: Forecasting, prevention.* Future of Humanity Institute, University of Oxford, Centre for the Study of Existential Risk, University of Cambridge, Center for a New American Security, Electronic Frontier Foundation, & OpenAI. https://arxiv.org/ftp/arxiv/papers/1802/1802.07228.pdf

Edelman. (2022). *2022 special report: Trust in the workplace.* Edelman. www.edelman.com/trust/2022-trust-barometer/special-report-trust-workplace

Eisikovits, N., & Feldman, D. (2021). *AI is killing choice and chance—Which means changing what it means to be human.* Nextgov/FCW. www.nextgov.com/ideas/2021/03/ai-killing-choice-and-chance-which-means-changing-what-it-means-be-human/172299/

Elgammal, A. (2020, May 27). The robot artists aren't coming. *The New York Times.* www.nytimes.com/2020/05/27/opinion/artificial-intelligence-art.html

Elkus, R., & Shivakumar, S. (2023). *A personal view on today's competitiveness challenges: "We Did it to ourselves."* Center for Strategic & International Studies. www.csis.org/blogs/perspectives-innovation/personal-view-todays-competitiveness-challenges-we-did-it-ourselves

Elluru, G. R., Horvitz, E., Howell, C., & Young, J. (2021, April 26). *Key considerations for the responsible development and fielding of artificial intelligence.* National Security Commission on Artificial Intelligence. https://arxiv.org/pdf/2108.12289

Ellwood, M. (2021, January 5). *The people who want to send smells through your TV.* BBC. https://bbc.com/future/article/20210104-the-reason-why-you-cant-smell-television-shows-yet

Emergent Risk International. (2022). *Strategic business analysis: United States: Violent crime trends upwards.* https://emergentriskinternational.com/

Errick, K. (2022). *AI's value to organizations parallels value to individuals, report finds.* Nextgov/FCW. www.nextgov.com/emerging-tech/2022/11/ais-value-organizations-parallels-value-individuals-report-finds/379200/

Errick, K. (2022). *Challenges in the space domain are becoming "more technologically focused," experts say.* Nextgov/FCW. www.nextgov.com/emerging-tech/2022/10/challenges-space-domain-are-becoming-more-technologically-focused-experts-say/378789/.

Errick, K. (2022). *Emerging tech training gets a $30M boost from NSF.* Nextgov/FCW. www.nextgov.com/emerging-tech/2022/10/emerging-tech-training-gets-30m-boost-nsf/378641/

Errick, K. (2022). *Federal agencies still face several cloud challenges, watchdog says.* Nextgov/FCW. www.nextgov.com/it-modernization/2022/09/federal-agencies-still-face-several-cloud-challenges-watchdog-says/377854/

Errick, K. (2022). *FTC debates whether data privacy concerns warrant market wide rules.* Nextgov/FCW. www.nextgov.com/analytics-data/2022/09/ftc-deba tes-whether-data-privacy-concerns-warrant-market-wide-rules/376916/

Errick, K. (2022). *Future astronaut suits could feature augmented reality.* Nextgov/ FCW. www.nextgov.com/emerging-tech/2022/12/future-astronaut-suits-could-feature-augmented-reality/380765/

Errick, K. (2022). *Good AI starts with a trained workforce, government experts say.* Nextgov/FCW. www.nextgov.com/emerging-tech/2022/11/good-ai-starts-trained-workforce-government-experts-say/380000/

Errick, K. (2022). *How government might work up to 3D-printed buildings.* Nextgov/FCW. www.nextgov.com/emerging-tech/2022/10/how-government-might-work-3d-printed-buildings/378886/.

Errick, K. (2022). *Interior's body camera policy is not finalized despite years of use, watchdog says.* Nextgov/FCW. www.nextgov.com/policy/2022/09/interiors-body-camera-policy-not-finalized-despite-years-use-watchdog-says/377408/.

Errick, K. (2022). *Lack of cloud backups poses a "real problem" for data protection, expert says.* Nextgov/FCW. www.nextgov.com/analytics-data/2022/12/lack-cloud-backups-poses-real-problem-data-protection-expert-says/381250/

Errick, K. (2022, August 11). *LOG4J vulnerability prompts lawmakers to examine agency cyber measures.* Nextgov/FCW. www.nextgov.com/cybersecurity/2022/08/log4j-vulnerability-prompts-lawmakers-examine-agency-cyber-measures/375727/

Errick, K. (2022). *NASA's out of this world tech advancements in 2022.* Nextgov/ FCW. www.nextgov.com/emerging-tech/2022/12/nasas-out-world-tech-advan cements-2022/381180/

Errick, K. (2022). *TSA wants to automate ID verification at checkpoint security.* Nextgov/FCW. www.nextgov.com/analytics-data/2022/12/tsa-wants-automate-id-verification-checkpoint-security/380494/

Errick, K. (2022). *Watchdog: Most agencies behind on personal data disclosure guidance.* Nextgov/FCW. www.nextgov.com/analytics-data/2022/12/watchdog-most-agencies-behind-personal-data-disclosure-guidance/381198/

Errick, K. (2023). *DHS calls for counter-drone information to help fight threats.* Nextgov/FCW. www.nextgov.com/emerging-tech/2023/01/dhs-calls-counter-drone-information-help-fight-threats/381667/

Errick, K. (2023). *IBM, NASA will use AI to improve climate change research.* Nextgov. www.nextgov.com/emerging-tech/2023/02/ibm-nasa-will-use-ai-impr ove-climate-change-research/382437/

Errick, K. (2023). *Launch of first 3D-printed rocket included innovative NASA alloy.* Nextgov/FCW. www.nextgov.com/emerging-tech/2023/05/launch-first-3d-printed-rocket-included-innovative-nasa-alloy/385924/

Errick, K. (2023). *Lawmakers introduce bill to tackle criminal and terrorist crypto activities.* Nextgov/FCW. www.nextgov.com/emerging-tech/2023/05/lawmak ers-introduce-bill-tackle-criminal-and-terrorist-crypto-activities/385811/

Errick, K. (2023, April 28). *NASA Quest Mission could revitalize supersonic travel, but quieter*. Nextgov/FCW. www.nextgov.com/emerging-tech/2023/04/nasa-quesst-mission-could-revitalize-supersonic-travel-quieter/385728/

Errick, K. (2023). *NIST wants to mitigate smart home telehealth cybersecurity risks*. Nextgov/FCW. www.nextgov.com/cxo-briefing/2023/04/nist-wants-mitigate-smart-home-telehealth-cybersecurity-risks/385217/

Errick, K. (2023, January 27). *Treasury looks for new tech to prove physical money is legit*. Nextgov/FCW. www.nextgov.com/emerging-tech/2023/01/treasury-looks-new-tech-prove-physical-money-legit/382319/

Errick, K. (2023). *"Very realistic" that humans will be on Mars in 20 years, NASA official says*. Nextgov/FCW. www.nextgov.com/emerging-tech/2023/01/very-realistic-humans-will-be-mars-20-years-nasa-official-says/381724/

Errick, K. (2023). *"We have nothing" showing UFOs are of alien origin, defense official says*. Nextgov/FCW. www.nextgov.com/technology-news/2023/01/we-have-nothing-showing-ufos-are-alien-origin-defense-official-says/381512/

Erwin, S. (2023). *DARPA launches initiative to help tech companies work on classified programs*. SpaceNews. https://spacenews.com/darpa-launches-initiative-to-help-tech-companies-work-on-classified-programs/

Espiner, T., & Sherman, N. (2023). *JP Morgan's Jamie Dimon warns world facing "most dangerous time in decades."* BBC. www.bbc.com/news/business-67104734

Estrin, D. (2022, January 18). *Israeli police used spyware to hack its own citizens, an Israeli newspaper reports*. NPR. www.npr.org/2022/01/18/1073828708/israel-spyware-citizens-nso-group

European Commission. (2019, April 8). *Ethics guidelines for trustworthy AI*. https://ec.europa.eu/futurium/en/ai-alliance-consultation.1.html

European Parliament. (2020). *Hearing on artificial intelligence in criminal law and its use by the police and judicial authorities in criminal matters*. Programme. www.europarl.europa.eu/committees/en/hearing-on-artificial-intelligence-in-cr/product-details/20200211CHE07061

European Parliamentary Reach Service Scientific Foresight Unit. (2021). *Digital automation and the future of work*.

European Union Agency for Fundamental Rights. (2019). *Facial recognition technology: Focus paper*.

European Union Agency for Fundamental Rights (FRA). (2020). *Facial recognition technology: Fundamental rights considerations in the context of law enforcement*.

Europol Innovation Lab. (2023). *The second quantum revolution—The impact of quantum computing and quantum technologies on law enforcement*. European Union Agency for Law Enforcement Cooperation. www.europol.europa.eu/publication-events/main-reports/second-quantum-revolution-impact-of-quantum-computing-and-quantum-technologies-law-enforcement

Europol Unclassified. (2017). *Crime in the age of technology*. www.europol.europa.eu/publications-events/main-reports/european-union-serious-and-organised-crime-threat-assessment-2017

Ewing, P. (2017). *Why is Russia helping anti-U.S. insurgents in Afghanistan?* NPR. www.npr.org/2017/02/13/515020244/why-is-russia-helping-anti-u-s-insurge nts-in-afghanistan

Executive Office of the President. (2019). Maintaining American leadership in artificial intelligence. *Federal Register, 84*(31), 3967–3972. www.federalregister. gov/documents/2019/02/14/2019-02544/maintaining-american-leadership-in-artificial-intelligence

Executive Office of the President. (2020). *Draft OMB memo on regulation of AI.* The White House. www.whitehouse.gov/wp-content/uploads/2020/01/Draft-OMB-Memo-on-Regulation-of-AI-1-7-19.pdf

Executive Office of the President of the United States. (2019). *2016–2019 progress report: Advancing artificial intelligence R&D.* www.nitrd.gov/pubs/AI-Resea rch-and-Development-Progress-Report-2016-2019.pdf

Executive Office of the President of the United States. (2022, June). *Information Technology Operating Plan.*

Faesen, L., Mayhew, E., Torossian, B., & Zensus, C. (2019, November 19). *Conflict in cyberspace: Parsing the threats and the state of international order in cyberspace.* The Hague Center for Strategic Studies. www.hcss.nl/pub/2019/ strategic-monitor-2019-2020/conflict-in-cyberspace/

Faesen, L., Sweijs, T., Klimburg, A., & Tesauro, G. (2022, April 6). *The promises and perils of a minimum cyber deterrence posture: Considerations for small and middle powers.* The Hague Centre for Strategic Studies. https://hcss.nl/wp-cont ent/uploads/2022/04/Cyber-Deterrence-Final.pdf

Farah, H., & Mason, R. (2023, August 8). Electoral Commission apologises for security breach involving UK voters' data | Information commissioner. *The Guardian.* www.theguardian.com/technology/2023/aug/08/uk-electoral-com mission-registers-targeted-by-hostile-hackers

Farid, H. (2022). *Text-to-image AI: Powerful, easy-to-use technology for making art—And fakes.* Nextgov/FCW. www.nextgov.com/ideas/2022/12/text-image-ai-powerful-easy-use-technology-making-art-and-fakes/380456/

Farivar, C., & Brewster, T. (2023, December 14). Google just killed warrants that give police access to location data. *Forbes.* www.forbes.com/sites/ cyrusfarivar/2023/12/14/google-just-killed-geofence-warrants-police-locat ion-data/

Farooq, U. (2024, February 2). *Police departments are turning to AI to sift through millions of hours of unreviewed body-cam footage.* Route Fifty. www.route-fifty.com/digital-government/2024/02/police-departments-are-turning-ai-sift-through-millions-hours-unreviewed-body-cam-footage/393876/

Farrington, D. P., Piza, E., Thomas, A., & Welsh, B. C. (2021). The internationalization of CCTV surveillance: Effects on crime and implications for emerging technologies. *International Journal of Comparative and Applied Criminal Justice, 46*, 81–102. www.crimrxiv.com/pub/sw8ljm5k/release/1

Farrow, R. (2021, January 8) An Air Force combat veteran breached the Senate. *The New Yorker.* www.newyorker.com/news/news-desk/an-air-force-combat-veteran-breached-the-senate

Farrow, R. (2022, April 18). How democracies spy on their citizens. *The New Yorker.* www.newyorker.com/magazine/2022/04/25/how-democracies-spy-on-their-citizens

FCW. (2022). *Machine learning on the job.* www.govexec.com/assets/machine-learning-job-fcwq322/portal/

FCW Electronic Records Management Workshop. (2022, September). *Digitization and automation: The path to efficiency.*

Federal Aviation Administration. (2018, February). *FAA strategic plan, FY 2019–2022.*

Federal Communications Commission. (2022). *Advanced methods to target and eliminate unlawful robocalls; call authentication trust anchor.* Federal Register. www.federalregister.gov/documents/2022/11/18/2022-25148/advanced-methods-to-target-and-eliminate-unlawful-robocalls-call-authentication-trust-anchor

Federal Data Strategy Development Team. (2021). *Federal data strategy 2021 action plan.* https://strategy.data.gov/assets/docs/2021-Federal-Data-Strategy-Action-Plan.pdf

Federal Trade Commission. (2022). *Commercial surveillance and data security rulemaking.* Kvgo. https://kvgo.com/ftc/commercial-surveillance-sep-8

Feiner, L. (2023). *Chinese hackers outnumber FBI cyber staff 50 to 1, bureau director says.* CNBC. www.cnbc.com/2023/04/28/chinese-hackers-outnumber-fbi-cyber-staff-50-to-1-director-wray-says.html

Ferguson-Walter, K. J., Fugate, S., & Gutzwiller, R. S. (2019, November). *Are cyber attackers thinking fast and slow? Exploratory analysis reveals evidence of decision-making biases teamers.* ResearchGate. www.researchgate.net/publication/337418480_Are_Cyber_Attackers_Thinking_Fast_and_Slow_Exploratory_Analysis_Reveals_Evidence_of_Decision-Making_Biases_in_Red_Teamers

Feuer, A., & Higgins, A. (2016, December 3). Extremists turn to a leader to protect western values: Vladimir Putin. *The New York Times.* www.nytimes.com/2016/12/03/world/americas/alt-right-vladimir-putin.html

Fick, N., & Miscik, J. (Co-Chairs). Segal, A., & Goldstein, G. M. (Project Directors). (2022, July). *Confronting reality in cyberspace: Foreign policy for a fragmented Internet.* Council on Foreign Relations. www.cfr.org/task-force-report/confronting-reality-in-cyberspace

Field, M. (2021, February 9). *As Trump's impeachment trial begins, the Russian network that helped him in 2016 taps his supporters on Gab.com.* Bulletin of the Atomic Scientists. https://thebulletin.org/2021/02/as-trumps-impeachment-trial-begins-the-russian-network-that-helped-him-in-2016-taps-his-supporters-on-gab-com/

Financial Crimes Enforcement Network. (2021). *Financial trend analysis: Ransomware trends in Bank Secrecy Act data between January 2021 and June 2021.*

Financial Crimes Enforcement Network. (2022). *FinCEN analysis reveals ransomware reporting in BSA filings increased significantly during the second half of 2021.* www.fincen.gov/news/news-releases/fincen-analysis-reveals-ransomware-reporting-bsa-filings-increased-significantly

Fischer, S. (2023). *Insider will start experimenting with AI to write articles.* Axios. www.axios.com/2023/04/13/insiders-newsroom-will-start-experimenting-with-ai

Fischer, S. (2023, January 24). *Newsrooms reckon with AI following CNET saga.* Axios. www.axios.com/2023/01/24/chatgpt-media-automation-cnet-saga

Fischer, S., & Baysinger, T. (2023). *Media summer apocalypse.* Axios. www.axios.com/2023/07/14/media-summer-apocalypse-hollywood-strikes

Fischer, S., & McGill, M. H. (2022, January 27). *Crypto leads to massive surge in online scams.* Axios. www.axios.com/2022/01/27/crypto-scam-ftc

Fiscutean, A. (2021, October 21). *Nixon's unheard moon-disaster speech is now a warning about the deepfake future.* ZDNet. www.zdnet.com/article/nixons-grim-moon-disaster-speech-is-a-now-a-warning-about-the-deepfake-future/

Fischer, S. (2023). *AI's hidden toll on our brains.* Axios. www.axios.com/2023/06/10/ai-mental-health-risks-misinformation

FitzGerald, J. (2022). *Floppy disks in Japan: Minister declares war on old-fashioned technology.* BBC. www.bbc.co.uk/news/world-asia-62749310

Fitzgerald, M. (2023). *As employers expand artificial intelligence in hiring, few states have rules.* Route Fifty. www.route-fifty.com/digital-government/2023/07/employers-expand-artificial-intelligence-hiring-few-states-have-rules/388561/

Fitzgerald, M. (2023). *What is artificial intelligence? Legislators are still looking for a definition.* Route Fifty. www.route-fifty.com/emerging-tech/2023/10/what-artificial-intelligence-legislators-are-still-looking-definition/391017/

Fitzpatrick, A. (2022, August 29). *Drones are sniffing out landmines in Ukraine.* Axios. www.axios.com/2022/08/29/drones-landmines-ukraine

Fitzpatrick, A. (2022). *This AI-powered stroller can drive itself.* Axios. www.axios.com/2022/10/06/ai-stroller-ella-gluxkind

Fitzpatrick, A. (2023, January 3). *Axios newsletters.* Axios. www.axios.com/newsletters

Fitzpatrick A. (2023). *Facial recognition's alarming pitfalls.* Axios. www.axios.com/2023/01/07/facial-recognition-issues-problems

Fitzpatrick, A. (2023). *"Flying car" gets FAA testing nod.* Axios. www.axios.com/2023/07/06/flying-car-alef-aeronautics

Fitzpatrick, A. (2023, February 3). *Fully autonomous passenger planes are inching closer to takeoff.* Axios. www.axios.com/2023/02/03/fully-autonomous-flight-planes

Fitzpatrick A., Kingson J., & Muller J. (2023). *Self-driving car fears on the rise.* Axios. www.axios.com/2023/03/03/self-driving-car-fears-poll

Fitzpatrick, A., Kingston, J., & Muller, J. (2023, January 24). *Robo-cat.* Axios.

Fitzpatrick, A., Kingston, J., & Muller, J. (2023, March 20). *Grocery bots.* Axios.

Fitzpatrick, A., Kingston, J., & Muller, J. (2023, March 22). *Google's ChatGPT rival advances.* Axios.

Fitzpatrick, A., Kingston, J., & Muller, J. (2023, May 16). *Anti-bird drones.* Axios.

Fitzpatrick, A., Kingston, J., & Muller, J. (2023, May 19). *Salad-slinging robot.* Axios.

Fitzpatrick, A., Kingston, J., & Muller, J. (2023). *Adobe's new Photoshop tools make fakery even easier.* Axios. www.axios.com/2023/05/23/adobe-photoshop-ai-fakery-deepfakes

Fitzpatrick, A., Kingston, J., & Muller, J. (2023). *AI impersonation ban.* Axios.

Fitzpatrick, A., Kingston, J., & Muller, J. (2023). *Chatbots at the drive-through.* Axios.

Fitzpatrick, A., Kingston, J., & Muller, J. (2023). *5G comes to hospitals.* Axios. www.axios.com/2023/05/30/coming-to-a-hospital-near-you-5g

Fitzpatrick, A., Kingston, J., & Muller, J. (2023). *Meet Abel, a robot with empathy.* Axios.

Fitzpatrick, A., Kingston, J., & Muller, J. (2023). *QR clothing labels.* Axios.

Fitzpatrick, A., Kingston, J., & Muller, J. (2023). *Who will lose jobs to AI?* Axios.

Fitzpatrick, A., Kingston, J., & Muller, J. (2024, January 31). *The hunt for quantum algorithms.* Axios.

Fitzpatrick, A., Kingson, J., & Muller, J. (2024, February 5). *New AI scam: "Audio-jacking."* Axios.

Fitzpatrick, A., Kingson, J. A., & Muller, J. (2024, March 28). *AI falls into "trough of disillusionment."* Axios. www.axios.com/newsletters/axios-whats-next-49b3afc3-f1e7-4356-a91e-409dd3932a92.html

Fitzpatrick, A., Kingson, J. A., & Muller, J. (2024, April 10). *Games as AI testing ground.* Axios. www.axios.com/newsletters/axios-whats-next-527917db-eb25-45cb-a73d-eeed227f1e81.html

Foley, C., Weaver, J., & Lewis, J. (2023). *CSIS panel: The future of quantum—Australia's national strategy.* Center for Strategic & International Studies. www.csis.org/events/future-quantum-australias-national-strategy

Formula 1. (2023). *Michael Schumacher: Seven-time F1 champion's family plan legal action after AI-generated "interview."* BBC. www.bbc.com/sport/formula1/65333115

Forrester Research. (2021, February 4). *AI drives the evolution of technology and data governance.* ZDNet. www.zdnet.com/article/ai-drives-the-evolution-of-technology-and-data-governance/

Fosco, M. (2018, October 30). *Will artificial intelligence save us from the next cyberattack?* Ozy. www.ozy.com/the-new-and-the-next/will-artificial-intelligence-save-us-from-the-next-cyberattack/88428/

Fox News. (2015, March 24). *Thousands sign WhiteHouse.gov petition for Alaska to secede—To Russia.* Fox News. www.foxnews.com/politics/thousands-sign-whitehouse-gov-petition-for-alaska-to-secede-to-russia

France 24. (2022). *Hackers leak Australian health records on dark web.* www.france24.com/en/live-news/20221109-hackers-leak-australian-health-records-on-dark-web

Franceschi-Bicchierai, L. (2022, August 17). *How a third-party SMS service was used to take over signal accounts.* Vice. www.vice.com/en/article/qjkvxv/how-a-third-party-sms-service-was-used-to-take-over-signal-accounts

Frank, J. (2021, December 22). *The Reith lectures. Stuart Russell—Living with artificial intelligence. AI: A future for humans—BBC sounds.* BBC. www.bbc.co.uk/programmes/m001216k

Franks, J. (2022). *Cloud computing: Federal agencies face four challenges.* U.S. GAO. www.gao.gov/products/gao-22-106195

Fried, I. (2023). *Generative AI can help with mundane tasks too.* Axios. www.axios.com/2023/04/17/generative-ai-adobe-tasks-efficiency

Freilich, C. (2022, April 27). *Israel's spyware sector will survive the NSO Pegasus scandal.* World Politics Review. www.worldpoliticsreview.com/despite-nso-pegasus-scandal-israel-s-cyber-sector-is-going-strong/

Fried, I. (2020, June 15). *Fresh concerns about AI bias in the age of COVID-19.* Axios. www.axios.com/2020/06/15/fresh-concerns-about-ai-bias-in-the-age-of-covid-19

Fried, I. (2021, February 10). *AR glasses are what comes after the smartphone.* Axios. www.axios.com/2021/02/10/ar-glasses-what-comes-after-smartphone

Fried, I. (2021, November 14). *Exclusive: IBM achieves quantum computing breakthrough.* Axios. www.axios.com/2021/11/14/ibm-quantum-comput ing-axios-hbo

Fried, I. (2021, December 15). *Log4j open-source flaw has put millions of systems at risk.* Axios. www.axios.com/2021/12/15/log4j-open-source-cybersecur ity-flaw

Fried, I. (2021, December 15). *Massive open-source flaw has put millions of systems at risk.* Axios. https://news.harvard.edu/gazette/story/2019/03/harvard-professor-says-surveillance-capitalism-is-undermining-democracy/

Fried, I. (2022, January 7). *CES 2022 brought pieces of the metaverse into view.* Axios. www.axios.com/2022/01/07/ces-2022-metaverse-pieces-vr

Fried, I. (2022, January 21). *Microsoft's deal for Activision Blizzard is all about the metaverse.* Axios. www.axios.com/2022/01/21/microsofts-metaverse-maneuver ing-activision-blizzard-deal

Fried, I. (2022, January 24). *IRS face recognition program raises hackles.* Axios. www.axios.com/2022/01/24/irs-face-recognition-hackles-id-me

Fried, I. (2022, February 9). *Battle over government use of face recognition rages on.* Axios. www.axios.com/2022/02/09/face-recognition-government-use-battle

Fried, I. (2022, October 7). *The walletless future is closer than ever.* Axios. www. axios.com/2022/10/07/walletless-future-travel-biometrics-identity-documents

Fried, I. (2022, December 2). *The smartest AI is dumb without people.* Axios. www.axios.com/2022/12/02/ai-smart-humans-in-loop-stanford

Fried, I. (2022, December 5). *Exclusive: Adobe will sell AI-made stock images.* Axios. www.axios.com/2022/12/05/adobe-ai-made-stock-images

Fried, I. (2023, January 4). *Microsoft's Bing search has big ChatGPT plans.* Axios. www.axios.com/2023/01/04/microsoft-bing-search-chatgpt-openai

Fried, I. (2023, January 19). *ChatGPT and generative AI are the talk of this year's Davos forum.* Axios. www.axios.com/2023/01/19/chatgpt-davos-2023-talk-ai-chatbot

Fried, I. (2023, January 31). *OpenAI releases tool to detect machine-written text.* Axios. www.axios.com/2023/01/31/openai-chatgpt-detector-tool-machine-writ ten-text

Fried, I. (2023, March 15). *When "scary good" AI gets even better.* Axios. www. axios.com/2023/03/15/gpt4-openai-chatgpt-new-version

Fried, I. (2023, April 19). *The global elite is excited and terrified by AI.* Axios. www.axios.com/2023/04/19/ai-ted-conference-global-elite

Fried, I. (2023, May 1). *AI stars in Hollywood's Writers Guild contract nego-tiations.* Axios. www.axios.com/2023/05/01/ai-hollywood-labor-negotiations-writers-guild

Fried, I. (2023, May 10). *Google debuts latest AI model, updated chatbot, Pixel devices.* Axios. www.axios.com/2023/05/10/google-palm-2-ai-io-conference

Fried, I. (2023, July 10). *How AI will turbocharge misinformation—And what we can do about it.* Axios. www.axios.com/2023/07/10/ai-misinformation-response-measures

Fried, I. (2023, December 6). *Apple, Google warn governments can spy on you via push notifications.* Axios. www.axios.com/2023/12/06/apple-google-requests-push-notification-data

Fried, I. (2023, December 13). *Exclusive: Biden team wades into open-source AI controversy.* Axios. www.axios.com/2023/12/13/open-source-ai-white-house-ntia

Fried, I. (2024, March 27). *Chatbot letdown: Hype hits rocky reality.* Axios. www.axios.com/2024/03/27/ai-chatbot-letdown-hype-reality

Fried, I. (2024, April 5). *For AI firms, anything "public" is fair game.* Axios. www.axios.com/2024/04/05/open-ai-training-data-public-available-meaning

Fried, I., & Rosenberg, S. (2023). *AI could choke on its own exhaust as it fills the web.* Axios. www.axios.com/2023/08/28/ai-content-flood-model-collapse

Fuller, T., & Metz, C. (2018, October 26). A.I. is helping scientists predict when and where the next big earthquake will be. *The New York Times.* www.nytimes.com/2018/10/26/technology/earthquake-predictions-artificial-intelligence.html

Fung, A., & Lessig, L. (2023). *How AI could take over elections—And undermine democracy.* Route Fifty. www.route-fifty.com/tech-data/2023/06/how-ai-could-take-over-elections-and-undermine-democracy/387059/

Funk, M. (2024, June 14). *How local government fraud has—and hasn't—changed since the pandemic.* Route Fifty. www.route-fifty.com/finance/2024/06/how-local-government-fraud-hasand-hasntchanged-pandemic/397385/

Future Lawyers. (2021, July 19). *Justice in the Imminent Age of Artificial Intelligence.* https://futurelawyers.in/justice-in-the-imminent-age-of-artificial-intelligence/

G7 France. (2019). *Biarritz strategy for an open, free, and secure digital transformation.* www.elysee.fr/admin/upload/default/0001/05/62a9221e66987d4e0d6ffcb058f3d2c649fc6d9d.pdf

Gagliordi, N. (2018, December 12). *How self-driving tractors, AI, and precision agriculture will save us from the impending food crisis.* ZDNet.

Gannon, K. (2020, July 2). *US, Russia share a complex and bloody history in Afghanistan.* AP NEWS. https://apnews.com/article/b4377be5308f230dbe2e3fa01029537f

GAO-22-106154. (2022). *Facial recognition technology: CBP traveler identity verification and efforts to address privacy issues.* U.S. GAO. www.gao.gov/products/gao-22-106154

Garcia, E. (2018, April 19). *The Artificial intelligence race: U.S. China and Russia.* Modern Diplomacy. https://moderndiplomacy.eu/2018/04/19/the-artificial-intelligence-race-u-s-china-and-russia/

Gardner, F. (2021, December 30). *What does future warfare look like? It's here already.* BBC. www.bbc.com/news/world-59755100

Gardner, F. (2022, January 27). *What is the quantum apocalypse and should we be scared?* BBC. www.bbc.com/news/technology-60144498

Gardner, T., & Satter, R. (2023). *U.S. Energy Dept gets two ransom notices as MOVEit hack claims more victims.* Reuters. www.reuters.com/technology/us-energy-dept-got-two-ransom-requests-cl0p-data-breach-2023-06-16/

Gariffo, M. (2021, December 16). *Cosmic rays could render quantum computing error correction techniques useless.* ZDNet. www.zdnet.com/article/cosmic-rays-could-render-quantum-computing-error-correction-techniques-useless/

Gariffo, M. (2022, January 18). *What is web3? Everything you need to know about the decentralized future of the internet.* ZDNet. www.zdnet.com/article/what-is-web3-everything-you-need-to-know-about-the-decentralised-future-of-the-internet/

Garman, B., & Tidy, J. (2022, August 25). *NATO investigates hacker sale of missile firm data.* BBC. www.bbc.com/news/technology-62672184

Garrison, B. (2023, January 11). *Regulating artificial intelligence requires balancing rights, innovation.* Just Security. www.justsecurity.org/84724/regulating-artificial-intelligence-requires-balancing-rights-innovation/

Gartenstein-Ross, D., Hodgson, S., & Clarke, C. P. (2020). *The Russian Imperial Movement (RIM) and its links to the transnational white supremacist extremist movement.* International Centre for Counter-Terrorism. https://icct.nl/publication/the-russian-imperial-movement-rim-and-its-links-to-the-transnational-white-supremacist-extremist-movement/

Garvie, C., & Moy, L. M. (2019). *Face Surveillance in the United States.* Georgetown Law Center on Privacy & Technology. www.americaunderwatch.com/

Gatlan, S. (2022). *Police dismantles criminal ring that hacked keyless cars.* BleepingComputer. www.bleepingcomputer.com/news/security/police-dismantles-criminal-ring-that-hacked-keyless-cars/

Gatlan, S. (2023). *CISA now warns critical infrastructure of ransomware-vulnerable devices.* BleepingComputer. www.bleepingcomputer.com/news/security/cisa-now-warns-critical-infrastructure-of-ransomware-vulnerable-devices/

Gatlan, S. (2023). *3CX confirms North Korean hackers behind supply chain attack.* BleepingComputer. www.bleepingcomputer.com/news/security/3cx-confirms-north-korean-hackers-behind-supply-chain-attack/

Gatlan, S. (2024, February 26). *Russian hackers shift to cloud attacks, US and allies warn.* BleepingCompter. www.bleepingcomputer.com/news/security/russian-hackers-shift-to-cloud-attacks-us-and-allies-warn/

Gawad, J., & Bonde, C. (2017). *Artificial intelligence: Future of medicine and healthcare.* BioChemistry: An Indian Journal, 11(2), 1–4.

Geman, B. (2021, May 10). *What to know about the colonial pipeline cyberattack.* Axios. www.axios.com/2021/05/10/colonial-pipeline-cyberattack-oil-what-know

General Services Administration Office of Government-wide Policy. (2021, January 5). *The digital worker identity playbook* (version 1.1). www.idmanagement.gov/playbooks/dw/

Gent, E. (2019). *A new anti-aging therapy is starting its first human trial—And it costs $1 million.* SingularityHub. https://singularityhub.com/2019/12/16/a-new-anti-aging-therapy-is-starting-its-first-human-trial-and-it-costs-1-million/

Gerken, T. (2023). *Banks warn of big increase in online scams.* BBC. www.bbc.com/news/technology-65486219.

Gerken, T., & McMahon, L. (2023, September 21). *Game of Thrones author sues ChatGPT owner OpenAI.* BBC. www.bbc.co.uk/news/technology-66866577

Gerken, T., & Rahman-Jones, I. (2023). *Rishi Sunak: AI firms cannot "mark their own homework."* BBC. www.bbc.com/news/technology-67285315

German, B. (2021, May 10). *What to know about the Colonial Pipeline cyberattack.* Axios. www.axios.com/2021/05/10/colonial-pipeline-cyberatt ack-oil-what-know

Gershgorn, D. (2018). *Amazon and Microsoft claim AI can read human emotions. Experts say the science is shaky.* Nextgov/FCW. www.nextgov.com/emerging-tech/2018/12/amazon-and-microsoft-claim-ai-can-read-human-emotions-expe rts-say-science-shaky/153414/

Gershgorn, D. (2018). *This is the week that the drone surveillance state became real.* Nextgov/FCW. www.nextgov.com/emerging-tech/2018/06/week-drone-surveillance-state-became-real/148847/

Gesser, A. (2023). *Balancing AI benefits and risks and whether boards need AI experts—Interview of Avi Gesser by FT's agenda.* Debevoise Data Blog. www. debevoisedatablog.com/2023/04/17/balancing-ai-benefits-and-risks-and-whet her-boards-need-ai-experts-interview-of-avi-gesser-by-fts-agenda/

Gesser, A., Brundage, S., Allaman, S., Muse, M., & Gaillard, L. (2023). *The value of having AI governance—Lessons from ChatGPT.* Debevoise Data Blog. www. debevoisedatablog.com/2023/04/05/the-value-of-having-ai-governance-lessons-from-chatgpt/

Gesser, A., Liebermann, E., Rubin, P., Skrzypczyk, J., Gressel, A., Roberts, M., Muse, M., & Runsten, M. (2022). *FTC proposed rulemaking part 4—Reducing risks associated with artificial intelligence.* Debevoise Data Blog. www.debevo isedatablog.com/2022/09/29/ftc-rulemaking-part-4-reducing-risks-associated-with-artificial-intelligence/

Gesser, A., Maddox, R., Brehmer, H., Gressel, A., Locwood, T., Scwartz, N., & Yonts, J. (2022). *Protecting AI models and data—The latest cybersecurity challenge.* Debevoise Data Blog. www.debevoisedatablog.com/2022/09/22/pro tecting-ai-models-and-data-the-latest-cybersecurity-challenge/

Gewirtz, D. (2023, September 7). *We're not ready for the impact of generative AI on elections.* ZDNet. www.zdnet.com/article/were-not-ready-for-the-impact-of-generative-ai-on-elections/

Gewirtz, D. (2023). *Will AI take programming jobs or turn programmers into AI managers?* ZDNet. www.zdnet.com/article/will-ai-take-programming-jobs-or-turn-programmers-into-ai-managers/

Gianchandani, E., & Parker, L. E. (2021, September 1). *Request for public comment: Seeking input on nationwide AI research resource implementation plan.* National Institutes of Health. https://nexus.od.nih.gov/all/2021/09/01/ request-for-public-comment-seeking-input-on-nationwide-ai-research-resource-implementation-plan/

Giaretta, A., & Dragoni, N. (2020). Community targeted phishing: A middle ground between massive and spear phishing through natural language gener-ation. In *Proceedings of 6th international conference in software engineering for defence applications: SEDA 2018* (pp. 86–93). Springer International Publishing.

Gibbs, S. (2017, August 20). Elon Musk leads 116 experts calling for outright ban of killer robots. *The Guardian.* www.theguardian.com/technology/2017/aug/20/ elon-musk-killer-robots-experts-outright-ban-lethal-autonomous-weapons-war

Gillum, J. (2023). *Leaked police files offer clues on how cops use data firms.* Bloomberg. www.bloomberg.com/news/articles/2023-01-25/hackers-claimed-to-breach-a-police-vendor-spilling-data-trove

Glaser, A. (2017, March 27). *Elon Musk wants to connect computers to your brain so we can keep up with robots.* Vox. www.vox.com/2017/3/27/15079226/elon-musk-computers-technology-brain-ai-artificial-intelligence-neural-lace

Glasure, E. (2018, December 11). *Artificial intelligence is the next big player in genomics.* BioSpace. www.biospace.com/article/artificial-intelligence-is-the-next-big-player-in-genomics/

Global Network on Extremism and Technology. (n.d.). *Extremist responses to coronavirus.* https://gnet-research.org/resources/extremist-responses-to-coro navirus/

Goasduff, L. (2019). *Gartner says 5.8 billion enterprise and automotive IoT endpoints will be in use in 2020.* Gartner. www.gartner.com/en/newsroom/press-releases/2019-08-29-gartner-says-5-8-billion-enterprise-and-automotive-io

Godon, S., & Rosenbach, E. (2022, February 15). America's cyber-reckoning: How to fix a failing strategy. *Foreign Affairs.* www.foreignaffairs.com/articles/united-states/2021-12-14/americas-cyber-reckoning

Goggin, B. (2023, January 1). *Wickr Me, Amazon's encrypted chat app, stops accepting new users.* NBC News. www.nbcnews.com/tech/tech-news/wickr-me-shut-down-new-user-amazon-encrypted-chat-app-stops-rcna63536

Goh, et al. (2021, March 4). *Multimodal neurons in artificial neural networks.* Distil. https://distill.pub/2021/multimodal-neurons/

Gold, A. (2022, April 23). *E.U. deal paves the way for strict Big Tech content rules.* Axios. www.axios.com/2022/04/23/eu-digital-services-act-tech-content-rules

Gold, A. (2023, January 30). *AI rockets ahead in vacuum of U.S. regulation.* Axios. www.axios.com/2023/01/30/ai-chatgpt-regulation-laws

Gold, A. (2023). *DOJ has eyes on AI, antitrust chief tells SXSW crowd.* Axios. www.axios.com/2023/03/13/doj-kanter-ai-artificial-intelligence-antitrust

Gold, A. (2023). *FTC opens probe into ChatGPT maker OpenAI.* Axios. www.axios.com/2023/07/13/ftc-investigate-openai-chatgpt

Gold, A. (2023). *FTC sues Amazon for "tricking and trapping" Prime customers.* Axios. www.axios.com/2023/06/21/ftc-lawsuit-amazon-prime

Gold, A. (2023). *How generative AI could generate more antisemitism.* Axios. www.axios.com/2023/05/25/generative-ai-antisemitism-bias

Gold, A. (2023). *Scoop: Ron Conway to convene tech execs on AI policy.* Axios. www.axios.com/2023/04/10/ron-conway-ai-policy-execs-convene

Gold, A. (2023). *Scoop: Schumer lays groundwork for Congress to regulate AI.* Axios. www.axios.com/2023/04/13/congress-regulate-ai-tech

Gold, A., & Heath, R. (2023). *White House gets AI firms to take safety pledge.* Axios. www.axios.com/2023/07/21/white-house-ai-firms-safety-pledge

Golden, A. (2023). *College students test drones for campus safety improvements.* Axios. www.axios.com/local/nw-arkansas/2023/03/10/arkansas-college-stude nts-droneup-campus-safety

Goldhill, O. (2018). *Police are using artificial intelligence to spot written lies.* Nextgov/FCW. www.nextgov.com/emerging-tech/2018/10/police-are-using-art ificial-intelligence-spot-written-lies/152388/

Goldman Sachs. (2022, November 15). *Humanoid robots: Sooner than you might think*. www.goldmansachs.com/intelligence/pages/humanoid-robots.html

Goldstein, E. (2023, August 4). *CISA cybersecurity strategic plan: Shifting the arc of national risk to create a safer future*. Cybersecurity and Infrastructure Security Agency. www.cisa.gov/news-events/news/cisa-cybersecurity-strategic-plan-shifting-arc-national-risk-create-safer-future

Goode, K., Kim, H.-M., & Deng, M. (2023, March). *Examining Singapore's AI Progress*. Center for Security and Emerging Technology (CSET). https://cset.geo rgetown.edu/publication/examining-singapores-ai-progress/

Goodin, D. (2022). *Numerous orgs hacked after installing weaponized open source apps*. ArsTechnica. https://arstechnica.com/information-technology/2022/09/north-korean-threat-actors-are-weaponizing-all-kinds-of-open-source-apps/

Goodin, D. (2023). *Feds seize 13 more DDoS-for-hire platforms in ongoing international crackdown*. ArsTechnica. https://arstechnica.com/information-technol ogy/2023/05/feds-seize-13-more-ddos-for-hire-platforms-in-ongoing-internatio nal-crackdown/

Goodin, D. (2023). *JumpCloud, an IT firm serving 200,000 orgs, says it was hacked by nation-state*. ArsTechnica. https://arstechnica.com/security/2023/07/jumpcloud-says-nation-state-hacker-breach-targeted-some-of-its-customers/

Goodwin, G. L. (2021, July 13). *Facial Recognition Technology: Federal Law Enforcement Agencies Should Have Better Awareness of Systems Used By Employees* (Testimony before the Subcommittee on Crime, Terrorism, and Homeland Security, Committee on the Judiciary, House of Representatives). United States Government Accountability Office.

Goodyear, J. (2022). An algorithm can predict future crimes with 90% accuracy. Here's why the creator thinks the tech won't be abused. *BBC Science Focus*. www.sciencefocus.com/news/algorithm-predict-future-crimes-90-accuracy-heres-why-creator-thinks-tech-wont-be-abused

Gordon, S., & Rosenbach, E. (2022, February 15). America's cyber-reckoning. *Foreign Affairs*. www.foreignaffairs.com/articles/united-states/2021-12-14/americas-cyber-reckoning

Gordon-Reed, A. (2020, August 31). America's original sin. *Foreign Affairs*. www. foreignaffairs.com/articles/united-states/2017-12-12/americas-original-si

Gottsegen, G. (2018, June 6). *Drones are now being trained to spot violent people in crowds*. CNET. www.cnet.com/news/ai-drones-are-being-trained-to-spot-violence-from-the-sky/

Goud, N. (2019, January 11). *AI to help British police detect fake crimes*. Cybersecurity Insiders. www.cybersecurity-insiders.com/ai-to-help-british-pol ice-detect-fake-crimes/

Grabosky, P. (2007). *Electronic crime*. Pearson Prentice Hall.

Grabosky, P., Smith, R. G., & Urbas, G. (2004). *Cyber criminals on trial*. Cambridge University.

Graham, E. (2022). *AI could help Congress schedule and find unexpected consensus, expert says*. Nextgov/FCW. www.nextgov.com/emerging-tech/2022/07/ai-could-help-congress-schedule-and-find-unexpected-consensus-expert-says/ 375105/

Graham, E. (2022). *Amazon admits to giving ring footage without owners' permission*. Nextgov/FCW. www.nextgov.com/analytics-data/2022/07/amazon-admits-giving-police-ring-footage-without-owners-permission/374480/

Graham, E. (2022). *Climate change poses threat to U.S. national security, GAO says*. Nextgov/FCW. www.nextgov.com/policy/2022/09/climate-change-poses-threat-us-national-security-gao-says/377330/

Graham, E. (2022). *DOD announces new contract awards for its "internet in space" effort*. Nextgov/FCW. www.nextgov.com/emerging-tech/2022/11/dod-announces-new-contract-awards-its-internet-space-effort/379240/

Graham, E. (2022). *DOD creates office to enhance investments in tech vital to national security*. Nextgov/FCW. www.nextgov.com/emerging-tech/2022/12/dod-creates-office-enhance-investments-tech-vital-national-security/380420/

Graham, E. (2022). *FCC moves to limit the number of spam and scam texts*. Nextgov/FCW. www.nextgov.com/policy/2022/10/fcc-moves-limit-number-spam-and-scam-texts/378200/

Graham, E. (2022). *FCC rule for blocking overseas robocalls receives approval*. Nextgov/FCW. www.nextgov.com/policy/2022/11/fcc-rule-blocking-overseas-robocalls-receives-approval/380060/

Graham, E. (2022). *Federal action is needed to protect consumer data, new report says*. Nextgov/FCW. www.nextgov.com/analytics-data/2022/09/federal-action-needed-protect-consumer-data-new-report-says/377089/

Graham, E. (2022). *House oversight Dems seeking data from social media companies about threats to law enforcement*. Nextgov/FCW. www.nextgov.com/analytics-data/2022/08/house-oversight-dems-seeking-data-social-media-companies-about-threats-law-enforcement/376201/

Graham, E. (2022). *Lockheed Martin, Verizon demonstrate capabilities of 5G-enabled drones for DOD*. Nextgov/FCW. www.nextgov.com/emerging-tech/2022/09/lockheed-martin-verizon-demonstrate-capabilities-5g-enabled-drones-dod/377795/

Graham, E. (2022). *Social media's national security implications draw lawmaker scrutiny*. Nextgov/FCW. www.nextgov.com/cybersecurity/2022/09/social-medias-national-security-implications-draw-lawmaker-scrutiny/377205/

Graham, E. (2023, April 24). *DHS outlines cyber priorities in release of delayed review*. Nextgov/FCW. www.nextgov.com/emerging-tech/2023/04/dhs-outlines-cyber-priorities-release-delayed-review/385557/

Graham, E. (2023, April 28). *DOD's frontline AI adoption still limited by network and data collection*. Nextgov/FCW. www.nextgov.com/artificial-intelligence/2023/04/dods-frontline-ai-adoption-still-limited-network-and-data-collection/385732/

Graham, E. (2023, May 22). *Lawmakers want DHS to assess national security risks of doxing*. Nextgov/FCW. www.nextgov.com/cybersecurity/2023/05/lawmakers-want-dhs-assess-national-security-risks-doxing/386642/

Graham, E. (2023, June 12). *House cyber panel's NDAA draft prioritizes commercial tech, expert engagement*. Nextgov/FCW. www.nextgov.com/cybersecurity/2023/06/house-cyber-panels-ndaa-draft-prioritizes-commercial-tech-expert-engagement/387441/

Graham, E. (2023, July 10). *Interior's cyber practices allow for easily crackable passwords, watchdog finds.* Nextgov/FCW. www.nextgov.com/cybersecurity/2023/01/interiors-cyber-practices-allow-easily-crackable-passwords-watchdog-finds/381620/

Graham, E. (2023, August 4). *FCC wants to use AI to measure commercial spectrum use.* Nextgov/FCW. www.nextgov.com/artificial-intelligence/2023/08/fcc-wants-use-ai-measure-commercial-spectrum-use/389148/

Graham, E. (2023, August 8). *GAO: IRS must enhance cyber oversight of third-party vendors, modernize online services.* Nextgov/FCW. www.nextgov.com/digital-government/2023/08/gao-irs-must-enhance-cyber-oversight-third-party-vendors-modernize-online-services/389229/

Graham, E. (2023, December 12). *Senate democrats seek to establish civil rights offices for AI.* Nextgov/FCW. www.nextgov.com/artificial-intelligence/2023/12/senate-democrats-seek-establish-civil-rights-offices-ai/392709/

Graham, E. (2023, December 19). *How agencies will leverage virtual reality, generative AI over the next 2 years.* Nextgov/FCW. www.nextgov.com/emerging-tech/2023/12/how-agencies-will-leverage-virtual-reality-generative-ai-over-next-2-years/392888/

Graham, E. (2023). *AI and China are "defining challenges of our time," CISA director says.* Nextgov/FCW. www.nextgov.com/emerging-tech/2023/05/ai-and-china-are-defining-challenges-our-time-cisa-director-says/386952/

Graham, E. (2023). *Biden administration examining how companies use AI to surveil employees.* Nextgov/FCW. www.nextgov.com/policy/2023/05/biden-administration-examining-how-companies-use-ai-surveil-employees/385883/

Graham, E. (2023). *Bipartisan bill seeks to safeguard US data from foreign exploitation.* Nextgov/FCW. www.nextgov.com/policy/2023/06/bipartisan-bill-seeks-safeguard-us-data-foreign-exploitation/387548/

Graham, E. (2023). *DHS unveils departmentwide body camera policy.* Nextgov/FCW. www.nextgov.com/policy/2023/05/dhs-unveils-departmentwide-body-camera-policy/386701/

Graham, E. (2023). *Digital authoritarianism poses "critical threat" to national security, Intel chief says.* Nextgov/FCW. www.nextgov.com/emerging-tech/2023/04/digital-authoritarianism-poses-critical-threat-national-security-intel-chief-says/385614/

Graham, E. (2023). *DOD's data integration experiments help to identify benefits and barriers to new tech.* Nextgov/FCW. www.nextgov.com/digital-government/2023/07/dods-data-integration-experiments-help-identify-benefits-and-barriers-new-tech/388744/

Graham, E. (2023). *DOD's zero trust initiative is a unique "unity of effort," Air Force CIO says.* Nextgov/FCW. www.nextgov.com/cybersecurity/2023/05/dods-zero-trust-initiative-unique-unity-effort-air-force-cio-says/386038/

Graham, E. (2023). *Enhanced information sharing with industry key to deterring digital threats, NSA cyber chief says.* Nextgov/FCW. www.nextgov.com/emerging-tech/2023/04/enhanced-information-sharing-industry-key-deterring-digital-threats-nsa-cyber-chief-says/385071/

Graham, E. (2023). *Evolving' CISA program helped agencies quickly respond to recent cyber incidents.* Nextgov/FCW. www.nextgov.com/cybersecurity/2023/07/evolving-cisa-program-helped-agencies-quickly-respond-recent-cyber-incidents/388782/

Graham, E. (2023). *House bill mandates disclosure of AI-generated content in political ads.* Nextgov/FCW. www.nextgov.com/emerging-tech/2023/05/house-bill-mandates-disclosure-ai-generated-content-political-ads/385935/

Graham, E. (2023). *House Dem sounds alarm about AI in political messaging.* Nextgov/FCW. www.nextgov.com/artificial-intelligence/2023/07/house-dem-sounds-alarm-about-ai-political-messaging/388599/

Graham, E. (2023). *Interior's cyber practices allow for easily crackable passwords, watchdog finds.* Nextgov/FCW. www.nextgov.com/cybersecurity/2023/01/interiors-cyber-practices-allow-easily-crackable-passwords-watchdog-finds/381620/

Graham, E. (2023). *Lack of emerging tech framework is "weakening" US stance against China, lawmakers warn.* Nextgov/FCW. www.nextgov.com/emerging-tech/2023/02/lack-emerging-tech-framework-weakening-us-stance-against-china-lawmakers-warn/382483/

Graham, E. (2023). *Lawmakers propose shoring up nuclear cyber standards ahead of NDAA markup.* Nextgov/FCW. www.nextgov.com/cybersecurity/2023/06/lawmakers-propose-shoring-nuclear-cyber-standards-ahead-ndaa-markup/387632/

Graham, E. (2023). *Lawmakers reintroduce legislation to bolster satellite cybersecurity.* Nextgov/FCW. www.nextgov.com/cybersecurity/2023/05/lawmakers-reintroduce-legislation-bolster-satellite-cybersecurity/385991/

Graham, E. (2023). *Majority of GAO's cyber recommendations since 2010 have gone unresolved.* Nextgov/FCW. www.nextgov.com/cybersecurity/2023/01/majority-gaos-cyber-recommendations-2010-have-gone-unresolved/382043/

Graham, E. (2023). *National cyber strategy seeks to shift burden from consumers to tech firms.* Nextgov/FCW. www.nextgov.com/cybersecurity/2023/03/national-cyber-strategy-seeks-shift-burden-consumers-tech-firms/383560/

Graham, E. (2023). *Schumer says "don't count Congress out" when it comes to regulating AI.* Nextgov/FCW. www.nextgov.com/artificial-intelligence/2023/06/schumer-says-dont-count-congress-out-when-it-comes-regulating-ai/387768/

Graham, E. (2023). *Unmonitored networks put US nuclear arsenal at risk, GAO finds.* Nextgov/FCW. www.nextgov.com/cybersecurity/2023/05/unmonitored-networks-put-us-nuclear-arsenal-risk-gao-finds/386910/

Graham, E. (2023). *US cyber diplomat calls for bolstering American advantage in Global Tech Policy.* Nextgov/FCW. www.nextgov.com/policy/2023/02/us-cyber-diplomat-calls-bolstering-american-advantage-global-tech-policy/382526/

Graham, E. (2024, January 2). *Bill sets transparency standards for AI models, including use of copyrighted material.* Nextgov/FCW. www.nextgov.com/artificial-intelligence/2024/01/bill-sets-transparency-standards-ai-models-including-use-copyrighted-material/393052/

Graham, E. (2024, January 29). *Stop funding predictive policing tech without "evidence standards," lawmakers tell DOJ.* Nextgov/FCW. www.nextgov.com/artificial-intelligence/2024/01/stop-funding-predictive-policing-tech-without-evidence-standards-lawmakers-tell-doj/393705/

Graham, E. (2024, January 29). *TSA uses "minimum" data to fine-tune its facial recognition, but some experts still worry.* Nextgov/FCW. www.nextgov.com/ emerging-tech/2024/01/tsa-uses-minimum-data-fine-tune-its-facial-recognition-some-experts-still-worry/393672/

Graham, E. (2024, February 5). *Autonomous tech featured in Senate border and foreign aid bill.* Nextgov/FCW. www.nextgov.com/emerging-tech/2024/02/aut onomous-tech-featured-senate-border-and-foreign-aid-bill/393931/

Graham, E. (2024, June 7). *Lawmakers look to restore TSA funding to speed screening tech deployment.* Nextgov/FCW. www.nextgov.com/modernization/ 2024/06/lawmakers-look-restore-tsa-funding-speed-screening-tech-deployment/ 397221/

Graham, E. G. (2023, March 14). *Increased remote work for many governments also raises cyber risks.* Route Fifty. www.route-fifty.com/tech-data/2023/03/ report-increased-remote-work-many-governments-also-raises-cyber-risks/ 383986/

Graham, E. G. (2023, March 21). *"Alarming content" from AI chatbots raises child safety concerns, Senator says.* NextGov. www.nextgov.com/artificial-intel ligence/2023/03/alarming-content-ai-chatbots-raises-child-safety-concerns-sena tor-says/384251/

Graph Convolution Network. (2022, June). *Data Lessons from COVID.*

Graph Convolution Network. (2022, August). *Smart city apps.*

Graph Convolution Network. (2023, February). *Phishing.*

Greely, H. (2018). *The end of sex and the future of human reproduction.* Harvard University Press. www.hup.harvard.edu/books/9780674984011

Greene, T. (2020, August 6). *Why "human-like" is a low bar for most AI projects.* The Next Web. https://thenextweb.com/neural/2020/08/06/why-human-like-is-a-low-bar-for-most-ai-projects/

Greenemeier, L. (2017, October 18). AI versus AI: Self-taught AlphaGo Zero vanquishes its predecessor. *Scientific American.* www.scientificamerican.com/ article/ai-versus-ai-self-taught-alphago-zero-vanquishes-its-predecessor/

Greig, J. (2021, December 13). *Kronos hit with ransomware, warns of data breach and "several week" outage.* ZDNet. www.zdnet.com/article/hr-platform-kro nos-brought-down-by-ransomware-attack-ukg-warns-of-data-breach/

Greig, J. (2021, December 14). *Virginia legislative agencies and commissions hit with ransomware attack.* ZDNet. www.zdnet.com/article/virginia-legislative-agencies-and-commissions-hit-with-ransomware-attack/

Greig, J. (2022, January 25). *Hackers hijacking Instagram accounts of companies and influencers, demanding ransom.* ZDNet. www.zdnet.com/article/hack ers-hijacking-instagram-accounts-of-companies-and-influencers-demanding-ransom/

Greig, J. (2022, January 26). *Report: Cybercriminals laundered at least $8.6 billion worth of cryptocurrency in 2021.* ZDNet. www.zdnet.com/finance/blockchain/ cybercriminals-laundered-at-least-8-6-billion-worth-of-cryptocurrency-in-2021/

Greig, J. (2023, January 12). *Fortinet warns of hackers targeting governments through VPN vulnerability.* The Record. https://therecord.media/fortinet-warns-of-hackers-targeting-governments-through-vpn-vulnerability

Greig, J. (2023, March 10). *AT&T says 9 million customers exposed in January vendor breach*. The Record. https://therecord.media/att-says-nine-million-expo sed-in-data-breach

Greig, J. (2023, April 6). *CISA director: AI cyber threats the "biggest issue we're going to deal with this century."* The Record. https://therecord.media/cisa-direc tor-ai-cyber-threats-the-biggest-of-the-century

Greig, J. (2023, July 18). *TJ Maxx, Shutterfly, TomTom latest organizations to confirm MOVEit breaches*. The Record. https://therecord.media/more-compan ies-confirm-moveit-related-data-incidents-shutterfly-tjmaxx-tomtom

Greig, J. (2023, July 31). *"Worm-like" botnet malware targeting popular Redis storage tool*. The Record. https://therecord.media/redis-malware-worm-botnet

Greig, J. (2023, August 9). *IRS confirms takedown of bulletproof hosting pro-vider Lolek*. The Record. https://therecord.media/lolek-bulletproof-hosting-seiz ure-fbi-irs

Grimm, E., & Stabile, J. (2020, February 6). *Confronting Russia's role in trans-national white supremacist extremism*. Just Security. www.justsecurity.org/ 68420/confronting-russias-role-in-transnational-white-supremacist-extremism/

Groll, E. (2023, March 20). *Chinese-linked hackers deployed the most zero-day vulnerabilities in 2022, researchers say*. CyberScoop. https://cyberscoop.com/ mandiant-zero-day-vulnerabilities-china/

Groll, E., & Vasquez, C. (2023, August 10). *Satellite hack on eve of Ukraine war was a coordinated, multi-pronged assault*. CyberScoop. https://cyberscoop.com/ viasat-ka-sat-hack-black-hat/

Gross, S. R., O'Brien, B., Hu, C., & Kennedy, E. (2014). Rate of false conviction of criminal defendants who are sentenced to death. *PNAS, 111*(20), 7230–7235. www.pnas.org/doi/10.1073/pnas.1306417111

Grossmann, I., Feinberg, M., Parker, D. C., Christakis, N. A., Tetlock, P. E., & Cunningham, W. A. (2023). AI and the transformation of social science research. *Science (New York, N.Y.), 380*(6650), 1108–1109. https://doi.org/10.1126/scie nce.adi1778

Guo, E., & Renaldi, A. (2022, April 6). Deception, exploited workers, and cash handouts: How Worldcoin recruited its first half a million test users. *MIT Technology Review*. www.technologyreview.com/2022/04/06/1048981/worldc oin-cryptocurrency-biometrics-web3/

Gutman-Argemi, C. (2023, April 12). Europe is paranoid about data but does nothing about spyware. *Foreign Policy*. https://foreignpolicy.com/2023/04/12/ europe-spyware-abuse-pegasus-data-privacy-hungary-spain/

Gyori, L., & Kreko, P. (2017). *Russian disinformation and extremism in Hungary | Warsaw Institute*. Warsaw Institute. https://warsawinstitute.org/russian-disinfo rmation-extremism-hungary/

Haan, K. (2023). Over 75% of consumers are concerned about misinformation from artificial intelligence. *Forbes*. www.forbes.com/advisor/business/artificial-intelligence-consumer-sentiment/

Habuka, H. (2023, February 14). *Japan's approach to A.I. regulation and its impact on the 2023 G7 presidency*. Center for Strategic & International Studies. www.csis.org/analysis/japans-approach-ai-regulation-and-its-impact-2023-g7-presidency

Halter, N. (2021, February 12). *Minneapolis bans police from using facial recognition tech.* Axios. www.axios.com/local/twin-cities/2021/02/12/minneapolis-poised-to-ban-police-from-using-facial-recognition-technology

Haltiwanger, J. (2017, November 9). *Russia's military has new robot tank it says fights better than human soldiers.* Yahoo Sports. https://sports.yahoo.com/russia-apos-military-robot-tank-184040234.html

Hambling, D. (2021, November 5). Drone used in attack on US electrical grid last year, report reveals. *New Scientist.* www.newscientist.com/article/2296480-drone-used-in-attack-on-us-electrical-grid-last-year-report-reveals/

Hamre, J. J., Lewis, J. A., & Allen, G. C. (2022, April 8). *Responsible AI in Global Context.* Center for Strategic & International Studies. www.csis.org/events/responsible-ai-global-context

Hannas, W. C., Chang, H. M., Chou, D. H., & Fleeger, B. (2022, July). *China's Advanced AI Research: Monitoring China's Paths to "General" Artificial Intelligence.* Center for Security and Emerging Technology. https://cset.georgetown.edu/publication/chinas-advanced-ai-research/

Hao, K. (2019, February 26). Why AI is a threat to democracy—And what we can do to stop it. *MIT Technology Review.* www.technologyreview.com/2019/02/26/66043/why-ai-is-a-threat-to-democracyand-what-we-can-do-to-stop-it

Hao, K. (2021, January 8). Five ways to make AI a greater force for good in 2021. *MIT Technology Review.* www.technologyreview.com/2021/01/08/1015907/ai-force-for-good-in-2021/

Hao, K. (2021, January 22). AI could make healthcare fairer—By helping us believe what patients say. *MIT Technology Review.* www.technologyreview.com/2021/01/22/1016577/ai-fairer-healthcare-patient-outcomes/

Harding, E. (2022, January 27). *Mover over JARVIS, meet OSCAR: Open source, Cloud based, AI-enabled reporting for the intelligence community.* Center for Strategic & International Studies (CSIS). www.csis.org/analysis/move-over-jarvis-meet-oscar

Harding, E. (2023). *From maybe-secure to responsible security: The new national cybersecurity strategy.* Center for Strategic & International Studies. www.csis.org/analyss/maybe-secure-responsible-security-new-national-cybersecurity-strategy

Harding, E. (2023, July 26). *Three ways a technological revolution will impact the intel community.* Defense News. www.defensenews.com/opinion/2023/07/26/three-ways-a-technological-revolution-will-impact-the-intel-community/

Harding, E., & Ghoorhoo, H. (2022). *Hard choices in a ransomware attack choices in a ransomware attack .* Center for Strategic & International Studies. www.csis.org/analysis/hard-choices-ransomware-attack

Harding, E., & Ghoorhoo, H. (2023, April). *Seven critical technologies for winning the next war.* Center for Strategic & International Studies. www.csis.org/analysis/seven-critical-technologies-winning-next-war

Haridy, R. (2018, February 22). *South Korea establishes research center to develop autonomous weapons.* New Atlas. https://newatlas.com/korea-ai-weapons-military-kaist-hanwha/53576/

Harris, R. (2020, June 22). *Why aren't people smarter? The dubious benefits of intelligence, real or artificial.* ZDNet. www.zdnet.com/article/why-arent-people-smarter/

Harris, S., Mekhennet, S., & Nakhlawi, R. (2021). Far-right groups make plans for protests and assaults before and after Inauguration Day. *The Washington Post.* www.washingtonpost.com/national-security/far-right-violent-plans-inauguration/2021/01/14/15668f16-567d-11eb-a817-e5e7f8a406d6_story.html

Harrison, M. (2023). *90% of online content will be AI-generated by 2026.* The Byte. https://futurism.com/the-byte/experts-90-online-content-ai-generated

Hart, K. (2023). *Facial recognition surges in retail stores.* Axios. www.axios.com/2021/07/19/facial-recognition-retail-surge

Harwell, D. (2018, November 23). Wanted: The "perfect babysitter." Must pass AI scan for respect and attitude. *The Washington Post.* www.washingtonpost.com/technology/2018/11/16/wanted-perfect-babysitter-must-pass-ai-scan-respect-attitude/

Harwell, D. (2019, December 19). Federal study confirms racial bias of many facial-recognition systems, cast doubt on their expanding use. *The Washington Post.* www.washingtonpost.com/technology/2019/12/19/federal-study-confirms-racial-bias-many-facial-recognition-systems-casts-doubt-their-expanding-use/

Hassold, C. (2022, December 12). *The double-edged sword of CHATGPT: How threat actors could ...—Abnormal.* Abnormal Security. https://abnormalsecurity.com/blog/double-edged-sword-of-chatgpt

Hate Speech International. (2017). *Neo-Nazis in the North: The Nordic Resistance Movement in* Finland, Sweden and Norway *(Investigating Extremism).* www.hate-speech.org/wp-content/uploads/2017/03/neo-nazis-in-the-north.pdf

Hawkins, A. J. (2023, February 14). *Hyundai and Kia forced to update software on millions of vehicles because of the viral TikTok challenge.* The Verge. www.theverge.com/2023/2/14/23599300/hyundai-kia-car-theft-software-update-free-tiktok-challenge

Hawkins, E. (2023, January 11). *Codeword marketing agency hires AI "interns."* Axios. www.axios.com/2023/01/11/marketing-ai-interns

Hayden, M. (2019). *Stephen Miller's affinity for white nationalism revealed in leaked emails.* Southern Poverty Law Center. www.splcenter.org/hatewatch/2019/11/12/stephen-millers-affinity-white-nationalism-revealed-leaked-emails

Hayden, M. (2019). *U.S. State Department Official Involved in White Nationalist Movement, Hatewatch Determines.* Southern Poverty Law Center. www.splcenter.org/gebert

Hayden, M. (2020). *U.S. White Nationalist Group Linked to Pro-Kremlin Propagandist.* Southern Poverty Law Center. www.splcenter.org/hatewatch/2020/10/06/us-white-nationalist-group-linked-pro-kremlin-propagandist

Health Matters. (n.d.). *Behind the latest advance in IVF treatment.* New York Presbyterian. https://healthmatters.nyp.org/behind-the-latest-advance-in-ivf-treatment/

Heath, R. (2023, May 11). *Democracy isn't ready for its AI test.* Axios. www.axios.com/2023/05/11/democracy-ai-artificial-intelligence-2024-elections

Heath, R. (2023, May 15). *AI's loneliness crisis.* Axios. www.axios.com/2023/05/15/ai-loneliness-crisis-mental-health-pets

Heath, R. (2023, August 8). *U.S. public opinion is evenly split on AI.* Axios. www.axios.com/2023/08/08/ai-divides-america-polls-chatgpt

Heath, R. (2023, December 11). *There's a big catch in the EU's landmark new AI law.* Axios. www.axios.com/2023/12/11/eu-ai-law-catch

Heath, R. (2023, December 20). *Child abuse images found in AI training data.* Axios. www.axios.com/2023/12/20/ai-training-data-child-abuse-images-stanford

Heath, R. (2023). *AI boom's big winners are all in four states.* Axios. www.axios.com/2023/07/24/ai-goldrush-concentrated-4-states

Heath, R. (2023). *AI productivity boost will hit banks, retail first, study finds.* Axios. www.axios.com/2023/06/14/ai-productivity-revolution-banks-retail

Heath, R. (2023). *AI's next battle: open or closed.* Axios. www.axios.com/2023/06/26/ais-next-battle-open-closed-chatgpt

Heath, R. (2023). *Another AI threat: The next pandemic.* Axios. www.axios.com/2023/06/16/pandemic-bioterror-ai-chatgpt-bioattacks

Heath, R. (2023). *China races ahead of U.S. on AI regulation.* Axios. www.axios.com/2023/05/08/china-ai-regulation-race

Heath, R. (2023). *What is private 5G and how industries are using it.* Axios. www.axios.com/2023/07/13/5g-private-networks

Heath, R. (2024, February 8). *FCC outlaws AI voices in robocall scams.* Axios. www.axios.com/2024/02/08/fcc-ai-robocalls-illegal

Heath, R. (2024, March 20). *AI-fueled scams target tax refunds.* Axios. www.axios.com/2024/03/20/tax-returns-scam-ai-cybersecurity

Heath, R. (2024, May 9). *Don't fear AI-driven "biosurveillance" experts say.* Axios. www.axios.com/2024/05/09/ai-superbugs-biosurveillance-fear-bio defense

Heath, R., & Morrone, M. (2023, December 27). *Generative AI will have another wild ride in 2024.* Axios. www.axios.com/2023/12/27/ai-predictions-tech-trends-2024-openai-chatgpt

Heaven, W. (2021, January 14). AIs that read sentences are now catching coronavirus mutations. *MIT Technology Review.* www.technologyreview.com/2021/01/14/1016162/ai-language-nlp-coronavirus-hiv-flu-mutations-antinbodies-immune-vaccines/

Heaven, W. (2021, February 5). Predictive policing is still racist—Whatever data is uses. *MIT Technology Review.* www.technologyreview.com/2021/02/05/1017560/predictive-policing-racist-algorithmic-bias-data-crime-predpol/

Helmus, T. C. (2018). *Russian social media influence: Understanding Russian propaganda in Eastern Europe.* RAND Corporation. www.rand.org/pubs/research_reports/RR2237.html

Helmus, T. C. (2022, July). *Artificial intelligence, deepfakes, and disinformation: A primer.* RAND Corporation. www.rand.org/pubs/perspectives/PEA1043-1.html

Hemsoth, N. (2021, January 11). *2021 could be the year of quantum drug discovery.* The Next platform. www.nextplatform.com/2021/01/11/2021-could-be-the-year-of-quantum-drug-discovery/

Herb, J., Perez, E., O'Sullivan, D., & Morales, M. (2020). *What we know about the extremists taking part in riots across the US.* CNN. www.cnn.com/2020/05/31/politics/outside-influence-extremists-riots-us/index.html

Hereid, A. (2022). *Why household robot servants are a lot harder to build than robotic vacuums and automated warehouse workers.* Nextgov/FCW. www.next gov.com/ideas/2022/09/why-household-robot-servants-are-lot-harder-build-robotic-vacuums-and-automated-warehouse-workers/376867/

Herr, T. (2020, October 19). *Securing the energy transition: Innovative cyber solutions for grid resiliency.* Atlantic Council. www.atlanticcouncil.org/event/securing-the-energy-transition/

Hicks, K. (2022, February). *Securing defense-critical supply chains: An action plan developed in response to President Biden's executive order 14017.* U.S. Department of Defense.

High-Level Expert Group on Artificial Intelligence (AI HLEG). (2019). *Ethics guidelines for trustworthy AI.* https://digital-strategy.ec.europa.eu/en/policies/expert-group-ai

Hill, J., McKenney, R., & Konkoly-Thege, K. (2023). *Moving toward an all-of-the-above approach to quantum cybersecurity.* Center for Strategic & International Studies. www.csis.org/analysis/moving-toward-all-above-approach-quantum-cybersecurity

Hiner, J. (2023, January 1). *CES 2023 preview: 4 big questions that will shape the week.* ZDNet. www.zdnet.com/article/ces-2023-preview-4-big-questions-that-will-shape-the-week/

Hiner, J. (2023, January 6). *Best of CES 2023: 6 innovations that will shape the future.* ZDNet. www.zdnet.com/article/best-of-ces-2023-innovations-that-will-shape-the-future/

Hiner, J. (2023, December 20). *ZDNet looks back on tech in 2023, and looks ahead to 2024.* ZDNet. www.zdnet.com/article/zdnet-looks-back-on-tech-in-2023-and-looks-ahead-to-2024/

Hines, A. (2021, February 2). *How normal people deployed facial recognition on Capitol Hill protesters.* Vice. www.vice.com/en/article/4ad5k3/how-normal-people-deployed-facial-recognition-on-capitol-hill-protesters

Holder, S. (2020, August 6). *In San Diego, smart streetlights spark surveillance reform.* CityLab. www.bloomberg.com/news/articles/2020-08-06/a-surveillance-standoff-over-smart-streetlights

Hollywood, J. S., Woods, D., Silberglitt, R., & Jackson, B. A. (2015). *Using future internet technologies to strengthen criminal justice.* RAND Corporation. www.rand.org/pubs/research_reports/RR928.html

Home Office News team. (2023, October 29). *Police use of facial recognition: Factsheet.* GOV.UK. https://homeofficemedia.blog.gov.uk/2023/10/29/police-use-of-facial-recognition-factsheet/

Homeland Security. (2022, December). *DHS S&T develops portable outdoor gunshot detection technology for law enforcement.* www.dhs.gov/science-and-tec hnology/news/2022/12/29/dhs-st-develops-portable-outdoor-gunshot-detection-technology-law-enforcement

Homeland Security Advisory Council. (2020, November 12). *Final report of the biometrics subcommittee.* www.dhs.gov/sites/default/files/publications/final_ hsac_biometrics_subcommittee_report_11-12-2020.pdf

Homeland Security Digital Library. (2020, December 22). *FEMA 2020 national preparedness report.*

Hooijdonk, R. (2021, September 9). *"Is there a problem, (robotic) officer?"* Richard Van Hooijdonk Blog. https://blog.richardvanhooijdonk.com/en/is-there-a-problem-robotic-officer/

Hooks, C. (2021, May 12). Elon Musk is turning Boca Chica into a space-travel hub. Not everyone is starstruck. *Texas Monthly.* www.texasmonthly.com/news-politics/elon-musk-boca-chica-starbase-texas/

Horn-Muller, A. (2023). *AI can now forecast the next food crisis.* Axios. www. axios.com/2023/03/10/ai-forecast-food-crisis

House of Lords, Justice and Home Affairs Committee. (2022). *Technology rules? The advent of new technologies in the justice system* (1st Report of Session 2021–22, HL Paper 180). Published by the Authority of the House of Lords. https:// committees.parliament.uk/publications/9453/documents/163029/default/

Howe, E. (2022). *The army can predict when some leaders are at risk of misconduct.* Nextgov/FCW. www.nextgov.com/emerging-tech/2022/10/army-can-pred ict-when-some-leaders-are-risk-misconduct/378498/

Howell, J., & Maimon, D. (2022). *Darknet markets generate millions in revenue selling stolen personal data, supply chain study finds.* Nextgov/FCW. www.next gov.com/ideas/2022/12/darknet-markets-generate-millions-revenue-selling-sto len-personal-data-supply-chain-study-finds/380615/

Howell, S. (2023, July 24). *Technology competition: A battle for brains.* Center for a New American Security. www.cnas.org/publications/reports/technology-comp etition-a-battle-for-brains

HRW. (2017, May 15). *China: Police DNA database threatens privacy.* Human Rights Watch. www.hrw.org/news/2017/05/15/china-police-dna-database-threatens-privacy

Huang, Z. (2018). *Chinese police are wearing sunglasses that can recognize faces.* Nextgov/FCW. www.nextgov.com/analytics-data/2018/02/chinese-police-are-wearing-sunglasses-can-recognize-faces/145886/

Hubbard, T., & Chawda, V. (2023). *Rethinking cybersecurity in a boundaryless world.* Nextgov/FCW. www.nextgov.com/ideas/2023/04/rethinking-cybersecur ity-boundaryless-world/385677/

Hughes, O. (2021, December 5). *Remote working jobs: 5 problems we need to solve in 2022.* ZDNet. www.zdnet.com/article/remote-working-jobs-5-probl ems-we-need-to-solve-in-2022/

Hughes, O. (2021, December 9). *Remote-working job surveillance is on the rise. for some, the impact could be devastating.* ZDNet. www.zdnet.com/article/rem ote-working-job-surveillance-is-on-the-rise-for-some-the-impact-could-be-deva stating/

Hughes, O. (2022, January 20). *Automation could make 12 million jobs redundant. here's who's most at risk.* ZDNet. www.zdnet.com/article/automation-could-make-12-million-jobs-redundant-heres-whos-most-at-risk/

Huntley, S. (2023). *Fog of war: How the Ukraine conflict transformed the cyber threat landscape.* Threat Analysis Group. https:/blog.google/threat-analysis-group/fog-of-war-how-the-ukraine-conflict-transformed-the-cyber-threat-landscape/

Huntley, S. (2024, February 6). *Buying spying: How the commercial surveillance industry works and what can be done about it.* Google Threat Analysis Group. https://blog.google/threat-analysis-group/commercial-surveillance-vendors-google-tag-report/

Hutson, M. (2023, November 30). Tiny robots made from human cells heal damaged tissue. *Nature.* www.nature.com/articles/d41586-023-03777-x

Hvistendahl, M. (2019, April 15). Can we stop AI outsmarting humanity? *The Guardian.* www.theguardian.com/technology/2019/mar/28/can-we-stop-robots-outsmarting-humanity-artificial-intelligence-singularity

Iaria, M. (2022, July 25). *Bunnings, Kmart temporarily turn off facial recognition technology as privacy probe continues.* news.com.au. www.news.com.au/technology/bunnings-temporarily-turns-off-facial-recognition-technology-as-privacy-probe-continues/news-story/02b1f7b37e92c3df4630a48053623679

IFR Press Releases. (2018, February 7). *Robot density rises globally.* International Federation of Robots. https://ifr.org/ifr-press-releases/news/robot-density-rises-globally

Igini, M. (2022, February 8). *Could the Bill Gates smart city lead the way for other cities to follow?* Earth.Org. https://earth.org/bill-gates-smart-city/

Ilascu, I. (2022). *Russian hackers use new info stealer malware against Ukrainian orgs.* BleepingComputer. www.bleepingcomputer.com/news/security/russian-hackers-use-new-info-stealer-malware-against-ukrainian-orgs/

Ilascu, I. (2023, January 3). *Ransomware impacts over 200 govt, edu, healthcare orgs in 2022.* BleepingComputer. www.bleepingcomputer.com/news/security/ransomware-impacts-over-200-govt-edu-healthcare-orgs-in-2022/

IMF. (2022, July 26). *World economic outlook update, July 2022: Gloomy and more uncertain.* www.imf.org/en/Publications/WEO/Issues/2022/07/26/world-economic-outlook-update-july-2022

InCyber. (2023). *AI deciphers passwords from keyboard sounds.* https://incyber.org/en/ai-deciphers-passwords-keyboard-sounds/

InCyber. (2023). *MOVEit vulnerability: The list of victims grows longer.* https://incyber.org/en/moveit-vulnerability-list-victims-grows-longer/

InCyber. (2023). *Phishing attack uses QR code.* https://incyber.org/en/phishing-attack-uses-qr-code/

Infoblox. (2023). *Dog hunt: Finding Decoy Dog toolkit via anomalous DNS traffic.* https://blogs.infoblox.com/cyber-threat-intelligence/cyber-threat-advisory/dog-hunt-finding-decoy-dog-toolkit-via-anomalous-dns-traffic/

InsideTrade.com. (2023, December 13). *Analyst: U.S.–EU trade frictions over artificial intelligence are likely.* https://insidetrade.com/daily-news/analyst-us-eu-trade-frictions-over-artificial-intelligence-are-likely

Inskeep, S., & Allam, H. (2021). *Examining domestic extremist threats to Americans and U.S. government [News].* NPR. www.npr.org/2021/02/02/963115515/examining-domestic-extremist-threats-to-americans-and-u-s-government

Inspector General U.S. Department of Defense. (2023, February 9). *Management advisory: The DoDs use of mobile applications* (Report No. DODIG-2023-041). www.dodig.mil/reports.html/Article/3294159/management-advisory-the-dods-use-of-mobile-applications-report-no-dodig-2023-041/

Intel RealSense. (2020, April 16). *How robotics is the next big thing. Intel RealSense Depth and Tracking Cameras.* www.intelrealsense.com/robotic-automation/amp/

Intel471. (2024, February 13). *How Discord is abused for cybercrime.* https://intel471.com/blog/how-discord-is-abused-for-cybercrime

International Organization of Security Commissions. (2021, October). *The use of artificial intelligence and machine learning by market intermediaries and asset managers: Final report.* www.iosco.org/library/pubdocs/pdf/IOSCOPD684.pdf

Internet Crime Complaint Center. (2022). *Scammers using computer-technical support impersonation scams to target victims and conduct wire transfers.* Federal Bureau of Investigation. www.ic3.gov/Media/Y2022/PSA221110.

Interpret. (2022, May 20). *Some views on basic systems for data.* https://interpret.csis.org/translations/some-views-on-basic-systems-for-data/

Ivanova, I., Turtelbloom, A., Fornaroli, F., Ishik, C., Brokopp, N.-E., Pesce, P., Bright, J., Gorajski, R., Gullová, Z., Tan, A., Latinov, A., & Westphal, N. (2022, January 3). *5G roll-out in the EU: delays in deployment of networks with security issues remaining unsolved.* European Court of Auditors.

Ivanti. (2023). *Government cybersecurity status report.* www.ivanti.com/resources/v/doc/ivi/2747/a856c631661d

Jafee, L., Depillis, L., Arnsdorf, I., & Mcswane, D. (2021). *Capitol rioters planned for weeks in plain sight. The police weren't ready.* Nextgov/FCW. www.nextgov.com/cxo-briefing/2021/01/capitol-rioters-planned-weeks-plain-sight-police-werent-ready/171246/

JAIC Public Affairs. (2020, November 13). *Build to scale: Maximizing AI/ML impact across the DOD. AI.mil—Accelerating DoD's adoption & integration of AI.* www.ai.mil/blog_11_13_20-build_to_scale_maximizing_al-ml_impact_across_the_dod.html

Jakubowska, E., Maryam, H., Mahmoudi, M. (2024, April 14). *Euroviews. Retrospective facial recognition surveillance conceals human rights abuses in plain sight.* Euronews. www.euronews.com/2023/04/14/retrospective-facial-recognition-surveillance-conceals-human-rights-abuses-in-plain-sight

Jalal, M. (2022, August 2). Twelve futuristic cities are being built around the world, from Saudi Arabia to China. *The National.* www.thenationalnews.com/arts-culture/2022/08/02/12-futuristic-cities-being-built-around-the-world-from-saudi-arabia-to-china/

Jamieson, L. (2021, August 12). *Incredible urban designs for the future.* Ozy. www.ozy.com/pg/newsletter/the-daily-dose/439094/

Janofsky, A. (2023). *Cyber agencies warn of new TrueBot malware variants targeting US and Canadian firms.* The Record. https://therecord.media/cyber-agencies-warn-of-truebot-malware-variants-us-canada

Jasper, M. (2020). *Critical update: Why having artificial intelligence talent is a national security issue.* Nextgov/FCW. www.nextgov.com/podcasts/2020/12/critical-update-why-having-artificial-intelligence-talent-national-security-issue/170976/

Jimenez, N. (2022). *Cyber-attacks on small firms: The US economy's "Achilles heel"?* BBC. www.bbc.co.uk/news/business-63260648

Joffre, T. (2020). Neo-Nazi Nordic Resistance Movement targets Jews on Yom Kippur. *The Jerusalem Post.* www.jpost.com/diaspora/neo-nazi-nordic-resistance-movement-targets-jews-on-yom-kippur-643809

Johnsen, B. (2021). 5 Terrorism trends to watch in 2021. *Homeland Security Today.* www.hstoday.us/subject-matter-areas/infrastructure-security/5-terrorism-trends-to-watch-in-2021/

Johnson, C. (2023, June 26). *The national security benefits of reallocating federal spectrum for 5G.* Center for Strategic & International Studies. www.csis.org/analysis/national-security-and-spectrum-5g

Joint Chiefs of Staff. (2018, July). *Joint Concept for Operating in the Information Environment* (JCOIE). www.jcs.mil/Portals/36/Documents/Doctrine/concepts/joint_concepts_jcoie.pdf

Joint Chiefs of Staff. (2019, June 3). *Competition Continuum.* www.jcs.mil/Portals/36/Documents/Doctrine/jdn_jg/jdn1_19.pdf

Joint Concept for Robotic and Autonomous Systems. (2015, December 8). *Update: Overall classification of this briefing is UNCLASSIFIED.*

Joint Research Centre on Transnational Crime (transcime). (n.d.). *International Ph.D. in Criminology (cycle Vx).* Università Cattolica del Sacro Cuore. www.transcrime.it/en/international-ph-d-in-criminology/

Jones, D. (2022). *TSA rolls out long-anticipated cyber directive for freight, passenger rail systems.* Cybersecurity Dive. www.cybersecuritydive.com/news/tsa-cyber-directive-freight-passenger-rail/634538/

Jones, D. (2023). *Dole says February ransomware attack breached data of almost 3,900 US workers.* Cybersecurity Dive. www.cybersecuritydive.com/news/dole-ransomware-breached-data-workers/653650/

Jones, J. (2023). *AI could automate 300 million jobs. Here's which are most (and least) at risk.* ZDNet. www.zdnet.com/article/ai-could-automate-25-of-all-jobs-heres-which-are-most-and-least-at-risk/

Jones, J. (2023). *US Chamber of Commerce pushes for AI regulation, warns it could disrupt economy.* ZDNet. www.zdnet.com/article/us-chamber-of-commerce-pushes-for-ai-regulation-warns-it-can-disrupt-economy/

Jones, K. (2022, October 18). *Without regulation, the metaverse will be like social media on steroids.* World Politics Review.

Jones, S. (2018). *The rise of far-right extremism in the United States.* Center for Strategic & International Studies. www.csis.org/analysis/rise-far-right-extremism-united-states

Jones, S. G., Doxsee, C., & Harrington, N. (2020). *The escalating terrorism problem in the United States* (CSIS BRIEFS, p. 10). Center for Strategic & International Studies. www.csis.org/analysis/escalating-terrorism-problem-uni ted-states

Jones, S. G., Doxsee, C., Harrington, N., Hwang, G., & Suber, J. (2020, October 22). *The war comes home: The evolution of domestic terrorism in the United States.* Center for Strategic & International Studies. https://csis-website-prod. s3.amazonaws.com/s3fs-public/publication/201021_Jones_WarComesH ome_Methodology.pdf

Joos, T. (2022). *The real threat of unconventional cyberattacks.* Incyber. https:// incyber.org/en/the-real-threat-of-unconventional-cyberattacks/

Jordan, J., & Toran-Burrell, A. (2023, March 20). *States have the resources to clear criminal records.* Route-fifty. www.route-fifty.com/workforce/2023/03/sta tes-have-resources-clear-criminal-records/384194/

Joy, L., & Nolan, J. (2016-2022). *Westworld* [TV series]. Kilter Films; Bad Robot; Jerry Weintraub Productions; Warner Bros Television.

Joyce, M. (2023, April 11). *A Conversation on Cybersecurity with NSA's Rob Joyce.* Center for Strategic & International Studies. www.csis.org/analysis/conve rsation-cybersecurity-nsas-rob-joyce

Kageyama, Y. (2022). *Robot that stocks drinks is newest thing at the corner store.* AP News. https://apnews.com/article/technology-japan-tokyo-376b88f650346 1497d94df46cc9c5d8c

Kang, D. (2018, November 6). *Chinese "gait recognition" tech IDs people by how they walk.* AP News. https://apnews.com/article/bf75dd1c26c947b7826d270a1 6e2658a

Kanowitz, S. (2022). *States face more nuanced cloud security challenges.* GCN. https://gcn.com/cybersecurity/2022/10/states-face-more-nuanced-cloud-secur ity-challenges/378851/

Kanowitz, S. (2023, May 30). *State DOT streamlines traffic monitoring.* Route Fifty. www.route-fifty.com/tech-data/2023/05/iot-network-streamlines-state-dot-traffic-monitoring/386902/

Kanowitz, S. (2023, June 23). *Air taxis are taking off. Cities should start planning now.* Route Fifty. www.route-fifty.com/infrastructure/2023/06/air-taxis-are-tak ing-cities-should-start-planning-now/387848/

Kanowitz, S. (2023, July 10). *Michigan to automatically expunge some criminal records under "clean slate" program.* Route Fifty. www.route-fifty.com/public-safety/2023/01/michigan-embraces-clean-slate-program-without-applications/ 382327/

Kanowitz, S. (2024, February 8). Shining a light on shadow AI. Route Fifty. www. route-fifty.com/cybersecurity/2024/02/shining-light-shadow-ai/394017/

Kapko, M. (2023). *White House considers ban on ransom payments, with caveats.* Cybersecurity Dive. www.cybersecuritydive.com/news/white-house-considers-ransom-payment-ban/649673/

Karako, T., & Dahlgren, M. (2022, February). *Complex air defense: Countering the hypersonic missile threat.* Center for Strategic & International Studies.

Kaufman, I., & Galvin, E. (2020, June 26). *How machine learning finds anomalies to catch financial cybercriminals.* The Next Web. https://thenextweb.com/neural/2020/06/26/how-machine-learning-combats-financial-cybercrime-syndication/

Keisner, C. A. (2016, December). *Breakthrough technologies—Robotics and IP.* WIPO. www.wipo.int/wipo_magazine/en/2016/06/article_0002.html

Kejriwal, M. (2023). *Don't bet with ChatGPT—Study shows language AIs often make irrational decisions.* Nextgov/FCW. www.nextgov.com/ideas/2023/04/dont-bet-chatgptstudy-shows-language-ais-often-make-irrational-decisions/385025/

Kelion, L. (2021, January 13). *Huawei patent mentions use of Uighur-spotting tech.* BBC. www.bbc.com/news/technology-55634388

Kelley, A. (2021). *Data broker sales to law enforcement violate fourth amendment, senator argues.* Nextgov/FCW. www.nextgov.com/policy/2021/12/data-broker-sales-law-enforcement-violate-fourth-amendment-senator-argues/359784/

Kelley, A. (2021). *Homeland security looking for ideas on AI, biological surveillance.* Nextgov/FCW. www.nextgov.com/emerging-tech/2021/11/homeland-security-looking-ideas-ai-biological-surveillance/187050/

Kelley, A. (2021). *U.S., Australian law enforcement enter into partnership against cybercrimes.* Nextgov/FCW. www.nextgov.com/cxo-briefing/2021/12/us-austral ian-law-enforcement-enter-partnership-against-cybercrimes/359942/

Kelley, A. (2022, August 17). *NIST to release a new playbook for A.I. best practices.* Nextgov/FCW. www.nextgov.com/emerging-tech/2022/08/nist-rele ase-new-playbook-ai-best-practices/375920/

Kelley, A. (2022). *A look into proposed tech amendments for the 2023 NDAA.* Nextgov/FCW. www.nextgov.com/emerging-tech/2022/10/look-proposed-tech-amendments-2023-ndaa/378788/

Kelley, A. (2022). *Accurate U.S. crime data demands more state participation.* Nextgov/FCW. www.nextgov.com/analytics-data/2022/08/accurate-us-crime-data-demands-more-state-participation/375415/

Kelley, A. (2022). *Agencies look to expand both automation tech and ai workforce.* Nextgov/FCW. www.nextgov.com/emerging-tech/2022/02/agencies-look-expand-both-automation-tech-and-ai-workforce/361843/

Kelley, A. (2022). *Agency recommends firmer data, algorithm regulations to protect online privacy.* Nextgov/FCW. www.nextgov.com/analytics-data/2022/11/agency-recommends-firmer-data-algorithm-regulations-protect-online-privacy/380079/

Kelley, A. (2022). *AI government hinges on supportive leadership and a "glass breaker" in charge.* Nextgov/FCW. www.nextgov.com/emerging-tech/2022/03/ai-government-hinges-supportive-leadership-and-glass-breaker-charge/363531/

Kelley, A. (2022). *AI is "no magical shortcut" FTC says in fighting disinformation online.* Nextgov/FCW. www.nextgov.com/emerging-tech/2022/06/ai-no-magi cal-shortcut-ftc-says-fighting-disinformation-online/368341/

Kelley, A. (2022). *Census targets data modernization, cybersecurity ahead of 2030 rollout.* Nextgov/FCW. www.nextgov.com/it-modernization/2022/11/census-targets-data-modernization-cybersecurity-ahead-2030-rollout/380140/

Kelley, A. (2022). *Compliance first, penalty second as feds implement crypto regulations.* Nextgov/FCW. www.nextgov.com/emerging-tech/2022/10/complia nce-first-penalty-second-feds-implement-crypto-regulations/379056/

Kelley, A. (2022). *Critical update: To bridge quantum's valley of death, labs need funding and workforce.* Nextgov/FCW. www.nextgov.com/podcasts/2022/06/ bridge-quantums-valley-death-labs-need-funding-and-workforce/367635/

Kelley, A. (2022). *Cryptocurrencies "could pose risks" to stability of US economy, treasury warns.* Nextgov/FCW. www.nextgov.com/emerging-tech/2022/10/crypt ocurrencies-could-pose-risks-stability-us-economy-treasury-warns/378149/

Kelley, A. (2022). *DHS launches "largest customer experience hiring initiative" with hundreds of technologist positions.* Nextgov/FCW. www.nextgov.com/tec hnology-news/2022/09/dhs-launches-largest-customer-experience-hiring-initiat ive-hundreds-technologist-positions/376971/

Kelley, A. (2022). *DHS to begin electric vehicle adoption for law enforcement.* Nextgov/FCW. www.nextgov.com/it-modernization/2022/09/dhs-begin-electric-vehicle-adoption-law-enforcement/377414/

Kelley, A. (2022). *DOE wants to bridge their "valley of death."* Nextgov/FCW. www.nextgov.com/emerging-tech/2022/11/doe-wants-bridge-their-valley-death/ 379431/

Kelley, A. (2022). *Global financial crimes organization releases guide on NFTs.* Nextgov/FCW. www.nextgov.com/emerging-tech/2022/04/global-financial-cri mes-organization-releases-guide-nfts/366272/

Kelley, A. (2022). *High-tech financial crimes warrant coordinated digital identity efforts, FinCEN warns.* Nextgov/FCW. www.nextgov.com/cybersecurity/2022/ 09/high-tech-financial-crimes-warrant-coordinated-digital-identity-efforts-fin cen-warns/376947

Kelley, A. (2022). *Justice officials release framework for policing crime in crypto space.* Nextgov/FCW. www.nextgov.com/emerging-tech/2022/09/justice-offici als-release-framework-policing-crime-crypto-space/377293/

Kelley, A. (2022). *Justice, EEOC release guide to prevent AI discrimination.* Nextgov/FCW. www.nextgov.com/emerging-tech/2022/05/justice-eeoc-release-guide-prevent-ai-discrimination/366887/

Kelley, A. (2022). *Many digital assets are "rife with risks," fed official warns.* Nextgov/FCW. www.nextgov.com/emerging-tech/2022/10/many-digital-assets-are-rife-risks-fed-official-warns/378359/

Kelley, A. (2022). *New Biden AI framework a "blueprint" for future regulations.* Nextgov/FCW. www.nextgov.com/emerging-tech/2022/10/bidens-new-ai-framework-blueprint-future-regulations/377992/

Kelley, A. (2022). *New US–EU data privacy framework focuses on limiting U.S. surveillance.* Nextgov/FCW. www.nextgov.com/analytics-data/2022/10/new-us-eu-data-privacy-framework-focuses-limiting-us-surveillance/378170/

Kelley, A. (2022). *NIST advocates human-centric focus of AI tech.* Nextgov/FCW. www.nextgov.com/emerging-tech/2022/03/nist-advocates-human-centric-focus-ai-tech/363331/

Kelley, A. (2022). *NIST announces new Internet of Things Advisory Board.* Nextgov/FCW. www.nextgov.com/emerging-tech/2022/10/nist-announces-new-internet-things-advisory-board/378861/

Kelley, A. (2022). *NIST to release new playbook for AI best practices.* Nextgov/ FCW. www.nextgov.com/emerging-tech/2022/08/nist-release-new-playbook-ai-best-practices/375920/

Kelley, A. (2022). *NSA releases post-quantum algorithms, aims for full implementation by 2035.* Nextgov/FCW. www.nextgov.com/cybersecurity/2022/ 09/nsa-releases-post-quantum-algorithms-aims-full-implementation-2035/ 376880/

Kelley, A. (2022). *Proposed bill would let people know when law enforcement is surveilling them.* Nextgov/FCW. www.nextgov.com/policy/2022/03/proposed-bill-would-let-people-know-when-law-enforcement-surveilling-them/363464/

Kelley, A. (2022). *Quantum tech's path to commercialization will be a 2023 NIST priority.* Nextgov/FCW. www.nextgov.com/emerging-tech/2022/12/quantum-techs-path-commercialization-will-be-2023-nist-priority/381203/

Kelley, A. (2022). *Regulatory agency issues first document addressing AI in nuclear operations.* Nextgov/FCW. www.nextgov.com/policy/2022/07/regulatory-age ncy-issues-first-document-addressing-ai-nuclear-operations/373961/

Kelley, A. (2022). *Report: Emerging tech has become a tool for government censorship.* Nextgov/FCW. www.nextgov.com/emerging-tech/2022/01/report-emerging-tech-has-become-tool-government-censorship/361300/

Kelley, A. (2022). *Report reveals surveillance abuses in educational technology.* Nextgov/FCW. www.nextgov.com/analytics-data/2022/03/report-reveals-surve illance-abuses-educational-technology/363860/

Kelley, A. (2022). *Standards development a "critical" issue for US–EU Trade and Tech Council.* Nextgov/FCW. www.nextgov.com/policy/2022/12/standards-development-critical-issue-us-eu-trade-and-tech-council/380846/

Kelley, A. (2022). *Technical standards work is a priority for White House international policy.* Nextgov/FCW. www.nextgov.com/policy/2022/09/technical-standards-work-priority-white-house-international-policy/377900/

Kelley, A. (2022). *Transportation department looks to AI to help modernize highways.* Nextgov/FCW. www.nextgov.com/emerging-tech/2022/11/transpo rtation-department-looks-ai-help-modernize-highways/379257/

Kelley, A. (2022). *U.S. joins France in new quantum tech partnership.* Nextgov/ FCW. www.nextgov.com/emerging-tech/2022/12/us-joins-france-new-quan tum-tech-

Kelley, A. (2022). *US must proactively participate in international AI standards-setting, officials warn.* Nextgov/FCW. www.nextgov.com/emerging-tech/2022/ 09/us-must-proactively-participate-international-ai-standards-setting-officials-warn/377851/

Kelley, A. (2022). *US–UK data sharing program goes into effect.* Nextgov/FCW. www.nextgov.com/technology-news/2022/10/us-uk-data-sharing-program-goes-effect/377978/

Kelley, A. (2022). *White House releases holistic digital asset regulatory framework.* Nextgov/FCW. www.nextgov.com/technology-news/2022/09/white-house-relea ses-holistic-digital-asset-regulatory-framework/377259/

Kelley, A. (2023, January 4). *State Department creates first office devoted to emerging technology* diplomacy. Nextgov/FCW. www.nextgov.com/emerging-tech/ 2023/01/state-department-creates-first-office-devoted-emerging-technology-diplomacy/381459/

Kelley, A. (2023, January 5). *FCC releases proposed rule to give drones more spectrum access.* Nextgov/FCW. www.nextgov.com/emerging-tech/2023/01/fcc-relea
ses-proposed-rule-give-drones-more-spectrum-access/381513/

Kelley, A. (2023, January 18). *Push for more quantum tech investment reaches World Economic Forum.* Nextgov/FCW. www.nextgov.com/emerging-tech/
2023/01/push-more-quantum-tech-investment-reaches-world-economic-forum/
381906/

Kelley, A. (2023, March 14). *GAO offers quantum guidance to federal agencies.* Nextgov/FCW. www.nextgov.com/emerging-tech/2023/03/gao-offers-quantum-
guidance-federal-agencies/383947/

Kelley, A. (2023, March 15). *"Multiple threat actors" used old exploit to access federal agency servers.* Nextgov/FCW. www.nextgov.com/cybersecurity/2023/
03/multiple-threat-actors-used-old-exploit-access-federal-agency-servers/
384041/

Kelley, A. (2023, March 16). *How international acquisitions can become a cybercrime frontier.* Nextgov/FCW. www.nextgov.com/cybersecurity/2023/03/how-
international-acquisitions-can-become-cybercrime-frontier/384047/

Kelley, A. (2023, March 16). *White House Tech Council launches Cyber-Physical Resilience Working Group.* Nextgov/FCW. www.nextgov.com/cybersecurity/
2023/03/white-house-tech-council-launches-cyber-physical-resilience-working-
group/384096/

Kelley, A. (2023, March 20). *CISA: Election security still under threat at cyber and physical level.* Nextgov/FCW. www.nextgov.com/cybersecurity/
2023/03/cisa-election-security-still-under-threat-cyber-and-physical-level/
384172/

Kelley, A. (2023, May 22). *Report estimates trillions in indirect losses would follow quantum computer hack.* Nextgov/FCW. www.nextgov.com/cybersecur
ity/2023/05/report-estimates-trillions-indirect-losses-would-follow-quantum-
computer-hack/386653/

Kelley, A. (2023, May 23). *White House releases new AI national frameworks, educator recommendations.* Nextgov/FCW. www.nextgov.com/artificial-intel
ligence/2023/05/white-house-releases-new-ai-national-frameworks-educator-
recommendations/386691/

Kelley, A. (2023, May 24). *Cyber agencies unveil updated ransomware guide.* Nextgov/FCW. www.nextgov.com/cybersecurity/2023/05/cyber-agencies-unveil-
updated-ransomware-guide/386737/

Kelley, A. (2023, May 24). *FDA announces contract for automation in drug performance analyses.* Nextgov/FCW. www.nextgov.com/artificial-intellige
nce/2023/05/fda-announces-contract-automation-drug-performance-analyses/
386714/

Kelley, A. (2023, June 9). *White House efforts to get data equity-ready will also support AI, official says.* Nextgov/FCW. www.nextgov.com/artificial-intellige
nce/2023/06/white-house-efforts-get-data-equity-ready-will-also-support-ai-
official-says/387375/

Kelley, A. (2023, July 10). *The future of quantum security will be encoded in light, researchers hope.* Nextgov/FCW. www.nextgov.com/cybersecurity/2023/01/fut ure-quantum-security-will-be-encoded-light-researchers-hope/382037/

Kelley, A. (2023, July 17). *NIST adds 40 potential quantum-resistant algorithms to growing roster.* Nextgov/FCW. www.nextgov.com/emerging-tech/2023/07/ nist-adds-40-potential-quantum-resistant-algorithms-growing-roster/388577/

Kelley, A. (2023, July 18). *White House announces new program to designate cyber-secure IoT devices.* Nextgov/FCW. www.nextgov.com/cybersecurity/2023/ 07/white-house-announces-new-program-designate-cyber-secure-iot-devices/ 388589/

Kelley, A. (2023, July 19). *White House seeks public insight to harmonize "inconsistent" cyber regulations.* Nextgov/FCW. www.nextgov.com/cybersecurity/ 2023/07/white-house-seeks-public-insight-harmonize-inconsistent-cyber-regu lations/388657/

Kelley, A. (2023, July 21). *Biden: New AI agreement will "shepherd" responsible innovation, but legislation still needed.* Nextgov/FCW. www.nextgov.com/artific ial-intelligence/2023/07/biden-new-ai-agreement-will-shepherd-responsible-inn ovation-legislation-still-needed/388745/

Kelley, A. (2023, July 28). *The world is "reentering an era of strategic competition" with cyber, official says.* Nextgov/FCW. www.nextgov.com/cybersecur ity/2023/07/world-reentering-era-strategic-competition-cyber-official-says/ 388921/

Kelley, A. (2023, August 2). *Tech officials caution on data security in public sector AI applications.* Nextgov/FCW. www.nextgov.com/artificial-intelligence/2023/ 08/tech-officials-caution-data-security-public-sector-ai-applications/389077/

Kelley, A. (2023, August 4). *CISA unveils plan to measure cybersecurity success.* Nextgov/FCW. www.nextgov.com/cybersecurity/2023/08/cisa-unveils-plan-measure-cybersecurity-success/389156/

Kelley, A. (2023, August 4). *NSF aims to drive democratization of AI with its funding.* Nextgov/FCW. www.nextgov.com/artificial-intelligence/2023/08/nsf-aims-drive-democratization-ai-its-funding/389153/

Kelley, A. (2023, August 9). *White House and DARPA challenge innovators to bring AI tools to cyber defense.* Nextgov/FCW. www.nextgov.com/artificial-intel ligence/2023/08/white-house-and-darpa-challenge-innovators-bring-ai-tools-cyber-defense/389265/

Kelley, A. (2023, November 22). *FTC votes to streamline investigations into AI products.* Nextgov/FCW. www.nextgov.com/artificial-intelligence/2023/11/ftc-votes-streamline-investigations-ai-products/392260/

Kelley, A. (2023, November 27). *US and UK release joint guidelines for secure-by-design AI.* Nextgov/FCW. www.nextgov.com/artificial-intelligence/2023/11/ us-and-uk-release-joint-guidelines-secure-design-ai/392284/

Kelley, A. (2023, December 15). *Government's quantum efforts are shifting to a near-term strategy.* Nextgov/FCW. www.nextgov.com/emerging-tech/2023/12/ governments-quantum-efforts-are-shifting-near-term-strategy/392810/

Kelley, A. (2023). *4 Agencies pledge enforcement against AI bias.* Nextgov/FCW. www.nextgov.com/emerging-tech/2023/04/4-agencies-pledge-enforcement-agai nst-ai-bias/385638/

Kelley, A. (2023). *Biden to meet with AI experts to talk regulation and safety.* Nextgov/FCW. www.nextgov.com/artificial-intelligence/2023/06/biden-meet-ai-experts-talk-regulation-and-safety/387666/

Kelley, A. (2023). *CFPB looks to existing law to regulate workplace surveillance tech.* Nextgov/FCW. www.nextgov.com/policy/2023/06/cfpb-looks-existing-law-regulate-workplace-surveillance-tech/387765/

Kelley, A. (2023). *CISA, FBI need data from cybercrime victims to support policy.* Nextgov/FCW. www.nextgov.com/cybersecurity/2023/05/cisa-fbi-need-data-cyb ercrime-victims-support-policy/386090/

Kelley, A. (2023). *CISA unveils plan to measure cybersecurity success.* Nextgov/ FCW. www.nextgov.com/cybersecurity/2023/08/cisa-unveils-plan-measure-cybersecurity-success/389156/

Kelley, A. (2023). *Crypto investor charged with market manipulation, defrauding over $100 million.* Nextgov/FCW. www.nextgov.com/technology-news/2023/ 02/crypto-investor-charged-market-manipulation-defrauding-over-100-million/ 382566/

Kelley, A. (2023). *Cyberattacks on Energy's National Labs draw lawmaker scrutiny.* Nextgov/FCW. www.nextgov.com/cybersecurity/2023/02/cyberattacks-energys-national-labs-draw-lawmaker-scrutiny/382503/

Kelley, A. (2023). *DHS announces first-ever AI task force.* Nextgov/FCW. www. nextgov.com/emerging-tech/2023/04/dhs-announces-first-ever-ai-task-force/ 385491/

Kelley, A. (2023). *DHS S&T and CISA forge deep partnership in emerging tech R&D.* Nextgov/FCW. www.nextgov.com/emerging-tech/2023/04/dhs-st-and-cisa-forge-deep-partnership-emerging-tech-rd/385375/

Kelley, A. (2023). *DHS to release AI guidance for critical infrastructure.* Nextgov/ FCW. www.nextgov.com/artificial-intelligence/2023/10/dhs-release-ai-guidance-critical-infrastructure/390979/

Kelley, A. (2023). *Emerging tech, misinformation dominate May transatlantic council talks.* Nextgov/FCW. www.nextgov.com/emerging-tech/2023/06/emerg ing-tech-misinformation-dominate-may-transatlantic-council-talks/387092/

Kelley, A. (2023). *Emerging technologies star in White House R&D priorities.* Nextgov/FCW. www.nextgov.com/emerging-tech/2023/08/emerging-technolog ies-star-white-house-rd-priorities/389505/

Kelley, A. (2023). *Energy allocates $16M for high-performance machine learning research.* Nextgov/FCW. www.nextgov.com/emerging-tech/2023/08/energy-allocates-16m-high-performance-machine-learning-research/389722/

Kelley, A. (2023). *Establishing international tech standards is "the issue of our time," lawmaker says.* Nextgov/FCW. www.nextgov.com/artificial-intelligence/ 2023/07/establishing-international-tech-standards-issue-our-time-lawmaker-says/388536/

Kelley, A. (2023). *EU approves US approach to safeguard transatlantic data flows.* Nextgov/FCW. www.nextgov.com/digital-government/2023/07/eu-approves-us-approach-safeguard-transatlantic-data-flows/388353/

Kelley, A. (2023). *Experts call for overhaul of "outdated" critical infrastructure cyber policy.* Nextgov/FCW. www.nextgov.com/cybersecurity/2023/06/experts-call-overhaul-outdated-critical-infrastructure-cyber-policy/387205/

Kelley, A. (2023). *FCC Chair: Spectrum authority and global policy are key priorities in the 5G era.* Nextgov/FCW. www.nextgov.com/emerging-tech/2023/07/fcc-chair-spectrum-authority-and-global-policy-are-key-priorities-5g-era/388817/

Kelley, A. (2023). *FCC releases proposed rule to give drones more spectrum access.* Nextgov/FCW. www.nextgov.com/emerging-tech/2023/01/fcc-releases-proposed-rule-give-drones-more-spectrum-access/381513/

Kelley, A. (2023). *Federal operation takes down sophisticated Russian malware.* Nextgov/FCW. www.nextgov.com/cybersecurity/2023/05/federal-operation-takes-down-sophisticated-russian-malware/386136/

Kelley, A. (2023). *First AI advisory committee report stresses getting regulatory balance right.* Nextgov/FCW. www.nextgov.com/artificial-intelligence/2023/06/first-ai-advisory-committee-report-stresses-importance-getting-regulatory-balance-right/387853/

Kelley, A. (2023). *First national standards strategy aims to keep U.S. competitive in emerging tech.* Nextgov/FCW. www.nextgov.com/cxo-briefing/2023/05/first-national-standards-strategy-aims-keep-us-competitive-emerging-tech/385964/

Kelley, A. (2023). *FTC charges Ring over "disregard" for customer data security.* Nextgov/FCW. www.nextgov.com/analytics-data/2023/06/ftc-charges-ring-over-disregard-customer-data-security/386993/

Kelley, A. (2023). *How NIST is helping to guide the government conversation on AI.* Nextgov/FCW. www.nextgov.com/artificial-intelligence/2023/07/how-nist-helping-guide-government-conversation-ai/388523/

Kelley, A. (2023). *How the US aims to tackle the "collective action problem" of ransomware.* Nextgov/FCW. www.nextgov.com/cybersecurity/2023/11/how-us-aims-tackle-collective-action-problem-ransomware/391783/

Kelley, A. (2023). *IRS needs better documentation for its cyber threat hunts, watchdog says.* Nextgov/FCW. www.nextgov.com/cybersecurity/2023/07/irs-needs-better-documentation-its-cyber-threat-hunts-watchdog-says/388790/

Kelley, A. (2023). *Justice to merge 2 offices in step with cyber implementation plan.* Nextgov/FCW. www.nextgov.com/cybersecurity/2023/07/justice-merge-2-offices-step-cyber-implementation-plan/388691/

Kelley, A. (2023). *Lawmakers introduce bill to keep AI from going nuclear.* Nextgov/FCW. www.nextgov.com/emerging-tech/2023/04/lawmakers-initiate-several-efforts-put-guardrails-ai-use/385711/

Kelley, A. (2023). *New AI agreement will "shepherd" responsible innovation, but legislation still needed.* Nextgov/FCW. www.nextgov.com/artificial-intelligence/2023/07/biden-new-ai-agreement-will-shepherd-responsible-innovation-legislation-still-needed/388745/

Kelley, A. (2023). *New AI research funding to focus on 6 areas.* Nextgov/FCW. www.nextgov.com/emerging-tech/2023/05/pentagon-wants-peer-inside-its-cloud-providers-infrastructure/386016/

Kelley, A. (2023). *New legislation seeks to upgrade commercial drone rules.* Nextgov/FCW.　www.nextgov.com/emerging-tech/2023/02/new-legislation-seeks-upgrade-commercial-drone-rules/382761/

Kelley, A. (2023). *NIST debuts long-anticipated AI risk management framework.* Nextgov/FCW. www.nextgov.com/emerging-tech/2023/01/nist-debuts-long-anti cipated-ai-risk-management-framework/382251/

Kelley, A. (2023). *NIST releases draft standards for 3 post-quantum encryption algorithms.* Nextgov/FCW. www.nextgov.com/emerging-tech/2023/08/nist-relea ses-draft-standards-3-post-quantum-encryption-algorithms/389709/

Kelley, A. (2023). *NTIA asks public how to measure safe AI systems.* Nextgov/ FCW.　www.nextgov.com/emerging-tech/2023/04/ntia-asks-public-how-to-meas ure-safe-ai-systems/385167/

Kelley, A. (2023). *OPM identifies over 50 skill sets to look for in federal AI workers.* Nextgov/FCW. www.nextgov.com/emerging-tech/2023/07/opm-identif ies-over-50-skill-sets-look-federal-ai-workers/388261/

Kelley, A. (2023). *Plan for federal AI research and development resource emphasizes diversity in innovation.* Nextgov/FCW. www.nextgov.com/emerg ing-tech/2023/01/plan-federal-ai-research-and-development-resource-emphasi zes-diversity-innovation/382144/

Kelley, A. (2023). *Public–private partnerships will be key in national quantum initiative reauthorization.* Nextgov/FCW. www.nextgov.com/emerging-tech/2023/ 05/public-private-partnerships-will-be-key-national-quantum-initiative-reau thorization/385894/

Kelley, A. (2023). *Scaling and talent development dominate Senate's AI-focused NDAA amendments.* Nextgov/FCW. www.nextgov.com/artificial-intelligence/ 2023/07/scaling-and-talent-development-dominate-senates-ai-focused-ndaa-amendments/388903/

Kelley, A. (2023). *SEC announces new cyber reporting rules for companies.* Nextgov/FCW. www.nextgov.com/cybersecurity/2023/07/sec-announces-new-cyber-reporting-rules-companies/388858/

Kelley, A. (2023). *Securing U.S. intellectual property "top priority" for federal law enforcement.* Nextgov/FCW. www.nextgov.com/cybersecurity/2023/05/secur ing-us-intellectual-property-top-priority-federal-law-enforcement/386777/

Kelley, A. (2023). *State-sponsored actors leading cause of cyber concern in public sector.* Nextgov/FCW. www.nextgov.com/cybersecurity/2023/05/state-sponso red-actors-leading-cause-cyber-concern-public-sector/386101/

Kelley, A. (2023). *Sweeping White House AI order includes mandate for commercial developers.* Nextgov/FCW. www.nextgov.com/artificial-intelligence/2023/ 10/sweeping-white-house-ai-order-includes-mandate-commercial-developers/ 391598/

Kelley, A. (2023). *7 Tech companies agree to White House's new trustworthy AI commitments.* Nextgov/FCW. www.nextgov.com/artificial-intelligence/2023/ 07/7-tech-companies-agree-white-houses-new-trustworthy-ai-commitments/ 388717/

Kelley, A. (2023). *Tech officials caution on data security in public sector AI applications.* Nextgov/FCW. www.nextgov.com/artificial-intelligence/2023/08/ tech-officials-caution-data-security-public-sector-ai-applications/389077/

Kelley, A. (2023). *Tech panel champions near-term quantum efforts in must-pass defense bill.* Nextgov/FCW. www.nextgov.com/emerging-tech/2023/06/tech-panel-champions-near-term-quantum-efforts-must-pass-defense-bill/387638/

Kelley, A. (2023). *The future of quantum security will be encoded in light, researchers hope.* Nextgov/FCW. www.nextgov.com/cybersecurity/2023/01/future-quantum-security-will-be-encoded-light-researchers-hope/382037

Kelley, A. (2023). *The Office of the Special Envoy for Critical and Emerging Technology will facilitate strategic partnerships to develop and regulate innovative tech.* Nextgov/FCW. www.nextgov.com/emerging-tech/2023/01/state-department-creates-first-office-devoted-emerging-technology-diplomacy/381459/

Kelley, A. (2023). *US "can't PSA our way out" of cyber vulnerability, CISA director says.* Nextgov/FCW. www.nextgov.com/cybersecurity/2023/06/us-cant-psa-our-way-out-cyber-vulnerability-cisa-director-says/387815/

Kelley, A. (2023). *US deploys tech diplomacy to cultivate leadership in emerging fields.* Nextgov/FCW. www.nextgov.com/policy/2023/05/us-deploys-tech-diplomacy-cultivate-leadership-emerging-fields/386971/

Kelley, A. (2023). *US must be more aware of "adversarial side" of AI, DHS official warns.* Nextgov/FCW. www.nextgov.com/emerging-tech/2023/04/us-must-be-more-aware-adversarial-side-ai-dhs-official-warns/385330/

Kelley, A. (2023). *U.S., South Korean agencies warn of state-sponsored spearphishing.* Nextgov/FCW. www.nextgov.com/cybersecurity/2023/06/us-south-korean-agencies-warn-state-sponsored-spearphishing/387067/

Kelley, A. (2023). *US teams up with partner nations to release smart city cyber guidance.* Nextgov/FCW. www.nextgov.com/cybersecurity/2023/04/us-teams-partner-nations-release-smart-city-cyber-guidance/385412/

Kelley, A. (2023). *White House announces new program to designate cyber-secure IoT devices.* Nextgov/FCW. www.nextgov.com/cybersecurity/2023/07/white-house-announces-new-program-designate-cyber-secure-iot-devices/388589/

Kelley, A. (2023). *White House cyber strategy can help mitigate AI dangers, official says.* Nextgov/FCW. www.nextgov.com/cybersecurity/2023/06/white-house-cyber-strategy-can-help-mitigate-ai-dangers-official-says/387266/

Kelley, A. (2023). *White House launches strategy to advance data privacy tech and processes.* Nextgov/FCW. www.nextgov.com/analytics-data/2023/03/white-house-launches-strategy-advance-data-privacy-tech-and-processes/384674/

Kelley, A. (2023). *White House releases new AI national frameworks, educator recommendations.* Nextgov/FCW. www.nextgov.com/emerging-tech/2023/05/white-house-releases-new-ai-national-frameworks-educator-recommendations/386691/

Kelley, A. (2023). *White House unveils $140M investment for responsible AI, upcoming agency guidance.* Nextgov/FCW. www.nextgov.com/emerging-tech/2023/05/white-house-unveils-140m-investment-responsible-ai-upcoming-guidance-agencies/385966/

Kelley, A. (2023). *Why 2 lawmakers turned to AI to advocate for its own regulation.* Nextgov/FCW. www.nextgov.com/emerging-tech/2023/02/why-2-lawmakers-turned-ai-advocate-its-own-regulation/382458/

Kelley, A. (2024, January 2). *Roberts: Legal field will be "significantly affected by AI."* Nextgov/FCW. www.nextgov.com/artificial-intelligence/2024/01/roberts-legal-field-will-be-significantly-affected-ai/393061/

Kelley, A. (2024, February 8). *Commerce announces AI safety consortium.* Nextgov/FCW. www.nextgov.com/artificial-intelligence/2024/02/commerce-announces-ai-safety-consortium/394038/

Kelley, A. K. (2023, March 21). *Quantum information technologies could be applied to the electrical grid for security and sustainability improvements.* Nextgov/FCW. www.nextgov.com/emerging-tech/2023/03/quantum-sensing-has-critical-potential-electrical-grid-officials-says/384259/

Kelley, K. (2023, November 22). *FCC adopts new rules for wireless providers to rein in SIM swapping.* Nextgov/FCW. https://therecord.media/fcc-new-rules-stop-sim-swapping

Kelley, L. (2022, June 6). *Russian ministry website appears hacked; Ria reports user's data protected.* Reuters. www.reuters.com/world/europe/russian-ministry-website-appears-hacked-ria-reports-users-data-protected-2022-06-06/

Kendall-Taylor, A., Frantz, E., & Wright, J. (2020, March). The digital dictators. *Foreign Affairs.* www.foreignaffairs.com/articles/china/2020-02-06/digital-dictators

Kennedy, T. (2022). *What will it take to end the public sector's cybersecurity talent gap?* Nextgov/FCW. www.nextgov.com/ideas/2022/09/what-will-it-take-end-public-sectors-cybersecurity-talent-gap/377668/

Kerr, F., & Manch, T. (2019, December 18). *Arrested New Zealand soldier with far-right ties was questioned after March 15 attacks.* Stuff. www.stuff.co.nz/national/118298650/arrested-new-zealand-soldier-with-farright-ties-was-questioned-after-march-15-attacks

Kerravala, Z. (2021, November 18). *Why conversational AI is now ready for prime time.* ZDNet. www.zdnet.com/article/why-conversational-ai-is-now-ready-for-prime-time/

Khogeer, K. (2023, August 7). *Zoom addresses privacy concerns raised by AI data collection language in terms of service.* NBS News. www.nbcnews.com/tech/innovation/zoom-ai-privacy-tos-terms-of-service-data-rcna98665

Khosravi, P., Kazemi, E., Zhan, Q., Malmsten, J., Toschi, M., Zisimopoulous, P., Sigaras, A., Lavery, S., Cooper, L., Hickman, C., Meseguer, M., Rosenwaks, Z., Elemento, O., Zaninovic, N., & Hajirasouliha, I. (2019). *Deep learning enables robust assessment and selection of human blastocysts after in vitro fertilization. Digital Medicine*, 2(21), 1–21. https://rdcu.be/dEVMq

Kim, C. (2022, July 23). *The slow-motion pace of crypto regulation.* Axios. www.axios.com/2022/07/23/crypto-regulation-legal-sec-united-states

Kim, V. (2022, January 12). How governments used the pandemic to normalize surveillance. *Los Angeles Times.* www.latimes.com/world-nation/story/2021-12-09/the-pandemic-brought-heightened-surveillance-to-save-lives-is-it-here-to-stay

Kine, P. (2024, May 16). *Putin and Xi plot sanction resistance.* POLITICO. www.politico.eu/newsletter/china-watcher/putin-and-xi-plot-sanction-resistance/

Kinetz, E. (2018, November 30). *In China, your car could be talking to the government.* AP News. https://apnews.com/article/4a749a4211904784826b45e812cff4ca

Kingson, J. (2022, July 8). *So, a robot walks into a nursing home....* Axios. www. axios.com/2022/07/08/robot-nursing-home-elderly-aging-health-robotics

Kingson, J. (2022, July 13). *New AI tools let you chat with your dead relatives.* Axios. www.axios.com/2022/07/13/artificial-intelligence-chatbots-dead-relati ves-grandma

Kingson, J. (2022, August 25). *"Cities of the future," built from scratch.* Axios. www.axios.com/2022/08/25/city-of-the-future-neom-telosa-lore-mbs

Kingson, J. (2023, January 30). *New AI tool instantly analyzes police bodycam footage.* Axios. www.axios.com/2023/01/30/police-tyre-nichols-bodycam-footage

Kingson J. (2023). *Religious leaders experiment with ChatGPT sermons.* Axios. www.axios.com/2023/03/10/pastors-chatgpt-sermons-rabbi-minister

Kingson, J. (2023). *Robots are your new office security guard.* Axios. www.axios. com/2023/03/03/security-robots-artificial-intelligence

Kingson, J. (2023). *Teachers and students warm up to ChatGPT.* Axios. www. axios.com/2023/03/07/chatgpt-teachers-students-schools

Kingson, J. A. (2021, March 4). *Sidewalk robots get legal rights as "pedestrians."* Axios. www.axios.com/2021/03/04/sidewalk-robots-legal-rights-pedestrians

Kingson, J. A. (2022, January 13). *The beauty business turns to augmented reality.* Axios. www.axios.com/2022/01/13/the-beauty-business-turns-to-augmented-reality

Kingson, J. A. (2022, January 26). *The future of retail: More self-service.* Axios. www.axios.com/2022/01/26/the-future-of-retail-more-self-service

Kingson, J. A. (2022, March 21). *The convenience of a "Smart Home" draws near.* Axios. www.axios.com/2022/03/21/the-convenience-of-a-smart-home-draws-near

Kingson, J. A. (2022, June 11). *Welcome to the summer of robots.* Axios. www. axios.com/2022/06/09/robots-kitchen-delivery-robotics

Kingson, J. A. (2023, January 13). *Friend or foe? Teachers debate ChatGPT.* Axios. www.axios.com/2023/01/13/chatgpt-schools-teachers-ai-debate

Kingson, J. A. (2023, February 2). *STEM who? The humanities mount a come-back.* Axios. www.axios.com/2023/02/02/humanities-stem-college

Kingson, J. A. (2023, December 5). *The first humanoid robot factory is about to open.* Axios. www.axios.com/2023/12/05/humanoid-robot-factory-agility-bipe dal-amazon

Kingson, J. (2021, February 11). *The future of smart cities is in street lights.* Axios. www.axios.com/2021/02/11/smart-cities-street-lights

Kingson, J. (2022). *Attack of the pizza-making robots.* Axios. www.axios.com/ 2022/10/04/robot-pizza

Kingson, J. (2022). *Google unfurls whiz-bang projects and vision for future of AI.* Axios. www.axios.com/2022/11/03/google-artificial-intelligence

Kingson, J. (2022). *"Matter" could solve smart homes' biggest problem.* Axios. www.axios.com/2022/11/04/matter-smart-home-iot-amazon-google-apple-devices

Kingson, J. (2022). *The rise of upscale portable lavatories.* Axios. www.axios.com/ 2022/12/09/portable-lavatories-toilets-luxury-bathroom-porta-potty

Kingson, J. (2022). *Trending crimes: "Check washing" and "mailbox fishing."* Axios. www.axios.com/2022/11/16/check-washing-mailbox-fishing

Kingson, J. (2023). *Alcohol sellers to start biometric scanning your face or palm to verify age.* Axios. www.axios.com/2023/07/25/alcohol-biometric-scan-face-palm-age-recognition

Kingson, J. (2023). *2D barcodes will revolutionize retail as we know it.* Axios. www.axios.com/2023/04/17/2d-barcode-transition-2027

Kingson, J. (2023). *Meet your new colleague: Apollo, the humanoid robot.* Axios. www.axios.com/2023/09/04/humanoid-robot-labor-warehouse-jobs-apollo-apptronik

Kingson, J. (2023). *We tried the video call of the future.* Axios. www.axios.com/2023/05/09/video-call-zoom-videoconferencing-teams

Kingston, J., Muller, J., & Fitzpatrick, A. (2023). Adobe's new Photoshop tools make fakery even easier. *Axios.* https://www.axios.com/2023/05/23/adobe-photoshop-ai-fakery-deepfakes

Kirchgaessner, S. (2023). Experts warn of new spyware threat targeting journalists and political figures. *The Guardian.* www.theguardian.com/technology/2023/apr/11/canadian-security-experts-warn-over-spyware-threat-to-rival-pegasus-citizen-lab

Kirchner, L. (2015, November 18). *What's the evidence mass surveillance works? Not much.* Pro Publica. www.propublica.org/article/whats-the-evidence-mass-surveillance-works-not-much

Kivunja, C. (2018). Distinguishing between theory, theoretical framework, and conceptual framework: A systematic review of lessons from the field. *International Journal of Higher Education, 7*(6), 44. https://doi.org/10.5430/ijhe.v7n6p44

Kleinman, Z. (2023). *AI "godfather" Yoshua Bengio feels "lost" over life's work.* BBC. www.bbc.com/news/technology-65760449

Kleinman, Z. (2023). *Artificial intelligence: Experts propose guidelines for safe systems.* BBC. www.bbc.com/news/technology-66225855

Kleinman, Z. (2023). *US Air Force denies AI drone attacked operator in test.* BBC. www.bbc.com/news/technology-65789916

Kleinman, Z., & Gerken, T. (2023). *Nick Clegg: AI language systems are "quite stupid."* BBC. www.bbc.com/news/technology-66238004

Kleinman, Z., & Vallance, C. (2023). *AI "godfather" Geoffrey Hinton warns of dangers as he quits Google.* BBC. www.bbc.com/news/world-us-canada-65452940

Kleinman, Z., Wain, P., & Swain, A. (2023). *Using AI for loans and mortgages is big risk, warns EU boss.* BBC. www.bbc.com/news/technology-65881389

Knutson, J. (2023). *Brokers selling military members' personal info.* Axios. www.axios.com/2023/11/06/military-data-sold-for-cents-cheap-privacy

Knutson, J. (2022, January 27). *Elon Musk says Tesla is prioritizing development of a robot that can perform human tasks.* Axios. www.axios.com/2022/01/27/musk-telsa-prioritizing-robot-development

Knutson, J. (2022, June 3). *Consumers report losing more than $1 billion from crypto scams since 2021, FTC says.* Axios. www.axios.com/2022/06/03/consumer-lost-1-billio-cryptocurrency-scams

Knutson, J. (2023, June 23). *How AI is helping scammers target victims in "sextortion" schemes.* Axios. www.axios.com/2023/06/23/artificial-intelligence-sexual-exploitation-children-technology

Knutson, J. (2023, December 4). *23andMe sees personal data on 6.9 million customers stolen by hackers.* Axios. www.axios.com/2023/12/04/23andme-customers-stolen-data

Knutson, J. (2024, March 29). *OpenAI reveals artificial intelligence tool to recreate human voices.* Axios. www.axios.com/2024/03/29/ai-recreate-person-voice-recording-openai

Koblentz, G. D. (2020). Emerging technologies and the future of CBRN terrorism. *The Washington Quarterly, 43,* 177–196.

Koebler, J. (2020, March 4). *The small company is turning Utah into a surveillance panopticon.* Vice. www.vice.com/en/article/k7exem/banjo-ai-company-utah-surveillance-panopticon

Kokalitcheva, K. (2023, December 8). *EU reaches landmark deal on world's first comprehensive AI regulation.* Axios. www.axios.com/2023/12/08/eu-ai-regulation-law-europe

Komas, N. (2023). *Meta's Threads app is a privacy nightmare that won't launch in EU yet.* TechCrunch. https://techcrunch.com/2023/07/05/threads-no-eu-launch/

Konkel, F. (2022). *Lawmakers call for end to government's use of facial recognition tech.* Nextgov/FCW. www.nextgov.com/policy/2022/02/lawmakers-call-end-governments-use-facial-recognition-tech/361781/

Konkel, F. (2022). *Lawmakers intro bill to ban TikTok in U.S.* Nextgov/FCW. www.nextgov.com/cxo-briefing/2022/12/lawmakers-intro-bill-ban-tiktok-us/380817/

Konkel, F. (2022). *49% of tech pros believe AI poses "existential threat" to humanity, per report.* Nextgov/FCW. www.nextgov.com/emerging-tech/2022/10/49-tech-pros-believe-ai-poses-existential-threat-humanity-report/378691/

Konkel, F. (2022). *Report: Ensure federal AI policies are aligned.* Nextgov/FCW. www.nextgov.com/policy/2022/01/report-ensure-federal-ai-policies-are-aligned/360698/https://www.nextgov.com/policy/2022/01/report-ensure-federal-ai-policies-are-aligned/360698/

Konkel, F. (2022). *Report: U.S. tops Government AI Readiness Index.* Nextgov/FCW. www.nextgov.com/emerging-tech/2022/01/report-us-tops-government-ai-readiness-index/361039/

Konkel, F. (2022). *Survey: AI "mission critical" to 70% of public sector IT decision makers.* Nextgov/FCW. www.nextgov.com/emerging-tech/2022/02/survey-ai-mission-critical-70-public-sector-it-decision-makers/362203/

Konkel, F. (2023, December 11). *GAO to release landmark AI report.* Nextgov/FCW. www.nextgov.com/artificial-intelligence/2023/12/gao-release-landmark-ai-report/392647/

Konkel, F. (2023). *Congress is "in learning mode" about AI, lawmakers say.* Nextgov/FCW. www.nextgov.com/emerging-tech/2023/06/congress-learning-mode-about-ai-lawmakers-say/387287/

Konkel, F. (2023). *3 in 4 Americans worry AI will take their jobs*. Nextgov/FCW. www.nextgov.com/emerging-tech/2023/04/3-4-americans-worried-ai-will-take-their-jobs/385615/

Konkel, F. (2023). *Lawmakers suggest "radical transparency" as key to shoring up US cyber posture*. Nextgov/FCW. www.nextgov.com/cybersecurity/2023/06/lawmakers-suggest-radical-transparency-key-shoring-us-cyber-posture/387492/

Konkel, F. (2023). *Microsoft unveils OpenAI service for government customers*. Route Fifty. www.route-fifty.com/tech-data/2023/06/microsoft-unveils-openai-service-government-customers/387293/

Konkel, F. (2023). *Proceed with caution: Industry advises a careful approach to generative AI*. Nextgov/FCW. www.nextgov.com/artificial-intelligence/2023/07/proceed-caution-industry-advises-careful-approach-generative-ai/388600/

Konkel, F. (2023). *Senator calls for cybersecurity audit of law enforcement wireless network*. Nextgov/FCW. www.nextgov.com/emerging-tech/2023/04/senator-calls-cybersecurity-audit-law-enforcement-wireless-network/385110/

Konkel, F. (2023). *US marshals to unveil "fully reconstituted system" following ransomware attack*. Nextgov/FCW. www.nextgov.com/cybersecurity/2023/05/us-marshals-unveil-fully-reconstituted-system-following-ransomware-attack/385866/

Konkel, F. (2023). *White House to hold "frank" discussion with top AI CEOs Thursday*. Nextgov/FCW. www.nextgov.com/emerging-tech/2023/05/white-house-hold-frank-discussion-top-ai-ceos-thursday/385929/

Kornbluh, K., & Trehu, J. (2023, March). *The new American foreign policy of technology: Promoting innovation, national security, and democratic values in a digital world*. German Marshall Fund. www.gmfus.org/news/new-american-foreign-policy-technology

Kramer, M. (2022). *Commercial satellites are the next front in space war*. Axios. www.axios.com/2022/11/01/starlink-ukraine-elon-musk-war-space

Kramer, M. (2023, January 17). *The growing space economy*. Axios. www.axios.com/newsletters/axios-space-c4cfb894-8174-4770-8fcb-703f927b59c1.html

Kramer, M. (2023, February 1). *Machine learning to find learned aliens*. Axios. www.axios.com/2023/02/01/machine-learning-alien-search

Kratsios, M. (2019, February 11). *Why the US needs a strategy for AI*. WIRED. www.wired.com/story/a-national-strategy-for-ai/

Krebs, B. (2021). *DDoS-Guard to forfeit internet space occupied by Parler*. Krebs on Security. https://krebsonsecurity.com/2021/01/ddos-guard-to-forfeit-internet-space-occupied-by-parler/

Krebs, B. (2023, January 9). *Identity thieves bypassed Experian security to view credit reports*. Krebs on Security. https://krebsonsecurity.com/2023/01/identity-thieves-bypassed-experian-security-to-view-credit-reports/

Krebs, B. (2023, February 28). *Hackers claim they breached T-Mobile more than 100 times in 2022*. Krebs on Security. https://krebsonsecurity.com/2023/02/hackers-claim-they-breached-t-mobile-more-than-100-times-in-2022/

Kreuze, J. (n.d.). *Smartphone-based diagnosis of crop diseases*. CIP International Potato Center. https://cipotato.org/cip_projects/smartphone-based-diagnosis-crop-diseases/

Krishnan, K. N. (2004). *Developing a police perspective and exploring the use of biometrics and other emerging technologies as an investigative tool in identity crimes.* U.S. Department of Justice Office of Justice Programs. www.ojp.gov/ncjrs/virtual-library/abstracts/developing-police-perspective-and-exploring-use-biometrics-and

Kuiper, J. (2017, May 22). *The long history and bright future of artificial intelligence in medicine.* Growth. https://growthevidence.com/joel-kuiper/

Kumar, R. (2022). *The same app can pose a bigger security and privacy threat depending on the country where you download it, study finds.* Nextgov/FCW. www.nextgov.com/ideas/2022/09/same-app-can-pose-bigger-security-and-privacy-threat-depending-country-where-you-download-it-study-finds/377817/

Kuntz, C. (2022, July 8). *Genomes: The era of purposeful manipulation begins.* Center for Strategic & International Studies. www.csis.org/analysis/genomes-era-purposeful-manipulation-begins

Kury, T. (2022). *What social media regulation could look like: Think of pipelines, not utilities.* Nextgov/FCW. www.nextgov.com/ideas/2022/12/what-social-media-regulation-could-look-think-pipelines-not-utilities/380927/

Kuzmenko, O. (2019, February 15). *"Defend the white race": American extremists being co-opted by Ukraine's far-right.* Bellingcat. www.bellingcat.com/news/uk-and-europe/2019/02/15/defend-the-white-race-american-extremists-being-co-opted-by-ukraines-far-right/

Latham, K. (2023). *CES 2023 preview: 4 big questions that will shape the week.* ZDNet. www.zdnet.com/article/ces-2023-preview-4-big-questions-that-will-shape-the-week/

Latham, K. (2023). *Flying boats and other tech for cleaner shipping.* BBC. www.bbc.com/news/business-63700540

Lawler, R. (2022, August 15). *Signal alerts 1,900 messaging users to a security threat from Twilio hackers—The attackers used their access to pull up three specific numbers.* The Verge. www.theverge.com/2022/8/15/23306949/signal-messaging-app-sms-twilio-data-breach-security-privacy

Lee, C. (2023, August 8). *Unmasking hypnotized AI: The hidden risks of large language models.* Security Intelligence. https://securityintelligence.com/posts/unmasking-hypnotized-ai-hidden-risks-large-language-models/

Lee, C. (2024, February 1). *Audio-jacking: Using generative AI to distort live audio transactions.* Security Intelligence. https://securityintelligence.com/posts/using-generative-ai-distort-live-audio-transactions/

Lee, M., Dimarogonas, J., Geist, E., Manuel, S., Schwankhart, R. A., & Downing, B. (2023). *Opportunities and risks of 5G military use in Europe.* RAND Corporation. www.rand.org/pubs/research_reports/RRA1351-2.html

Legare, R. (2023, February 16). *Justice Department targets threats to U.S. innovation, warns of China's "weaponization of data."* CBS News. www.cbsnews.com/news/justice-department-china-data-disruptive-technology-strike-force-lisa-monaco/

Lempinenl, E. (2021, January 8). *Biden must mount campaign against right-wing extremists, says Berkeley expert.* Berkeley News. https://news.berkeley.edu/2021/01/07/biden-must-mount-campaign-against-right-wing-extremists-says-berkeley-expert/

Leprince-Ringuet, D. (2020, April 1). *AI vs your career? What artificial intelligence will really do to the future of work.* ZDNet. www.zdnet.com/article/ai-vs-your-career-what-artificial-intelligence-will-really-do-to-the-future-of-work/

Leprince-Ringuet, D. (2020, July 20). *2084: What happens when artificial intelligence meets Big Brother.* ZDNet. www.zdnet.com/article/2084-what-happens-when-artificial-intelligence-meets-big-brother/

Leprince-Ringuet, D. (2020, August 5). *Evil AI: These are the 20 most dangerous crimes that artificial intelligence will create.* ZDNet. www.zdnet.com/article/evil-ai-these-are-the-20-most-dangerous-crimes-that-artificial-intelligence-will-create/

Leprince-Ringuet, D. (2021, January 6). *Facial recognition: Now algorithms can see through face masks.* ZDNet. www.zdnet.com/article/facial-recognition-now-algorithms-can-see-through-face-masks/

Leprince-Ringuet, D. (2021, January 29). *US, China or Europe? Here's who is really winning the global race for AI.* ZDNet. www.zdnet.com/article/us-china-or-europe-heres-who-is-really-winning-the-global-race-for-ai/

Leprince-Ringuet, D. (2021, December 22). *Quantum computers: Eight ways quantum computing is going to change the world.* ZDNet. www.zdnet.com/article/quantum-computers-eight-ways-quantum-computing-is-going-to-change-the-world/

Levine, A. S. (2023, February 3). In the face of attacks, TikTok tries to charm its critics with transparency. *Forbes.* www.forbes.com/sites/alexandralevine/2023/02/02/tiktok-transparency-center/

LeVine, S. (2019, March 20). *A paradise for the age of the techno-autocrat.* Axios www.axios.com/2019/03/20/us-china-artificial-intelligence-surveillance

LeVine, S., & Waddell, K. (2019, March 1). *The big American robot push.* Axios. www.axios.com/2019/03/01/the-big-american-robot-push

Levinson, K. (2022). *Machine learning digs into states' archives.* Route Fifty. www.route-fifty.com/tech-data/2022/12/machine-learning-digs-states-archives/381234/

Levinson, K. (2023). *AI in the workplace: Local officials explore responsible use.* Route Fifty. www.route-fifty.com/digital-government/2023/06/ai-workplace-local-officials-explore-responsible-use/387088/

Levinson, K. (2023). *Drones enlisted for real-time monitoring of public events.* Route Fifty. www.route-fifty.com/management/2023/06/drones-enlisted-real-time-monitoring-public-events/388065/

Levinson, K. (2023). *Homelessness could have a 3D-printed solution.* Route Fifty. www.route-fifty.com/emerging-tech/2023/07/homelessness-could-have-3d-printed-solution/388442/

Levinson, K. (2023). *Justice launches $8M smart policing grant program.* Route Fifty. www.route-fifty.com/public-safety/2023/03/justice-launches-8m-smart-policing-grant-program/383933/

Levinson, K. (2024, February 9). *Deepfake porn: The ugly side of generative AI, and what states can do about it.* Route Fifty. www.route-fifty.com/digital-government/2024/02/deepfake-porn-ugly-side-generative-ai-and-what-states-can-do-about-it/394089/

Lewis, A. C. (2022, February 15). *Driving while baked? Inside the high-tech quest to find out.* Wired.Com. www.wired.com/story/weed-dui-test/

Lewis, A. J., Force, H. J., & Tahan, C. (2023). *The future of quantum—Driving innovation and security from the government.* Center for Strategic & International Studies. www.csis.org/events/future-quantum-driving-innovation-and-security-government

Lewis, A. J., & Painter, C. (2022, August 15). *Placing cyber diplomacy at the top of the agenda.* Center for Strategic & International Studies. www.csis.org/node/66558

Lewis, J. (2022, June 23). *The cyber real world and multilateralism: Inside cyber diplomacy.* CSIS Podcasts. www.csis.org/podcasts/inside-cyber-diplomacy/cyber-real-world-and-multilateralism

Lewis, J. (2023). *AI and rumors of impending doom.* Center for Strategic & International Studies. www.csis.org/analysis/ai-and-rumors-impending-doom

Lewis, J., & Crumpler, W. (2021, February 3). *Questions about facial recognition.* Center for Strategic & International Studies. www.csis.org/analysis/questions-about-facial-recognition

Lewis, J., Moody, D., Merzbacher, C., & McMarty, B. (2022). *The Future of Quantum—Public/Private collaboration for innovation and adoption.* Center for Strategic & International Studies. www.csis.org/events/future-quantum-publicprivate-collaboration-innovation-and-adoption

Lewis, J., & Painter, C. (2023). *Implementing cyber confidence-building measures.* Center for Strategic & International Studies. www.csis.org/podcasts/inside-cyber-diplomacy/implementing-cyber-confidence-building-measures

Lewis, J. A. (2022, January 20). *Holding malicious cyber actors accountable.* Center for Strategic & International Studies. www.csis.org/events/holding-malicious-cyber-actors-accountable

Lewis, J. A. (2022, February 4). *Russia and the threat of massive cyberattack.* Center for Strategic & International Studies. www.csis.org/analysis/russia-and-threat-massive-cyberattack

Lewis, J. A. (2022, November). *Tech regulation can harm national security.* Center for Strategic & International Studies. www.csis.org/analysis/tech-regulation-can-harm-national-security

Lewis, J. A. (2022, December 9). *Emerging technologies: Regulation and innovation.* Center for Strategic & International Studies. www.csis.org/podcasts/does-not-compute/emerging-technologies-regulation-and-innovation

Lewis, J. A., Lostri, E., & Cheng, C. (2022, February 15). *AI strategies and autonomous vehicles development.* Center for Strategic & International Studies. www.csis.org/analysis/ai-strategies-and-autonomous-vehicles-development

Lewis, J. A., & Painter, C. (2022, August 15). *Placing cyber diplomacy at the top of the agenda.* Center for Strategic & International Studies. www.csis.org/node/66558

Letter from the Office of the Utah State Auditor John Dougall, to Attorney General the Hon. Sean Reyes, Re: Limited Review of Banjo (26 March 2021): https://reporting.auditor.utah.gov/servlet/servlet.FileDownload?file=0151K000004 2i9lQAA

Liang, A. (2022). *US chip makers hit by new China export rule.* BBC. www.bbc.co.uk/news/business-62747401

Liautaud, S., & Sweetingham, L. (2021). *The power of ethics: How to make good choices in a complicated world.* Simon & Schuster.

Licato, J. (2023, April 24). *AI-generated spam may soon be flooding your inbox— And it will be personalized to be especially persuasive.* Nextgov/FCW. www.nextgov.com/ideas/2023/04/ai-generated-spam-may-soon-be-flooding-your-inbox and-it-will-be-personalized-be-especially-persuasive/385521/

Limbago, A. L. (n.d.). *Data sovereignty in a reglobalized world.* GRC Outlook. https://grcoutlook.com/data-sovereignty-in-a-reglobalized-world/

Limotta, M. (2020). *How AI will help the U.S. to Mars and beyond.* Nextgov/FCW. www.nextgov.com/ideas/2020/12/how-ai-will-help-us-mars-and-beyond/170935/

Lisbona, N. (2022, January 31). *True story? lie detection systems go high-tech.* BBC. www.bbc.com/news/business-60153129

Lloreda, C. (2023). Scientists use AI to decipher words and sentences from brain scans. *Science AAAS.* www.science.org/content/article/scientists-use-ai-decipher-words-and-sentences-brain-scans

Lofgren, M. (2016, October 31). Trump, Putin, and the Alt-Right International. *The Atlantic.* www.theatlantic.com/international/archive/2016/10/trump-putin-alt-right-comintern/506015/

Lohn, A., & Jackson, K. (2022). *Will AI make cyber swords or shields?* Center for Security and Emerging Technology. https://cset.georgetown.edu/publication/will-ai-make-cyber-swords-or-shields/

Lopez, T. D. (2020, February 25). *DOD adopts 5 principles of artificial intelligence ethics.* U.S. Department of Defense. www.defense.gov/News/News-Stories/article/article/2094085/dod-adopts-5-principles-of-artificial-intelligence-ethics/

Lucia, B. (2018). *Artificial intelligence for policing stirs ethics concerns.* Nextgov/FCW. www.nextgov.com/analytics-data/2018/04/artificial-intelligence-policing-stirs-ethics-concerns/147822/

Lyngaas, S. (2022, December 20). *Iran and Russia were too distracted to meddle in midterm elections, US general says.* CNN. www.cnn.com/2022/12/19/politics/iran-russia-cyber-command-midterm-elections/index.html

Lyngaas, S. (2023, August 5). *"This isn't some random dude with a duffel bag": To catch fentanyl traffickers, feds dig into crypto markets.* CNN. www.cnn.com/2023/08/05/politics/fentanyl-cryptocurrency-cartels-federal-agents-catch-up/index.html

Lyngaas, S. (2023, August 10). *Homeland Security report details how teen hackers exploited security weaknesses in some of the world's biggest companies.* CNN. www.cnn.com/2023/08/10/politics/dhs-hacking-report

Maass, D. (2020, September 18). *Three interactive tools for understanding police surveillance.* Electronic Frontier Foundation. www.eff.org/deeplinks/2020/09/three-interactive-tools-understanding-police-surveillance

Macaulay, T. (2020, April 27). *UK spies must ramp up use of AI to fight new threats, says report.* The Next Web. https://thenextweb.com/neural/2020/04/27/uk-spies-must-ramp-up-use-of-ai-to-fight-new-threats-says-report/

Macaulay, T. (2020, July 6). *Can AI convincingly answer existential questions?* The Next Web. https://thenextweb.com/neural/2020/07/06/study-tests-whether-ai-can-convincingly-answer-existential-questions/

Macaulay, T. (2020, July 29). *Scientists use AI to predict what makes a successful relationship.* The Next Web. https://thenextweb.com/neural/2020/07/29/scientists-use-ai-to-predict-what-makes-a-successful-relationship/

Macdonals, A. (2022). *Alcohol retailer deploys ITL's biometric age verification to more stores as pilot ends.* Biometric Update. www.biometricupdate.com/202206/alcohol-retailer-deploys-itls-biometric-age-verification-to-more-stores-as-pilot-ends

Machani, A. (2022, October 18). *A lawless cyberspace hurts young people the most.* World Politics Review. www.worldpoliticsreview.com/to-protect-teens-social-media-needs-international-governance/

Machine Learning and Artificial Intelligence Subcommittee of the National Science and Technology Council. (2022, July). *Lessons Learned from federal use of Cloud computing to support artificial intelligence research and development.* www.whitehouse.gov/wp-content/uploads/2022/07/07-2022-Lessons-Learned-Cloud-for-AI-July2022.pdf

Macnak, M. (2023). *How agencies can automate data extraction at scale.* Route Fifty. www.route-fifty.com/tech-data/2023/05/how-agencies-can-automate-data-extraction-scale/386934/

Maddox, T. (2020, March 2). *CIO Jury: Artificial intelligence and machine learning an essential part of cybersecurity.* ZDNet. www.zdnet.com/article/cio-jury-artificial-intelligence-and-machine-learning-an-essential-part-of-cybersecurity/

Mailes, G., Carrasco, M., & Arcuri, A. (2021, April). *The global trust imperative.* BCG & Salesforce. https://web-assets.bcg.com/bf/de/d2a310054cd8891fd7f8cd95452b/the-global-trust-imperative-salesforce-bcg-whitepaper.pdf

Maillet, D. C., McGrail, K., Nelson, A. H., Paprice, P. A., & Schull, M. J. (2023, December 12). *Want to know if your data are managed responsibly? Here are 15 questions to help you find out.* Route Fifty. www.route-fifty.com/digital-government/2023/12/want-know-if-your-data-are-managed-responsibly-here-are-15-questions-help-you-find-out/392695/

Maittelsteadt, M. (2021, February). *AI verification: Mechanisms to ensure AI arms control compliance CSET issue brief.* Center for Security and Emerging Technology.

Malbec, N. (2023, July 3). *NewSpace: New frontiers and new challenges for cybersecurity.* InCyber News. https://incyber.org/en/newspace-new-frontiers-new-challenges-for-cybersecurity/

Malekos Smith, Z. L. (2022, March 13). *There are tradeoffs in governing the metaverse.* Center for Strategic & International Studies. www.csis.org/analysis/there-are-tradeoffs-governing-metaverse

Mallenbaum, C. (2023, December 24). *Lab-grown diamonds go luxury—And rock the industry.* Axios. www.axios.com/2023/12/24/diamonds-lab-grown-natural-price-cartier-dousset

Malloy, D. (2017, August 8). *Could the biggest win for taxpayers be artificial intelligence?* Ozy. www.ozy.com/news-and-politics/could-the-biggest-win-for-taxpayers-be-artificial-intelligence/79771/

Malloy, D. (2020, July 19). *What no one will tell you about robots.* Ozy. www.ozy.com/the-new-and-the-next/what-no-one-will-tell-you-about-robots/359012/

Maluchandani, N., & Shanahan, J. (2022). *Software- defined warfare: Architecting the DOD's transition to the digital age.* Center for Strategic & International Studies. www.csis.org/analysis/software-defined-warfare-architecting-dods-transition-digital-age

Manen, H. V., Schaffrath, J., Sweijs, T., & Wijk, K. V. (2020, January 25). *What world do we live in? An analysis of global geodynamic trends.* The Hague Centre for Strategic Studies. www.hcss.nl/pub/2019/strategic-monitor-2019-2020/what-world-do-we-live-in/

Manyika, S. L. (2018, March 2). *Is she a superhero for artificial intelligence?* Ozy. www.ozy.com/the-new-and-the-next/is-she-a-superhero-for-artificial-intelligence/83698/

Marcellino, W., Beauchamp-Mustafaga, N., Kerrigan, A., Chao, L. N., & Smith, J. (2023). *The rise of generative AI and the coming era of social media manipulation 3.0: Next-generation Chinese astroturfing and coping with ubiquitous AI.* RAND Corporation. www.rand.org/pubs/perspectives/PEA2679-1.html

Marchant, G. (2019). *"Soft Law" Governance of Artificial Intelligence.* https://escholarship.org/uc/item/0jq252ks

Marino, K. (2022, January 21). *The Federal Reserve is open to creating a digital dollar.* Axios. www.axios.com/2022/01/21/the-federal-reserve-is-open-to-creating-a-digital-dollar

Markay, L. (2022). *Political pros turn to AI in cash race.* Axios. www.axios.com/2022/10/07/ai-becomes-a-political-super-weapon

Markou, C. (2017, May 16). *Why using AI to sentence criminals is a dangerous idea.* The Conversation. https://theconversation.com/amp/why-using-ai-to-sentence-criminals-is-a-dangerous-idea-77734

Markus Giesler. (2020). *What makes us buy into AI?* www.mgiesler.com/blog/buy-ai

Martin, A. (2023). *Genesis market gang tries to sell platform after FBI disruption.* The Record. https://therecord.media/genesis-market-fraud-platform-for-sale-dark-web

Martin, N. R. (2020). *Cracking open The Base.* The Informant. www.informant.news/p/cracking-open-the-base

Martindale, D. (2005, October 1). One face, one neuron. *Scientific American.* www.scientificamerican.com/article/one-face-one-neuron/

Martinho-Truswell, E. (2018, January 26). How AI could help the public sector. *Harvard Business Review.* https://hbr.org/2018/01/how-ai-could-help-the-public-sector

Marx, P. (2018, November 19). Learning to love robots. *The New Yorker.* www.newyorker.com/magazine/2018/11/26/learning-to-love-robots

Mason, D., & Pearson, J. (2023). *Ransomware attack on data firm ION could take days to fix—Sources.* Reuters. www.reuters.com/technology/ransomware-attack-data-firm-ion-could-take-days-fix-sources-2023-02-02/

Matishak, M. (2021). *New Senate intel chief wants to reimagine "decimated" spy agency.* POLITICO. www.politico.com/news/2021/02/04/mark-warner-senate-intel-interview-466087

Matyszczyk, C. (2021, January 25). *That cute robot comp can instantly work out who you are.* ZDNet. www.zdnet.com/article/that-cute-robot-cop-can-instantly-work-out-who-you-are/

Matyszczyk, C. (2021, January 29). *I've just seen the future of technology and you may not like it.* ZDNet. www.zdnet.com/article/ive-just-seen-the-future-of-technology-and-you-may-not-love-i

Matyszczyk, C. (2022, July 2). *A Starbucks barista proved we trust robots more than people—Have we sunk to this? It seems we have.* ZDNet. www.zdnet.com/article/a-starbucks-barista-just-proved-we-trust-robots-more-than-people/

Matyszczyk, C. (2022, September 3). *McDonald's just threw technology out the window (well, the customers did).* ZDNet. www.zdnet.com/article/mcdonalds-just-threw-technology-out-the-window-well-its-customers-did/

Matyszczyk, C. (2023, January 8). *One of America's most hated companies hired a security robot. It didn't go well.* ZDNet. www.zdnet.com/article/one-of-americas-most-hated-companies-hired-a-security-robot-it-didnt-go-well/

Matyszczyk, C. (2023, March 4). *McDonald's drive-thru robot made a mistake. Then it all got ridiculous.* ZDNet. www.zdnet.com/article/mcdonalds-drive-thru-robot-made-a-mistake-then-it-all-got-ridiculous/

Maxwell, T. (2018, December 21). *Robots are the future, and we don't trust them.* PBS. www.pbs.org/newshour/amp/economy/making-sense/robots-are-the-future-and-we-dont-trust-them

Maynard, A. (2021). *Elon Musk's Tesla Bot raises serious concerns—But probably not the ones you think.* Nextgov/FCW. www.nextgov.com/ideas/2021/09/elon-musks-tesla-bot-raises-serious-concerns-probably-not-ones-you-think/185202/

Maynard, A. (2022, June 13). *"Jurassic World" scientists still haven't learned that just because you can doesn't mean you should—Real-world genetic engineers can learn from the cautionary tale.* Nextgov/FCW. www.nextgov.com/emerging-tech/2022/06/jurassic-world-scientists-still-havent-learned-just-because-you-can-doesnt-mean-you-should-real-world-genetic-engineers-can-learn-cautionary-tale/368086/

Mazmanian, A. (2023). *Biden signs AI order but stresses need for legislation.* Nextgov/FCW. www.nextgov.com/artificial-intelligence/2023/10/biden-signs-ai-order-stresses-need-legislation/391622/

Mazmanian, A. (2023). *Bipartisan bill proposes blue-ribbon panel to address AI risks, regulations.* Nextgov/FCW. www.nextgov.com/artificial-intelligence/2023/06/bipartisan-bill-proposes-blue-ribbon-panel-address-ai-risks-regulations/387696/

Mazmanian, A. (2023). *Spy agencies acquire commercial data with little coordination and few controls.* Nextgov/FCW. www.nextgov.com/analytics-data/2023/06/spy-agencies-acquire-commercial-data-little-coordination-and-few-controls/387489/.

Mazzocco, I. (2022, July 27). *The AI-surveillance symbiosis in China.* Big Data China. https://bigdatachina.csis.org/the-ai-surveillance-symbiosis-in-china/

McAleenan, K. (2019). *Strategic framework for countering terrorism and targeted violence* (p. 40). Department of Homeland Security.

McCallum, S. (2023). *Revenge and deepfake porn laws to be toughened.* BBC. www.bbc.com/news/technology-66021643

McCallum, S., & Kleinman, Z. (2023). *US announces "strongest global action yet" on AI safety.* BBC. www.bbc.com/news/technology-67261284

McCallum, S., & Vallance, C. (2022, August 25). *Start-up denies using tech to turn call center accents "white."* BBC. www.bbc.com/news/technology-62633188

McCallum, S., & Vallance, C. (2023). *News: ChatGPT-maker U-turns on threat to leave EU over AI law.* BBC. www.bbc.com/news/technology-65708114

McCallum, S., & Vallance, C. (2023). *Prototype "brain-like" chip promises greener AI, says tech giant.* BBC. www.bbc.com/news/technology-66465230

McCullom, R. (2023). *Robot police dogs are on patrol, but who's holding the leash?* Route Fifty. www.route-fifty.com/digital-government/2023/09/robot-pol ice-dogs-are-patrol-whos-holding-leash/389978/

McFarland, T., & McCormack, T. (2014). *Mind the gap: Can developers of autonomous weapons systems be liable for war crimes?* The United State Naval War College.

McFate, M. (2022). *Network visibility proves its worth in defending against cyber attacks.* Riverbed. www.riverbed.com/blogs/network-visibility-proves-worth/

McGee, M. K. (2022, December). *A plan to address future healthcare cyber challenges.* Government Information Security. www.bankinfosecurity.com/int erviews/plan-to-address-future-healthcare-cyber-challenges-greg-garcia-i-5192

McGloughlin, J. (2023, December 27). *4 steps to prepare for the coming quantum onslaught.* Nextgov/FCW. www.nextgov.com/ideas/2023/12/4-steps-prepare-coming-quantum-onslaught/392836/

McGuire, M. R., & Holt, T. (2017). *The routledge handbook of technology, crime and justice.* Routledge International Handbooks. www.routledge.com/The-Routledge-Handbook-of-Technology-Crime-and-Justice/McGuire-Holt/p/book/9780367581404

McIntyre, C. (2019, May 8). *Transforming the finance sector.* University of Oxford. www.research.ox.ac.uk/article/2019-05-08-transforming-the-finance-sector

McKendrick, J. (2018, December 12). *Time to instill trust and confidence in artificial intelligence.* ZDNet. www.zdnet.com/article/instilling-trust-and-confidence-in-artificial-intelligence/

McKendrick, J. (2020, February 15). *7 business areas ripe for an artificial intelligence boost.* ZDNet. www.zdnet.com/article/7-business-areas-ripe-for-an-artific ial-intelligence-boost/

McKendrick, J. (2023). *AI and advanced applications are straining current technology infrastructures.* ZDNet. www.zdnet.com/article/ai-and-advanced-appli cations-may-strain-current-technology-infrastructures-to-their-limits/

McKendrick, J. (2023). *More skills are needed to help AI plug skills gaps.* ZDNet. www.zdnet.com/article/more-skills-needed-to-help-ai-plug-skills-gaps/

McLellan, C. (2022, August 5). *Digital transformation in 2022 and beyond: These are the key trends.* ZDNet. www.zdnet.com/article/digital-transformation-in-2022-and-beyond-these-are-the-key-trends/

McLellan, C. (2022, October 12). *What is the metaverse, and who will build it?* ZDNet. www.zdnet.com/article/what-is-the-metaverse-and-who-will-build-it/

McLennan, M., & Zurich Insurance Group. (2024, January). *The global risks report 2024 19th edition insight report*. World Economic Forum.

McIntosh, S. (2024, February 7). *Martin Scorsese says immersive screening experiences can weaken films*. BBC. www.bbc.co.uk/news/entertainment-arts-68215163

McMahon, L. (2022, June 9). *Ministry of Defence acquires government's first quantum computer*. BBC. www.bbc.com/news/technology-61647134

McMahon, S., & O'Dowd, P. (2021, January 11). *Watchdog group warns far-right extremists feel emboldened, view Capitol mob as a "watershed moment."* Wbur. www.wbur.org/hereandnow/2021/01/11/inauguration-violence-capitol-trump

McMallum, S. (2022). *Is it goodbye—finally—to the fax machine?* BBC. www.bbc.co.uk/news/technology-63472371

McMallum, S., & Clarke, J. (2023). *What is AI, is it dangerous and what jobs are at risk?* BBC. www.bbc.com/news/technology-65855333

McManus, S. (2023). *Why it matters where your data is stored*. BBC. www.bbc.com/news/business-66310714

McPherson, S. (2022). *Scene graph technology: High-impact use cases for government*. Nextgov/FCW. www.nextgov.com/ideas/2022/04/scene-graph-technology-high-impact-use-cases-government/365607/

Medeiros, M. (2017, March 7). *Intellectual property strategy for artificial intelligence*. IP Osgoode. www.iposgoode.ca/2017/03/intellectual-property-strategy-for-artificial-intelligence/

Mehrotra, D. (2023, January 11). *A police app exposed secret details about raids and suspects*. WIRED. www.wired.com/story/sweepwizard-police-raids-data-exposure/

Mellon, D. (2020). *App tells you who's collecting your data and why*. Futurity. www.futurity.org/iot-assistant-app-privacy-data-2290022-2/

Meta. (n.d.). *The metaverse is having impact today*.

Metz, C. (2017, May 23). *An improved AlphaGo wins its first game against the world's top Go player*. WIRED. www.wired.com/2017/05/revamped-alphago-wins-first-game-chinese-go-grandmaster/

Meunier, A. (2023). *Will orbital data centers soon be a reality?* InCyber. https://incyber.org/en/will-orbital-data-centers-soon-be-a-reality/

Meyer, J. (2020, June 5). Russian "terrorists" training German Neo-Nazi youth in combat—Reports. *The Moscow Times*. www.themoscowtimes.com/2020/06/05/russian-terrorists-training-german-neo-nazi-youth-in-combat-reports-a70497

Michel, C. (2016). *How Russia surpassed Germany to become the racist ideal for Trump-loving white supremacists*. Quartz. https://qz.com/869938/how-russia-surpassed-germany-to-become-the-dangerous-new-role-model-for-trump-loving-american-white-supremacists/

Michel, C. (2017). *How Russia became the leader of the global Christian right*. POLITICO. https://politi.co/2KgFMxg

Michel, C. (2017). *Russian, American white nationalists raise their flags in Washington*. ThinkProgress. https://archive.thinkprogress.org/russian-american-nationalists-washington-5bd15fd18eaf/

Michel, H. (2021, February 4). *There are spying eyes everywhere—And now they share a brain.* WIRED. www.wired.com/story/there-are-spying-eyes-everywh ere-and-now-they-share-a-brain/

Microsoft. (2022, August). *Extortion economics; ransomwares new business model.* https://query.prod.cms.rt.microsoft.com/cms/api/am/binary/ RE54L7v

Microsoft Security. (2022). *Extortion economics.* Microsoft. www.microsoft.com/ en-us/security/business/security-insider/anatomy-of-an-external-attack-surface/ extortion-economics/

Microsoft Threat Intelligence. (2023, May 19). *The confidence game: Shifting tactics fuel surge in business email compromise.* www.microsoft.com/en-us/secur ity/business/security-insider/reports/cyber-signals/shifting-tactics-fuel-surge-in-business-email-compromise/

Microsoft Threat Intelligence. (2023, August 2). *Midnight Blizzard conducts targeted social engineering over Microsoft Teams.* www.microsoft.com/en-us/ security/blog/2023/08/02/midnight-blizzard-conducts-targeted-social-engineer ing-over-microsoft-teams/

Middlebury Institute of International Studies at Monterey. (2020). *The Russian imperial movement and coronavirus.* The Center on Terrorism, Extremism, and Counterterrorism. www.middlebury.edu/institute/academics/centers-initiatives/ ctec/ctec-publications/russian-imperial-movement-and-covid-19

Miller, E. (2023). *Wireless for government operated industrial networks; how to choose the Best-Fit over a Force-Fit.* CISCO.

Miller, J. (2023, January 5). *Axios newsletters.* Axios. www.axios.com/news letters

Miller, K. M. (2007, January). The impact of DNA and other technology on the criminal justice system: Improvements and complications, *Albany Law Journal of Science & Technology, 17,* 87–125.

Miller, M. (2024, March 25). *Officials plan for new age of cyber threats to satellites.* POLITICO. www.politico.com/news/2024/03/25/satellite-cyber-thr eat-00148672

Miller, S. (2022). *Updated digital forensics database speeds criminal investigations.* Nextgov/FCW. www.nextgov.com/cxo-briefing/2022/06/updated-digital-forens ics-database-speeds-criminal-investigations/368809/

Miller, S. (2023, January 24). *What motivates remote workers to protect IT assets?* Nextgov/FCW. www.nextgov.com/emerging-tech/2023/01/what-motivates-rem ote-workers-protect-it-assets/381896/

Miller, S. (2023, June 1). *Digital driver's licenses expand.* Route Fifty. www.route fifty.com/tech-data/2023/06/digital-drivers-licenses-expand/387031/

Miller, S. (2024, January 29). *Data literacy 101: Building a public sector work force for the future.* Route Fifty. www.route-fifty.com/digital-government/2024/ 01/data-literacy-101-building-public-sector-workforce-future/393694/

Miller-Idriss, C., & Koehler, D. (2021, February 10). A plan to beat back the far right. *Foreign Affairs.* www.foreignaffairs.com/articles/united-states/2021-02-03/plan-beat-back-far-right

Moniz, E., Nunn, S., Schieffer, B., & Schwartz, A. H. (2021, December 8). *Nuclear weapons: The growing risk*. Center for Strategic & International Studies. www. csis.org/analysis/nuclear-weapons-growing-risk

Monks, K. (2014, August 12). *Spy satellites fighting crime from space*. CNN. www.cnn.com/2014/08/11/tech/innovation/spy-satellites-fighting-crime-from-space/index.html

Montellaro, Z. (2024, March 11). *America's election chiefs are worried AI is coming for them*. POLITICO. www.politico.com/news/2024/03/11/secretary-state-ai-election-misinformation-00146137

Morgan Stanley. (2020, October 1). *Could a computer think like a human?* www. morganstanley.com/ideas/quantum-neuromorphic-computer-processing

Morison, J., & Harkens, A. (2019). Re-engineering justice? Robot judges, computerized courts, and (semi) automated legal decision-making. *Legal Studies*, 39(4), 618–635. https://doi.org/10.1017/lst.2019.5

Morris, B. (2023). *How long until a robot is doing your dishes?* BBC. www.bbc. com/news/business-66288309

Morrish, L. (2023). *A face recognition site crawled the web for dead people's photos*. WIRED. www.wired.com/story/a-face-recognition-site-crawled-the-web-for-dead-peoples-photos/

Mucha, S. (2021). *Biden issues executive order following mounting cyberattacks*. Axios. www.axios.com/2021/05/12/biden-executive-order-cyberattacks

Mufson, S. (2014, February 7). Why an AK-47 may be a bigger threat to the electricity grid than a cyberattack. *The Washington Post*. www.washingtonpost. com/news/wonk/wp/2014/02/07/why-an-ak-47-may-be-a-bigger-threat-to-the-electricity-grid-than-a-cyberattack/

Mulchandani, C., & Shanahan, J. (2022, September 6). *Software- defined warfare: architecting the DOD's transition to the digital age*. Center For Strategic & International Studies. www.csis.org/analysis/software-defined-warfare-architecting-dods-transition-digital-age

Muller, J. (2019, February 1). *Tomorrow's cars need a new kind of workforce*. Axios. www.axios.com/2019/02/01/self-driving-cars-skills-gap

Muller, J. (2021, April 26). *Self-driving cars speed forward while safety rules lag*. Axios. www.axios.com/2021/04/26/self-driving-cars-tesla-crashes-safety

Muller, J. (2022, January 4). *Deere unveils autonomous tractor to transform agriculture*. Axios. www.axios.com/2022/01/04/deeres-driverless-tractor-gives-stressed-farmers-a-new-tool

Muller, J. (2022, January 11). *Tesla setting lets you drive like a jerk*. Axios. www. axios.com/2022/01/11/your-tesla-could-drive-like-a-jerk

Muller, J. (2022, February 1). *With big trials in North Carolina and Texas, drone delivery is about to take off*. Axios. www.axios.com/2022/02/01/home-medicine-drone-delivery-2022

Muller, J. (2022, February 3). *Where to encounter some of the first self-driving vehicles*. Axios. www.axios.com/2022/02/03/where-to-encounter-some-of-the-first-self-driving-vehicles

Muller, J. (2022, February 10). *We tried it: A pizza vending machine.* Axios. www.axios.com/2022/02/10/we-tried-it-a-pizza-vending-machine

Muller, J. (2022, May 18). *Why driverless cars can't go everywhere yet.* Axios. www.axios.com/2022/05/18/driverless-cars-robotaxis-waymo-automated-vehicles

Muller, J. (2022, June 10). *Flying taxis, delivery drones and more are finally taking off.* Axios. www.axios.com/2022/06/10/flying-taxis

Muller, J. (2022, September 26). *Meet the "vertiport," where you'll go to hail an air taxi.* Axios. www.axios.com/2022/09/26/vertiport-flying-taxi

Muller, J. (2022, October 28). *Buttigieg: Self-driving cars could be safer.* Axios. www.axios.com/2022/10/28/pete-buttigieg-self-driving-cars

Muller, J. (2022, November 9). *Your next car might not drive if you've been drinking.* Axios. www.axios.com/2022/11/09/drunk-driving-sensors

Muller, J. (2022, November 17). *Amazon can't get enough human workers—So here come the robots.* Axios. www.axios.com/2022/11/17/amazon-robots

Muller, J. (2022, November 23). *Cruise, Waymo push robotaxis amid doubts about self-driving tech.* Axios. www.axios.com/2022/11/23/cruise-waymo-robotaxis-ford-gm-autonomous-vehicles

Muller, J. (2023, March 17). *Autonomous cars could help millions of disabled Americans find jobs, study finds.* Axios. www.axios.com/2023/03/17/autonomous-cars-disabled-americans-jobs

Muller, J. (2023, August 29). *Robotaxis hit the accelerator in growing list of cities nationwide.* Axios. www.axios.com/2023/08/29/cities-testing-self-driving-driverless-taxis-robotaxi-waymo

Muller, J. (2023, November 29). *Detroit's newest road can charge electric cars as they travel on it.* Axios. www.axios.com/2023/11/29/detroit-electric-roadway

Muller, J. (2024, January 2). *2024 will be a breakout year for delivery drones.* Axios. www.axios.com/2024/01/02/delivery-drones-2024-amazon-zipline-wing

Muller, J. (2024, January 12). *Chatty cars, swappable bodies: Future of transportation on display at CES.* Axios. www.axios.com/2024/01/12/ces-2024-cars-ai-honda-kia

Muller, V. C. (2020, April 30). *Ethics of artificial intelligence and robotics.* Stanford Encyclopedia of Philosophy. https://plato.stanford.edu/entries/ethics-ai/

Mulligan, K. (2021, January 19). *The United States could be in the early days of a domestic insurgency.* Center for American Progress. www.americanprogress.org/issues/security/news/2021/01/19/494758/united-states-early-days-domestic-insurgency/

Murakami, K. (2023, August 8). *Unless states act soon, the "AI rich" will "only get richer."* Route Fifty. www.route-fifty.com/emerging-tech/2023/08/unless-states-act-soon-ai-rich-will-only-get-richer/389224/

Murakami, K. (2023, August 11). *Regulate AI? Here's what states need to know.* Route Fifty. www.route-fifty.com/digital-government/2023/08/regulate-ai-heres-what-states-need-know/389359/

Muro, M., Jacobs, J., & Liu, S. (2023). *Building AI cities: How to spread the benefits of an emerging technology across more of America.* Brookings. www.brookings.edu/articles/building-ai-cities-how-to-spread-the-benefits-of-an-emerging-technology-across-more-of-america/

Murray, D. (2024, April 14). *Police use of retrospective facial recognition technology: A step change in surveillance capability necessitating an evolution of the human rights law framework.* Modern Law Review, 87, 833–863. https://doi.org/10.1111/1468-2230.12862

Myers, B. (2022, July 21). *New Orleans City Council approves police use of facial recognition, reversing earlier ban.* Nola. www.nola.com/news/crime_police/artic le_d31cb51a-090c-11ed-8929-7bc8922a7d0d.html

NAACP. (n.d.). *Artificial intelligence in predictive policing issue brief.* https:// naacp.org/resources/artificial-intelligence-predictive-policing-issue-brief

Nakashima, E. (2018, January 12). Russian military was behind "NotPetya" cyberattack in Ukraine, CIA concludes. *The Washington Post.* www.washing tonpost.com/world/national-security/russian-military-was-behind-notpetya-cyberattack-in-ukraine-cia-concludes/2018/01/12/048d8506-f7ca-11e7-b34a-b85626af34ef_story.html

Nakashima, E., & Starks, T. (2023). U.S. national cyber strategy to stress Biden push on regulation. *The Washington Post.* www.washingtonpost.com/national-security/2023/01/05/biden-cyber-strategy-hacking/

Narayanan, M., & Schoeberl, C. (2023, June). *A matrix for selecting responsible AI frameworks.* Center for Security and Emerging Technology. https://cset.geo rgetown.edu/publication/a-matrix-for-selecting-responsible-ai-frameworks/

Nasheri, H. (2005). Economic espionage and industrial spying. Cambridge University Press. https://assets.cambridge.org/97805218/35824/frontmatter/ 9780521835824_frontmatter.pdf

Nasheri, H. (2012). *New developments in intelligence and espionage.* World Politics Review.

Nasheri, H. (2018). The impact of intellectual property theft on national and global security. In: Reichel, P., & Randa, R. (eds.), *Transnational Crime and Global Security* (Vol. 1). Praeger.

Nasheri, H. (2021, December 21). *The dumb and the dangerous road ahead.* United Nations Interregional Crime and Justice Research Institute.

Nasheri, H. (2023, May). *State-sponsored economic espionage in cyberspace: Risks and preparedness, in cybercrime in the pandemic digital age and beyond* (Chang, L. Y.-C., Sarre, R., & Smith, R. G., Eds.). Springer International Publishing.

National Aeronautics and Space Administration Office of Inspector General. (2023, May 3). *NASA's management of its artificial intelligence capabilities.* https://oig.nasa.gov/docs/IG-23-012.pdf

National Artificial Intelligence Advisory Committee. (2023, May). *National artificial intelligence advisory committee year 1 report 2023.* www.ai.gov/wp-cont ent/uploads/2023/05/NAIAC-Report-Year1.pdf

National Artificial Intelligence Initiative Office. (2021, September 8). *Department of Commerce establishes National Artificial Intelligence Advisory Committee.* National Artificial Intelligence Initiative. www.ai.gov/department-of-commerce-establishes-national-artificial-intelligence-advisory-committee/

National Cyber Security Centre. (2024, January 24). *Global ransomware threat expected to rise with AI, NCSC warns.* www.ncsc.gov.uk/news/global-ransomw are-threat-expected-to-rise-with-ai

National Development and Reform Commission. (2022, March 21). *Some views on basic systems for data.* Center for Strategic & International Studies. https://interpret.csis.org/translations/some-views-on-basic-systems-for-data/

National Institute of Food and Agriculture. (2021). *Artificial intelligence.* https://nifa.usda.gov/artificial-intelligence

National Institute of Standards and Technology. (2021, October 15). *Draft—Taxonomy of AI risk.* www.nist.gov/system/files/documents/2021/10/15/taxonomy_AI_risks.pdf

National Institute of Standards and Technology. (2022, August 18). *NIST AI RMF playbook FAQs.* www.nist.gov/itl/ai-risk-management-framework/nist-ai-rmf-playbook-faqs

National Institute of Standards and Technology, U.S. Department of Commerce. (2022). *Towards a standard for identifying and managing bias in artificial intelligence.* https://nvlpubs.nist.gov/nistpubs/SpecialPublications/NIST.SP.1270.pdf

National Institute of Standards and Technology, U.S. Department of Commerce (NIST). (2023). *Artificial Intelligence Risk Management Framework (AI RMF 1.0).* https://nvlpubs.nist.gov/nistpubs/ai/NIST.AI.100-1.pdf

National Science and Technology Council. (2016, October). *The national artificial intelligence research and development strategic plan.* www.nitrd.gov/pubs/national_ai_rd_strategic_plan.pdf

National Science and Technology Council. (2018, December). *Charting a course for success: America's strategy for STEM education.* www.energy.gov/sites/prod/files/2019/05/f62/STEM-Education-Strategic-Plan-2018.pdf

National Science and Technology Council. (2019, June). *The national artificial intelligence research and development strategic plan: 2019 update.* www.nitrd.gov/pubs/National-AI-RD-Strategy-2019.pdf

National Science and Technology Council. (2021, December). *Networking and information technology R&D program and the National Artificial Intelligence Initiative Office: Supplement to the President's FY2022 budget.* www.nitrd.gov/pubs/FY2022-NITRD-NAIIO-Supplement.pdf

National Security Agency. (2022, September). *Announcing the Commercial National Security Algorithm Suite 2.0.* https://media.defense.gov/2022/Sep/07/2003071834/-1/-1/0/CSA_CNSA_2.0_ALGORITHMS_.PDF

National Security Commission on Artificial Intelligence. (2019, July 31). *Initial report.* www.nscai.gov/wp-content/uploads/2021/01/NSCAI_Initial-Report-to-Congress_July-2019.pdf

National Security Commission on Artificial Intelligence. (2019, November). *Interim report.* www.nscai.gov/wp-content/uploads/2021/01/NSCAI-Interim-Report-for-Congress_201911.pdf

National Security Commission on Artificial Intelligence. (2020, March). *First quarter recommendations.* www.nscai.gov/wp-content/uploads/2021/01/NSCAI-First-Quarter-Recommendations.pdf

National Security Commission on Artificial Intelligence. (2020, July 22). *Key considerations for responsible development & fielding of artificial intelligence abridged version.*

National Security Commission on Artificial Intelligence. (2020, October). *Interim report and third quarter recommendations*. www.nscai.gov/wp-content/uploads/2021/01/NSCAI-Interim-Report-and-Third-Quarter-Recommendations.pdf

National Security Commission on Artificial Intelligence. (2020). *Mitigating economic impacts of the COVID-19 pandemic and preserving U.S. Strategic competitiveness in artificial intelligence*. www.nscai.gov/wp-content/uploads/2021/01/NSCAI_White-Paper_Mitigating-Economic-Impacts-of-the-Covid-19-Pandemic.pdf

National Security Commission on Artificial Intelligence. (2021, January). *Summary of the National Security Commission on Artificial Intelligences (NSCAI) second quarter recommendations*. www.nscai.gov/wp-content/uploads/2021/01/Summary-of-NSCAI-Q2-Recommendations.pdf

National Security Commission on Artificial Intelligence. (2021). *Final report*. www.nscai.gov/wp-content/uploads/2021/03/Full-Report-Digital-1.pdf

National Security Commission on Artificial Intelligence. (2021). *Message from the Chairman and Vice Chairman*. https://irp.fas.org/offdocs/ai-commission.pdf

National Security Commission on Artificial Intelligence. (2021). *The Role of AI technology in pandemic response and preparedness: Recommended investments and initiatives* (White Paper Series on Pandemic Response and Preparedness, No. 3).

National Security Commission on Artificial Intelligence. (n.d.). *Privacy and ethics recommendations for putting applications developed to mitigate COVID-19*.

National Security Institute. (2022, December 20). *The SCIF year-in-review—National security predictions for 2023*. Medium. https://thescif.org/the-scif-year-in-review-national-security-predictions-for-2022-a2d2f1483b9d

NBC News. (2014, August 15). *Future tech? Autonomous killer robots are already here*. www.nbcnews.com/tech/security/future-tech-autonomous-killer-robots-are-already-here-n105656

Networking & Information Technology Research and Development Subcommittee and the Machine Learning & Artificial Intelligence Subcommittee of the National Science & Technology Council. (2020, March). *Artificial intelligence and cybersecurity: Opportunities and challenges*. www.nitrd.gov/pubs/AI-CS-Tech-Summary-2020.pdf

New Hampshire Department of Justice. (2024, February 6). *Voter suppression AI robocall investigation update*. www.doj.nh.gov/news/2024/20240122-voter-robocall.html

Newell, B. (2021). *Body cameras help monitor police but can invade people's privacy*. Nextgov/FCW. www.nextgov.com/ideas/2021/05/body-cameras-help-monitor-police-can-invade-peoples-privacy/174282/

Newman, B. (2015). *Artificial intelligence poses a greater risk to IP than humans do*. TechCrunch. https://techcrunch.com/2015/12/31/artificial-intelligence-poses-a-greater-risk-to-ip-than-humans-do/

Newman, L., & Burgess, M. (2023). *The biggest hack of 2023 keeps getting bigger*. WIRED UK. www.wired.com/story/moveit-breach-victims/

News18. (2020, February 14). *New Zealand police inducts first AI-based cop named Ella into its force*. www.news18.com/amp/news/buzz/new-zealand-pol ice-inducts-first-ai-based-cop-named-ella-into-its-force-2501293.html

News18. (2020, April 29). *Will AI take over the world? Robots may carry out all human works by 2050, says experts*. www.news18.com/amp/news/buzz/will-rob ots-take-over-the-world-ai-may-carry-out-all-human-works-by-2050-says-expe rts-2597733.html

Nextgov/FCW. (2022, October). *The state of cybersecurity*. www.nextgov.com/ass ets/the-state-of-cybersecurity-ngq422/portal/

Nextgov/FCW. (2022, December). *3 ways Google Cloud helps government improve human services with AI*. www.nextgov.com/sponsors/2022/12/3-ways-google-cloud-helps-government-improve-human-services-ai/380839/

Nextgov/FCW. (2022). *Automation in action*. www.nextgov.com/assets/automat ion-action-ngq322/portal/

Nextgov/FCW. (n.d.). *Quantum-mania across government; the emerging technology has the attention of the federal*. www.nextgov.com/assets/quantum-mania-across-government-ngq123/portal/

Nhede, N. (2017). *Does artificial intelligence have the potential to eliminate the risk of utility cyber-attacks?* Smart Energy International.

Nichols, G. (2020, August 17). *AI-based traffic management gets green light*. ZDNet. www.zdnet.com/article/ai-based-traffic-management-gets-green-light/

Nichols, G. (2020, December 18). *Forecast 2021: Artificial intelligence during COVID and beyond*. ZDNet. www.zdnet.com/article/forecast-for-2021-artific ial-intelligence-during-covid-and-beyond/

Nichols, G. (2020, December 29). *Expressive robotics is breathing "life" into machines*. ZDNet. www.zdnet.com/article/expressive-robotics-is-breathing-life-into-machines/

Nichols, G. (2021, February 9). *How AI (not automation) will revolutionize commercial trucking*. ZDNet. www.zdnet.com/article/why-ai-not-automation-will-revolutionize-commercial-trucking/

Nichols, G. (2021, November 30). *Robots in 2022: Six robotics predictions from industry-leading humans*. ZDNet. www.zdnet.com/article/2022-robotics-pred ictions-from-industry-leading-execs/

Nichols, G. (2021, December 9). *Pirate-hunting drone monitors crime on the high seas*. ZDNet. www.zdnet.com/article/pirate-hunting-drone-monit ors-crime-on-high-seas/

Nichols, G. (2021, December 22). *2022: A major revolution in robotics*. ZDNet. www.zdnet.com/article/2022-prediction-a-major-revolution-in-robotics/

Nichols, G. (2021, December 23). *2022 resolution: How to stop worrying and welcome the Robots*. ZDNet. www.zdnet.com/article/are-robots-here-to-stay-amid-staff-shortages/

Nichols, G. (2022, January 11). *Has AI found a treatment for Fragile X*. ZDNet. www.zdnet.com/article/has-ai-found-a-treatment-for-fragile-x/

Nichols, G. (2022, January 27). *Should robots be able to deliver booze?* ZDNet. www.zdnet.com/article/should-robots-be-able-to-deliver-booze/

Nichols, G. (2022, February 2). *Electric sheep turns old lawnmowers into robots.* ZDNet. www.zdnet.com/article/electric-sheep-turns-old-lawnmowers-into-robots/

Nichols, G. (2022, February 10). *With lead in China, RoboTaxi maker turns sights on U.S.* ZDNet. www.zdnet.com/article/with-lead-in-china-robotaxi-maker-turns-sights-on-us/

Nichols, G. (2022, February 17). *Robot fry cook gets job at 100 White Castle locations.* ZDNet. www.zdnet.com/article/robot-fry-cook-gets-job-at-100-white-castle-locations/

Nichols, G. (2022, June 24). *No really, robots are about to take A LOT of jobs.* ZDNet. www.zdnet.com/article/no-really-robots-are-about-to-take-a-lot-of-jobs/

Nichols, G. (2022, July 8). *Two robots just cut a deal to bake and deliver your pizzas.* ZDNet. www.zdnet.com/article/two-robots-just-cut-a-deal-to-bake-and-deliver-your-pizzas/

Nichols, G. (2022, August 16). *Elon Musk drops details about Tesla's humanoid robot.* ZDNet. www.zdnet.com/article/elon-musk-drops-details-about-teslas-humanoid-robot/

Nichols, G. (2022, September 9). *Robots have rushed in to fill jobs people don't want. What happens if recession hits?* ZDNet. www.zdnet.com/article/robots-have-rushed-in-to-fill-jobs-people-dont-want-what-happens-if-recession-hits/

Nicol, W. (2017, April 18). *Automated agriculture: Can robots, drones, and AI save us from starvation?* Digital Trends. www.digitaltrends.com/cool-tech/automated-agriculture-can-robots-drones-ai-save-us-from-starvation/

Nimmo, B., & Hutchins, E. (2023, March). *Phase-based tactical analysis of online operations.* Carnegie Endowment for International Peace. https://carneg ieendowment.org/2023/03/16/phase-based-tactical-analysis-of-online-operati ons-pub-89275

Noorzai, R., Sahinkaya, E., & Sarwan, R. (2020). *Afghan lawmakers: Russian support to Taliban no secret.* Voice of America. www.voanews.com/extremism-watch/afghan-lawmakers-russian-support-taliban-no-secret

NordVPN. (2023). *Dark web market case study.* https://nordvpn.com/research-lab/dark-web-case-study/

Nouwens, M. (2021, February). *China's digital silk road: Integration into national IT infrastructure and wider implications for western defense industries.* The International Institute for Strategic Studies. www.iiss.org/en/research-paper/2021/02/china-digital-silk-road-implications-for-defence-industry/

Noyan, O. (2022, February 1). *Big Tech opposes Germany's enhanced hate speech law.* Euractiv. www.euractiv.com/section/digital/news/german-reinforcement-of-hate-speech-law-faces-opposition-from-big-online-platforms/

Nylen, L. (2021, December 26). *Big Tech's next monopoly game: Building the car of the future.* POLITICO. www.politico.com/news/magazine/2021/12/27/self-driving-car-big-tech-monopoly-525867

O'Brien, J. T., & Nelson, C. (2020). *Assessing the risks posed by the convergence of artificial intelligence and biotechnology. Health Security, 18*(3), 219–227. https://doi.org/10.1089/hs.2019.0122

Odell, M. (2014, September 24). *Are robots going to destroy us all?* Esquire. www. esquire.com/uk/culture/news/a7074/robots-mankind-future/

ODNI. (2023). *IARPA leads first-of-its-kind effort to fashion smart clothing.* www.dni.gov/index.php/newsroom/press-releases/press-releases-2023/3717-iarpa-leads-first-of-its-kind-effort-to-fashion-smart-clothing

O'Dwyer, G. (2023, July 7). *Sweden, Finland eye quantum tech leap amid call for official strategy.* Defense News. www.defensenews.com/industry/techwatch/2023/07/07/sweden-finland-eye-quantum-tech-leap-amid-call-for-official-strategy/

O'Grady, M. (2022, January 18). *Twenty-five percent of Europe-5 jobs are at risk from automation; 12 million jobs will be lost by 2040.* Forrester. www.forrester.com/blogs/twenty-five-percent-of-europe-5-jobs-are-at-risk-from-automation-12-million-jobs-will-be-lost-by-2040/

O'Neill, P. H. (2020, September 21). CIA's new tech recruiting pitch: More patents, more profits. *MIT Technology Review.* www.technologyreview.com/2020/09/21/1008654/cias-new-tech-recruiting-pitch-more-patents-more-profits/

O'Neill, P. H. (2021, November 24). NSO was about to sell hacking tools to France. now it's in crisis. *MIT Technology Review.* www.technologyreview.com/2021/11/23/1040509/france-macron-nso-in-crisis-sanctions/

Offenhartz, J. (2021, April 29). *NYPD sending its "Creepy" robot dog to the farm upstate.* Gothamist. https://gothamist.com/news/nypd-sending-its-creepy-robot-dog-farm-upstate

Office of Educational Technology. (2023, May). *Artificial intelligence and the future of teaching and learning; insights and recommendations.* https://tech.ed.gov/ai-future-of-teaching-and-learning/

Office of the Chief Economist IP Data Highlights. (2020, October). *Inventing AI: Tracing the diffusion of artificial intelligence with U.S. Patents* (IP Data Highlights, Number 5). www.uspto.gov/sites/default/files/documents/OCE-DH-AI.pdf

Office of the Director of National Intelligence. (2016). *Reducing your digital footprint.* www.dni.gov/files/NCSC/documents/campaign/Counterintelligence_Tips_Digitalfootprint.pdf

Office of the Director of National Intelligence. (2019). *The aim initiative; a strategy for augmenting intelligence using machines.* www.dni.gov/files/ODNI/Documents/AIM-Strategy.pdf

Office of the Director of National Intelligence. (2021, April 9). *Annual threat assessment of the US intelligence community.*

Office of the Director of National Intelligence. (2022, January 27). *Senior Advisory group panel on commercially available information.*

Office of the Director of National Intelligence. (2022, February). *Annual threat assessment of the US intelligence community.*

Office of the Director of National Intelligence. (2023, February 6). *Annual threat assessment of the US intelligence community.*

Office of the Press Secretary. (2013, February 12). *Presidential Policy Directive—Critical Infrastructure Security and Resilience.* The White House. https://obamawhitehouse.archives.gov/the-press-office/2013/02/12/presidential-policy-directive-critical-infrastructure-security-and-resil

Office of the State Auditor. (2021, March 26). *Letter from the Office of the Utah State Auditor John Dougall, to Attorney General the Hon Sean Reyes, Re: Limited Review of Banjo.*

Office on Drugs and Crime. (n.d.). *Cybercrime.* United Nations. www.unodc.org/unodc/en/cybercrime/index.html

Ogunleye, I. (2022, August). *AI's redress problem: Recommendations to improve consumer protection from artificial intelligence.* UC Berkeley Center for Long-Term Cybersecurity. https://cltc.berkeley.edu/publication/cltc-white-paper-ais-redress-problem/

Oliver, N. (2023, January 9). *Virginia is getting ready for flying cars.* Axios. www.axios.com/local/richmond/2023/01/09/flying-cars-virginia-jetson

Optiv Security. (2023, February 1). *The state of ransomware: 2022 in review.* www.optiv.com/insights/discover/blog/state-ransomware-2022-review

Ortiz, S. (2022, August 11). *Top 25 emerging technologies: Which ones will live up to the hype?* ZDNet. www.zdnet.com/article/25-emerging-technologies-to-watch/

Ortiz, S. (2022, August 22). *Can AI serve as a "great equalizer" in the real estate industry?* ZDNet. www.zdnet.com/article/can-ai-serve-as-a-great-equalizer-in-the-real-estate-industry/

Ortiz, S. (2023, August 9). *ChatGPT answers more than half of software engineering questions incorrectly.* ZDNet. www.zdnet.com/article/chatgpt-answers-more-than-half-of-software-engineering-questions-incorrectly/

Ortiz, S. (2023, September 15). *What is ChatGPT and why does it matter? Here's everything you need to know.* ZDNet. www.zdnet.com/article/what-is-chatgpt-and-why-does-it-matter-heres-everything-you-need-to-know/

Ortiz, S. (2023). *Expedia adds new AI features to improve your travel planning. Here's how.* ZDNet. www.zdnet.com/article/expedia-adds-new-ai-features-to-improve-your-travel-planning-heres-how/

Ortiz, S. (2023). *Generative AI might soon face some major copyright limitations from the EU.* ZDNet. www.zdnet.com/article/generative-ai-might-soon-face-some-major-copyright-limitations-from-eu/

Ortiz, S. (2023). *Scammers are using AI to impersonate your loved ones. Here's what to watch out for.* ZDNet. www.zdnet.com/article/scammers-are-using-ai-to-impersonate-your-loved-ones-heres-what-to-watch-for/

Osborne, C. (2018, June 13). *Researchers develop artificial intelligence system to watch you through walls.* ZDNet. www.zdnet.com/article/researchers-develop-artificial-intelligence-system-to-see-you-through-walls/

Osborne, C. (2018, October 29). *The police are now using artificial intelligence to spot fake robbery claims.* ZDNet. www.zdnet.com/article/law-enforcement-is-using-artificial-intelligence-to-spot-fake-confessions/

Osborne, C. (2018, November 7). *This is how artificial intelligence will become weaponized in future cyberattacks.* ZDNet. www.zdnet.com/article/this-is-how-artificial-intelligence-will-become-weaponized-in-future-cyberattacks/

Osborne, C. (2019, January 24). *Artificial intelligence will become the next new human right.* ZDNet. www.zdnet.com/article/artificial-intelligence-will-become-the-next-new-human-right/

Osborne, C. (2020, August 17). *Controversial facial recognition tech firm Clearview AI inks deal with ICE.* ZDNet. www.zdnet.com/article/controversial-facial-recognition-tech-firm-clearview-ai-inks-deal-with-ice/

Osborne, C. (2021, December 22). *Ransomware in 2022: We're all screwed.* ZDNet. www.zdnet.com/article/ransomware-in-2022-were-all-screwed/

Osborne, C. (2021, December 31). *Copycat and fad hackers will be the bane of supply chain security in 2022.* ZDNet. www.zdnet.com/article/copycat-and-fad-hackers-will-be-the-bane-of-supply-chain-security-in-2022/

Osborne, C. (2021, December 31). *The biggest data breaches, hacks of 2021.* ZDNet. www.zdnet.com/article/the-biggest-data-breaches-of-2021/

Osborne, C. (2022, June 6). *Ransomware attacks have dropped. And gangs are attacking each other's victims.* ZDNet. www.zdnet.com/article/ransomware-atta cks-have-dropped-and-gangs-are-attacking-each-others-victims/

Ozdemir, D., Paleja, A., Papadopoulos, L., & McFadden, C. (2021, August 17). *AI could send you to jail: How algorithms are changing justice.* Interesting Engineering. https://amp.interestingengineering.com/how-algorithms-are-chang ing-justice

Page, C. (2023). *Dish says ransomware gang stole almost 300,000 employee records.* TechCrunch. https://tcrn.ch/3WqnxMh

Page, C. (2023). *Ransomware attack forces Dallas to shut down courts, disrupts some 911 services.* TechCrunch. https://tcrn.ch/3ASeZE4

Page, C., & Whittaker, Z. (2023). *Hackers publish sensitive employee data stolen during CommScope ransomware attack.* TechCrunch. https://tcrn.ch/41ePclb

Palmai, K., & Smale, W. (2021, December 20). *The robot chefs that can cook your Christmas dinner.* BBC. www.bbc.com/news/business-59651334

Palmer, D. (2020, March 2). *AI is changing everything about cybersecurity, for better and for worse.* ZDNet. www.zdnet.com/article/ai-is-changing-everything-about-cybersecurity-f

Palmer, D. (2021, December 8). *Everyone is burned out. that's becoming a security nightmare.* ZDNet. www.zdnet.com/article/everyone-is-burned-out-thats-becom ing-a-security-nightmare/

Palmer, D. (2022, January 6). *Cybersecurity training isn't working. and hacking attacks are only getting worse.* ZDNet. www.zdnet.com/article/your-cybers ecurity-training-needs-improvement-because-hacking-attacks-are-only-gett ing-worse/

Palmer, D. (2022, February 1). *Ransomware: Is the party almost over for the cyber crooks?* ZDNet. www.zdnet.com/article/ransomware-is-the-party-almost-over-for-the-cyber-crooks/

Palmer, D. (2022, February 7). *Ransomware gangs are changing their tactics that could prove very expensive for some victims.* ZDNet. www.zdnet.com/article/ ransomware-gangs-are-changing-their-tactics-that-could-prove-very-expensive-for-some-victims/

Palmer, D. (2022, April 21). *FBI warning: Ransomware gangs are going after this lucrative but unexpected target.* ZDNet. www.zdnet.com/article/fbi-warning-ransomware-gangs-are-going-after-this-lucrative-but-unexpected-target/

Palmer, D. (2022, September 27). *Hackers are testing a destructive new way to make ransomware attacks more effective.* ZDNet. www.zdnet.com/article/ hackers-are-testing-a-destructive-new-way-to-make-ransomware-attacks-more-effective/

Palmer, D. (2022, November 17). *Not patched Log4j yet? Assume attackers are in your network, say CISA and FBI.* ZDNet. www.zdnet.com/article/cybers ecurity-warning-if-youve-not-patched-log4j-yet-assume-attackers-are-in-your-network/

Palmer, D. (2022, June 20). *Ransomware attacks: This is the data that cybercriminals really want to steal.* ZDNet. www.zdnet.com/article/ransomware-attacks-this-is-the-data-that-cyber-criminals-really-want-to-steal/

Palmer, D. (2022, December 12). *This evasive new cyberattack can bypass air-gapped systems to steal data from the most sensitive networks.* ZDNet. www.zdnet.com/article/this-evasive-new-cyberattack-can-bypass-air-gapped-systems-to-steal-data-from-the-most-sensitive-networks/

Palmer, D. (2023, January 9). *People are already trying to get ChatGPT to write malware.* ZDNet. www.zdnet.com/article/people-are-already-trying-to-get-chat gpt-to-write-malware/

Panagiotopolous, V. (2022). *Soccer fans, you're being watched.* WIRED. www. wired.com/story/soccer-world-cup-biometric-surveillance/

Pandey, E. (2022, January 7). *Tech is finally killing long lines.* Axios. www.axios. com/2022/01/07/virtual-line-queue-technology

Pandey, E. (2022, August 31). *Demystifying AI.* Axios. www.axios.com/2022/09/ 01/demystifying-artificial-intelligence-ai-machine-learning

Pandey, E., & Hart, K. (2019, November 20). *AI is coming for white-collar workers.* Axios. www.axios.com/ai-white-collar-workers-jobs-8384884a-f2e9-4633-91ee-ae90445f91be.html

Pandit, R. (2018, May 21). India now wants artificial intelligence-based weapon systems. *The Times of India.* https://timesofindia.indiatimes.com/india/india-moves-to-develop-ai-based-military-systems/articleshow/64250232.cms

Pardijs, S., & Dina, D. (2016, June 27). *The world according to Europe's insurgent parties: Putin, migration and people power.* European Council on Foreign Relations (ECFR). https://ecfr.eu/publication/the_world_according_to_europes_insurgent_parties7055/

Patel, H., & Marin, L. (2023). *Addressing human security: 150 investable trends.* Barclays. www.ib.barclays/our-insights/investing-with-human-security-in-mind-150-trends.html

Patterson, D. (2023). *ChatGPT is more like an "alien intelligence" than a human brain, says futurist.* ZDNet. www.zdnet.com/article/chatgpt-is-more-like-an-alien-intelligence-than-a-human-brain-says-futurist/

Patterson, D. (2023). *Real-time deepfake detection: How Intel Labs uses AI to fight misinformation.* ZDNet. www.zdnet.com/article/real-time-deepfake-detect ion-how-intel-labs-uses-ai-to-fight-misinformation/

Palo Alto Network (2022, March). *2022 Unit 42 Ransomware Threat Report.* https:// mysecuritymarketplace.com/reports/unit-42-ransomware-threat-report-2022/

Peng, Y. (2022, April 26). *Fundamentals to observe for maintaining and shaping national security in the new era—Study the outline for studying the overall National Security Outlook.* Center for Strategic & International Studies. https:// interpret.csis.org/translations/fundamentals-to-observe-for-maintaining-and-shaping-national-security-in-the-new-era-study-the-outline-for-studying-the-overall-national-security-outlook/

Perano, U., & Daly, K. (2020, January 20). *Google CEO calls for balanced regulations on artificial intelligence.* Axios. www.axios.com/2020/01/20/google-ceo-pichai-artificial-intelligence

Perez, E., & Lyngaas, S. (2023, February 17). *Exclusive: FBI says it has "contained" cyber incident on bureau's computer network.* CNN. www.cnn.com/2023/02/17/politics/fbi-cyber-incident-computer-network/index.html

Perlow, J. (2021, December 6). *"The Beatles: Get Back" shows that deepfake tech isn't always evil.* ZDNet. www.zdnet.com/article/the-beatles-get-back-shows-that-deepfake-tech-isnt-always-evil/

Perrigo, B. (2023). OpenAI could quit Europe over new AI rules, CEO Altman Warns. *Time.* https://time.com/6282325/sam-altman-openai-eu/

Perry, P. (2016, May 10). *How artificial intelligence will revolutionize healthcare.* Big Think. https://bigthink.com/philip-perry/how-artificial-intelligence-will-revolutionize-healthcare

Peters, N. (2022). *Nobel-winning quantum weirdness undergirds an emerging high-tech industry, promising better ways of encrypting communications and imaging your body.* Nextgov/FCW. www.nextgov.com/ideas/2022/10/nobel-winning-quantum-weirdness-undergirds-emerging-high-tech-industry-promising-better-ways-encrypting-communications-and-imaging-your-body/378244/

Piper, K. (2022). *The case for taking AI seriously as a threat to humanity.* Vox. www.vox.com/future-perfect/2018/12/21/18126576/ai-artificial-intelligence-machine-learning-safety-alignment

Palmer, D. (2022, October 12). *The metaverse is coming, and the security threats have already arrived.* ZDNet. www.zdnet.com/article/the-metaverse-is-coming-and-the-security-threats-have-already-arrived/

Pollet, M. (2022). *French court backs fraud detection programme based on "freely accessible" data.* EURACTIV. www.euractiv.com/section/digital/news/frances-highest-court-oks-governments-online-data-collection-experiment/

Pollock, B. (2019, August 5). *How robots will save the human race.* Automation World. www.automationworld.com/factory/robotics/blog/13320046/how-robots-will-save-the-human-race

Porter, T. (2020). *Russia could exploit its ties with US white nationalist groups to encourage election violence, experts warn.* Business Insider. www.businessinsider.com/russia-foment-election-violence-us-far-right-ties-experts-2020-9

Presidio Federal. (2023, June 20). *AI boosts security and operational capability.* Nextgov/FCW. https://fcw.com/sponsors/sponsor-content/2023/06/ai-boosts-security-and-operational-capability/387349/

Presidio Federal. (2023). *How automation can advance federal agencies in 2023.* Red Hat. https://presidiofederal.com/wp-content/uploads/2023/01/PF_Red Hat_How-Automation-Can-Advance-Agencies_FNL.pdf

Primack, D. (2023). *Here come the robot doctors.* Axios. www.axios.com/2023/01/18/chatgpt-ai-health-care-doctors

Probasco, E. S., & Toney, A. S. (2023, July). *Who Cares About Trust? Clusters of Research on Trustworthy AI.* Center for Security and Emerging Technology. https://cset.georgetown.edu/publication/who-cares-about-trust/

PWC. Economic impact [online]. Available from: https://www.pwc.com/us/en/forensic-services/publications/assets/economic-impact.pdf

Radesky, S., & Spring, J. (2023, August 3). *A call to action: Bolster UEFI cybersecurity now.* Cybersecurity and Infrastructure Security Agency. www.cisa.gov/news-events/news/call-action-bolster-uefi-cybersecurity-now

Radford, A. (2023). *Kuwait news outlet unveils AI-generated presenter Fedha.* BBC. www.bbc.com/news/world-middle-east-65238950

Rainie, L., Funk, C., Anderson, M., & Tyson, A. (2022). *How Americans think about AI.* Pew Research Center. www.pewresearch.org/internet/2022/03/17/how-americans-think-about-artificial-intelligence/

Rajghatta, C. (2020). Going against Donald Trump, FBI warns of white extremism, Russian interference in elections—Times of India. *The Times of India.* https://timesofindia.indiatimes.com/world/us/going-against-donald-trump-fbi-warns-of-white-extremism-russian-interference-in-elections/articleshow/78191344.cms

Ranger, S. (2022). *Cloud computing means big opportunities—And big threats.* ZDNet. www.zdnet.com/article/cloud-computing-security-where-it-is-where-its-going/

Ranger, S. (2022). *Remote work has changed everything. And it's still getting weirder.* ZDNet. www.zdnet.com/home-and-office/work-life/remote-work-has-changed-everything-and-its-still-getting-weirder/

Ranger, S. (2022). *The Future of the Web: The good, the bad and the very weird.* ZDNet. www.zdnet.com/article/the-future-of-the-web-the-good-the-bad-and-the-very-weird/

Ranger, S. (2022). *Three tech trends on the verge of a breakthrough in 2023.* ZDNet. www.zdnet.com/home-and-office/work-life/three-tech-trends-on-the-verge-of-a-breakthrough-in-2023/

Raskin, S., & Woods, A. (2021, April 15). De Blasio says "we should rethink" NYPD's robot dog over public concerns. *The New York Post.* https://nypost.com/2021/04/14/de-blasio-we-should-rethink-nypds-robot-dog-over-public-concerns/

Ray, T. (2019, November 8). *Will AI ever "understand" satire?* ZDNet. www.zdnet.com/article/will-ai-ever-understand-satire/

Ray, T. (2020, April 4). *AI runs smack up against a big data problem in COVID-19 diagnosis.* ZDNet. www.zdnet.com/article/ai-runs-smack-up-against-a-big-data-problem-in-covid-19-diagnosis/

Ray, T. (2021, December 17). *TikTok doesn't read your mind, it makes your mind.* ZDNet. www.zdnet.com/article/tiktok-doesnt-read-your-mind-it-makes-your-mind/

Ray, T. (2022, February 11). *The AI edge chip market is on fire, kindled by "staggering" VC funding.* ZDNet. www.zdnet.com/article/the-ai-edge-infere nce-chip-market-is-raging/

Ray, T. (2022, February 23). *Meta's Zuckerberg: "AI is perhaps the most important foundational technology of our time."* ZDNet. www.zdnet.com/arti cle/metas-zuckerberg-ai-is-perhaps-the-most-important-foundational-technol ogy-of-our-time/

Ray, T. (2022, November 2). *The new Turing test: Are you human?* ZDNet. www.zdnet.com/article/the-new-turing-test-are-you-human/

Ray, T. (2022, December 26). *Machines that think like humans: Everything to know about AGI and AI Debate 3.* ZDNet. www.zdnet.com/article/ai-debate-3-everything-you-need-to-know-about-artificial-general-intelligence/

Ray, T. (2023, January 23). *ChatGPT is "not particularly innovative," and "nothing revolutionary," says Meta's chief AI scientist.* ZDNet. www.zdnet.com/article/chatgpt-is-not-particularly-innovative-and-nothing-revolutionary-says-metas-chief-ai-scientist/

Ray, T. (2023, August 25). *AI's multi-view wave is coming, and it will be powerful.* ZDNet. www.zdnet.com/article/ais-multi-view-wave-is-coming-and-it-will-be-powerful/

Re, G. (2020, May 31). *Susan Rice makes claim Russians could be behind violent George Floyd demonstrations.* Fox News. www.foxnews.com/politics/susan-rice-suggests-russians-behind-violent-george-floyd-demonstrations

Re, M. R., & Solow-Niederman, A. (2019). *Developing artificially intelligent justice.* https://law.stanford.edu/wp-content/uploads/2019/08/Re-Solow-Niederman_20190808.pdf

Read, M. (2021). *Russia's role in stoking right-wing extremism in the west.* Stratfor. article/russia-s-role-stoking-right-wing-extremism-west

Red Hat. (2021). *Edge computing for the Department of Defense; overmatch near-peer adversaries with AI decision advantage.* https://static.carahsoft.com/concrete/files/6316/2611/6660/Edge_Computing_for_the_Department_of_Defense.pdf

Reed, T. (2023). *Health care's cyber defenses fall short.* Axios. www.axios.com/2023/07/12/health-cares-cyber-defenses

Reed, T. (2023). *Hospitals could be one cyberattack away from closure.* Axios. www.axios.com/2023/06/16/hospitals-cyberattack-away-closure

Reinharz, S. (2018, April 24). 5 AI trends you should be using to improve physical aecurity. *Security Magazine.* www.securitymagazine.com/articles/88943-ai-trends-you-should-be-using-to-improve-physical-security

Reuters. (2023, January 9). *U.S. Supreme Court lets Metas WhatsApp pursue "Pegasus" spyware suit.* www.reuters.com/legal/us-supreme-court-lets-metas-whatsapp-pursue-pegasus-spyware-suit-2023-01-09/

Reuters. (2023, July 10). *Spain's High Court shelves Israeli spyware probe on lack of cooperation.* www.reuters.com/world/europe/spains-high-court-shelves-israeli-spyware-probe-lack-cooperation-2023-07-10/

Richardson, J., Oueid, R., & Merzbacher, C. (2023). *The future of quantum—Building a global market.* Center for Strategic & International Studies. www.csis.org/events/future-quantum-building-global-market

Richberg, J. (2022). *AI-powered automation can be both a part of the problem and part of the solution.* Nextgov/FCW. www.nextgov.com/ideas/2022/01/ai-powered-automation-can-be-both-part-problem-and-part-solution/360294/

Rid, T. (2016, October 20). *How Russia pulled off the biggest election hack in U.S. history.* Esquire. www.esquire.com/news-politics/a49791/russian-dnc-emails-hacked/

Riley, T. (2022). *White House announces new surveillance guardrails to meet EU Privacy Shield expectations*. CyberScoop. https://cyberscoop.com/white-house-announces-new-surveillance-guardrails-to-meet-eu-privacy-shield-expectations/

Riley, T. (2023). *A year after Dobbs, federal privacy legislation to protect abortion seekers remains stalled*. CyberScoop. https://cyberscoop.com/dobbs-privacy-legislation-abortion-congress/

Riley, T. (2023). *Critics suggest intelligence agencies should get a warrant for FISA searches*. CyberScoop. https://cyberscoop.com/fisa-section-702-congress-reform/

Riley, T. (2023). *Cryptocurrency hacks shot up in 2022, amounting to almost $4 billion in losses*. CyberScoop. www.cyberscoop.com/cryptocurrency-hacks-2022/

Riley, T. (2023, May 17). *FTC says popular fertility app gave advertisers pregnancy data without permission*. CyberScoop. https://cyberscoop.com/ftc-fertility-app-pregnancy-data/

Riley, T. (2023). *Section 702 data led to State Department warnings about North Korean IT scams, official says*. CyberScoop. https://cyberscoop.com/section-702-fisa-state-north-korea/

Riley, T. (2023). *Sen. Warner: AI firms should put security at the center of their work*. CyberScoop. https://cyberscoop.com/mark-warner-ai-security-meta-microsoft-open-ai/

Rincon, P. (2021, November 17). *IBM claims advance in quantum computing*. BBC. www.bbc.com/news/science-environment-59320073

Riotta, C. (2022). *CISA sets voluntary cyber performance targets for critical infrastructure*. Nextgov/FCW. www.nextgov.com/cybersecurity/2022/10/cisa-sets-voluntary-cyber-performance-targets-critical-infrastructure/378994/

Riotta, C. (2023, June 7). *Public sector apps face widespread security challenges, report reveals*. Nextgov/FCW. www.nextgov.com/cybersecurity/2023/06/public-sector-apps-face-widespread-security-challenges-report-reveals/387251/

Riotta, C. (2023, July 31). *US is falling behind in global digital leadership, report says*. Nextgov/FCW. www.nextgov.com/digital-government/2023/07/us-falling-behind-global-digital-leadership-report-says/389000/

Riotta, C. (2023, August 2). *House panel probes China-linked email hacks*. Nextgov/FCW. www.nextgov.com/cybersecurity/2023/08/house-panel-probes-china-linked-email-hacks/389078/

Riotta, C. (2023, August 3). *Report reveals "sudden surge" in cyberattacks targeting government agencies*. Nextgov/FCW. www.nextgov.com/cybersecurity/2023/08/report-reveals-sudden-surge-cyberattacks-targeting-government-agencies/389105/

Riotta, C. (2023, August 8). *Space agencies are reforming acquisition to accelerate commercial tech integration*. Nextgov/FCW. www.nextgov.com/acquisition/2023/08/space-agencies-are-reforming-acquisition-accelerate-commercial-tech-integration/389239/

Riotta, C. (2023). *CISA's new directive targets devices that can be configured over public internet*. Nextgov/FCW. www.nextgov.com/cybersecurity/2023/06/cisas-new-directive-targets-devices-can-be-configured-over-public-internet/387488/

Riotta, C. (2023). *DHS cyber review board to examine China-linked cyberattacks of Microsoft.* Nextgov/FCW. www.nextgov.com/cybersecurity/2023/08/dhs-cyber-review-board-examine-china-linked-cyberattacks-microsoft/389351/

Riotta, C. (2023). *Federal vision to streamline cyber incident reporting expected this summer.* Nextgov/FCW. www.nextgov.com/cybersecurity/2023/06/federal-vision-streamline-cyber-incident-reporting-expected-summer/387023/

Riotta, C. (2023). *Feds want to help prevent cyberattacks on the water sector.* Route Fifty. www.route-fifty.com/infrastructure/2023/06/nist-wants-help-prev ent-major-cyberattack-water-sector/387832/

Riotta, C. (2023). *Industry leaders urge Congress to enact responsible AI regulations.* Nextgov/FCW. www.nextgov.com/artificial-intelligence/2023/09/ industry-leaders-urge-congress-enact-responsible-ai-regulations/390252/

Riotta, C. (2023). *Nation-state actors are exploiting AI for discord and attacks, DHS warns.* Nextgov/FCW. www.nextgov.com/cybersecurity/2023/09/nation-state-actors-are-exploiting-ai-discord-and-attacks-dhs-warns/390376/

Riotta, C. (2023). *New bill would give CISA greater cyber outreach responsibilities.* Nextgov/FCW. www.nextgov.com/cybersecurity/2023/06/new-bill-would-give-cisa-greater-cyber-outreach-responsibilities/387473/

Riotta, C. (2023). *NIST launches new working group to tackle AI risks.* Nextgov/FCW. www.nextgov.com/emerging-tech/2023/06/nist-launches-new-working-group-tackle-ai-risks/387855/

Riotta, C. (2023). *No "systemic risk" to government networks from latest breach, CISA says.* Nextgov/FCW. www.nextgov.com/cybersecurity/2023/06/cyberatt ack-hits-several-federal-agencies-drawing-all-hands-call-response/387579/

Riotta, C. (2023). *Ransomware gang exploits critical vulnerability in popular file transfer software.* Nextgov/FCW. www.nextgov.com/cybersecurity/2023/06/ ransomware-gang-exploits-critical-vulnerability-popular-file-transfer-software/ 387256/

Riotta, C., & Alms, N. (2023). *White House cyber implementation plan looks to ramp up resilience.* Nextgov/FCW. www.nextgov.com/cybersecurity/2023/07/ new-white-house-cyber-implementation-plan-looks-ramp-resilience/388450/

Ritchie, H. (2023). *Microsoft: Chinese hackers hit key US bases on Guam.* BBC. www.bbc.com/news/world-asia-65705198

Robinson, T., & Bridgewater, S. (2023). *Highlights from the RAeS Future Combat Air & Space Capabilities Summit.* Royal Aeronautical Society. www.aerosoci ety.com/news/highlights-from-the-raes-future-combat-air-space-capabilities-summit/

Robotics4EU. (2022). *Project overview: Robotics technology influences every aspect of work and home.* Robotics4eu. www.robotics4eu.eu/project-overview/

Rose, I. (2023). *The workers already replaced by artificial intelligence.* BBC. www.bbc.com/news/business-65906521

Rosenberg, S. (2022, May 6). *Apple, Google, Microsoft take new step toward a password-free world.* Axios. www.axios.com/2022/05/06/apple-google-micros oft-password-free-world

Rosenberg, S. (2022, June 13). *Chatbot AI has a mind of its own, Google engineer claims.* Axios. www.axios.com/2022/06/13/google-engineer-ai-sentient-lamda-chatbot

Rosenberg, S. (2022, July 25). *Sunset of the social network.* Axios. www.axios. com/2022/07/25/sunset-social-network-facebook-tiktok

Rosenberg, S. (2022, September 12). *AI-generated images open multiple cans of worms.* Axios. www.axios.com/2022/09/12/ai-images-ethics-dall-e-2-stable-diffusion

Rosenberg, S. (2022, December 14). *Tech's year of big endings.* Axios. www.axios. com/2022/12/14/tech-year-endings-2022-downturn

Rosenberg, S. (2023, January 24). *What ChatGPT can't do.* Axios. www.axios. com/2023/01/24/chatgpt-errors-ai-limitations

Rosenberg, S. (2023, February 6). *Tech giants rush to put Chatbot to work.* Axios. www.axios.com/2023/02/06/chatgpt-tech-giants-generative-ai

Rosenberg, S. (2023). *Battle for the soul of a new web.* Axios.

Rosenberg, S. (2023). *In AI arms race, ethics may be the first casualty.* Axios. www.axios.com/2023/01/31/chatgpt-ai-arms-race-ethics-competition

Rosenberg, S. (2024, February 28). *AI brings us a new kind of bug.* Axios.

Rosenberg, S. (2024, May 16). *Doomers have lost the AI fight.* Axios.

Rosenberg, S. (2024, May 17). *AI eats the web.* Axios.

Rosenthal, E. (2022). *Who's responsible if a Tesla on autopilot kills someone?* Nextgov/FCW. www.nextgov.com/ideas/2022/03/whos-responsible-if-tesla-autopilot-kills-someone/363111/

Rotella, S. (2021, January 10). *Domestic terrorism: A more urgent threat, but weaker laws.* The CT Mirror. https://ctmirror.org/2021/01/10/domestic-terror ism-a-more-urgent-threat-but-weaker-laws/

Rotella, S. (2021). *Global right-wing extremism networks are growing.* The U.S. is just now catching up. ProPublica. www.propublica.org/article/glo bal-right-wing-extremism-networks-are-growing-the-u-s-is-just-now-catch ing-up

Roth-Johnson, L. (2014, July 9). *With DARPA support, Lawrence Lab seeks to develop brain implant to treat memory loss.* KQED. www.kqed.org/science/ 19142/with-darpa-support-lawrence-lab-seeks-to-develop-brain-implant-to-treat-memory-loss

Roudik, P. (2015). *Legal provisions on fighting extremism: Russia.* Library of Congress. www.loc.gov/law/help/fighting-extremism/russia.php

Route Fifty. (2022, October). *The state and local cybersecurity landscape: A update on threats and solutions.* www.route-fifty.com/assets/cybersecurity-landscape-threats-and-solutions/portal/

Route Fifty. (2022, December). *Workforce development.* www.route-fifty.com/ass ets/rf-workforce-development-q4-2022/portal/

Routledge International Handbooks. (2020, May 19). *Mitigating economic impacts of the COVID-19 pandemic and preserving U.S. strategic competitiveness in artificial intelligence: White Paper series on pandemic response and preparedness, No. 2.*

Routledge International Handbooks. (2022, July). *Key considerations for responsible development and fielding of artificial intelligence; abridged version.* National Security Commission on Artificial Intelligence.

Rubio, I. (2022). Sci-fi no more: Introducing the contact lenses of the future. *Science & Tech EL PAÍS English Edition.* https://english.elpais.com/science-tech/2022-10-27/sci-fi-no-more-this-is-what-the-contact-lenses-of-the-future-will-do-for-you.html

Rundle, J. (2022, August 18). Lloyd's to exclude catastrophic nation-backed cyberattacks from insurance coverage. *The Wall Street Journal.* www.wsj.com/articles/lloyds-to-exclude-catastrophic-nation-backed-cyberattacks-from-insura nce-coverage-11660861586

Ruoti, S. (2022). *How QR codes work and what makes them dangerous—A computer scientist explains.* Nextgov/FCW. www.nextgov.com/cxo-briefing/2022/04/how-qr-codes-work-and-what-makes-them-dangerous-computer-scientist-explains/364147/

Ruoti, S. (2022). *What is proof-of-stake? A computer scientist explains a new way to make cryptocurrencies, NFTs and metaverse transactions.* Nextgov/FCW. www.nextgov.com/ideas/2022/09/what-proof-stake-computer-scientist-expla ins-new-way-make-cryptocurrencies-nfts-and-metaverse-transactions/377107/

Russia Matters. (2017). *Did the US government support Chechen separatism?* https://russiamatters.org/node/20317

Russia Today. (2017, December 24). *Brains over bucks: Putin hints AI may be key to Russia beating US in defense despite budget gap.* www.rt.com/news/414 107-putin-military-ai-hint/

Russo, M., & Wessner, C. (2023). *Collaboration is essential for the west to catch up on technology and ensure the future of democracy.* Center for Strategic & International Studies. www.csis.org/blogs/perspectives-innovation/collaborat ion-essential-west-catch-technology-and-ensure-future

Sabin, S. (2022, December 2). *DHS board starts investigating Lapsus$ teen hacker group.* Axios. www.axios.com/2022/12/02/dhs-board-teen-hackers-lapsus

Sabin, S. (2022, December 9). *One year later, the widespread Log4j threat lingers on.* Axios. www.axios.com/2022/12/09/log4j-year-anniversary-cybersecurity

Sabin, S. (2022, December 20). *1 big thing: 2022's easy, breezy hacking spree.* Axios. www.axios.com/2022/12/20/hacking-cybersecurity-2022-review

Sabin, S. (2022). *1 big thing: Cyber diplomacy takes center stage.* Axios.

Sabin, S. (2022). *Cybercriminals won't become AI experts overnight.* Axios. www. axios.com/2023/05/02/cybercriminals-ai-experts-defenders

Sabin, S. (2022). *37 governments pledge not to harbor ransomware criminals.* Axios. www.axios.com/2022/11/01/37-governments-band-together-against-ran somware

Sabin, S. (2022). *Mandiant uncovers sophisticated spy campaign.* Axios. www. axios.com/2022/09/30/mandiant-spy-campaign-vmware-virtual-computer

Sabin, S. (2022). *More states ban TikTok on government devices.* Axios. www. axios.com/local/salt-lake-city/2022/12/12/utah-bans-tiktok-state-owned-devi ces-cybersecurity

Sabin, S. (2022). *The double-edged sword of post-ransomware comms.* Axios. www.axios.com/2022/12/13/rackspace-ransomware-cybersecurity-commun ication

Sabin, S. (2022). *Zero-trust testing lab opens in Maryland.* Axios.

Sabin, S. (2023, January 3). *Axios newsletters.* Axios. www.axios.com/newsletters

Sabin, S. (2023, January 6). *Axios newsletters.* Axios. www.axios.com/newsletters

Sabin, S. (2023, January 10). *1 Fun thing.* Axios.

Sabin, S. (2023, January 17). *A government surveillance power in the hot seat.* Axios.

Sabin, S. (2023, January 20). *Axios newsletters.* Axios. www.axios.com/news letters

Sabin, S. (2023, January 26). *FBI shuts down servers, website tied to notorious ransomware gang.* Axios. www.axios.com/2023/01/26/fbi-ransomware-gang-hive-shutdown

Sabin, S. (2023, January 27). *Charted: Nearly 2,000 data compromises.* Axios.

Sabin, S. (2023, January 27). *NSO tries to make its case in D.C.* Axios.

Sabin, S. (2023, February 1). *School districts in Tucson, Nantucket are responding to active ransomware attacks.* Axios. www.axios.com/2023/02/01/school-distri cts-ransomware-tucson-nantucket

Sabin, S. (2023, February 7). *What to know about the VMware server attacks.* Axios.

Sabin, S. (2023, March 21). *1 big thing: OpenAI CEO's eye-scanning plan to replace passwords.* Axios.

Sabin, S. (2023, March 21). *Data breach leak site shuts down.* Axios.

Sabin, S. (2023, April 14). *Thousands compromised in ChatGPT-themed scheme.* Axios.

Sabin, S. (2023, May 19). *Fighting the rise of "infostealer" malware.* Axios.

Sabin, S. (2023, May 19). *Law enforcement if fighting the rise of "infostealer" malware.* Axios. www.axios.com/2023/05/19/infostealer-malware-cybersecurity

Sabin, S. (2023, May 19). *Microsoft warns of an overlooked cybercrime.* Axios.

Sabin, S. (2023, August 8). *IBM researchers easily trick ChatGPT to hack.* Axios.

Sabin, S. (2023, August 9). *U.S. taps cyber pros to develop AI cybersecurity tools.* Axios. www.axios.com/2023/08/09/darpa-cybersecurity-challenge-ai-tools

Sabin, S. (2023, September 1). *Elon Musk's X eyes biometric data collection.* Axios.

Sabin, S. (2023, December 5). *CEO says insider risk management needs to be disrupted.* Axios. www.axios.com/2023/12/05/insider-risk-management-dtex

Sabin, S. (2023, December 12). *How holiday scammers could get help from AI.* Axios. www.axios.com/2023/12/12/beware-chatgpt-holiday-scams

Sabin, S. (2023, December 16). *Lawmakers push surveillance debate to 2024.* Axios. www.axios.com/2023/12/16/fisa-surveillance-section-702-2024

Sabin, S. (2023). *A hidden network for nation-state cyberattacks.* Axios.

Sabin, S. (2023). *A new cybersecurity label for smart devices.* Axios.

Sabin, S. (2023). *An alternative to protect against quantum.* Axios.

Sabin, S. (2023). *1 big thing: A different kind of supply chain attack.* Axios.

Sabin, S. (2023). *1 big thing: Averting quantum's encryption apocalypse.* Axios.

Sabin, S. (2023). *1 big thing: Biden cyber strategy picks a fight with ransomware.* Axios.

Sabin, S. (2023). *1 big thing: Braving the zero-trust future.* Axios.

Sabin, S. (2023). *1 big thing: Generative AI is making voice scams easier to believe.* Axios.

Sabin, S. (2023). *1 big thing: Hackers could get help from the new AI chatbot.* Axios.

Sabin, S. (2023). *1 big thing: Login codes need a security upgrade.* Axios.

Sabin, S. (2023). *1 big thing: New security flaw's slow-burn perils.* Axios.

Sabin, S. (2023). *1 big thing: NSA and Cyber Command weigh divorce.* Axios.

Sabin, S. (2023). *1 big thing: Ransomware gangs cut to the chase.* Axios.

Sabin, S. (2023). *1 big thing: Researchers start playing spyware whack-a-mole.* Axios.

Sabin, S. (2023). *1 big thing: The Biden cybersecurity team's united front.* Axios.

Sabin, S. (2023). *Colonial Pipeline ransomware attack's unexpected legacy.* Axios.

Sabin, S. (2023). *Companies want to keep ChatGPT away from their secrets.* Axios.

Sabin, S. (2023). *Cyber Command, CISA unveil secret joint operations.* Axios. www.axios.com/2023/04/25/cyber-command-cisa-secret-operations

Sabin, S. (2023). *DHS board investigates teen hacker group.* Axios.

Sabin, S. (2023). *DOJ seizes Genesis Market that facilitated sale of more than 80 million account passwords.* Axios. www.axios.com/2023/04/05/doj-genesis-market-stolen-passwords-cybersecurity

Sabin, S. (2023). *Encryption faces legal threats around the globe.* Axios.

Sabin, S. (2023). *EU–U.S. data pact kicks off new sharing era.* Axios.

Sabin, S. (2023). *Generative AI is making voice scams easier to believe.* Axios.

Sabin, S. (2023). *Getting around FBI takedowns.* Axios.

Sabin, S. (2023). *Hackers head to the cloud.* Axios.

Sabin, S. (2023). *Hackers launch malware on small-biz routers.* Axios.

Sabin, S. (2023). *Hackers were busy this holiday season.* Axios.

Sabin, S. (2023). *Hackers zero in on under-resourced cities and towns.* Axios.

Sabin, S. (2023). *Inside the labs protecting U.S. critical infrastructure.* Axios.

Sabin, S. (2023). *Israel–Hamas hacks slow down but go global.* Axios.

Sabin, S. (2023). *LockBit's not-so-great, very busy month.* Axios.

Sabin, S. (2023). *Meta targets accounts tied to spyware.* Axios.

Sabin, S. (2023). *MOVEit breach fuels ransomware spree.* Axios.

Sabin, S. (2023). *MOVEit vulnerabilities keep piling up.* Axios.

Sabin, S. (2023). *NAS's plea to keep key surveillance power.* Axios.

Sabin, S. (2023). *New hackers using old tricks in Ukraine.* Axios.

Sabin, S. (2023). *North Korean hackers linked to IT firm breach.* Axios.

Sabin, S. (2023). *NSA's new project takes aim at foreign AI hacks.* Axios.

Sabin, S. (2023). *Privacy leader urges surveillance reform.* Axios.

Sabin, S. (2023). *Protecting your identity after MOVEit breaches.* Axios.

Sabin, S. (2023). *Ransomware gang threatens to leak Reddit data.* Axios.

Sabin, S. (2023). *Ransomware gangs fine-tune extreme blackmail tactics.* Axios.

Sabin, S. (2023). *Realizing the ChatGPT nightmare.* Axios.

Sabin, S. (2023). *Sanctions fuel boom in illicit crypto activity.* Axios.

Sabin, S. (2023). *Social-engineering scams get more sophisticated.* Axios.

Sabin, S. (2023). *Telecom's "extreme" password leaks.* Axios.

Sabin, S. (2023). *The bigger critical systems headache.* Axios.

Sabin, S. (2023). *Two spyware vendors put on trade blacklist.* Axios.

Sabin, S. (2023). *White House cyber regs enter a new phase.* Axios.

Sabin, S. (2023). *Why "don't pay ransom" pledges are so hard.* Axios.

Sabin, S. (2024, January 5). *Thermo Fisher halts DNA kit sales in Tibet.* Axios. www.axios.com/2024/01/03/tibet-thermo-fisher-halts-dna-collection-kit-sales

Sabin, S. (2024, January 16). *Predicting the hurdles for AI security policy.* Axios.

Sabin, S. (2024, January 23). *Cyber basics keep haunting major companies.* Axios.

Sabin, S. (2024, February 2). *The latest AI threat: Hijacking phone calls.* Axios.

Sabin, S. (2024, February 6). *1 big thing: Small spyware companies are a big problem.* Axios.

Sabin, S. (2024, February 13). *1 big thing: How Discord is becoming a hacker hotbed.* Axios.

Sabin, S. (2024, February 13). *Record fraud losses in 2023.* Axios.

Sabin, S. (2024, February 27). *China had "persistent" access to U.S. critical infrastructure.* Axios. www.axios.com/2024/02/07/china-volt-typhoon-critical-cyber attacks

Sabin, S. (2024, March 19). *Six countries join U.S. global spyware pact.* Axios.

Sabin, S. (2024, March 22). *1 big thing: Generative AI puts GPU security in the spotlight.* Axios. www.axios.com/newsletters/axios-codebook-423d2412-7b0d-4c5f-aebe-2aa13061490a.html

Sabin, S. (2024, April 5). *Hackers force AI chatbots to break their rules.* Axios.

Sabin, S. (2024, April 26). *1 big thing: AI models inch closer to hacking on their own.* Axios.

Sabin, S. (2024, May 3). *Surveillance looms over pro-Palestinian campus protests.* Axios. www.axios.com/2024/05/03/student-pro-palestine-encampments-cam pus-surveillance

Sadeghi, M. (2024, June 18). *Top 10 generative AI models mimic Russian disinformation claims a third of the time, citing Moscow-created fake local news sites as authoritative sources.* NewsGuard. www.newsguardtech.com/special-reports/generative-ai-models-mimic-russian-disinformation-cite-fake-news

Sagoff, J. (2022, January 24). *Argonne scientists use artificial intelligence to improve airplane manufacturing.* Argonne National Laboratory. www.anl.gov/article/argonne-scientists-use-artificial-intelligence-to-improve-airplane-manufacturing

Sahota, N. (2019, February 9). Will A.I. put lawyers out of business? *Forbes.*

Sakellariadis, J. (2023). *Biden admin's cloud security problem: "It could take down the internet like a stack of dominos."* POLITICO. www.politico.com/news/2023/03/10/white-house-cloud-overhaul-00086595

Sakellariadis, J. (2023). *FBI digital sting against Hive cybercrime group shows the promise—and limits—of hacking hackers.* POLITICO. www.politico.com/news/2023/07/04/fbi-digital-sting-shows-the-promise-and-limits-of-hacking-hackers-00104545

Salmon, F. (2023). *Cars' "unmatched power" to spy on drivers.* Axios. www.axios.com/2023/09/08/car-data-privacy-record-listen-mozilla-report

Salmon, F. (2024, March 18). *The era of the AI home broker approaches.* Axios. www.axios.com/2024/03/18/ai-home-broker-real-estate-housing

Salter, C. (2022, June 24). The smart city is a perpetually unrealized utopia. *MIT Technology Review.* www.technologyreview.com/2022/06/24/1053969/smart-city-unrealized-utopia/

Salter, J. (2023). *Thousands of remote IT workers sent wages to North Korea.* AP News.

Salvaterra, N. (2019, October 13). Oil and gas companies turn to AI to cut costs. *The Wall Street Journal.* www.wsj.com/articles/oil-and-gas-companies-turn-to-ai-to-cut-costs-11571018460

Samuels, M. (2021, December 9). *Robotic process automation: This is how to stop your workers from resenting the Bots.* ZDNet. www.zdnet.com/article/robotic-process-automation-this-is-how-to-stop-your-workers-from-resenting-the-bots/

Sancho, D., & Fuentes, M. R. (2023). *Inside the Halls of a Cybercrime Business.* Trend Micro Research.

Sandel, M. (2024, January 25). *Will tech change what it means to be human? And does it matter?* Harvard Gazette. https://news.harvard.edu/gazette/story/2024/01/will-tech-change-what-it-means-to-be-human-and-does-it-matter/

Sandia National Laboratories. (2022). *News releases: Sandia studies vulnerabilities of electric vehicle charging infrastructure.* Sandia National Laboratories. https://newsreleases.sandia.gov/ev_security/

Santos, D., Bunce, D., & Galiette, A. (2023). *Royal ransomware's spree against U.S. cities.* Unit 42. https://unit42.paloaltonetworks.com/royal-ransomware/

Santos, M. (2022, August 11). *Below old Seattle Macy's, Amazon plans to test robots.* Axios. www.axios.com/local/seattle/2022/08/11/seattle-macys-amazon-test-robots

Sapiro, M. (2022, February 7). *A conversation with Jake Sullivan: National security advisor.* YouTube. https://m.youtube.com/watch?v=CIwQn2vwh0o&feature=youtu.be

Saric, I. (2022, February 7). *IRS to end use of facial recognition program.* Axios. www.axios.com/2022/02/07/irs-end-facial-recognition

Saric, I. (2022, August 8). *Police departments struggle with staffing shortages.* Axios. www.axios.com/2022/08/08/police-department-staff-shortage

Saric, I. (2023, March 19). *School districts sue tech giants over youth mental health crisis.* Axios. www.axios.com/2023/03/19/school-social-media-youth-mental-health

Saric, I. (2023, March 27). *Biden moves to limit government use of commercial spyware.* Axios. www.axios.com/2023/03/27/biden-commercial-spyware-executive-order

Satter, R. (2023, December 13). *How cybercriminals are using Wyoming shell companies for global hacks.* Reuters. www.reuters.com/technology/cybersecurity/how-cybercriminals-are-using-wyoming-shell-companies-global-hacks-2023-12-12/

Schawbel, D. (2019, November 15). *How artificial intelligence is redefining the role of manager.* World Economic Forum. www.weforum.org/agenda/2019/11/how-artificial-intelligence-is-redefining-the-role-of-manager/

Scher, P. L. (2021, December 16). *J.P. Morgan International Council: Safeguarding business and national infrastructure.* JPMorgan Chase & Co. www.jpmorganchase.com/news-stories/jpmc-international-council-safeguarding-business-and-national-infrastructure

Schneider, S. (2019). Mind design: could you merge with artificial intelligence? *BBC Science Focus Magazine.* www.sciencefocus.com/future-technology/mind-design-could-you-merge-with-artificial-intelligence/.

Schneier, B., & Sanders, N. (2023). *AI could shore up democracy—Here's one way.* Belfer Center for Science and International Affairs. www.belfercenter.org/publication/ai-could-shore-democracy-heres-one-way

Schumer, C., Pritxker, T., & Allen, G. (2023). *Senator Chuck Schumer launches SAFE innovation in the AI age at CSIS.* Center for Science and International Affairs. www.csis.org/events/sen-chuck-schumer-launches-safe-innovation-ai-age-csis

Schwartz, C. (2023). *Deepfakes: Events that never happened could influence the 2024 presidential election.* Route Fifty. www.route-fifty.com/emerging-tech/2023/07/deepfakes-events-never-happened-could-influence-2024-presidential-election/388642/

Schwartz, R., Down, L., Jonas, A., & Tabassi, E. (2021, June). *A proposal for identifying and managing bias within artificial intelligence* (Draft NIST Special Publication 1270). U.S. Department of Commerce. https://nvlpubs.nist.gov/nistpubs/SpecialPublications/NIST.SP.1270-draft.pdf

Science and Technology DHS. (2022). *Feature article: Implementing mobile driver's licenses: Not as easy as you think.* Department of Homeland Security. www.dhs.gov/science-and-technology/news/2022/03/29/feature-article-implementing-mobile-drivers-licenses-not-easy-you-think

Science Council of the National Oceanic and Atmospheric Administration. (2020). *NDAA Artificial Intelligence Strategy: Analytics for next-generation earth science.* https://sciencecouncil.noaa.gov/wp-content/uploads/2023/04/2020-AI-Strategy.pdf

Science Focus. (2018). Can an algorithm deliver justice? *BBC Science Focus Magazine.* www.sciencefocus.com/future-technology/can-an-algorithm-deliver-justice/

Scoblic, J. (2023). *Strategic foresight in U.S agencies.* New America. www.newamerica.org/future-security/reports/strategic-foresight-in-us-agencies/

Segal, S. (2023, April 18). *Spring meetings readout: Outcomes and next steps.* Center for Strategic & International Studies. www.csis.org/analysis/spring-meetings-readout-outcomes-and-next-steps

Seger, E. (2021). *The greatest security threat of the post-truth age.* BBC. www.bbc.com/future/article/20210209-the-greatest-security-threat-of-the-post-truth-age

Select Committee on Artificial Intelligence of the National Science and Technology Council. (2020, November 17). *Recommendations for leveraging cloud computing resources for federally funded artificial intelligence research and development.* www.nitrd.gov/pubs/Recommendations-Cloud-AI-RD-Nov2020.pdf

Senate RPC. (2019, November 20). *Facial recognition: Potential and risk.* www.rpc.senate.gov/policy-papers/facial-recognition-potential-and-risk

Shapero, J. (2022, March 21). *Biden warns Russia "exploring options" for cyberattacks.* Axios. www.axios.com/2022/03/21/biden-russian-cyberattacks

Sharma, A. (2023, March 21). *Clop ransomware claims Saks Fifth Avenue; retailer says mock data stolen.* BleepingComputer. www.bleepingcomputer.com/news/security/clop-ransomware-claims-saks-fifth-avenue-retailer-says-mock-data-stolen/

Shea, M. (2023, August 7). *Is there a sinister side to the rise of female robots?* BBC. www.bbc.com/future/article/20230804-is-there-a-sinister-side-to-the-rise-of-female-robots

Shekhovtsov, A. (2015, September 15). *Russian politicians building an international extreme right alliance. Anton Shekhovtsov's Blog.* http://anton-shek hovtsov.blogspot.com/2015/09/russian-politicians-building.html

Shekhovtsov, A. (2015). *Russian politicians building an international extreme right alliance.* Interpreter. www.interpretermag.com/russian-politicians-build ing-an-international-extreme-right-alliance/

Sherman, J. (2019, March 6). Stop calling artificial intelligence research an "arms race." *The Washington Post.* www.washingtonpost.com/outlook/2019/03/06/ stop-calling-artificial-intelligence-research-an-arms-race/

Sherman, J. (2019, March 14). *Why the U.S. needs a National Artificial Intelligence Strategy.* World Politics Review. www.worldpoliticsreview.com/why-the-u-s-needs-a-national-artificial-intelligence-strategy/

Sherman, J. (2020, April 23). *The troubling rise of facial recognition technology in democracies.* World Politics Review. www.worldpoliticsreview.com/articles/ 28707/the-troubling-rise-of-ai-facial-recognition-technology-in-democracies

Shipman, M. (2023). *Do traffic signals need a fourth light for self-driving cars?* Nextgov/FCW. www.nextgov.com/ideas/2023/02/do-traffic-signals-need-fourth-light-self-driving-cars/382707/

Shivakumar, S., & Wessner, C. (2023). *CHIPS, Childcare, and National Security.* Center for Strategic & International Studies. www.csis.org/blogs/perspectives-innovation/chips-childcare-and-national-security

Shrestha, D. (2019, April 1). *How artificial intelligence will impact scientific research.* Medium. https://fusemachines.medium.com/how-artificial-intellige nce-will-impact-scientific-research-4e6f4face1ae

Shuster, S., & Perrigo, B. (2021). How a white-supremacist militia uses Facebook to radicalize and train new members. *Time.* https://time.com/5926750/azov-far-right-movement-facebook/

SI, M. (2022). *Clearer terms required in driverless tech.* Chinadaily.com. www.chi nadaily.com.cn/a/202209/26/WS6330ddb3a310fd2b29e799a6.html

Signe, L. (2023). *Fixing the global digital divide and digital access gap.* Brookings. www.brookings.edu/articles/fixing-the-global-digital-divide-and-digital-acc ess-gap/

Simonite, T. (2019, May 16). *How tech companies are shaping the rules governing AI.* WIRED. www.wired.com/story/how-tech-companies-shaping-rules-govern ing-ai

Simonite, T. (2019, June 11). *This new poker bot can beat multiple pros—At once.* WIRED. www.wired.com/story/new-poker-bot-beat-multiple-pros/

Singh, A. (2023). *World's first "robot lawyer" will soon defend a human in court.* The Swaddle. https://theswaddle.com/worlds-first-robot-lawyer-will-soon-def end-a-human-in-court/

Singleton, T., Gerken, T., & McMahon, L. (2023). *How a chatbot encouraged a man who wanted to kill the Queen.* BBC. www.bbc.com/news/technology-67012224

Slevin, C. (2022). *Ex-NSA worker charged with trying to sell US secrets.* AP News. https://apnews.com/article/nsa-russia-spy-classified-colorado-dalke-51c4b13ef 035f3dca8b62c433e6149d5

Slow, O. (2023). *Brics ministers call for rebalancing of global order away from West*. BBC. www.bbc.com/news/world-africa-65784030

Smalley, S. (2022, August 18). *Cyber Command's rotation "problem" exacerbates talent shortage amid growing digital threat*. CyberScoop. www.cyberscoop.com/military-rotation-norms-challenge-cyber-command/

Smith, C. S. (2019, December 18). The machines are learning, and so are the students. *The New York Times*. www.nytimes.com/2019/12/18/education/artific ial-intelligence-tutors-teachers.html

Smith, R. G., Cheung, R., et al. (2015). *Cybercrime risks and responses: Eastern and western perspectives* (Palgrave studies in cybercrime and cybersecurity). Palgrave Macmillan. www.crimeandjustice.org.uk/sites/crimeandjustice.org.uk/files/09627250408553240.pdf

Smith, R. G., Sarre, R., Chang, L. Y.-C., & Lau, L. Y.-C. (Eds.). (2023). *Cybercrime in the pandemic digital age and beyond*. (Palgrave studies in cybercrime and cybersecurity). Palgrave Macmillan. https://doi.org/10.1007/978-3-031-29107-4

Smith, T. (2023). *RadioGPT brings AI to the airwaves*. Axios. www.axios.com/local/cleveland/2023/03/07/ai-radio

Smith, Z. M. (2022). *The political reality inside metaverse cities*. Center for Strategic & International Studies. www.csis.org/analysis/political-reality-inside-metaverse-cities

Snow, J. (2017, July 20). *This AI traffic system in Pittsburgh has reduced travel time by 25%*. Smart Cities Dive. www.smartcitiesdive.com/news/this-ai-traffic-system-in-pittsburgh-has-reduced-travel-time-by-25/447494/

Snowflake. (2023). *5 ways state and local governments deliver superior services and insights with Snowflake*. www.snowflake.com/resource/5-ways-state-and-local-governments-deliver-superior-services-and-insights-with-snowflake/

Snyder, A. (2023, May 2). *AI leader says field's new territory is promising but risky*. Axios. www.axios.com/2023/03/02/demis-hassabis-deepmind-ai-new-territory

Snyder, A. (2023, June 22). *Social scientists look to AI*. Axios.

Snyder, A. (2024, April 4). *AI-aided inventions raise patent questions*. Axios. www.axios.com/newsletters/axios-science-e9cb5da2-0d75-4523-a1b7-da6b0 f0ec1b7.html

Snyder, A. (2024, April 11). *AI's flawed human yardstick*. Axios. www.axios.com/2024/04/11/ai-human-intelligence-smart-elon-musk

Solana, A. (2020, August 21). *AI may not predict the next pandemic, but big data and machine learning can fight this one*. ZDNet. www.zdnet.com/article/ai-may-not-predict-the-next-pandemic-but-big-data-and-machine-learning-are-key-to-fighting-this-one/

Solana, A. (2022, January 11). *2021 was a terrible year for cybersecurity. without action, 2022 could be even worse*. ZDNet. www.zdnet.com/article/2021-was-a-terrible-year-for-cybersecurity-without-action-2022-could-be-even-worse/

Solana, A. (2023, July 27). *Banks in the Metaverse can't lend you money yet, but they still want to sell you the dream*. ZDNet. www.zdnet.com/article/banks-in-the-metaverse-cant-lend-you-money-yet-but-they-still-want-to-sell-you-the-dream/

Solis, B. (2020, May 20). *Now hiring AI futurists: It's time for artificial intelligence to take a seat in the C-Suite.* ZDNet. www.zdnet.com/article/now-hiring-ai-futurists-in-an-era-of-covid-19-its-time-for-artificial-intellige nce-to-take-a-seat-in-the-c-suite/

Solomon, A. (2022, July 29). *For his new Smart Desert City, billionaire Marc Lore eyes Nevada, Utah, and Arizona.* Smart Cities Dive. www.smartcitiesdive.com/news/for-his-new-smart-desert-city-billionaire-marc-lore-eyes-nevada-utah-and/628483/

Solomon, H. (2021, February 3). *Clearview AI violated rights of Canadians with facial recognition tech, say privacy commissioners.* IT World Canada. www. itworldcanada.com/article/clearview-ai-violated-privacy-rights-of-canadians-with-facial-recognition-tech-say-privacy-commissioners/441698

Solomon, H. (2022). *Canada should limit police use of facial recognition technology, say privacy commissioners.* IT World Canada. www.itworldcanada. com/article/canada-should-limit-police-use-of-facial-recognition-technology-say-privacy-commissioners/482311

Sommer, W. (2020, January 23). *Feds arrest "crying Nazi" Chris Cantwell on threat charges.* The Daily Beast. www.thedailybeast.com/feds-arrest-crying-nazi-chris-cantwell-on-threat-charges

South, T. (2022, August 2). Big changes ahead for how troops battle future chemical, biological threats. *ArmyTimes.* www.armytimes.com/news/2022/08/02/big-changes-ahead-for-how-troops-battle-future-chemical-biological-threats/

Spaudling, S., & Silvers, R. (2022). *DHS cyber priorities for the coming year: A conversation with Under Secretary Rob Silvers.* Center for Strategic & International Studies. www.csis.org/events/dhs-cyber-priorities-coming-year-conversation-under-secretary-rob-silvers

Special Competitive Studies Project. (2022, September). *Mid-decade challenges to national competitiveness.* www.scsp.ai/2022/09/special-competitive-studies-proj ect-releases-first-report-sept-12-2022/

Spectrum Enterprise. (2021). *Strengthen government cybersecurity with unified threat management.* https://enterprise.spectrum.com/insights/resource-center/ executive-briefs/strengthen-government-cybersecurity-with-unified-threat-man agement.html

Spectrum News. (2020). *DHS report says white supremacist groups are deadliest US terror threat.* www.baynews9.com/fl/tampa/news/2020/10/07/white-supr emacist-groups-pose-greatest-us-domestic-terror-threat

Spencer, D., Cole, M., Joyce, S., Whittaker, X., & Stuart, M. (2021, January). *Digital automation and the future of work.* European Parliament. www.europ arl.europa.eu/RegData/etudes/STUD/2021/656311/EPRS_STU(2021)656 311(ANN1)_EN.pdf

Spielberg, S. (2002). *Minority report.* Twentieth Century Fox.

Spy Cloud. (2022). *Fortune 1000 identity exposure report.* https://engage.spycl oud.com/rs/713-WIP-737/images/spycloud-report-2022-fortune-1000-identity-exposure-report.pdf

Starks, T., & Schaffer, A. (2022). The White House is on a cyber bender. *The Washington Post.* www.washingtonpost.com/politics/2022/09/16/white-house-is-cyber-bender/

Starr, S. (2023). *Why Dayton quit ShotSpotter, a surveillance tool many cities still embrace.* Route Fifty. www.route-fifty.com/public-safety/2023/07/why-dayton-quit-shotspotter-surveillance-tool-many-cities-still-embrace/388603/

Stathis, J. (2023). *How to spot a credit card skimmer at gas pumps and avoid getting scammed.* Readers Digest. www.rd.com/article/gas-pump-skimmer/

Statt, N. (2020, June 11). *Microsoft won't sell facial recognition to police until Congress passes new privacy law.* The Verge. www.theverge.com/21288053/microsoft-facial-recognition-police-law-enforcement-pledge-regulation

Stein, S. (2022). *The metaverse's biggest unknown: Where we go from here.* ZDNet. www.zdnet.com/article/the-metaverses-biggest-unknown-where-we-go-from-here/

Steinmetz, K. F., & Yar, M. (2019). *Cybercrime and society* (3rd ed.). Sage.

Stengel, R. (2020). We should be as worried about domestic disinformation as we are about international campaigns. *Time.* https://time.com/5860215/domestic-disinformation-growing-menace-america/

Stewart, D., Buchholz, S., Bucaille, A., & Crossan, G. (2021, November 30). *Quantum computing in 2022: Newsful, but how useful?* Deloitte Insights. www2.deloitte.com/xe/en/insights/industry/technology/technology-media-and-telecom-predictions/2022/future-of-quantum-computing.html

Stoecklin, M. (2018, August 8). *DeepLocker: How AI can power a stealthy new breed of malware.* Security Intelligence. https://securityintelligence.com/deeploc ker-how-ai-can-power-a-stealthy-new-breed-of-malware/

Stojkovski, B. (2020, April 21). *Artificial intelligence: How machine-learning jobs are giving refugees a future in tech.* ZDNet. www.zdnet.com/article/artificial-intelligence-how-machine-learning-jobs-are-giving-refugees-a-fut ure-in-tech/

Stokel-Walker, C. (2022). AI bot ChatGPT writes smart essays—Should professors worry? *Nature.* www.nature.com/articles/d41586-022-04397-7

Stokel-Walker, C. (2023). *AI safety: How close is global regulation of artificial intelligence really?* Axios. www.bbc.com/future/article/20231107-why-global-regulation-of-artificial-intelligence-is-still-a-long-way-off

Stone, N. (2023). *Bitsight identifies nearly 100,000 exposed industrial control systems.* Bitsight. www.bitsight.com/blog/bitsight-identifies-nearly-100000-exposed-industrial-control-systems

Stransky, S. (2021, January 15). *The 2021 NDAA, White supremacy and domestic extremism.* Lawfare. www.lawfareblog.com/2021-ndaa-white-supremacy-and-domestic-extremism

Strategic Technologies Program. (2023). *The future of quantum—Developing a system ready for quantum.* Center for Strategic International Studies. www.csis. org/events/future-quantum-developing-system-ready-quantum

Stuart, E. (2023). *A federal program looks to connect smart buildings with smart policy.* Route Fifty. www.route-fifty.com/infrastructure/2023/03/new-federal-program-looks-connect-smart-buildings-smart-policy/383930/

Subcommittee on Investigations and Oversight. (2022, June 29). *Privacy in the age of biometrics.* Committee on Science, Space, and Technology. https://science. house.gov/hearings/privacy-in-the-age-of-biometrics

Subramanian, S., & Ward, M. (2022, October 8). *2022 Deloitte-NASCIO cybersecurity study*. Deloitte Insights. www2.deloitte.com/us/en/insights/indus try/public-sector/2022-deloitte-nascio-study-cybersecurity-post-pandemic.html

Superior Transcriptions LLC. (2023, April 18). *Report launch: Seven critical technologies for winning the next war*. Center for Strategic International Studies.

Susarla, A. (2022). *What the world would lose with the demise of Twitter: Valuable Eyewitness accounts and raw data on human behavior, as well as a habitat for trolls*. Nextgov/FCW. www.nextgov.com/ideas/2022/11/what-world-would-lose-demise-twitter-valuable-eyewitness-accounts-and-raw-data-human-behav ior-well-habitat-trolls/379978/

Tanium. (2020). *Whole of state 101: Navigating funding and change management obstacles.*

Tar, J. (2023). *Several French media block OpenAI's GPTBot over data collection concerns*. EURACTIV. www.euractiv.com/section/artificial-intelligence/news/ several-french-media-block-openais-gptbot-over-data-collection-concerns/

Taylor, D. (2023). *Quantum continues to heat up as the Netherlands' QuantWare lands 6 million*. Tech.eu. www.tech.eu/2023/03/09/quantum-continues-to-heat-up-as-the-netherlands-quantware-lands-6-million/

Teale, C. (2022, August 24). *Make A.I. accountable by adding redress tools, researchers* say. Nextgov/FCW. www.nextgov.com/emerging-tech/2022/08/ make-ai-accountable-adding-redress-tools-researchers-say/376119/

Teale, C. (2022). *Public employees expect more fraud, waste and abuse*. Route Fifty. www.route-fifty.com/management/2022/12/expect-even-more-fraud-waste-and-abuse/380884/

Teale, C. (2022). *The next era of data-driven local government*. Route Fifty. www. route-fifty.com/tech-data/2022/11/next-era-data-driven-local-government/ 380156/

Teale, C. (2022). *Transit agency pilots gun detection tech*. Route Fifty. www.route-fifty.com/tech-data/2022/12/transit-agency-pilots-gun-detection-tech/380492/

Teale, C. (2023, January 20). *Automated vehicles coming to Ohio roads*. Route Fifty. www.route-fifty.com/tech-data/2023/01/automated-vehicles-coming-ohio-roads/382039/

Teale, C. (2023, March 17). *The latest version's greater "steerability" allows users to vary the style and tone of the generated text to make scams even harder to detect*. Route-Fifty. www.route-fifty.com/digital-government/2023/03/chatgpt-could-make-phishing-more-sophisticated/384154/

Teale, C. (2023, July 10). *Cyberattack turns up the heat on common security problems*. Route Fifty. www.route-fifty.com/tech-data/2023/01/cyberattack-turns-heat-common-security-problems/381655/

Teale, C. (2023, November 7). *DELETE Act closes "big loophole" and tightens regulations on data brokers*. Route Fifty. www.route-fifty.com/digital-governm ent/2023/11/delete-act-closes-big-loophole-and-tightens-regulations-data-brok ers/391855/

Teale, C. (2023, December 12). *Without good data, government AI tools will just be "garbage in, garbage out."* Route Fifty. www.route-fifty.com/emerging-tech/ 2023/12/without-good-data-government-ai-tools-will-just-be-garbage-garbage-out/392699/

Teale, C. (2023, December 14). *2024 to bring "shifts" in government tech.* Route Fifty. www.route-fifty.com/digital-government/2023/12/2024-bring-shifts-gov ernment-tech/392776/

Teale, C. (2023, December 28). *After an action-packed year, 2024 will be another blockbuster year for AI.* Route Fifty. www.route-fifty.com/emerging-tech/2023/ 12/after-action-packed-year-2024-will-be-another-blockbuster-year-ai/392984/

Teale, C. (2023). *Agency execs strive to maintain modernization momentum.* Route Fifty. www.route-fifty.com/digital-government/2023/07/agency-execs-str ive-maintain-modernization-momentum/388386/

Teale, C. (2023). *AI will bring dramatic change in the next three years, say local government IT execs.* Route Fifty. www.route-fifty.com/emerging-tech/2023/09/ai-will-bring-dramatic-change-next-three-years-say-local-government-it-execs/390569/

Teale, C. (2023). *ChatGPT could make phishing more sophisticated.* Route Fifty. www.route-fifty.com/cybersecurity/2023/03/chatgpt-could-make-phishing-more-sophisticated/384088/

Teale, C. (2023). *Cyberattack turns up the heat on common security problems.* Route Fifty. www.route-fifty.com/tech-data/2023/01/cyberattack-turns-heat-common-security-problems/381655/

Teale, C. (2023). *Don't fear AI but prepare for its wider use.* Route Fifty. www. route-fifty.com/cybersecurity/2023/06/dont-fear-ai-prepare-its-wider-use/ 388103/

Teale, C. (2023). *EVs rev up cybersecurity challenges.* Route Fifty. www.route-fifty.com/tech-data/2023/05/evs-rev-up-cybersecurity-challenges/385830/

Teale, C. (2023). *Governor paves the way for an "AI Bill of Rights."* Route Fifty. www.route-fifty.com/tech-data/2023/06/governor-signs-bill-paving-way-state-level-ai-bill-rights/387470/

Teale, C. (2023). *New York City to weigh strict facial recognition ban.* Route Fifty. www.route-fifty.com/tech-data/2023/04/new-york-city-weigh-strict-facial-reco gnition-ban/385384/

Teale, C. (2023). *Passwordless security gains ground.* Route Fifty. www.route-fifty.com/digital-government/2023/06/passwordless-security-gains-ground-aut hentication/387687/

Teale, C. (2023). *Public sector slow to respond to cyberattacks, report finds.* Route Fifty. www.route-fifty.com/cybersecurity/2023/07/public-sector-slow-respond-cyberattacks-report-finds/388818/

Teale, C. (2023). *Smart cities need a new mindset, not just new technology.* Route Fifty. www.route-fifty.com/digital-government/2023/09/smart-cities-need-new-mindset-not-just-new-technology/390465/

Teale, C. (2023). *States wrestle with AI-driven future.* Route Fifty. www.route-fifty.com/emerging-tech/2023/10/states-wrestle-ai-driven-future/391201/

Teale, C. (2024, February 2). *As privacy conversations become mainstream, data protection laws gain traction.* Route Fifty. www.route-fifty.com/digital-governm ent/2024/02/new-jersey-latest-state-enact-data-privacy-protections/393890/

Teale, C. (2024, February 5). *Who should be in charge of protecting our water systems from cyber threats?* Route Fifty. www.route-fifty.com/cybersecurity/ 2024/02/who-should-be-charge-protecting-our-water-systems-cyber-threats/ 393927/

Team Chainalysis. (2023, August 17). *Ransomware revenue down as more victims refuse to pay.* Chainalysis. www.chainalysis.com/blog/crypto-ransomware-reve nue-down-as-victims-refuse-to-pay/

Team State Blog. (2022). *Jobs lost to automation statistics in 2022.* TeamStage. https://teamstage.io/jobs-lost-to-automation-statistics/

Tech Republic. (n.d.). *5 internet of things (IoT) innovations.* www.techr epublic.com/resource-library/whitepapers/5-internet-of-things-iot-innovati ons-free-pdf/

Tech Republic Premium. (2015). *Artificial intelligence and IT: The good, the bad and the scary.* www.techrepublic.com/resource-library/research/artificial-intel ligence-and-it-the-good-the-bad-and-the-scary-techrepublic-premium/

Techerati. (2019, July 16). *AI and cyber security: Separating hype from reality.* www.techerati.com/features-hub/opinions/ai-and-cyber-security-separating-hype-from-reality/

Technavio Blog. (2019, July 25). *Artificial intelligence in cyber security: How is AI transforming cyber security?* Technavio. https://blog.technavio.org/blog/art ificial-intelligence-in-cyber-security

Temperton, J. (2016, June 7). *Beer brewed with the help of AI? Yup, that's now a thing.* WIRED. www.wired.co.uk/article/beer-brewed-by-ai-intelligentx

Temple-Raston, D. (2023). *A "worst nightmare" cyberattack: The untold story of the SolarWinds hack.* NPR. www.npr.org/2021/04/16/985439655/a-worst-nightmare-cyberattack-the-untold-story-of-the-solarwinds-hack

Tham, I. (2022). Rules to tackle online harm in Singapore could be rolled out as early as 2023. *The Straits Times.* www.straitstimes.com/tech/tech-news/rules-to-tackle-online-harm-in-singapore-to-be-rolled-out-as-early-as-2023

Thanaraj, A. (2018, September 14). *Can robots be prosecuted for a crime?* University of Cumbria. www.cumbria.ac.uk/blog/articles/can-robots-be-prosecu ted-for-a-crime.php

The Alan Turing Institute. (2021). *AI ecosystem survey: Informing the national AI strategy summary report.* www.turing.ac.uk/sites/default/files/2021-09/ai-strat egy-survey_results_020921.pdf

The American Academy of Diplomacy. (2022, February). *Bringing America's multilateral diplomacy into the 21st century.* www.academyofdiplomacy.org/ wp-content/uploads/2022/03/Bringing-Americas-Multilateral-Diplomacy-into-the-21st-Century-FINAL.pdf

The Center for Long-Term Resilience. (2021, June). *Future proof: The opportunity to transform the UK's resilience to extreme risks.*

The Crown Secretary of State for Digital, Culture, Media and Sport. (2022, July). *Establishing a pro-innovation approach to regulating AI: An overview of the UK's emerging approach.* Secretary of State for Digital, Culture, Media and Sport by Command of Her Majesty. www.gov.uk/government/publications/ establishing-a-pro-innovation-approach-to-regulating-ai/establishing-a-pro-inn ovation-approach-to-regulating-ai-policy-statement

The Department of Homeland Security. (2023, April 24). *Privacy impact assessmentfor TSA unmanned aircraft systems*. DHS Reference No. DHS/TSA/PIA-043.

The Economist. (2024, June 20). *How AI is changing warfare*. www.economist.com/briefing/2024/06/20/how-ai-is-changing-warfare

The Hacker News. (2023). *Credential theft is (still) a top attack method*. https://thehackernews.com/2022/08/credential-theft-is-still-top-attack.html

The Intelligence Community. (2022). *Principles of artificial intelligence ethics for the intelligence community*. Intelgov. www.intelligence.gov/principles-of-artific ial-intelligence-ethics-for-the-intelligence-community

The National Counterintelligence and Security Center. (2021, October). *Protecting critical and emerging U.S. technologies from foreign threats*.

The National Intelligence Council. (2021, March). *Global trends 2040*. www.dni.gov/files/ODNI/documents/assessments/GlobalTrends_2040.pdf

The National Security Commission on Artificial Intelligence. (2021). *The final report*. www.nscai.gov/wp-content/uploads/2021/03/Full-Report-Digital-1.pdf

The Networking & Information Technology R&D Program. (2020, June). *Artificial intelligence and cybersecurity: A detailed technical workshop report*.

The President's National Security Telecommunications Advisory Committee (NSTAC). (2023). *Strategy for increasing trust in the information and communications technology and services ecosystem*.

The Secretary of the State for Science, Innovation and Technology. (2023, March). *A pro-innovation approach to AI regulation*. www.gov.uk/government/publicati ons/ai-regulation-a-pro-innovation-approach/white-paper

The Stack. (2022, April 4). *Technology use in the justice system is a "Wild West" warn Peers*. https://thestack.technology/police-ai-toolsnew-technologies-in-the-justice-system/

The Stack. (2022, April 5). *New technologies in the justice system are a "threat to a fair trial."* https://thestack.technology/police-ai-toolsnew-technologies-in-the-justice-system/

The Sufan Center. (2019). *White supremacy extremism: The transnational rise of the violent white supremacist movement* (pp. 1–60). https://thesoufancenter.org/wp-content/uploads/2019/09/Report-by-The-Soufan-Center-White-Supremacy-Extremism-The-Transnational-Rise-of-The-Violent-White-Supremacist-Movem ent.pdf

The White House. (2018, May 10). *Summary of the 2018 White House Summit on artificial intelligence for American industry*.

The White House. (2019, September 9). *Summary of the 2019 White House Summit on artificial intelligence in government*.

The White House. (2020). *Guidance for regulation of artificial intelligence applications*. www.whitehouse.gov/wp-content/uploads/2020/01/Draft-OMB-Memo-on-Regulation-of-AI-1-7-19.pdf

The White House. (2022, January 11). *White House Office of Science & Technology Policy releases Scientific Integrity Task Force Report.* www.whiteho use.gov/ostp/news-updates/2022/01/11/white-house-office-of-science-technol ogy-policy-releases-scientific-integrity-task-force-report/

The White House. (2022, March 25). *Fact Sheet: United States and European Commission announce trans-Atlantic data privacy framework.* www.whi tehouse.gov/briefing-room/statements-releases/2022/03/25/fact-sheet-uni ted-states-and-european-commission-announce-trans-atlantic-data-privacy-framework/

The White House. (2022, May 16). *U.S.–EU Joint Statement of the Trade and Technology Council.* www.whitehouse.gov/briefing-room/statements-releases/ 2022/12/05/u-s-eu-joint-statement-of-the-trade-and-technology-council/

The White House. (2022, October). *Blueprint for an AI Bill of Rights: Making automated systems work for the American people.*

The White House. (2022, October). *Fact sheet: Biden-Harris administration delivers on strengthening America's cybersecurity.* www.whitehouse.gov/brief ing-room/statements-releases/2022/10/11/fact-sheet-biden-harris-administrat ion-delivers-on-strengthening-americas-cybersecurity/

The White House. (2022, October). *National security strategy.*

The White House. (2022, November 18). *Migrating to post-quantum cryptography.*

The White House. (2023, March). *National cybersecurity strategy.*

The White House. (2023, May 20). *G7 leaders' statement on economic resilience and economic security.* www.whitehouse.gov/briefing-room/statements-relea ses/2023/05/20/g7-leaders-statement-on-economic-resilience-and-economic-security/

The White House. (2023, July). *National cybersecurity strategy implementa-tion plan.*

The White House. (2023, July 6). *The AI in Government Act of 2020—Artificial intelligence competencies.* www.whitehouse.gov/wp-content/uploads/2023/11/ AI-in-Government-Memo-draft-for-public-review.pdf

The White House. (2023, July 23). *National cyber workforce and educa-tion strategy.* www.whitehouse.gov/wp-content/uploads/2023/07/NCWES-2023.07.31.pdf

The White House. (2023, November). *Advancing governance, innovation, and risk management for agency use of artificial intelligence.*

The White House. (2023). *Fact sheet: Biden-Harris administration secures voluntary commitments from leading artificial intelligence companies to manage the risks posed by AI.* www.whitehouse.gov/briefing-room/stateme nts-releases/2023/07/21/fact-sheet-biden-harris-administration-secures-volunt ary-commitments-from-leading-artificial-intelligence-companies-to-man age-the-risks-posed-by-ai/

The White House. (2023). *Fact sheet: Biden-Harris administration takes new steps to advance responsible artificial intelligence research, development, and deploy-ment.* www.whitehouse.gov/briefing-room/statements-releases/2023/05/23/fact-sheet-biden-harris-administration-takes-new-steps-to-advance-responsible-art ificial-intelligence-research-development-and-deployment/

The White House Office of Science and Technology Policy. (2020, February). *American artificial intelligence initiative: year one annual report.* www.nitrd. gov/nitrdgroups/images/c/c1/American-AI-Initiative-One-Year-Annual-Rep ort.pdf

Thieme, M. (2023, August 7). *5 federal use cases for generative AI.* Nextgov/FCW. www.nextgov.com/ideas/2023/08/5-federal-use-cases-generative-ai/389165/

Thierry, G. (2023, July 31). *Giving AI direct control over anything is a bad idea— Here's how it could do us real harm.* The Conversation. https://theconversation. com/giving-ai-direct-control-over-anything-is-a-bad-idea-heres-how-it-could- do-us-real-harm-210168

Thomas, M. G. (2021, December 6). *The age of digital divination.* SAPIENS. www.sapiens.org/culture/digital-divination/

Thompson, N. (2018, March 31). *Emmanuel Macron talks to WIRED about France's AI strategy.* WIRED. www.wired.com/story/emmanuel-macron-talks- to-wired-about-frances-ai-strategy/

Tidy, J. (2022). *Australian police to Medibank hackers: "We know who you are."* BBC. www.bbc.co.uk/news/technology-63596691

Tidy, J. (2022). *Billions being spent in metaverse land grab.* BBC. www.bbc.co.uk/ news/technology-63488059

Tidy, J. (2022). *IHG hack: "Vindictive" couple deleted hotel chain data for fun.* BBC. www.bbc.co.uk/news/technology-62937678

Tidy, J. (2022). *Stolen $3bn Bitcoin mystery ends with popcorn tin discovery.* BBC. www.bbc.co.uk/news/technology-63547765

Tidy, J. (2023). *E2E encryption: Should Big Tech be able to read people's messages?* BBC. www.bbc.com/news/technology-66099040

Tidy, J. (2023). *Hacker gang Clop publishes victim names on dark web.* BBC. www.bbc.com/news/business-65924327

Tidy, J. (2023). *MOVEit hack: BBC, BA, and Boots among cyber-attack victims.* BBC. www.bbc.com/news/technology-65814104

Tidy, J. (2023). *MOVEit hack: What action can data-breach victims take?* BBC. www.bbc.com/news/technology-65820603

Tidy, J. (2023). *Pedophiles using AI to turn singers and film stars into kids.* BBC. www.bbc.com/news/technology-67172231

Tidy, J. (2023). *Why is it so rare to hear about Western cyber-attacks?* BBC. www. bbc.com/news/technology-65977742

Tidy, J., & Garman, B. (2022, August 26). *Nato investigates hacker sale of missile firm data.* BBC. www.bbc.com/news/technology-62672184

Tidy, J., & Gerken, T. (2022, August 11). *NHS IT supplier held to ransom by hackers.* BBC. www.bbc.com/news/technology-62506039

Totilo, S. (2023). *Roblox to begin interviewing some job candidates inside Roblox.* Axios. www.axios.com/2023/08/10/roblox-job-interviews-virtual-recruiting

Toulas, B. (2023, February 14). *New "MortalKombat" ransomware targets systems in the U.S.* BleepingComputer. www.bleepingcomputer.com/news/secur ity/new-mortalkombat-ransomware-targets-systems-in-the-us/

Toulas, B. (2023, February 15). *GitHub Copilot update stops AI model from revealing secrets.* BleepingComputer. www.bleepingcomputer.com/news/secur ity/github-copilot-update-stops-ai-model-from-revealing-secrets/

Toulas, B. (2023). *PayPal accounts breached in large-scale credential stuffing attack*. BleepingComputer. www.bleepingcomputer.com/news/security/paypal-accounts-breached-in-large-scale-credential-stuffing-attack/

Toulas, B. (2023). *RomCom hackers target NATO Summit attendees in phishing attacks*. BleepingComputer. www.bleepingcomputer.com/news/security/rom com-hackers-target-nato-summit-attendees-in-phishing-attacks/

Trakimavicius, L. (2019, February 6). *Leveraging AI to transform power grid security*. Atlantic Council. www.atlanticcouncil.org/blogs/new-atlanticist/lev eraging-ai-to-transform-power-grid-security/

Tran, P. (2018, March 16). *France to increase investment in AI for future weapon systems*. Defense News. www.defensenews.com/intel-geoint/2018/03/16/france-to-increase-investment-in-ai-for-future-weapon-systems/

Treasury Inspector General for Tax Administration. (2023, March 7). *The enterprise case management system did not consistently meet cloud security requirements* (Report No. 2021-20-018).

Treisman, R. (2024, July 11). *Bread and bullets: Some Southern supermartkets now sell ammo out of vending machines*. NPR. www.npr.org/2024/07/11/nx-s1-5033748/ammunition-vending-machines-grocery-stores

Trump, D. (2019, February 14). *Federal Register: Maintaining American leadership in Artificial Intelligence Executive Order 13859*. Federal Register. www.federalregister.gov/documents/2019/02/14/2019-02544/maintaining-american-leadership-in-artificial-intelligence

Tucker, P. (2014, December 31). *The military's new year's resolution for artificial intelligence*. Defense One. www.defenseone.com/technology/2014/12/militarys-new-years-resolution-artificial-intelligence/102102/

Tucker, P. (2019). *Here come AI-enabled cameras meant to sense crime before it occurs*. Nextgov/FCW. www.nextgov.com/emerging-tech/2019/04/here-come-ai-enabled-cameras-meant-sense-crime-it-occurs/156532/

Tucker, P. (2020). *Spies like AI: The future of artificial intelligence for the U.S. intelligence community*. Nextgov/FCW. www.nextgov.com/emerging-tech/2020/01/spies-ai-future-artificial-intelligence-us-intelligence-community/162683/

Tucker, P. (2022). *How will the military use 5G? A new drone experiment offers clues*. Nextgov/FCW. www.nextgov.com/cxo-briefing/2022/09/how-will-milit ary-use-5g-new-drone-experiment-offers-clues/377751/

Tucker, P. (2022). *The U.S. military is buying electric Jet-ski robots*. Nextgov/FCW. www.nextgov.com/emerging-tech/2022/09/military-buying-electric-jet-ski-rob ots/377565/

Tucker, P. (2023, July 10). *When may a robot kill? New DOD policy tries to clarify*. Nextgov/FCW. www.nextgov.com/cxo-briefing/2023/01/when-may-robot-kill-new-dod-policy-tries-clarify/382280/

Tucker, P. (2023). *AI is supposed to become smarter over time. ChatGPT can become dumber*. Nextgov/FCW. www.nextgov.com/artificial-intelligence/2023/07/ai-supposed-become-smarter-over-time-chatgpt-can-become-dumber/388878/

Tucker, P. (2023). *The Pentagon's AI chief is "scared to death" of ChatGPT*. Nextgov/FCW. www.nextgov.com/emerging-tech/2023/05/pentagons-ai-chief-scared-death-chatgpt/385969/

Tuman, A. (2019, December 27). *The growing role of technology in criminal justice.* TMC Net. www.tmcnet.com/topics/articles/2019/12/27/444108-grow ing-role-technology-criminal-justice.htm

Tung, L. (2021, December 8). *NASA has a new system to spot asteroids that might hit the Earth.* ZDNet. www.zdnet.com/article/nasa-has-a-new-system-to-spot-asteroids-that-might-hit-the-earth/

Tung, L. (2021, December 20). *Scammers grabbed $7.7 billion worth of cryptocurrency in 2021, say researchers.* ZDNet. www.zdnet.com/article/scamm ers-grabbed-7-7-billion-worth-of-cryptocurrency-in-2021-say-researchers/

Tung, L. (2021, December 21). *Police found 225 million stolen passwords hidden on a hacked cloud server. is yours one of them?* ZDNet. www.zdnet.com/arti cle/police-found-225-million-stolen-passwords-hidden-on-a-hacked-cloud-ser ver-is-yours-one-of-them/

Tung, L. (2022, January 6). *Supercomputing: Now Europe wants to be a big player too.* ZDNet. www.zdnet.com/article/eu-wants-a-massive-supercomputer-for-quantum-computing/

Tung, L. (2022, January 10). *Ransomware warning: Cyber criminals are mailing out USB drives that install malware.* ZDNet. www.zdnet.com/article/fbi-cybercr iminals-are-mailing-out-usb-drives-that-will-install-ransomware/

Tung, L. (2022, January 19). *FBI warning: Crooks are using fake QR codes to steal your passwords and money.* ZDNet. www.zdnet.com/article/fbi-warning-crooks-are-using-fake-qr-codes-to-steal-your-passwords-and-money/

Tung, L. (2022, February 2). *FBI warning: Scammers are posting fake job ads on networking sites to steal your money and identity.* ZDNet. www.zdnet.com/ article/fbi-warning-scammers-are-posting-fake-job-ads-on-networking-sites-to-steal-your-money-and-identity/

Tung, L. (2022, February 3). *Bad news for developers? this AI is getting very good at writing code.* ZDNet. www.zdnet.com/article/bad-news-for-developers-deepminds-ai-is-getting-good-at-writing-code/

Tung, L. (2022, February 21). *FBI: Now scammers are using fake video meetings to steal your money.* ZDNet. www.zdnet.com/article/fbi-now-scammers-are-using-fake-video-meetings-to-steal-your-money/

Tung, L. (2022, June 15). *A tiny botnet launched the largest DDOS attack on record.* ZDNet. www.zdnet.com/article/a-tiny-botnet-launched-the-largest-ddos-attack-on-record/

Tung, L. (2022, July 26). *NASA's cute space robots just hit another milestone.* ZDNet. www.zdnet.com/article/nasas-cute-space-robots-just-hit-another-milestone/

Tung, L. (2022, September 30). *Microsoft: Hackers are using open source soft-ware and fake jobs in phishing attacks.* ZDNet. www.zdnet.com/article/micros oft-hackers-using-open-source-software-and-fake-jobs-in-phishing-attacks/

Tung, L. (2023, January 4). *ChatGPT's next big challenge: Helping Microsoft to challenge Google search.* ZDNet. www.zdnet.com/article/chatgpts-next-big-challenge-helping-microsoft-to-challenge-google-search/

Tung, L. (2023, January 23). *Scientists use Wi-Fi routers to see humans through walls.* ZDNet. www.zdnet.com/article/scientists-use-wi-fi-routers-to-see-hum ans-through-walls/

Tunney, C. (2022, June 14). *New federal bill would compel key industries to bolster cyber security—Or pay the price.* CBC. www.cbc.ca/news/politics/cyberatta cks-bill-1.6487826

Turing, A. M. (1950). Computing machinery and intelligence. *Mind, 49,* 433–460. https://redirect.cs.umbc.edu/courses/471/papers/turing.pdf

Turnbull, T. (2022, July 13). *Australia probes retail giants Bunnings and Kmart over customer "faceprints."* BBC. www.bbc.com/news/world-australia-62145154

Turner, J. (2022). *The right way to monitor your employee productivity.* Gartner. www.gartner.com/en/articles/the-right-way-to-monitor-your-employee-productivity

Tyko, K. (2022, June 17). *IRS turns to voice bots to cut down taxpayers' wait times.* Axios. www.axios.com/2022/06/17/irs-tax-payment-phone-call-bots

UK AI Council. (2021, January). *AI roadmap.* https://assets.publishing.service.gov. uk/media/5ff3bc6e8fa8f53b76ccee23/AI_Council_AI_Roadmap.pdf

Unian.net. (2021, May 2). *U.S. Senate to examine Russia's influence on antigovernment extremists.* www.unian.info/world/moscow-s-role-senate-to-examine-russia-s-influence-on-extremists-11311418.html

United Nations Counter-Terrorism Committee Executive Directorate (UNCTED). (2021). *Emerging trends and recent evolution of the threat posed by ISIS/AL-Qaeda inspired terrorismin Europe: A spotlight on the terrorist profile(s), incitement techniques, vulnerable targets and potential impact of COVID-19—Summary report.*

United Nations Intelligence Crime and Justice Research Institution. (n.d.). *The Dumb and dangerous road ahead.* Ghent University.

United Nations Interregional Crime and Justice Research Institute. (2019). *Artificial intelligence and robotics for law enforcement.* https://unicri.it/artific ial-intelligence-and-robotics-law-enforcement

United Nations Interregional Crime and Justice Research Institute & International Criminal Police Organization. (2020). *Towards responsible AI innovation.* https://unicri.it/sites/default/files/2020-07/UNICRI-INTERPOL_Report_ Towards_Responsible_AI_Innovation_0.pdf

United Nations Office of Counter-Terrorism. (2021, June 25). *Science, technology, and innovation: Understanding advancements from the perspective of countering weapons of mass destruction terrorism.* https://unicri.it/News/New-Report-Science-Innovation-Countering-WMD-Terrorism

United Nations Office of Counter-Terrorism & United Nations Interregional Crime and Justice Research Institute. (2021). *Countering terrorism online with AI.* www.un.org/counterterrorism/sites/www.un.org.counterterrorism/files/cou ntering-terrorism-online-with-ai-uncct-unicri-report-web.pdf

United Nations Office on Drugs and Crime. (2020). *Darknet cybercrime threats to Southeast Asia.*

United States Department of Defense. (2022, March). *Summary of the Joint All-Domain Command (JADC2) & control strategy.*

United States Department of Health and Human Services. (2021, September). *Trustworthy AI (TAI) Playbook.*

United States Government Accountability Office. (2020, July). *Facial recognition technology: Privacy and accuracy issues related to commercial uses* (Report to Congressional Requesters, Accessible Version).

United States Government Accountability Office. (2021, June). *Artificial intelligence: An accountability framework for federal agencies and other entities* (GAO-21-519SP). www.gao.gov/assets/gao-21-519sp.pdf

United States Government Accountability Office. (2021, June). *Homeland Security: DHS needs to fully implement key practices in acquiring biometric identity management system* (Report to Congressional Requesters).

United States Government Accountability Office. (2021, August). *Facial recognition technology: Current and planned uses by federal agencies* (Report No. GAO-21-526). www.gao.gov/assets/gao-21-526.pdf

United States Government Accountability Office. (2022, February). *Artificial intelligence status of developing and acquiring capabilities for weapon systems.*

United States Government Accountability Office. (2022, October). *Critical infrastructure protection: Additional federal coordination is needed to enhance K-12 cybersecurity.*

United States Government Accountability Office. (2023, July 13). *Preliminary results show federal buildings remain underutilized due to longstanding challenges and increased telework.*

United States Intelligence Community. (2020). *Artificial intelligence ethics framework for the intelligence community.*

United States of America Department of State. (2021, September). *Enterprise data strategy: Empowering data informed diplomacy.* www.state.gov/wp-content/uploads/2021/09/Reference-EDS-Accessible.pdf

University of Bonn. (2019, June 6). How artificial intelligence can help detect rare diseases. *Science Daily.* www.sciencedaily.com/releases/2019/06/190606133805.htm

U.S. Agency of International Development. (2022, May). *USAID artificial intelligence action plan.* www.usaid.gov/sites/default/files/2022-05/USAID_Artificial_Intelligence_Action_Plan.pdf

U.S. Chamber of Commerce. (2022). *Chamber Comments on artificial intelligence export competitiveness.* www.uschamber.com/international/chamber-comments-on-artificial-intelligence-export-competitiveness

U.S. Chamber Staff. (2022). *Ensuring ethical AI.* U.S. Chamber of Commerce. www.uschamber.com/technology/how-to-make-ai-more-ethical-transparent-and-useful-for-everyone

U.S. Cyber Command. (2022, August 18). *"Partnership in Action": Croatian, U.S. cyber defenders hunting malicious actors.* www.cybercom.mil/Media/News/Article/3131961/partnership-in-action-croatian-us-cyber-defenders-hunting-for-malicious-actors/

U.S. Department of Commerce. (2024, February 29). *Citing national security concerns, Biden-Harris administration announces inquiry into connected vehicles.* www.commerce.gov/news/press-releases/2024/02/citing-national-security-concerns-biden-harris-administration-announces

U.S. Department of Defense. (2023, June 1). *North Korea using social engineering to enable hacking of think tanks, academia, and media.* https://media.defense.gov/2023/Jun/01/2003234055/-1/-1/0/JOINT_CSA_DPRK_SOCIAL_ENGINEERING.PDF

U.S. Department of Energy. (2021, November 10). *Artificial intelligence & technology office.* Energy.gov.

U.S. Department of Energy. (2021, December 2). *AI and ML enable efficient and effective real-time decisions in carbon capture and storage.* Energy.gov. www.energy.gov/ai/articles/ai-and-ml-enable-efficient-and-effective-real-time-decisions-carbon-capture-and-storage

U.S. Department of Energy. (2021, December 15). *Department of Energy Focus Group—Managing the convergence of AI and immersive technologies.* Energy. gov. www.energy.gov/ai/articles/department-energy-focus-group-managing-convergence-ai-and-immersive-technologies

U.S. Department of Energy. (2021). *AI innovation incubator.* Data Science Institute. https://data-science.llnl.gov/ai3

U.S. Department of Energy. (2022). *Artificial intelligence and autonomous systems research and development and implementation roadmap.*

U.S. Department of Health and Human Services. (2021, September). *Trustworthy AI (TAI) playbook.*

U.S. Department of Homeland Security. (2020, December). *U.S. Department of Homeland Security Artificial Intelligence Strategy.* www.dhs.gov/sites/default/files/publications/dhs_ai_strategy.pdf

U.S. Department of Homeland Security. (2023, September 14). *Homeland threat assessment 2024.* www.dhs.gov/sites/default/files/2023-09/23_0913_ia_23-333-ia_u_homeland-threat-assessment-2024_508C_V6_13Sep23.pdf

U.S. Department of Justice Office of the Chief Information Officer. (2019, February). *Data Strategy for the U.S. Department of Justice.* www.justice.gov/archives/jmd/page/file/1135081/download

U.S. Department of Justice Office of the Chief Information Officer. (2020, December). *Artificial Intelligence Strategy for the U.S. Department of Justice.* www.justice.gov/jmd/page/file/1364706/download

U.S. Department of State. (2020). *Pillars of Russia's disinformation and propaganda ecosystem* (p. 77).

U.S. Department of State. (2021, September). *Enterprise Data Strategy: Empowering data informed diplomacy.*

U.S. Department of State. (2023, January 4). *Establishing the Office of the Special Envoy for Critical and Emerging Technology.* www.state.gov/establishing-the-office-of-the-special-envoy-for-critical-and-emerging-technology/

U.S. Department of the Treasury. (2022). *Potential federal insurance response to catastrophic cyber incidents.* Federal Register. www.federalregister.gov/documents/2022/09/29/2022-21133/potential-federal-insurance-response-to-catastrophic-cyber-incidents

U.S. Department of the Treasury. (2024, March). *Managing artificial intelligence-specific cybersecurity risks in the financial services sector.* https://home.treasury.gov/system/files/136/Managing-Artificial-Intelligence-Specific-Cybersecurity-Risks-In-The-Financial-Services-Sector.pdf

U.S. Department of Transportation. (2018, October). *Preparing for the future of transportation: Automated vehicles 3.0.* www.transportation.gov/av/3

U.S. Department of Transportation. (2020, January). *Ensuring American leadership in automated vehicle technologies: Automated vehicles 4.0* www.transportation.gov/sites/dot.gov/files/2020-02/EnsuringAmericanLeadershipAVTech4.pdf

U.S. Equal Employment Opportunity Commission. (2022). *The Americans with Disabilities Act and the use of software, algorithms, and artificial intelligence to assess job applicants and employees.* www.eeoc.gov/laws/guidance/americans-disabilities-act-and-use-software-algorithms-and-artificial-intelligence

U.S. General Services Administration. (2022). *Virtual inspections provide a remote eye on key work during pandemic.* www.gsa.gov/blog/2021/09/03/virtual-inspections-provide-a-remote-eye-on-key-work-during-pandemic

U.S. Government. (2019, February 11). *Maintaining American leadership in artificial intelligence.* www.govinfo.gov/content/pkg/DCPD-201900073/pdf/DCPD-201900073.pdf

U.S. Government Accountability Office. (2021, July 13). *Facial recognition technology: Federal law enforcement agencies should have better awareness of systems used by employees* (GAO-21-105309). www.gao.gov/products/gao-21-105309

U.S. Government Accountability Office. (2021, November 19). *Digital services: Considerations for a federal academy to develop a pipeline of digital staff.* www.gao.gov/assets/gao-22-105388.pdf

U.S. Government Accountability Office. (2022, July 27). *Facial recognition technology: CBP traveler identity verification and efforts to address privacy issues.* www.gao.gov/products/gao-22-106154

U.S. Government Accountability Office. (2022, September). *Cloud computing: Federal agencies face four challenges.* www.gao.gov/assets/gao-22-106195.pdf

U.S. Government Accountability Office. (2023, January 31). *Cybersecurity high-risk series: Challenges in establishing a comprehensive cybersecurity strategy and performing effective oversight.* www.gao.gov/products/gao-23-106428

U.S. Government Publishing Office. (2019, September 20). *Confronting violent white supremacy (Part III): Addressing the transnational terrorist threat.* https://oversight.house.gov/legislation/hearings/joint-national-security-and-civil-rights-civil-liberties-subcommittee-hearing-0

U.S. Senate. (2022, September 29). *Texts of Senate amendment 6391. In Congressional Record* (Vol. 168, pp. S5912). Congress.gov. www.congress.gov/congressional-record/volume-168/issue-158/senate-section/article/S5912-1

U.S. Senate Committee on Homeland Security & Governmental Affairs. (n.d.). *Homepage.* www.hsgac.senate.gov/

UTSA. (2022). *UTSA researcher part of team protecting EV charging stations from cyberattacks.* www.utsa.edu/today/2022/01/story/elias-bou-harb-ev-charging-stations-cyberattacks.html

Uzialko, A. (2019, February 26). *Workplace automation is everywhere, and it's not just about robots.* Business News Daily. www.businessnewsdaily.com/9835-automation-tech-workforce.html

Valích, L. (2022). *Data from friends and strangers show where you are*. Nextgov/ FCW. www.nextgov.com/emerging-tech/2022/04/data-friends-and-strangers-show-where-you-are/365593/

Vallance, C. (2022, July 23). *World Cup to use drones to help protect stadiums*. BBC. www.bbc.com/news/technology-62243427

Vallance, C. (2022, November 9). *3D printed guns: Warnings over growing threat of 3D firearms*. BBC. www.bbc.co.uk/news/technology-63495123

Vallance, C. (2023, January 18). *Microsoft to cut 10,000 jobs as spending slows*. BBC. www.bbc.co.uk/news/technology-64317078

Vallance, C. (2023). *AI could worsen cyber-threats, report warns*. BBC. www.bbc.com/news/technology-67221117

Vallance, C. (2023). *Artificial intelligence could lead to extinction, experts warn*. BBC. www.bbc.com/news/uk-65746524

Vallance, C. (2023). *Face search company Clearview AI overturns UK privacy fine*. BBC. www.bbc.com/news/technology-67133157

Vallance, C. (2023). *Google company unveils drone delivery-network ambition*. BBC. www.bbc.co.uk/news/technology-64891005

Vallance, C. (2023). *Meta scientist Yann LeCun says AI won't destroy jobs forever*. BBC. www.bbc.com/news/technology-65886125

Vallance, C. (2023). *Minister attacks Meta boss over Facebook message encryption plan*. BBC. www.bbc.com/news/technology-65686989

Vallance, C. (2023). *Powerful artificial-intelligence ban possible, government adviser warns*. BBC. www.bbc.com/news/technology-65779181

Vallance, C. (2023). *Sarah Silverman sues OpenAI and Meta*. BBC. www.bbc.com/news/technology-66164228

Vallance, C., & McMahon, L. (2023). *Amazon takes on Microsoft as it invests*. BBC. www.bbc.com/news/technology-66914338

Van Sprang, M. (2014, October 10). *Watson and other impossible grand challenges*. IBM. www.ibm.com/blogs/think/nl-en/2014/10/20/watson-and-other-impossible-grand-challenges/

Vasquez, C. (2022, December 16). *CISA researchers: Russia's Fancy Bear infiltrated the US satellite network*. CyberScoop. https://cyberscoop.com/apt28-fancy-bear-satellite/

Vasquez, C. (2022). *DHS secretary says US faces "a new kind of warfare."* Cyberscoop. www.cyberscoop.com/dhs-mayorkas-cybersecurity/

Vasquez, C. (2023, January 26). *Cybercriminals scam two federal agencies via remote desktop tool, CISA warns*. CyberScoop. https://cyberscoop.com/cisa-federal-agency-refund-scam-remote-software/

Vasquez, C. (2023). *Mysterious malware designed to cripple industrial systems linked to Russia*. CyberScoop. https://cyberscoop.com/russia-ics-malware-cosmicenergy/

Veer, R. V.-D. (2019, December 11). *Terrorism in the age of technology*. ICCT. www.icct.nl/publication/terrorism-age-technology

Venkataramakrishnan, S. (2021, December 5). Why ethics must be built into tech development. *Financial Times*. www.ft.com/content/43a6a1ab-3f52-43c5-af67-b4e7a1251bde

Veracode. (2023). *Securing the future: Unveiling the state of software security in the public sector*. www.veracode.com/sites/default/files/pdf/resources/reports/veracode-state-of-software-security-2023-public-sector.pdf

Verizon. (2022). *2022 data breach investigations report*. www.verizon.com/business/resources/Tb79/reports/dbir/2022-data-breach-investigations-report-dbir.pdf

Verma, P. (2023). They thought loved ones were calling for help. It was an AI scam. *The Washington Post*. www.washingtonpost.com/technology/2023/03/05/ai-voice-scam/

Vicens, A. (2023, December 13). *Microsoft seizes infrastructure of top cybercrime group*. CyberScoop. https://cyberscoop.com/microsoft-seizes-infrastructure-of-top-cybercrime-group/

Vicens, A. (2024, January 31). *Pentagon investigating theft of sensitive files by ransomware group*. CyberScoop. https://cyberscoop.com/technica-pentagon-alphv-ransomware/

Victor, D. G. (2019, January 10). *How artificial intelligence will affect the future of energy and climate*. Brookings. www.brookings.edu/research/how-artificial-intelligence-will-affect-the-future-of-energy-and-climate/

Vincent, B. (2020, November 3). *Critical update: What a treasury office is learning from its blockchain projects*. Nextgov/FCW. www.nextgov.com/podcasts/2020/11/critical-update-what-treasury-office-learning-its-blockchain-projects/169736/

Vincent, B. (2020). *Senator questions how clearview AI's facial recognition tech is put to use on protesters*. Nextgov/FCW. www.nextgov.com/emerging-tech/2020/06/senator-questions-how-clearview-ais-facial-recognition-tech-put-use-protesters/166026/

Vincent, B. (2021). *Biden issues executive order to bolster nation's cybersecurity*. Nextgov/FCW. www.nextgov.com/cybersecurity/2021/05/biden-issues-executive-order-bolster-nations-cybersecurity/174004/

Vincent, B. (2021). *Critical update: How to develop apps for supercomputers that don't exist yet*. Nextgov/FCW. www.nextgov.com/podcasts/2021/06/critical-update-how-develop-apps-supercomputers-dont-exist-yet/174400/

Vincent, B. (2021). *Critical update: Let's talk about UFOs*. Nexgov/FCW. www.nextgov.com/podcasts/2021/03/critical-update-lets-talk-about-ufos/172536/

Vincent, B. (2021). *Democrats question Justice Department on use of predictive policing algorithms*. Nextgov/FCW. www.nextgov.com/policy/2021/04/democrats-question-justice-department-use-predictive-policing-algorithms/173419/

Vincent, B. (2021). *NSA director: Evolving cyber threats require deeper public–private partnerships*. Nextgov/FCW. www.nextgov.com/cybersecurity/2021/11/nsa-director-evolving-cyber-threats-require-deeper-public-private-partnerships/186918/

Vincent, B. (2022). *AI algorithms could rapidly deploy to the battlefield under new initiative*. Nextgov/FCW. www.nextgov.com/emerging-tech/2022/02/ai-algorithms-could-rapidly-deploy-battlefield-under-new-initiative/361790/

Vincent, B. (2022). *AI could match "fingerprints" of texts to their authors, under new intelligence program.* Nextgov/FCW. www.nextgov.com/emerging-tech/2022/02/ai-could-match-fingerprints-texts-their-authors-under-new-intellige nce-program/361850/

Vincent, B. (2022). *Air Force moves to drive computer vision research and development.* Nextgov/FCW. www.nextgov.com/emerging-tech/2022/02/air-force-moves-drive-computer-vision-research-and-development/362077/

Vincent, B. (2022). *Critical update: Inching closer to the long-awaited, next generation of supercomputers.* Nextgov/FCW. www.nextgov.com/podcasts/2022/03/critical-update-inching-closer-long-awaited-next-generation-supercomputers/363420/

Vincent, B. (2022). *Critical update: Revisiting the government's evolving-but-still-complicated relationship with UFOs.* Nextgov/FCW. www.nextgov.com/podca sts/2022/02/critical-update-revisiting-governments-evolving-still-complicated-relationship-ufos/362251/

Vincent, B. (2022). *Enforcement feds want augmented reality to monitor U.S./Mexico* Border. Nextgov/FCW. www.nextgov.com/emerging-tech/2021/08/drug-enforcement-feds-want-augmented-reality-monitor-usmexico-border/184636/

Vincent, J. (2016, December 20). *Artificial intelligence is going to make it easier than ever to fake images and video.* The Verge. www.theverge.com/2016/12/20/14022958/ai-image-manipulation-creation-fakes-audio-video

Vincent, J. (2017, July 12). *New AI research makes it easier to create fake footage of someone speaking.* The Verge. www.theverge.com/2017/7/12/15957844/ai-fake-video-audio-speech-obama

Vinopal, C., & Stabley, J. (2021, January 13). *How the U.S. Capitol attack highlights the challenges of thwarting online right-wing extremism.* PBS NewsHour. www.pbs.org/newshour/politics/how-the-u-s-capitol-attack-highlig hts-the-challenges-of-thwarting-online-right-wing-extremism

Violino, B. (2018, November 12). *Digital transformation in 2019: AI, robotics, and IoT to play starring roles.* ZDNet. www.zdnet.com/article/digital-transfo rmation-in-2019-ai-robotics-and-iot-to-play-starring-roles/

Vock, D. C. (2023, December 13). *Will new car technology stop people from driving drunk?* Route Fifty. www.route-fifty.com/emerging-tech/2023/12/will-new-car-technology-stop-people-driving-drunk/392742/

Vogel, M. (2019, May 1). *How bias creeps into health care AI.* Axios. www.axios.com/2019/05/01/how-bias-creeps-into-health-care-ai

Vogels, E. A., Gelles-Watnick, R., & Massarat, N. (2022, August 10). *Teens, Social Media and Technology 2022.* Pew Research Center. www.pewresearch.org/inter net/2022/08/10/teens-social-media-and-technology-2022/

Wachowski, L. (2021). *The Matrix Resurrections.* Warner Bros.

Wachowski, L., & Wachowski, L. (1999). *The Matrix.* Warner Bros.

Wachowski, L., & Wachowski, L. (2003). *The Matrix Reloaded.* Warner Bros.

Wachowski, L., & Wachowski, L. (2003). *The Matrix Revolutions.* Warner Bros.

Waddell, K. (2018, June 27). *AI might need a therapist, too.* Axios. www.axios.com/2018/06/27/ai-might-need-a-psychologist-1529700757

Waddell, K. (2018, October 14). *Will AI make us dumb?* Axios. www.axios.com/ artificial-intelligence-human-brain-critical-thinking-ability-1a17e87e-2a17-4dae-8371-f56d58a76812.html

Waddell, K. (2019, February 6). *AI takes on a children's game.* Axios. www.axios. com/2019/02/06/ai-learning-common-sense-pictionary

Waddell, K. (2019, February 11). *Trump to lay out an AI plan.* Axios. www.axios. com/2019/02/11/trump-us-ai-strategy-china

Waddell, K. (2019, February 21). *Keeping AI away from the bad guys.* Axios. www.axios.com/2019/02/21/keeping-ai-away-from-bad-guys

Waddell, K. (2019, June 14). *AI is "awakening" surveillance cameras.* Axios. www.axios.com/ai-surveillance-video-analysis-839b5bfb-a252-4641-9613-96eb3c88021c.html

Waddell, K. (2019, July 24). *The global race between China and U.S. to set the rules for AI.* Axios. www.axios.com/2019/07/14/artificial-intelligence-china-uni ted-states

Wain, P. (2023, May 9). *Apple co-founder says AI may make scams harder to spot.* BBC. www.bbc.com/news/technology-65496150

Wain, P. (2023, August 5). *Chatbots: Why does White House want hackers to trick AI?* BBC. www.bbc.co.uk/news/technology-66404069

Wait, P. (2021). *Economist calls for deeper examination of AI's risks.* Nextgov/ FCW. www.nextgov.com/policy/2021/12/economist-calls-deeper-examination-ais-risks/359730/

Walden, K., Neuberger, A., & Lewis, J. (2023). *The Biden–Harries administration's national cybersecurity strategy.* Center for Strategic & International Studies. www.csis.org/events/biden-harries-administration-national-cybersecurity-strategy

Wales, B. (2023). *CIRCIA at one year: A look behind the scenes.* Cybersecurity & Infrastructure Security Agency. www.cisa.gov/news-events/news/circia-one-year-look-behind-scenes

Wall, C., & Lostri, E. (2022, February 15). *The European Union's Digital Markets Act: A primer.* Center for Strategic & International Studies. www.csis.org/analy sis/european-unions-digital-markets-act-primer

Wall, D. S. (2007). *Cybercrime: The transformation of crime in the information age* (1st ed.). Cambridge: Polity.

Walsh, B. (2019, June 24). *Axios future.* Axios.

Walsh, B. (2020, July 22). *The continuing problem of AI bias.* Axios. www.axios. com/2020/07/22/artificial-intelligence-bias-gender-race-religion

Walsh, B. (2020, August 29). *Elon Musk's Neuralink wants to read your brain.* Axios. www.axios.com/2020/08/29/elon-musk-neuralink-brain-computer-interface

Walsh, B. (2020, October 7). *The electrical grid will be exposed to cyberattacks as it becomes connected to the internet.* Axios. www.axios.com/2020/10/07/pro tecting-smarter-grid-cyberattacks

Walsh, B. (2021, January 5). *OpenAI's new model can draw images from a written description.* Axios. www.axios.com/2021/01/05/openai-artificial-intelligence-model-images-dall-e

Walsh, B. (2021, February 13). *The coming conflict over facial recognition.* Axios. www.axios.com/2021/02/13/facial-recognition-capitol-hill-riots-regulation

Walsh, B. (2021, November 17). *AI will "change the nature of war."* Axios. www.axios.com/2021/11/17/robert-work-artificial-intelligence-warfare

Walsh, B. (2021, November 17). *Americans are confused about AI.* Axios. www.axios.com/2021/11/17/survey-american-atittudes-artificial-intelligence

Walsh, B. (2021, November 17). *Taming the wild west of AI hiring tools.* Axios. www.axios.com/2021/11/17/ai-hiring-tools-audit-laws

Walsh, B. (2021, December 22). *Balancing the benefits and risks of new technology.* Axios. www.axios.com/2021/12/22/technology-innovation-pandemic-progress

Wan, J. (2023). *FBI warns of public "juice jacking" charging stations that steal your data. How to stay protected.* ZDNet. www.zdnet.com/article/fbi-warns-of-juice-jacking-charging-stations-in-public-areas-how-to-stay-protected/

Washington Examiner. (2021, February 11). *Senate committee should examine all types of political violence.* www.washingtonexaminer.com/opinion/editorials/senate-committee-should-examine-all-types-of-political-violence

Watkins, J. (2017, August 28). *Ozy poll: Are we ready for robot teachers.* Ozy. www.ozy.com/news-and-politics/ozy-poll-are-we-ready-for-robot-teachers/80095/

Wattenbarger, M. (2021, January 2021). *Where surveillance cameras work, but the justice system doesn't.* Rest of World. https://restofworld.org/2021/mexico-city-security-theater/

Watts, C. (2017, October 31). *Extremist content and Russian disinformation online: Working with tech to find solutions.* Foreign Policy Research Institute. www.fpri.org/article/2017/10/extremist-content-russian-disinformation-online-working-tech-find-solutions/

Watts, C. (2024, June 2). *How Russia is trying to disrupt the 2024 Paris Olympic Games.* Microsoft on the Issues. https://blogs.microsoft.com/on-the-issues/2024/06/02/russia-cyber-bots-disinformation-2024-paris-olympics/

Way, E. (2022, July 5). *Robots are everywhere in Charlotte.* Axios. www.axios.com/local/charlotte/2022/07/05/robots-are-everywhere-in-charlotte-296978

Webster, G., Creemers, R., Triolo, P., & Kania, E. (2017, August 1). *Full translation: China's "New generation artificial intelligence development plan" (2017).* New America. www.newamerica.org/cybersecurity-initiative/blog/chinas-plan-lead-ai-purpose-prospects-and-problems/

Wei, M. (2022, February 24). *Taking solid steps in the construction of manufacturing power and a cyberpower: New achievements in China's industry and information technology development since the 18th party congress.* Interpret Center for Strategic & International Studies. https://interpret.csis.org/translations/taking-solid-steps-in-the-construction-of-a-manufacturing-power-and-a-cyberpower-new-achievements-in-chinas-industry-and-information-technology-development-since-the-18th-party-congress/

Weijiang, F. (2022, June 16). *The theoretical foundation of the global security initiative—The holistic view of national security.* Interpret Center for Strategic & International Studies. https://interpret.csis.org/translations/the-theoretical-foundation-of-the-global-security-initiative-the-holistic-view-of-national-security/

Weil, E. (2023). *You are not a parrot and ChatGPT is nothing like a human.* New York Intelligencer. https://nymag.com/intelligencer/article/ai-artificial-intel ligence-chatbots-emily-m-bender.html

Weill, K. (2018, July 26). *American racists look for allies in Russia.* The Daily Beast. www.thedailybeast.com/american-racists-look-for-allies-in-russia

Weinstein, E., & Luong, N. (2023, February). *U.S. outbound investment into Chinese AI companies.* Center for Security and Emerging Technology (CSET). https://cset.georgetown.edu/publication/u-s-outbound-investment-into-chinese-ai-companies/

Weisburd, A., Watts, C., & Berger, J. (2016, November 6). *Trolling for Trump: How Russia is trying to destroy our democracy.* War on the Rocks. https://waront herocks.com/2016/11/trolling-for-trump-how-russia-is-trying-to-destroy-our-democracy/

Wendling, M. (2022). *The truth about "medbeds"—A miracle cure that doesn't exist.* BBC. www.bbc.co.uk/news/blogs-trending-64070190

Wertheimer, T. (2022, July 23). *Blake Lemoine: Google fires engineer who said AI tech has feelings.* BBC. www.bbc.com/news/technology-62275326

Wesslau, F. (2016, October 19). *Putin's friends in Europe.* European Council on Foreign Relations (ECFR). https://ecfr.eu/article/commentary_putins_friends_in _europe7153/

West Monroe Partners. (2021, August). *Your operating model: Moving from traditional to digital.* www.westmonroe.com/perspectives/resource/your-operating-model-moving-from-traditional-to-digital

Whittaker, Z. (2022). *Xnspy stalkerware spied on thousands of iPhones and Android devices.* TechCrunch. https://techcrunch.com/2022/12/12/xnspy-stal kerware-iphone-android/

Whittaker, Z. (2023). *Another huge US medical data breach confirmed after Fortra mass-hack.* TechCrunch. https://techcrunch.com/2023/06/09/intellihartx-data-breach-fortra-ransomware/

Whittaker, Z. (2023). *Microsoft lost its keys, and the government got hacked.* TechCrunch. https://techcrunch.com/2023/07/17/microsoft-lost-keys-governm ent-hacked/

Whitwam, R. (2017, May 22). *Dubai set to deploy its first robotic cop.* ExtremeTech. www.extremetech.com/extreme/249675-dubai-set-deploy-first-robotic-cop

Wiggers, K. (2022, July 27). *Commercial image-generating AI raises thorny legal issues.* TechCrunch. https://techcrunch.com/2022/07/22/commercial-image-gen erating-ai-raises-all-sorts-of-thorny-legal-issues/

Wiggers, K. (2023). *OpenAI forms team to study "catastrophic" AI risks, including nuclear threats.* TechCrunch. https://techcrunch.com/2023/10/26/openai-forms-team-to-study-catastrophic-risks-including-nuclear-threats/

Williams, J. (2017, March 29). *Robots of the future: First robot cop to join Dubai Police Force in May.* Newsweek. www.newsweek.com/robots-police-task-2017-dubai-571119

Williams, L. (2022). *A wireless intelligence community "on the horizon," official says.* Nextgov/FCW. www.nextgov.com/emerging-tech/2022/12/wireless-intel ligence-community-horizon-official-says/381065/.

Williams, L. (2022). *It's finally here: Pentagon releases plan to keep hackers out of its networks.* Nextgov/FCW. www.nextgov.com/cybersecurity/2022/11/its-fina lly-here-pentagon-releases-plan-keep-hackers-out-its-networks/380157/

Williams, L. (2022). *Let's make it easier to share top-secret data with allies, Intel leader says.* Nextgov/FCW. www.nextgov.com/cxo-briefing/2022/12/lets-make-it-easier-share-top-secret-data-allies-intel-leader-says/380924/

Williams, L. (2023). *Get serious about data, US intelligence leaders tell agencies.* Nextgov/FCW. www.nextgov.com/analytics-data/2023/07/get-serious-about-data-us-intelligence-leaders-tell-agencies/388614/

Williams, L. (2023). *Outlines upcoming contractor cybersecurity plan.* Nextgov/FCW. www.nextgov.com/cxo-briefing/2023/05/pentagon-outlines-upcoming-contractor-cybersecurity-plan/386617/

Williamson, L. (2022). *Calais migrants: Smugglers cause fresh problems for police.* BBC. www.bbc.co.uk/news/world-europe-63119180

Wilson, J. (2020, January 24). Revealed: The true identity of the leader of an American neo-Nazi terror group. *The Guardian.* www.theguardian.com/world/2020/jan/23/revealed-the-true-identity-of-the-leader-of-americas-neo-nazi-terror-group

Withers, R. (2020, October 5). A.I. job interviews are taking the *"human" out of human resources.* Slate. https://slate.com/technology/2020/10/artificial-intellige nce-job-interviews.html

Wojno, M. (2021, December 6). *Brace yourself for these five top data breach trends in 2022, Experian warns.* ZDNet. www.zdnet.com/article/experian-relea ses-data-breach-industry-forecast-for-2022/

Wojno, M. (2022, January 18). *The future of money.* ZDNet. www.zdnet.com/ finance/blockchain/the-future-of-money-where-blockchain-and-cryptocurre ncy-will-take-us-next/

Wong, J. (2017). *People are scared of artificial intelligence for all the wrong reasons.* Nextgov/FCW. www.nextgov.com/emerging-tech/2017/04/people-are-scared-artificial-intelligence-all-wrong-reasons/137286/

Woodruff-Swan, B. (2023). *DHS has a program gathering domestic intelligence— And virtually no one knows about it.* POLITICO. www.politico.com/news/ 2023/03/06/dhs-domestic-intelligence-program-00085544

Worldcoin. (2023, March 14). *Introducing World ID and SDK.* https://worldcoin. org/blog/announcements/introducing-world-id-and-sdk

WPR Insights. (2022, June 27). *WPR insights: The promise and perils of Big Tech.* www.worldpoliticsreview.com/tech-ethics-artificial-intelligence-regulation-and-killer-drones/

Wright, G. (2023). *Amazon to pay $25m over child privacy violations.* BBC. www. bbc.com/news/technology-65772154

Wright, N. D. (Ed.). (2019). *Artificial intelligence, China, Russia, and the global order.* Maxwell Air Force Base, Alabama: Air University Press. www.airuni versity.af.edu/Portals/10/AUPress/Books/B_0161_WRIGHT_ARTIFICIAL_ INTELLIGENCE_CHINA_RUSSIA_AND_THE_GLOBAL_ORDER.PDF

WTTW News. (2021). *Capitol attack reflects US extremist evolution over decades.* https://news.wttw.com/2021/01/23/capitol-attack-reflects-us-extremist-evolut ion-over-decades

Xiangyang, C., Chungling, D., & Liqun, H. (2022, May 9). *Deep comprehension of the global security initiative: Coordinating our own security and common security.* Interpret Center for Strategic & International Studies. https://interpret. csis.org/translations/deep-comprehension-of-the-global-security-initiative-coord inating-our-own-security-and-common-security/

Xingrui, M. (2022, April 21). *Adhere to the overall National Security Outlook— Provide a strong guarantee for the realization of social stability and long-term stability in Xinjiang.* Interpret Center for Strategic & International Studies. https://interpret.csis.org/translations/adhere-to-the-overall-national-security-outlook-provide-a-strong-guarantee-for-the-realization-of-social-stability-and-long-term-stability-in-xinjiang/

Xu, A. (2023). *As deepfake fraud permeates China, authorities target political challenges posed by AI.* VOA China. www.voanews.com/a/as-deepfake-fraud-permeates-china-authorities-target-political-challenges-posed-by-ai-/7137 321.html

Yi, W. (2022, June 1). *Strengthen solidarity and cooperation, improve global governance—Video address by Wang Yi at the opening of the China–Russia high-level think tank forum.* Interpret Center for Strategic & International Studies. https://interpret.csis.org/translations/strengthen-solidarity-and-coop eration-improve-global-governance-video-address-by-wang-yi-at-the-opening-of-the-china-russia-high-level-think-tank-forum/

Ying, W. (2022, January 8). *Shutting algorithms into a legal cage.* Interpret Center for Strategic & International Studies. https://interpret.csis.org/translations/shutt ing-algorithms-into-a-legal-cage/

Yongsheng, T. (2022, January 15). *The international security situation in 2021: Unstable factors increase, uncertain risks rise.* Interpret Center for Strategic & International Studies. https://interpret.csis.org/translations/the-international-security-situation-in-2021-unstable-factors-increase-uncertain-risks-rise/

YouTube. (2022). *House science, space, and technology hearing on managing the risks of artificial intelligence.* https://m.youtube.com/watch?t=4132&v=xKbh 6Cv7oHA&feature=youtu.be

YouTube. (2022). *Responsible AI in a global context.* YouTube. www.youtube. com/watch?v=BVxF6jT9WAU

Yu, E. (2022). *Uber security breach "looks bad," potentially compromising all systems.* ZDNet. www.zdnet.com/article/uber-security-breach-looks-bad-pote ntially-compromising-all-systems/

Yu, E. (2023, March 13). *ChatGPT's most lauded capability also brings big risk to businesses.* ZDNet. www.zdnet.com/article/most-lauded-chatgpt-capability-also-brings-big-risk-to-businesses/

Yu, E. (2023, August 11). *75% of businesses are implementing or considering bans on ChatGPT.* ZDNet. www.zdnet.com/article/75-of-businesses-are-imple menting-or-considering-bans-on-chatgpt/

Zappone, C. (2016, June 14). Donald Trump–Vladimir Putin: Russia's information war meets the US election. *The Sydney Morning Herald.* www.smh.com. au/world/north-america/trumpputin-russias-information-war-meets-the-us-elect ion-20160609-gpf4sm.html

Zaraska, M. (2021, December 8). *The tomatoes at the forefront of a food revolution*. BBC. www.bbc.com/future/article/20211207-the-tomatoes-at-the-forefront-of-a-food-revolution

Zarkadakis, G. (2019). The rise of the conscious machines: How far should we take AI? *BBC Science Focus Magazine*. www.sciencefocus.com/future-technology/the-rise-of-the-conscious-machines-how-far-should-we-take-ai/

Zarrelli, N. (2016). *Human eyes might not notice a good forgery, but computers could*. Altaobscura. www.atlasobscura.com/articles/human-eyes-might-not-notice-a-good-forgery-but-computers-could

Zaveri, M. (2021, April 14). N.Y.P.D.'s robot dog returns to work, touching off a backlash. *The New York Times*. www.nytimes.com/2021/04/14/nyregion/robot-dog-nypd.html

Zegart, A. (2022, December 20). Open secrets Ukraine and the next intelligence revolution. *Foreign Affairs*. www.foreignaffairs.com/world/open-secrets-ukraine-intelligence-revolution-amy-zegart

Zeitchik, S. (2021, November 19). A Utah Company says it revolutionized truth-telling technology. Experts are highly skeptical. *The Washington Post*. www.washingtonpost.com/technology/2021/11/15/lie-detector-eye-movements-converus/

Zillman, C. (2021, April 24). *Scientists warn that robots and artificial intelligence could eliminate work*. Fortune. https://fortune.com/2016/02/15/robots-artificial-intelligence-work/amp/

Zoom. (2022). *How virtual care can help curb the behavioral health crisis*. www.govexec.com/media/zoom_how_virtual_care_can_help_curb_the_behavioral_health_crisis_10.21.pdf

Zulhusni, M. (2022). *Sharjah gets the world's first government-backed metaverse city*. TechWire. https://techwireasia.com/2022/10/anything-is-possible-as-sharjah-gets-the-worlds-first-government-backed-metaverse-city/

Zurcher, A. (2020, April 6). *Russian white supremacists are terrorists says Trump*. BBC. www.bbc.com/news/world-us-canada-52186185

Index

Printed in the United States
by Baker & Taylor Publisher Services